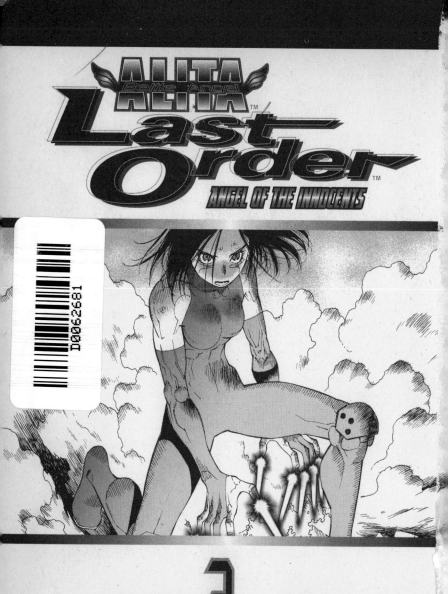

Battle Angel ALITA

ALITA™ Last Order™

ANGEL OF THE INNOCENTS

2

STORY & ART BY YUKITO KISHIRO

The Story Thus Far...

At the end of the eight-volume Battle Angel Alita series, beautiful cyborg Alita dies a noble death and seems to have finally become truly human. But her arch-foe, Desty Nova, and his assistant, Jim, have resurrected her inside a body as stunning as before, but even more powerful!

Newly awakened Alita sets out on a quest to find her old friends, but the world in which she finds herself is terrible to behold. Nova has exposed the city of Tiphares' terrible secret: after adolescence, everyone's brain is exchanged for a bio-chip! Driven insane by this revelation, Tiphares' adults are hunting down their own children to spill their precious organic brains!

As the reluctant protector of a band of surviving children, Alita is beset by one of her replicants, Sechs. After the battle, Nova invites her to tag along on a trip to the space city Ketheres, where Alita might meet the friends from her dreams and confirm that they aren't just figments of her imagination. But she declines, because she first wants to find the friends from her memories...

Meanwhile, Jim activates his greatest creation, a monster robot named Sachumodo, to guard the surviving children. But when more of the horrors of Tiphares are revealed to him, he too goes over the edge and prepares to unleash the monster's force on innocent and guilty alike.

At that very moment, his former guardian shoots an arrow through his neck....

BATTLE ANGEL ALITA:
LAST ORDER VOL. 2
Angel of the Innocents
Action Editon

Story & Art by
Yukito Kishiro

English Adaptation by
Fred Burke

Translation/Lillian Olsen
Touch-up & Lettering/Susan Daigle-Leach & Adam Symons
Cover & Graphics Design/Sean Lee
Editor/Annette Roman

Managing Editor/Annette Roman
Director of Production/Noboru Watanabe
VP of Publishing/Alvin Lu
Sr. Director of Acquisitions/Rika Inouye
VP of Sales & Marketing/Liza Coppola
Publisher/Hyoe Narita

First published in Japan in 2000 by SHUEISHA Inc., Tokyo.
English translation rights in the United States of America and Canada arranged by SHUEISHA, Inc.

Printed in Canada.

Published by VIZ MEDIA, LLC
P.O. Box 77064
San Francisco, CA 94107

Action Edition
10 9 8 7 6 5 4 3 2
First printing, October 2003
Second printing, June 2005

store.viz.com

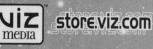

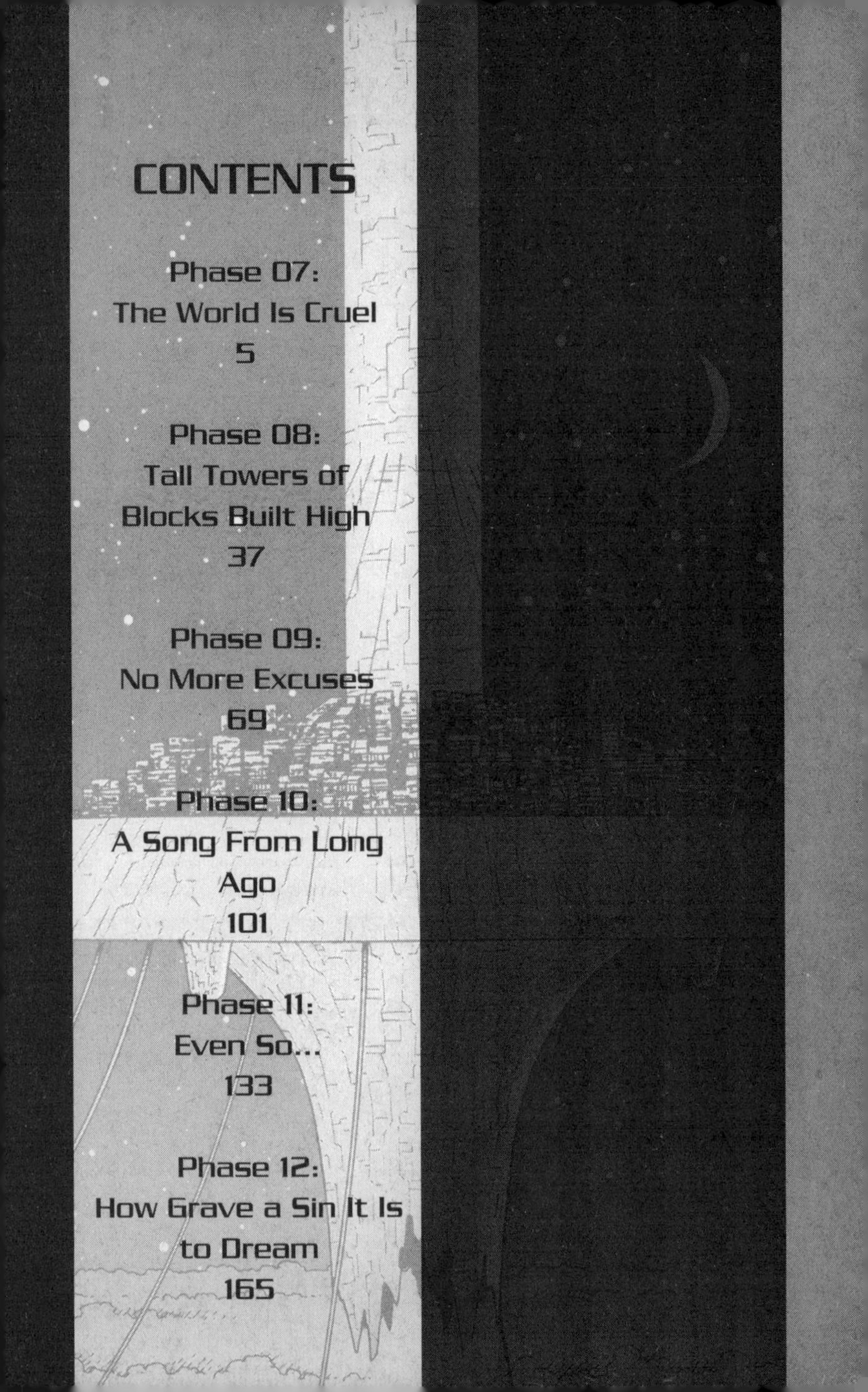

CONTENTS

PHASE 07
The World Is Cruel

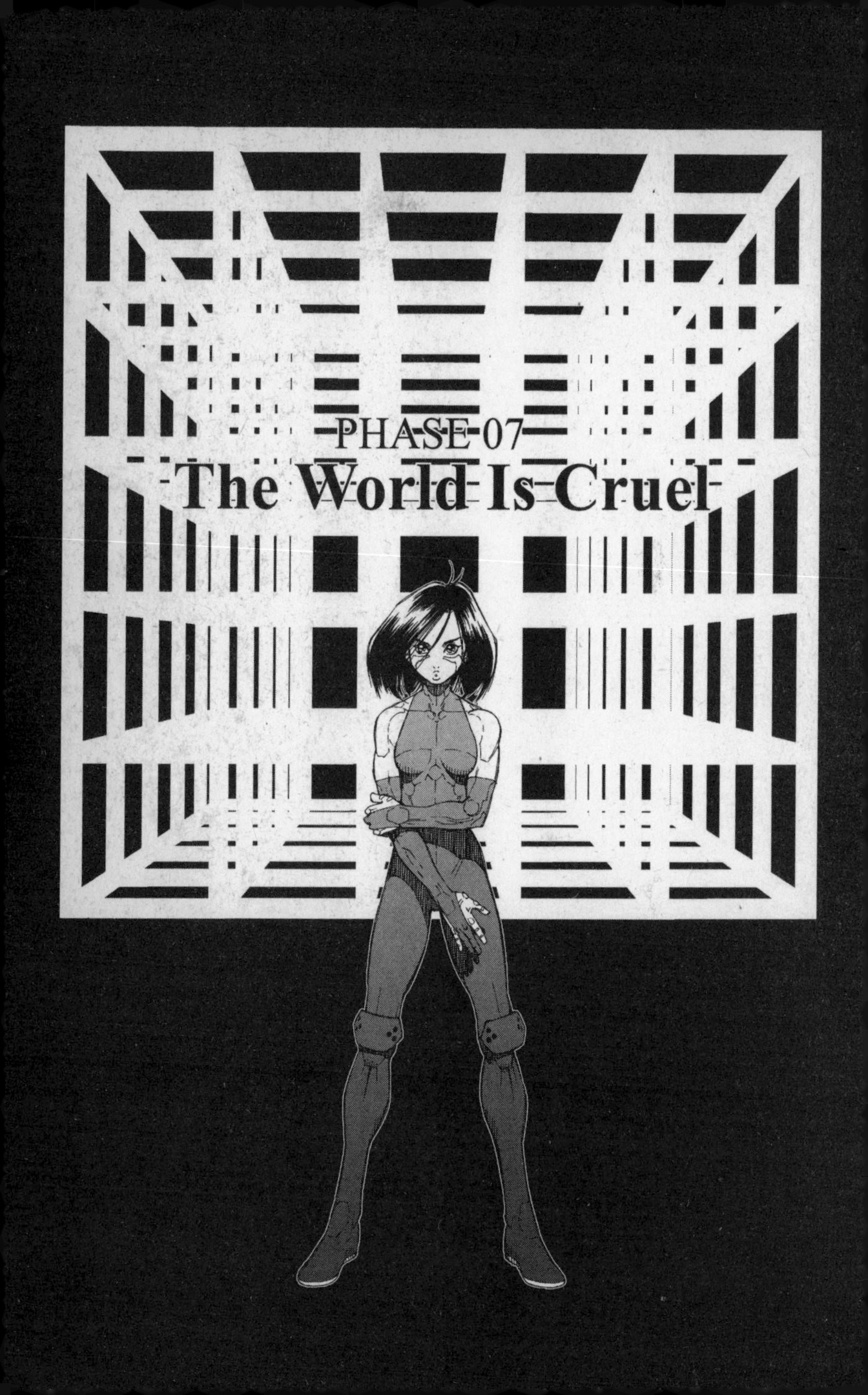

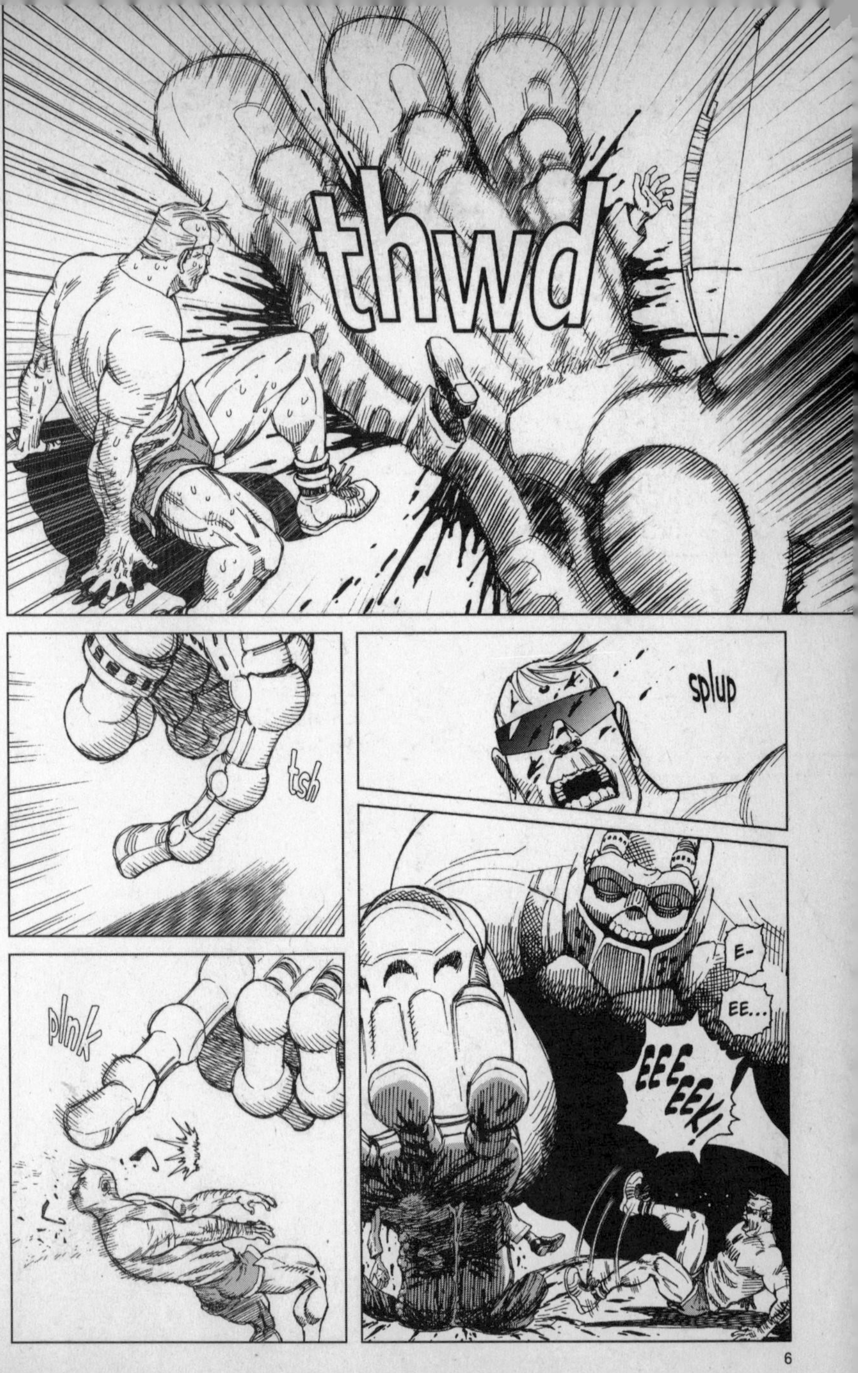
thwd
splup
tsh
E-
EE...
EEEEEK!
plnk

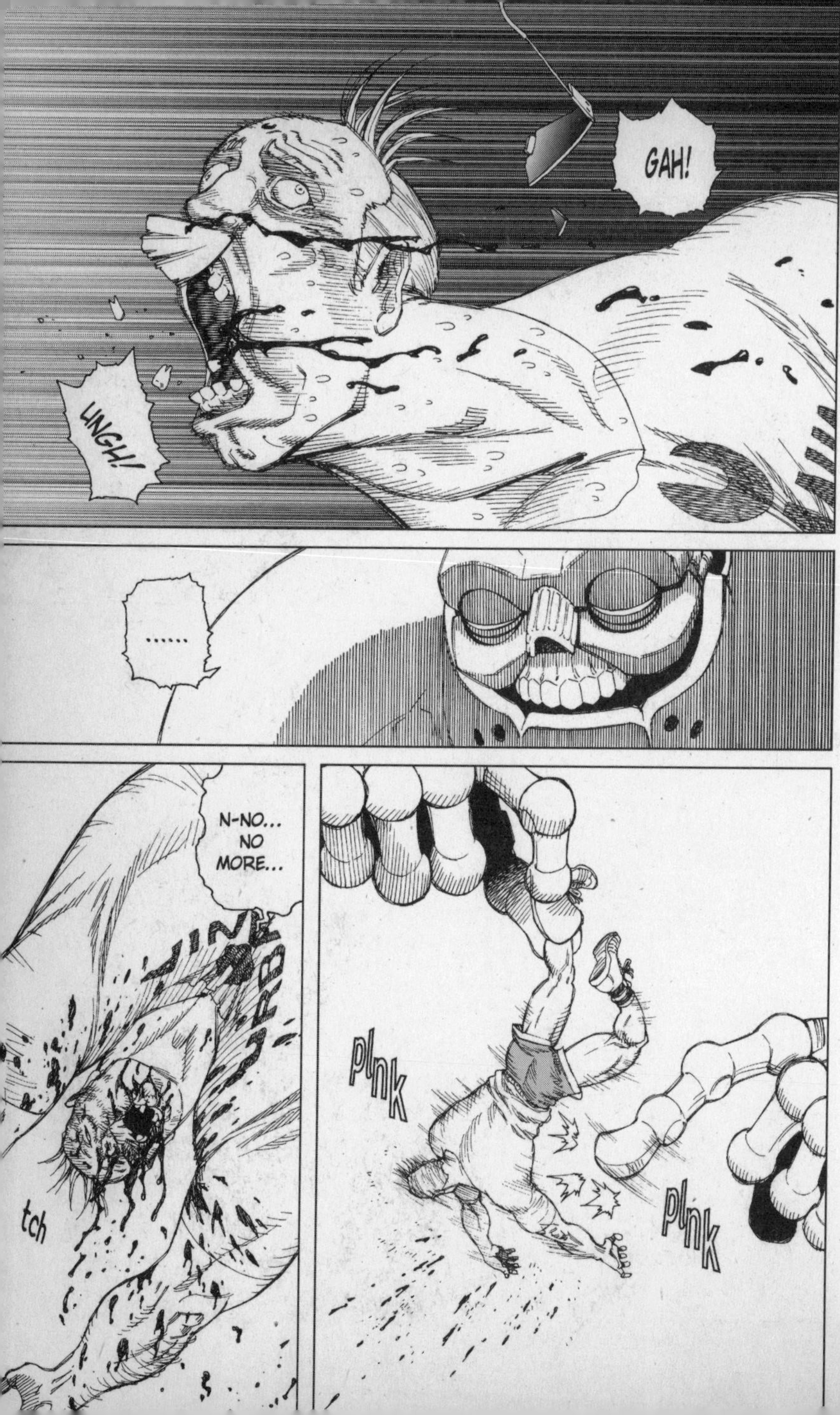
GAH!
UNGH!
......
plink
plink
N-NO... NO MORE...
tch

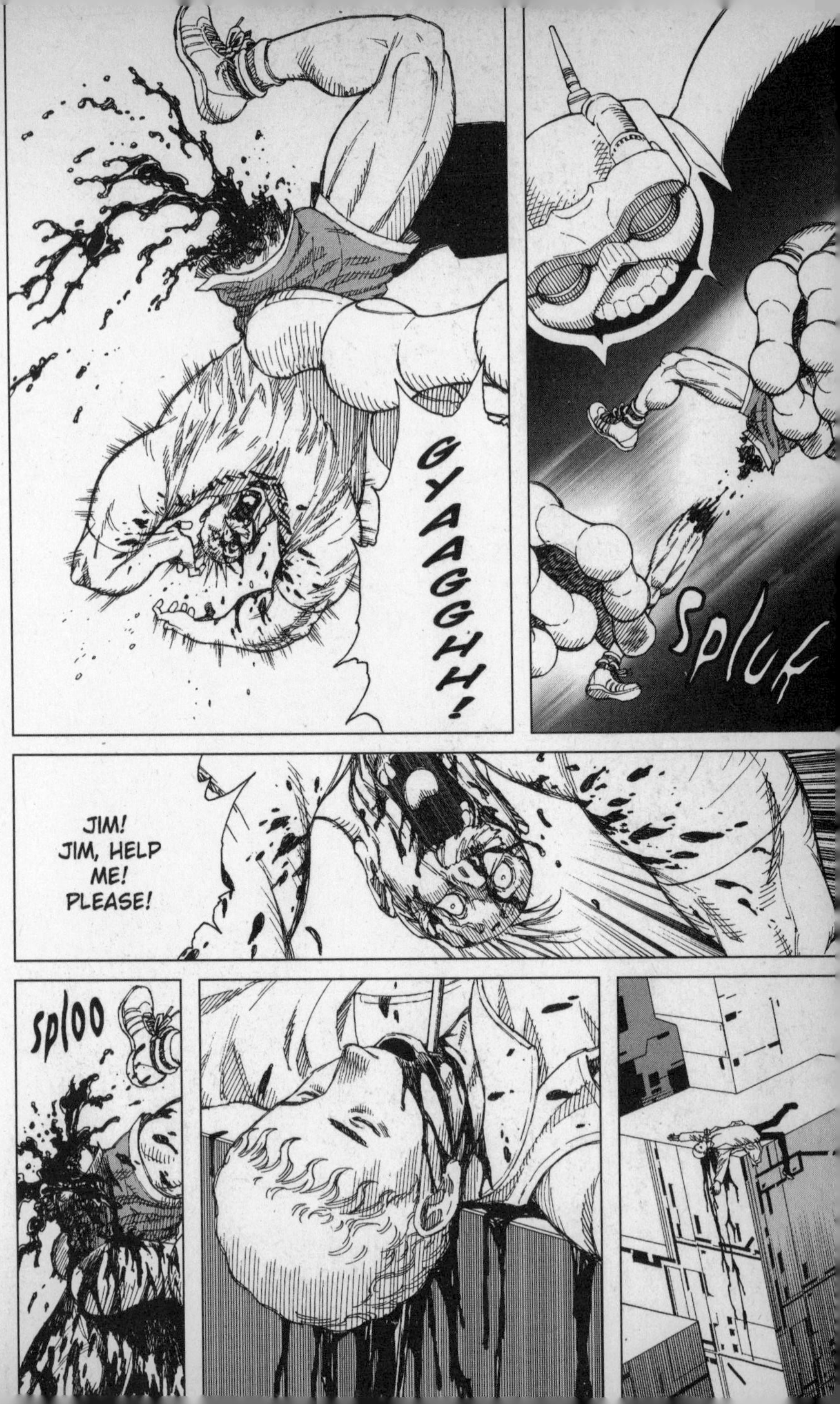
SPLUK
GYAAGGHH!
JIM! JIM, HELP ME! PLEASE!
SPLOO

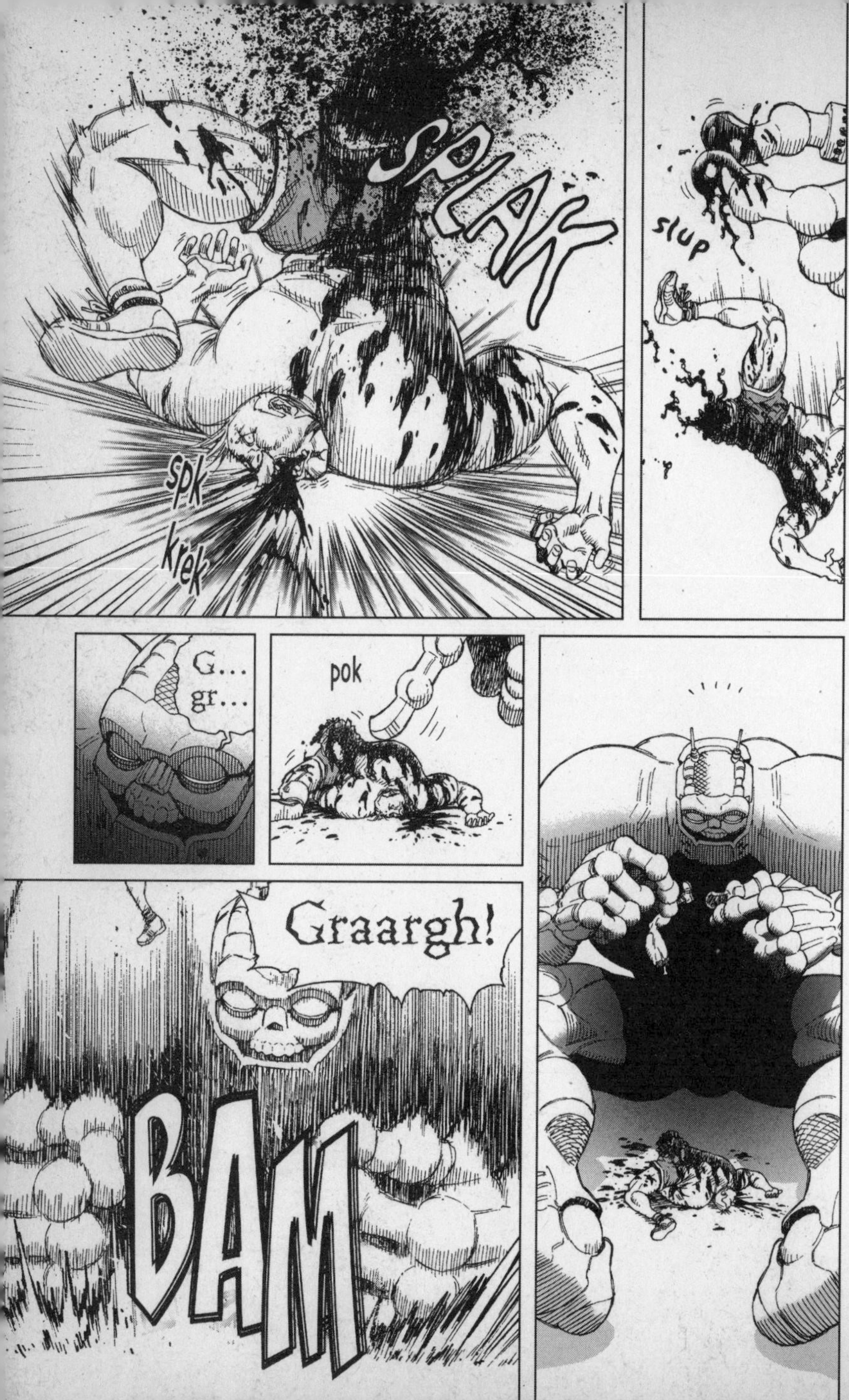
slup
SPLAK
spk
krek
pok
G... gr...
Graargh!
BAM

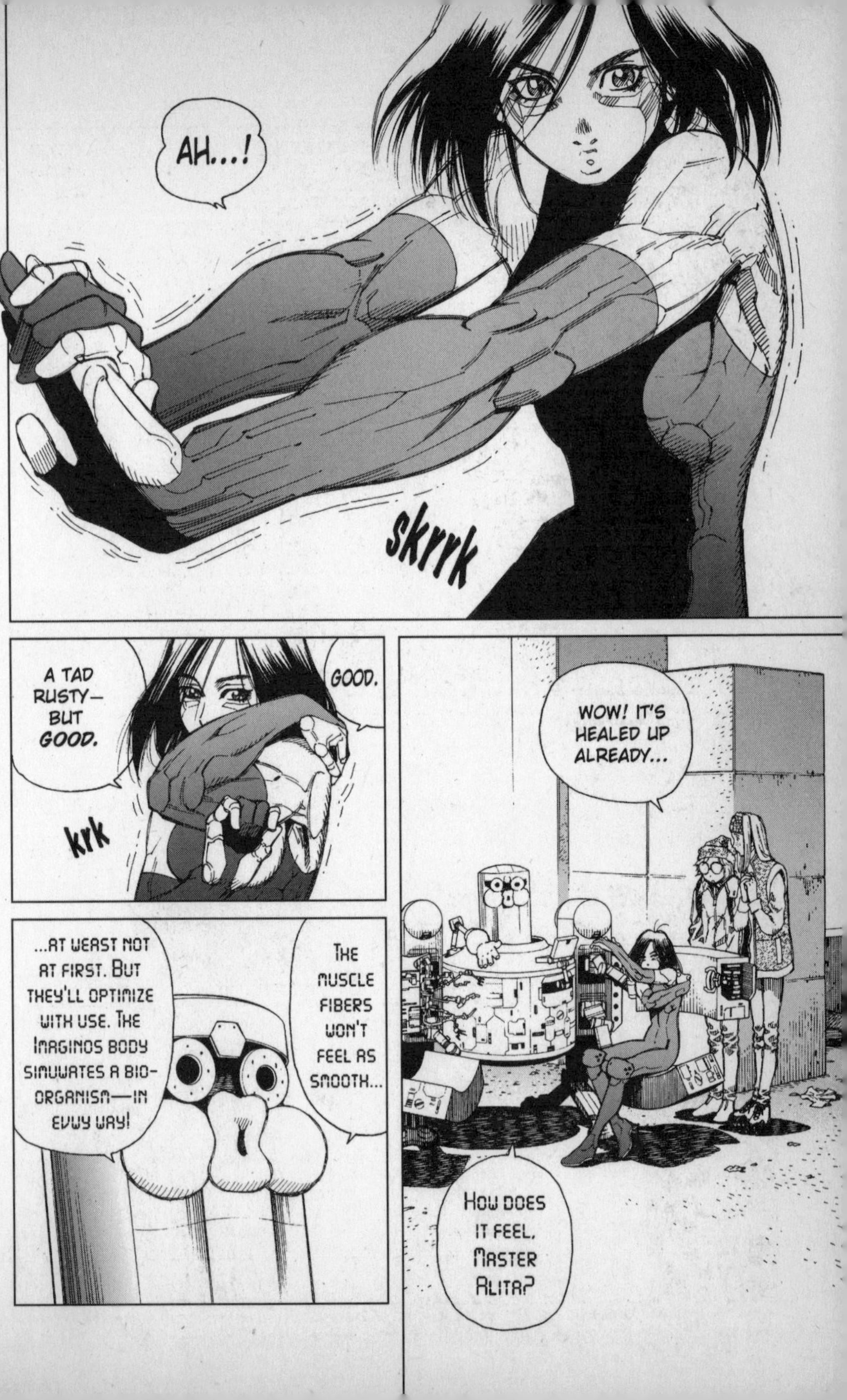
AH...!
skrrk
WOW! IT'S HEALED UP ALREADY...
HOW DOES IT FEEL, MASTER ALITA?
GOOD.
A TAD RUSTY— BUT GOOD.
krk
THE MUSCLE FIBERS WON'T FEEL AS SMOOTH...
...AT WEAST NOT AT FIRST. BUT THEY'LL OPTIMIZE WITH USE. THE IMAGINOS BODY SIMUWATES A BIO-ORGANISM—IN EVWY WAY!

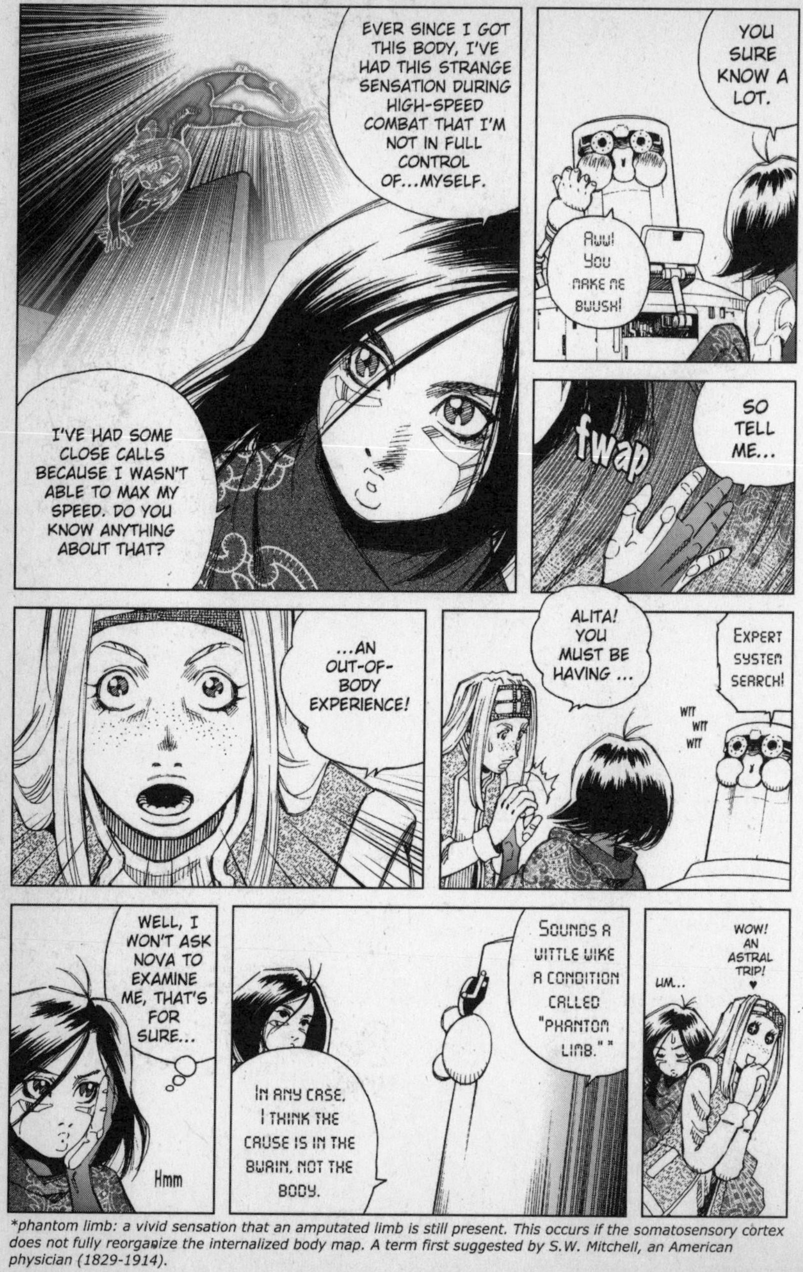
YOU SURE KNOW A LOT.
Aww! You make me bwush!
SO TELL ME...
fwap
EVER SINCE I GOT THIS BODY, I'VE HAD THIS STRANGE SENSATION DURING HIGH-SPEED COMBAT THAT I'M NOT IN FULL CONTROL OF...MYSELF.
I'VE HAD SOME CLOSE CALLS BECAUSE I WASN'T ABLE TO MAX MY SPEED. DO YOU KNOW ANYTHING ABOUT THAT?
Expert system search!
WIT WIT WIT
ALITA! YOU MUST BE HAVING ...
...AN OUT-OF-BODY EXPERIENCE!
WOW! AN ASTRAL TRIP! ♥
UM...
Sounds a wittle wike a condition called "phantom limb." *
In any case, I think the cause is in the bwain, not the body.
WELL, I WON'T ASK NOVA TO EXAMINE ME, THAT'S FOR SURE...
Hmm

*phantom limb: a vivid sensation that an amputated limb is still present. This occurs if the somatosensory cortex does not fully reorganize the internalized body map. A term first suggested by S.W. Mitchell, an American physician (1829-1914).

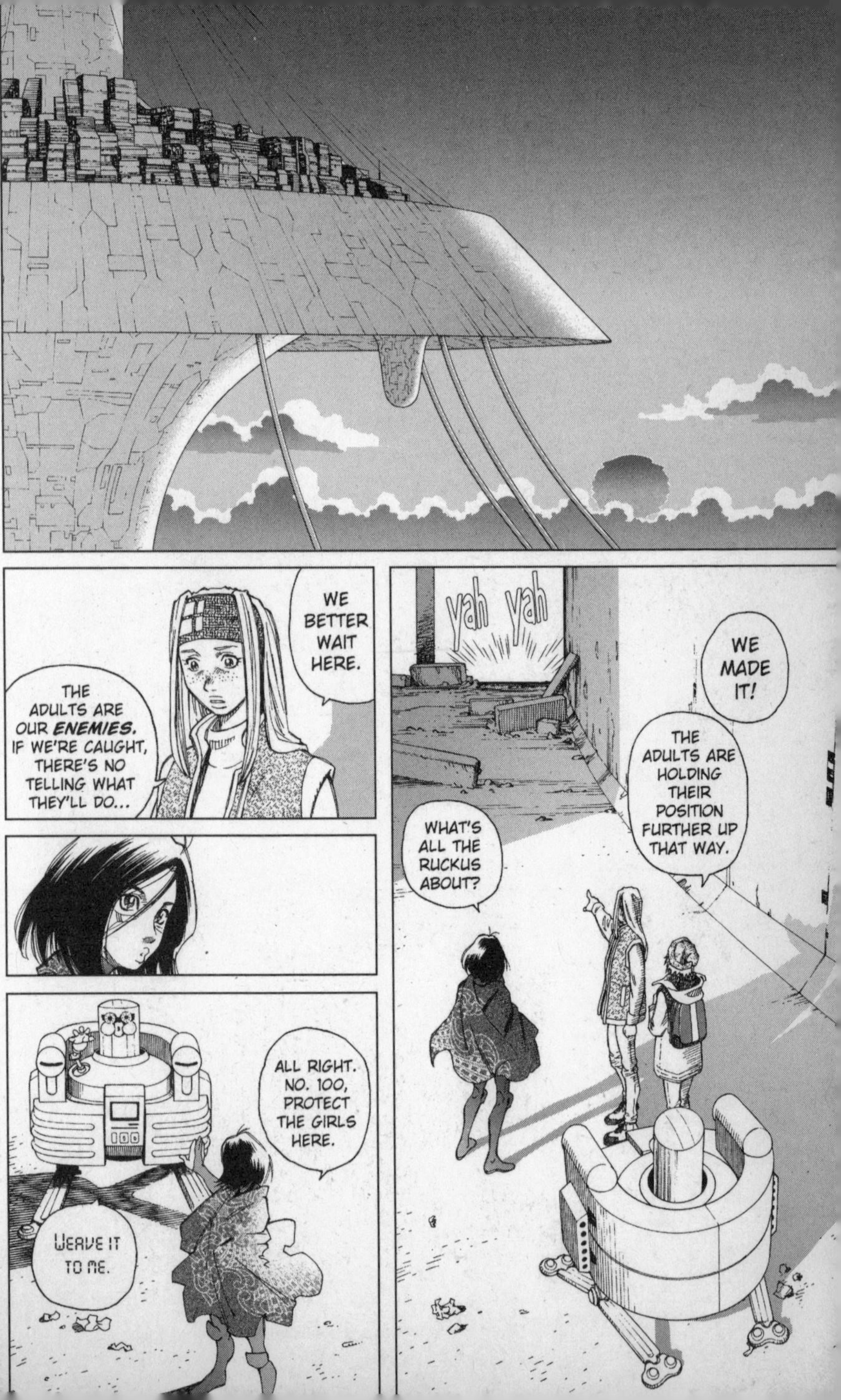
yah yah
WE MADE IT!
THE ADULTS ARE HOLDING THEIR POSITION FURTHER UP THAT WAY.
WHAT'S ALL THE RUCKUS ABOUT?
WE BETTER WAIT HERE.
THE ADULTS ARE OUR ENEMIES. IF WE'RE CAUGHT, THERE'S NO TELLING WHAT THEY'LL DO...
ALL RIGHT. NO. 100, PROTECT THE GIRLS HERE.
WEAVE IT TO ME.

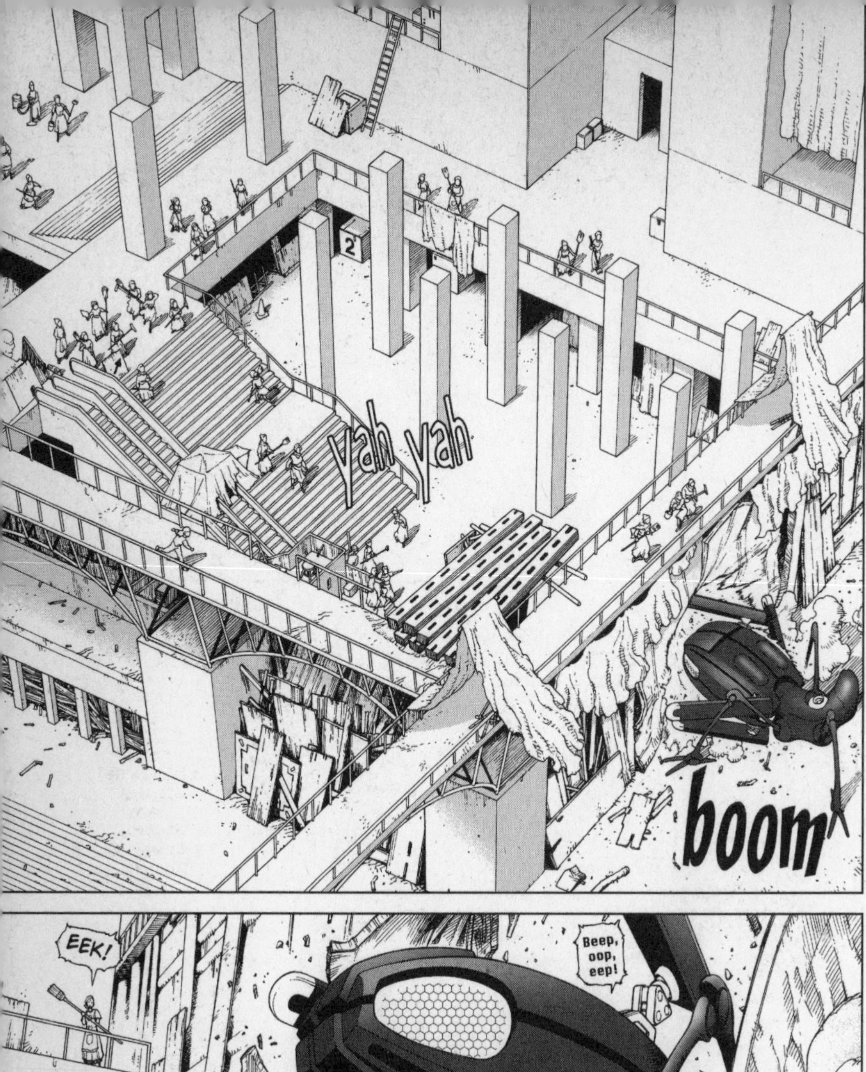
yah yah
boom
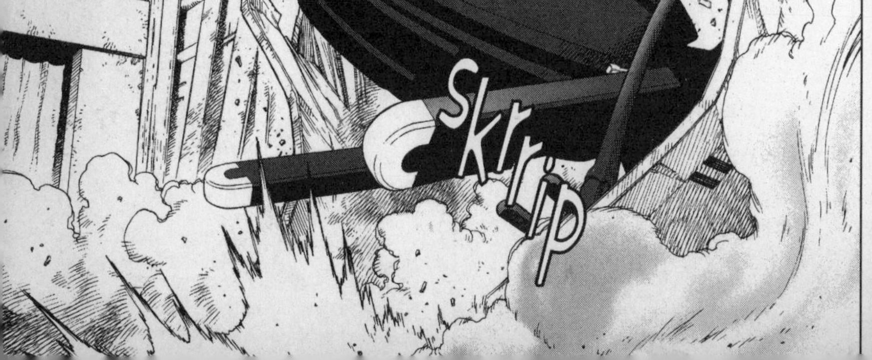
Beep, oop, eep!
EEK!
skrrip

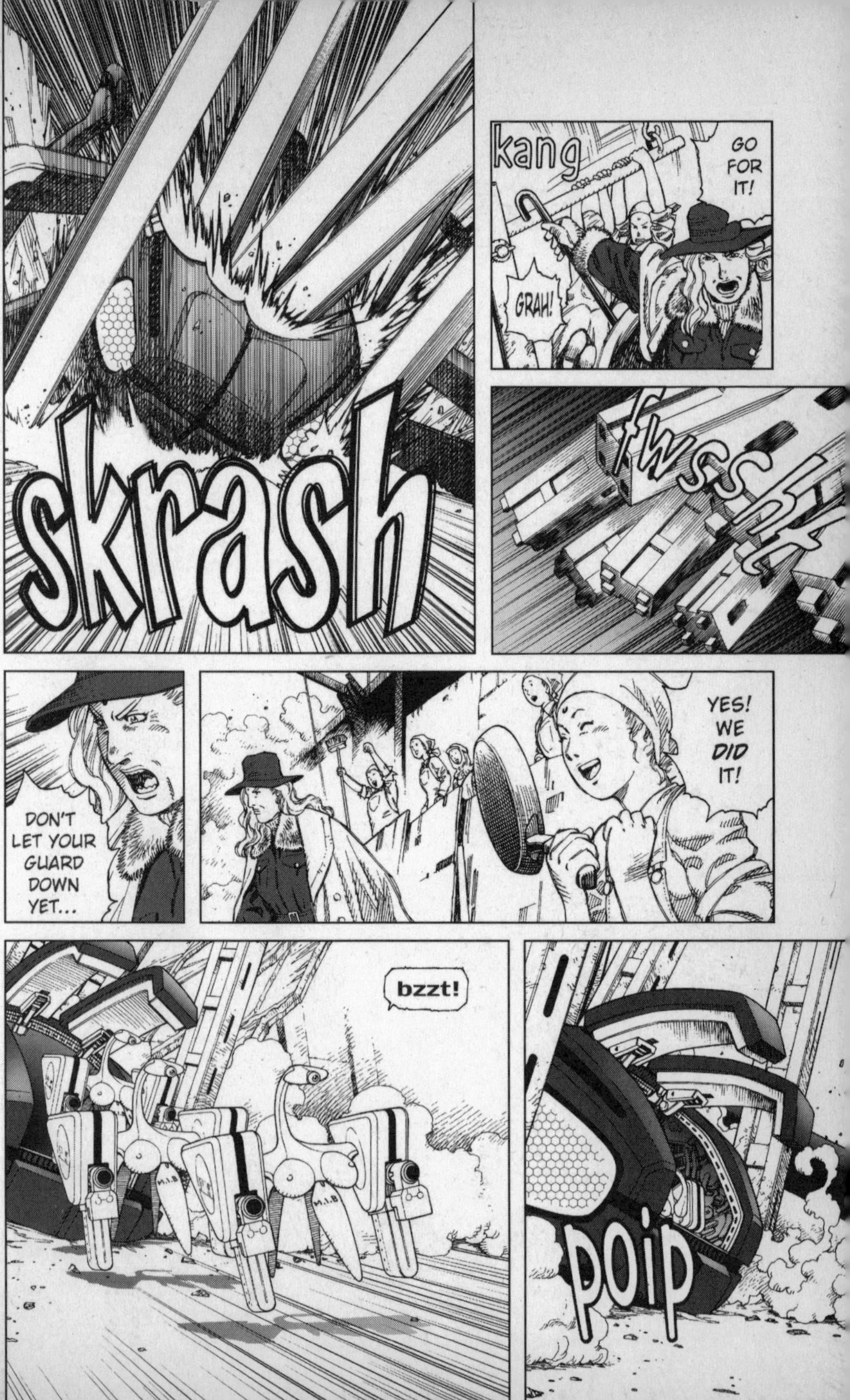
kang
GO FOR IT!
GRAH!
fwssht
skrash
YES! WE DID IT!
DON'T LET YOUR GUARD DOWN YET...
poip
bzzt!

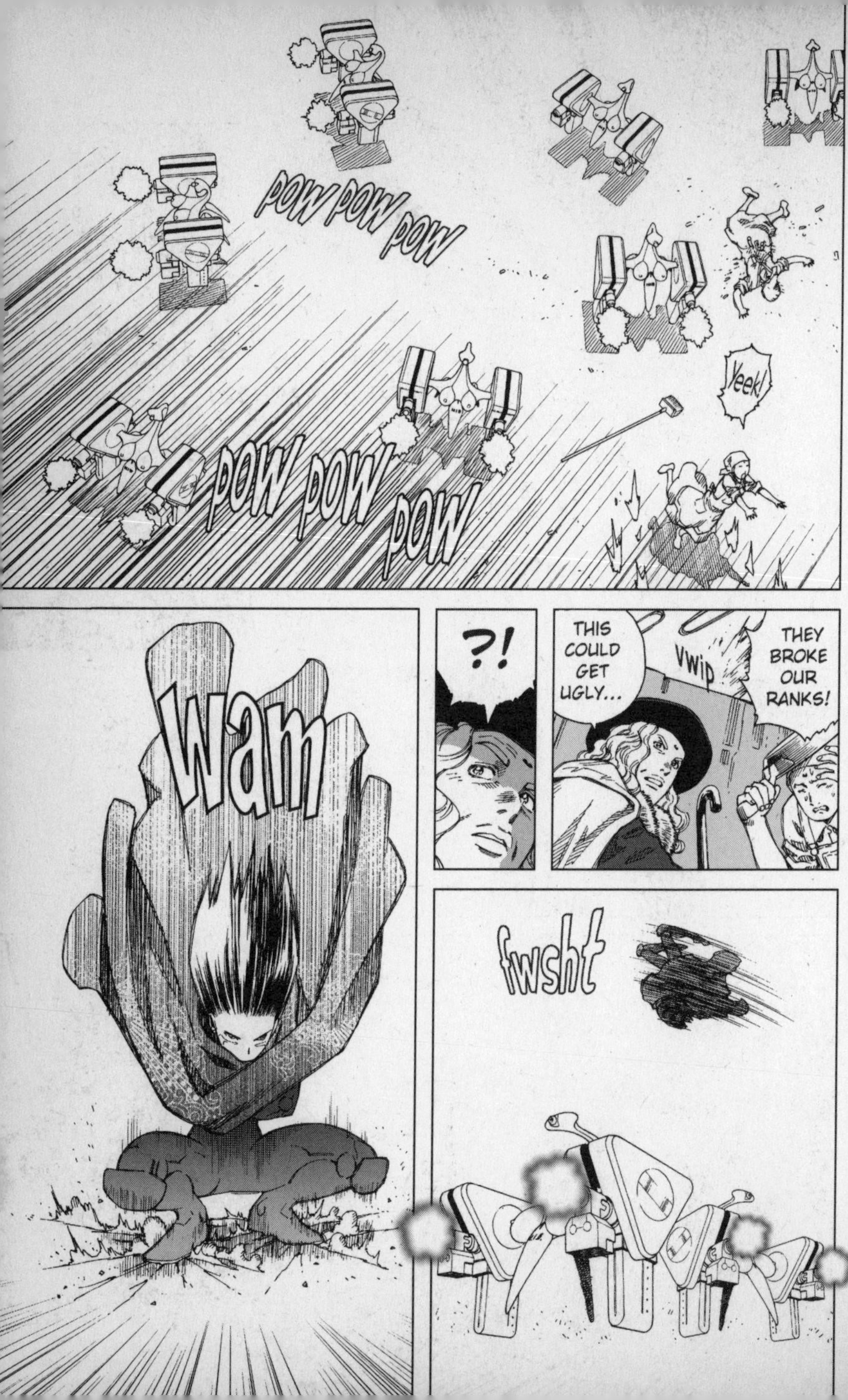
pow pow pow
Yeek!
pow pow pow
THEY BROKE OUR RANKS!
Vwip
THIS COULD GET UGLY...
?!
fwsht
wam

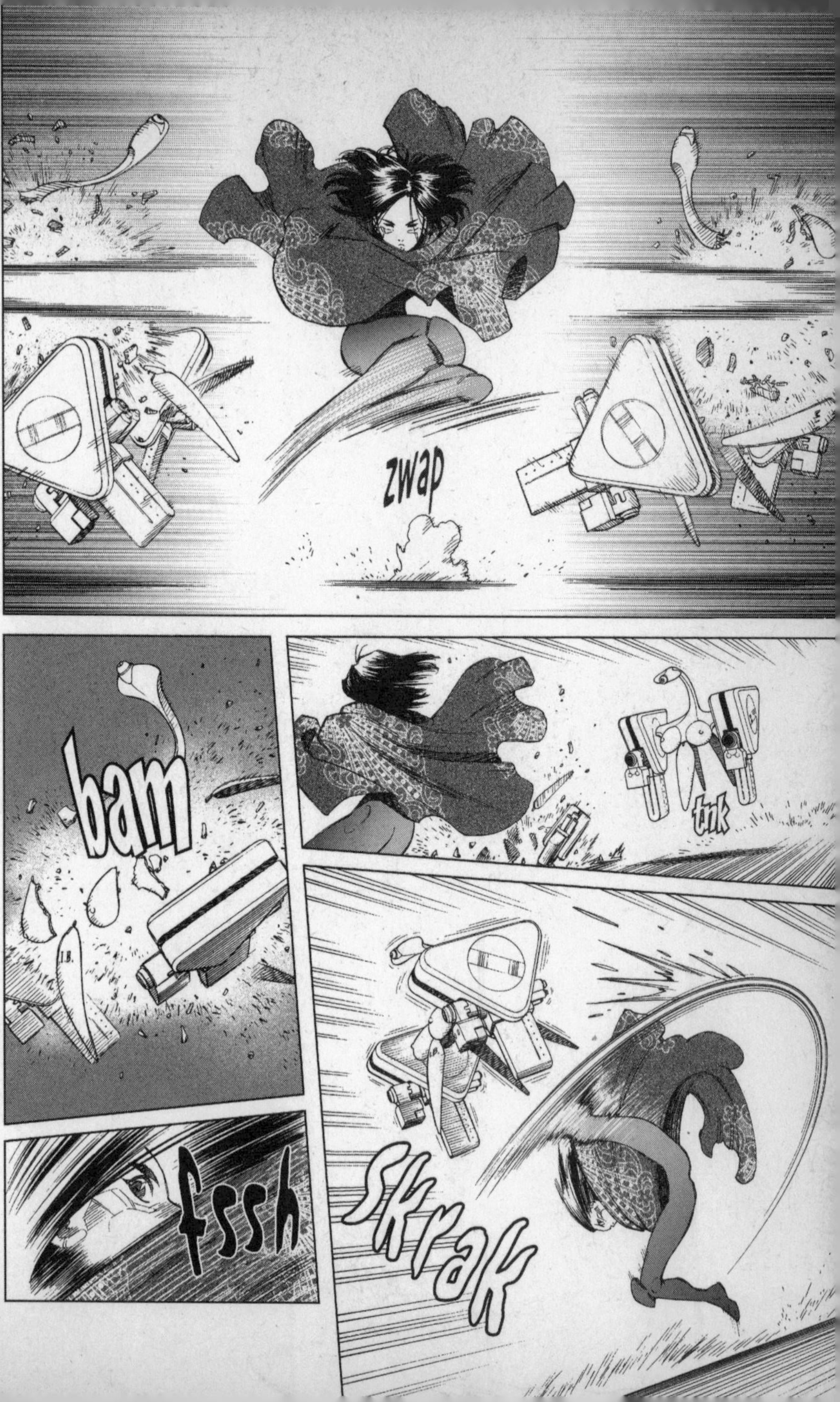
zwap
tnk
bam
Skrak
fssh

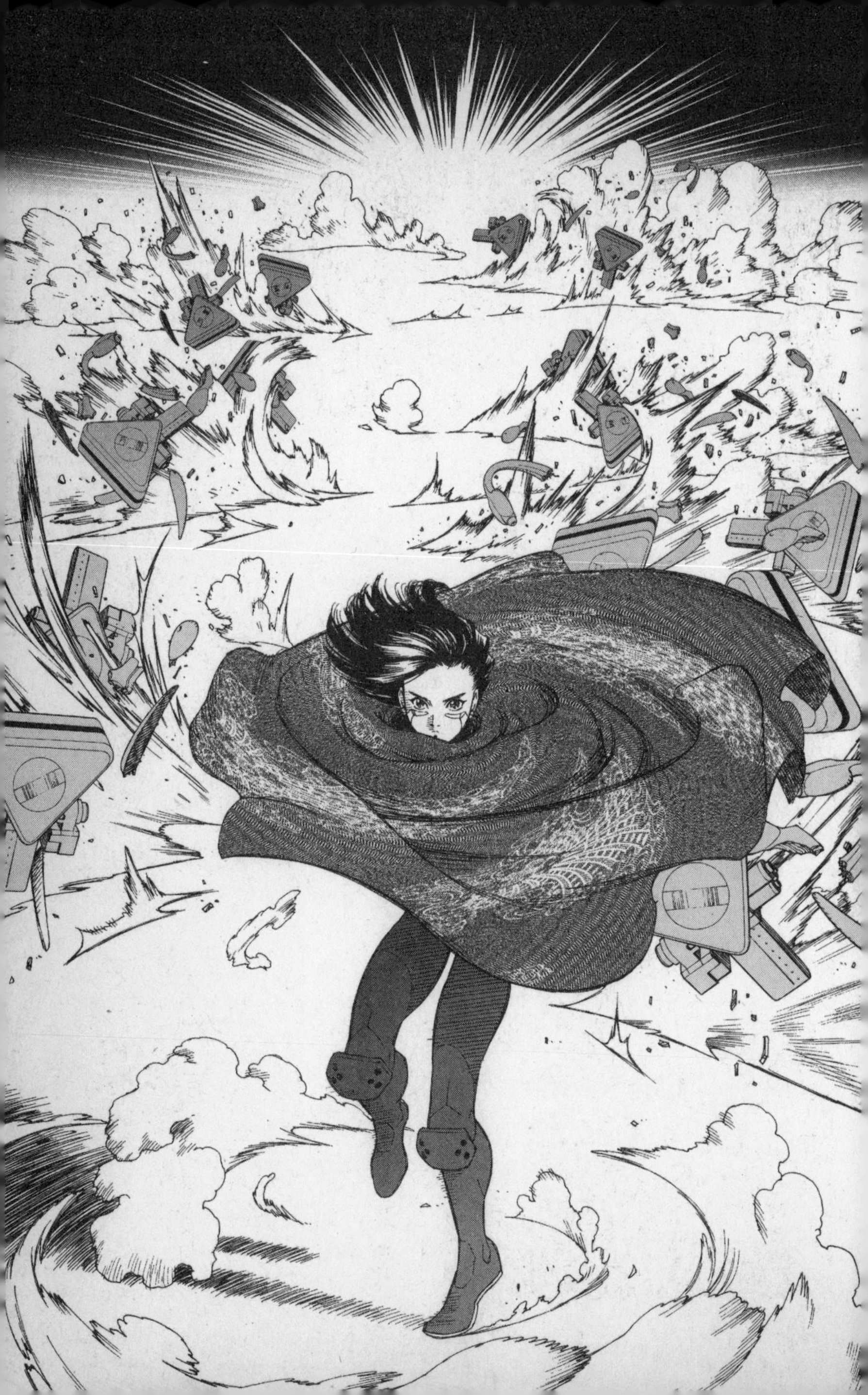

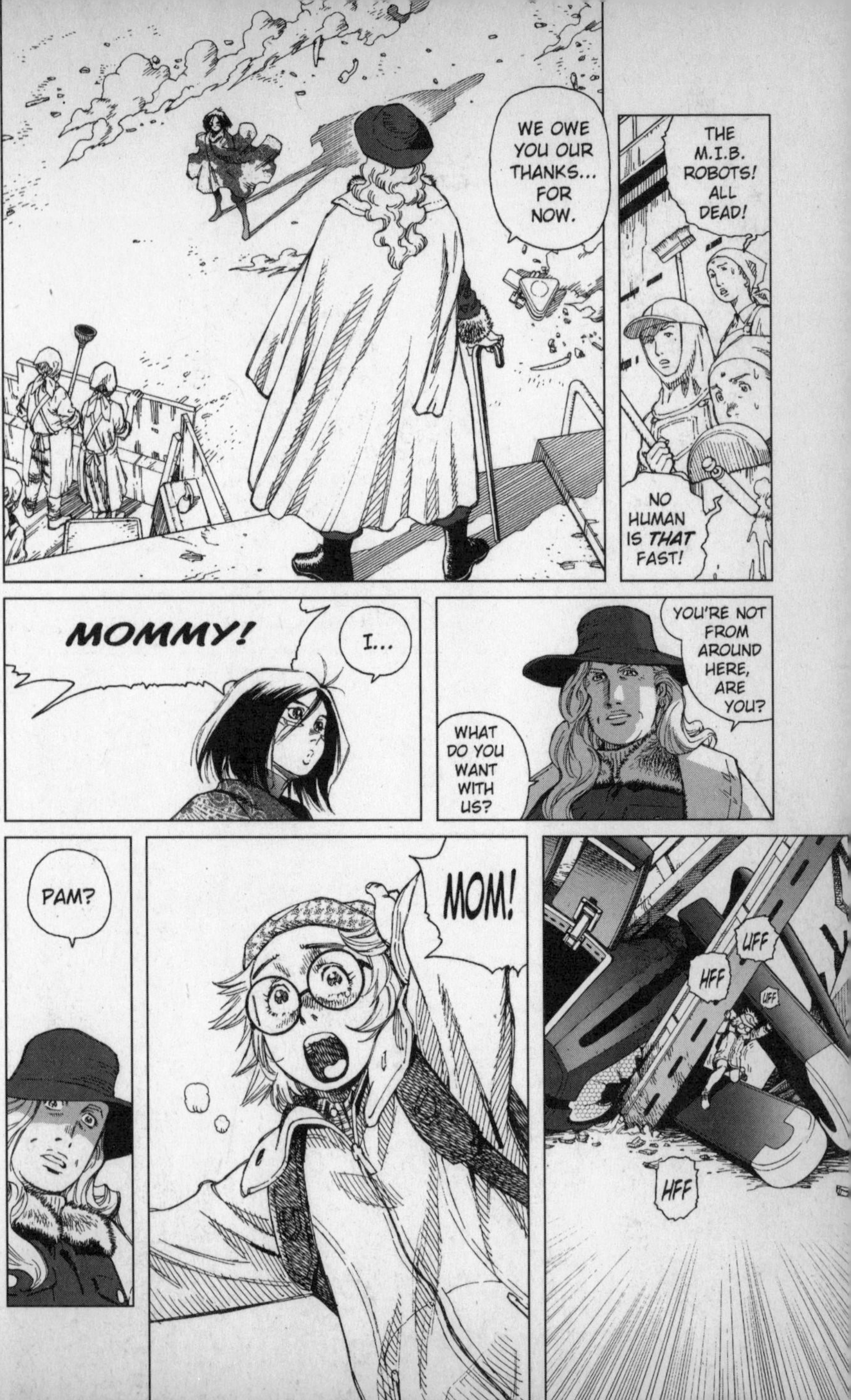
THE M.I.B. ROBOTS! ALL DEAD!
NO HUMAN IS *THAT* FAST!
WE OWE YOU OUR THANKS... FOR NOW.
YOU'RE NOT FROM AROUND HERE, ARE YOU?
WHAT DO YOU WANT WITH US?
I...
MOMMY!
UFF
HFF
UFF
HFF
MOM!
PAM?

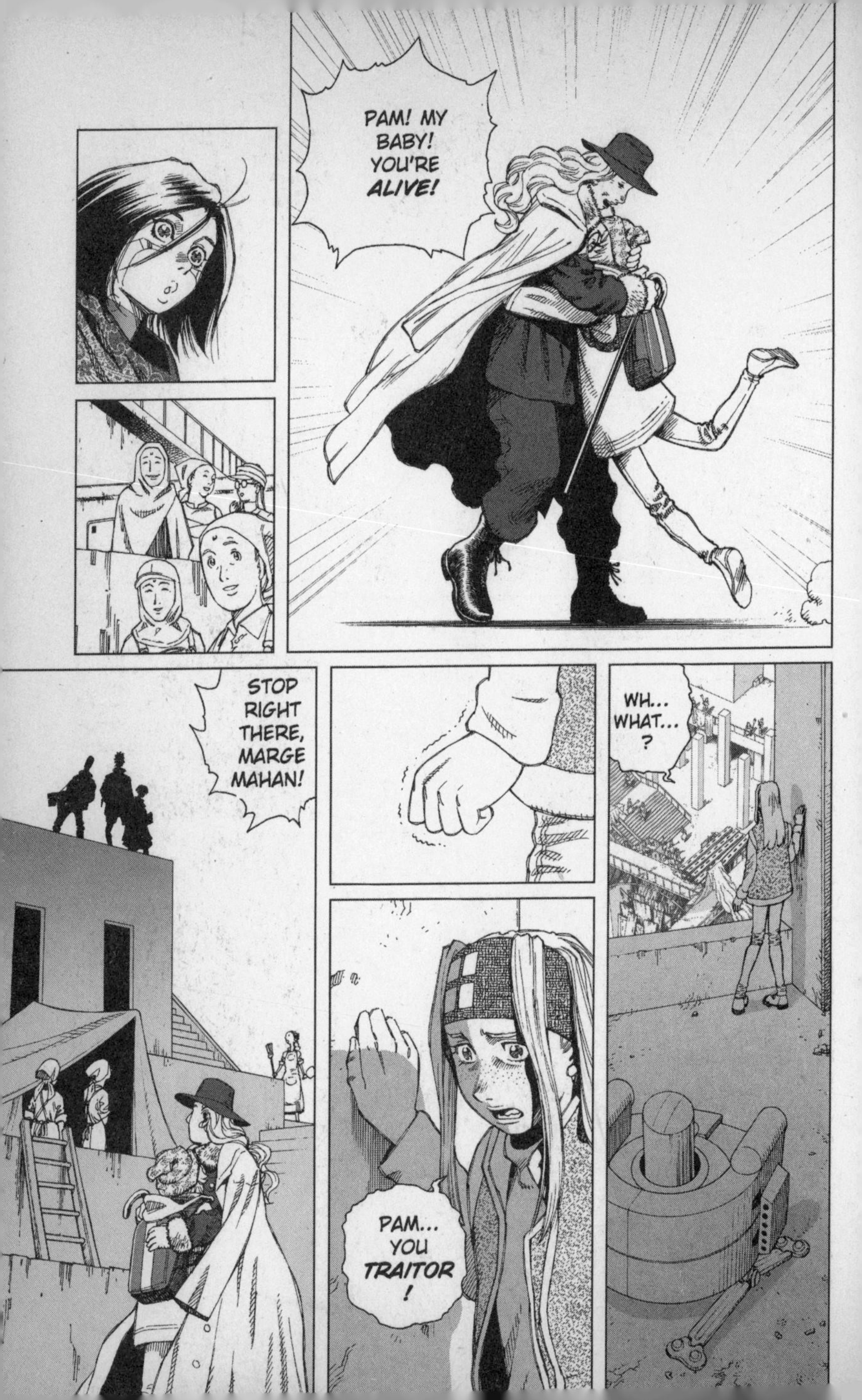
PAM! MY BABY! YOU'RE *ALIVE!*
WH... WHAT... ?
PAM... YOU *TRAITOR* !
STOP RIGHT THERE, MARGE MAHAN!

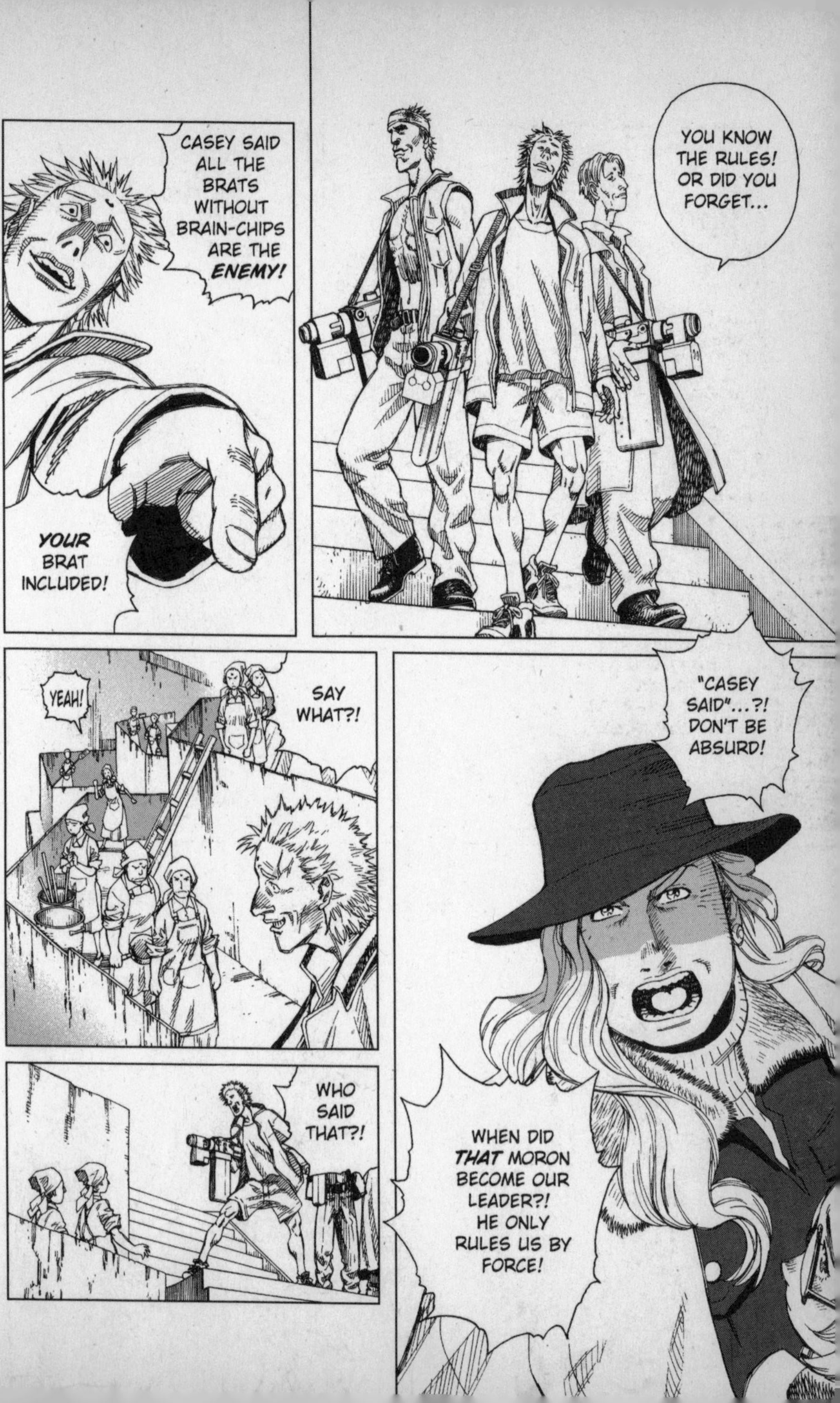
YOU KNOW THE RULES! OR DID YOU FORGET...
CASEY SAID ALL THE BRATS WITHOUT BRAIN-CHIPS ARE THE ENEMY!
YOUR BRAT INCLUDED!
"CASEY SAID"...?! DON'T BE ABSURD!
WHEN DID THAT MORON BECOME OUR LEADER?! HE ONLY RULES US BY FORCE!
SAY WHAT?!
YEAH!
WHO SAID THAT?!

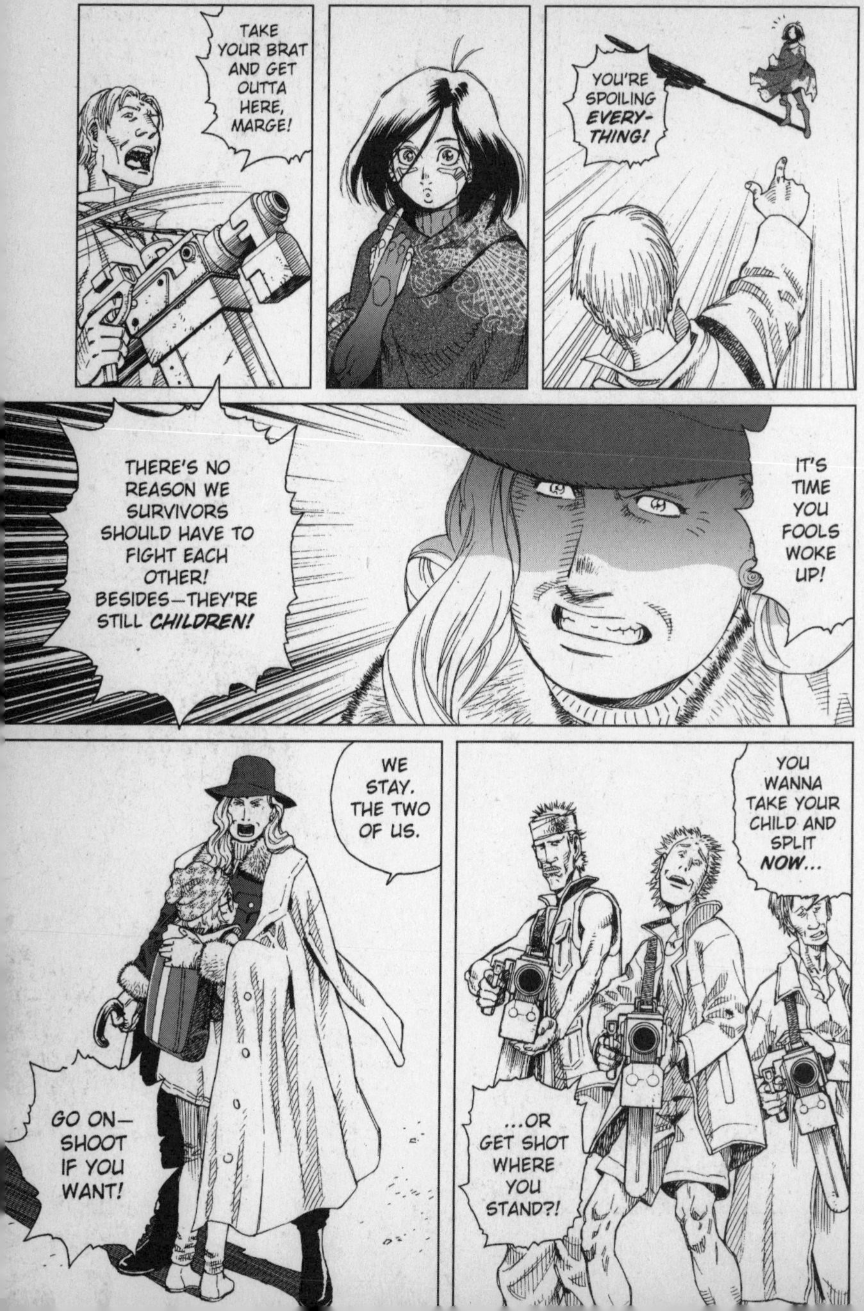
YOU'RE SPOILING EVERYTHING!
TAKE YOUR BRAT AND GET OUTTA HERE, MARGE!
IT'S TIME YOU FOOLS WOKE UP!
THERE'S NO REASON WE SURVIVORS SHOULD HAVE TO FIGHT EACH OTHER! BESIDES—THEY'RE STILL CHILDREN!
YOU WANNA TAKE YOUR CHILD AND SPLIT NOW...
...OR GET SHOT WHERE YOU STAND?!
WE STAY. THE TWO OF US.
GO ON— SHOOT IF YOU WANT!

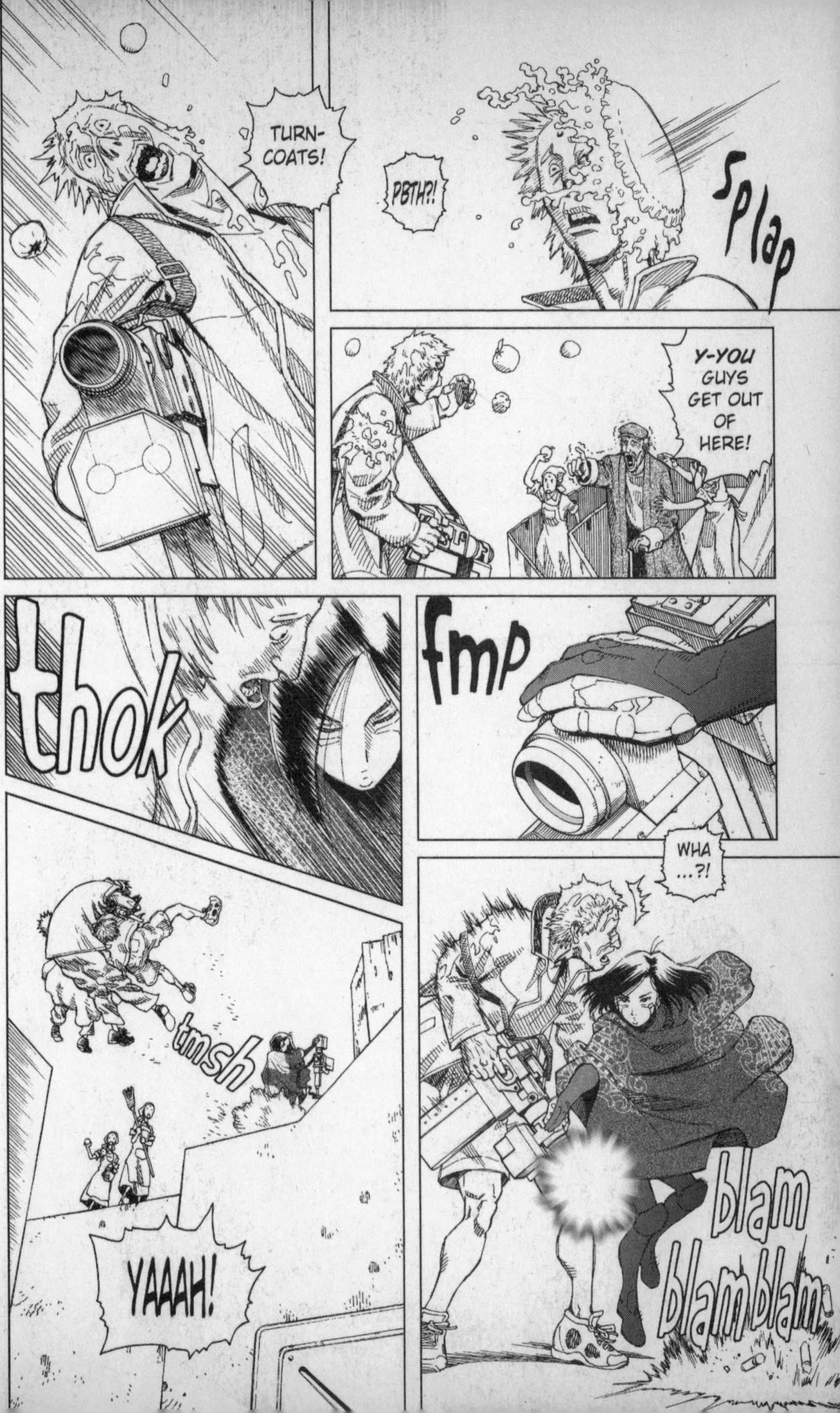
Splap
PBTH?!
Y-YOU GUYS GET OUT OF HERE!
TURN-COATS!
fmp
thok
WHA ...?!
blam
blamblam
tmsh
YAAAH!

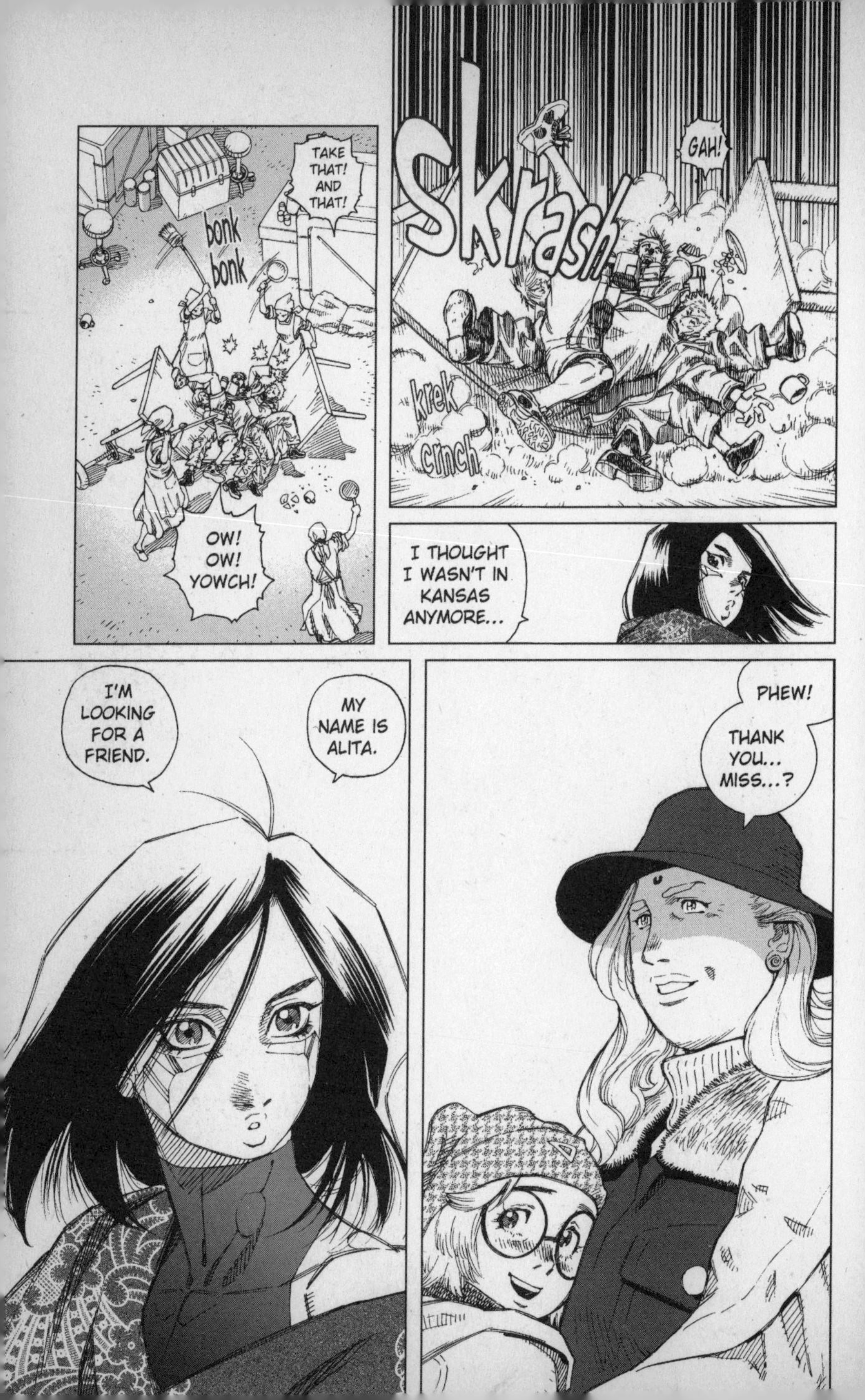
GAH!
Skrash
krek
crnch
I THOUGHT I WASN'T IN KANSAS ANYMORE...
TAKE THAT! AND THAT!
bonk
bonk
OW! OW! YOWCH!
PHEW!
THANK YOU... MISS...?
MY NAME IS ALITA.
I'M LOOKING FOR A FRIEND.

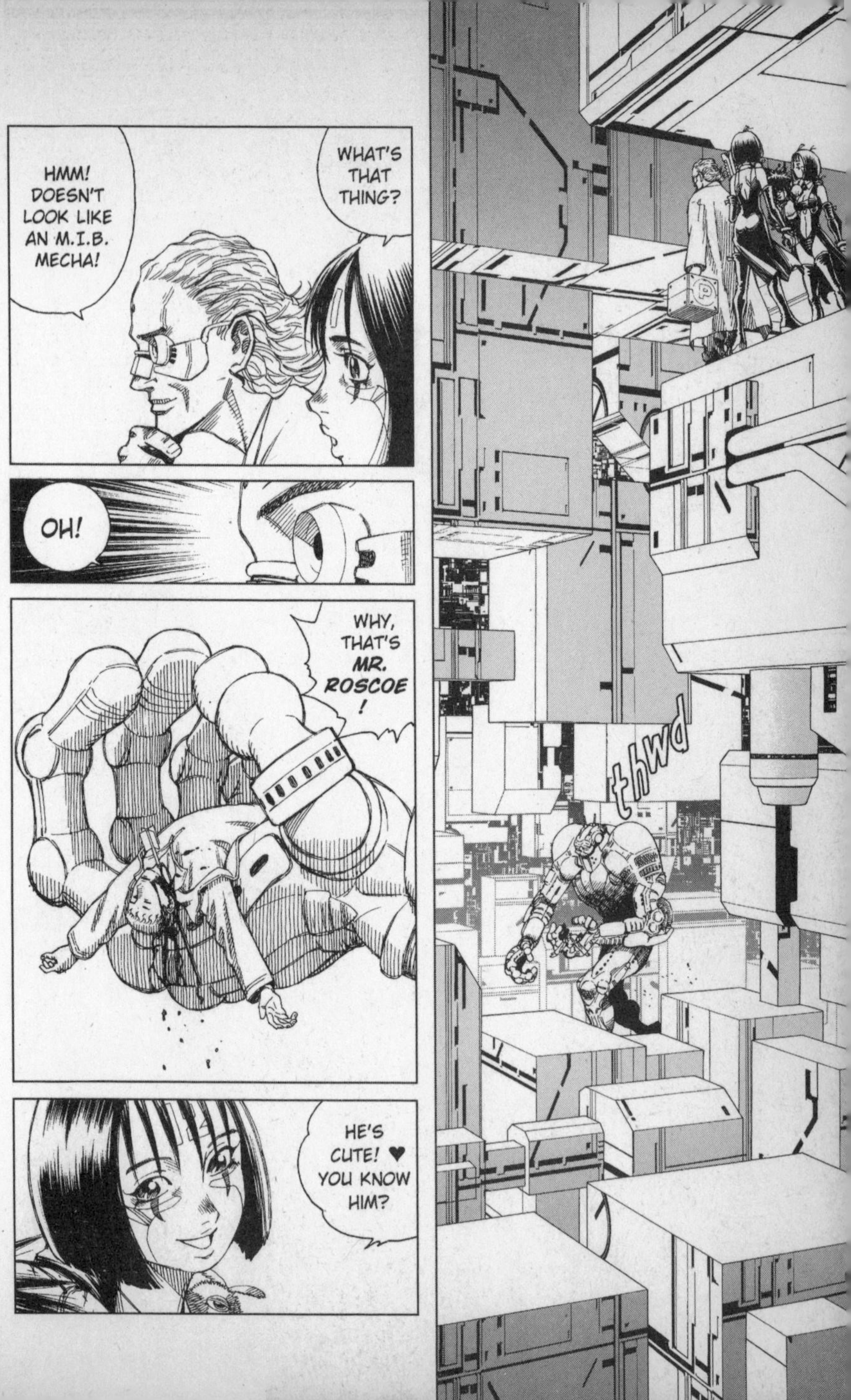
thwd
WHAT'S THAT THING?
HMM! DOESN'T LOOK LIKE AN M.I.B. MECHA!
OH!
WHY, THAT'S **MR. ROSCOE**!
HE'S CUTE! ♥ YOU KNOW HIM?

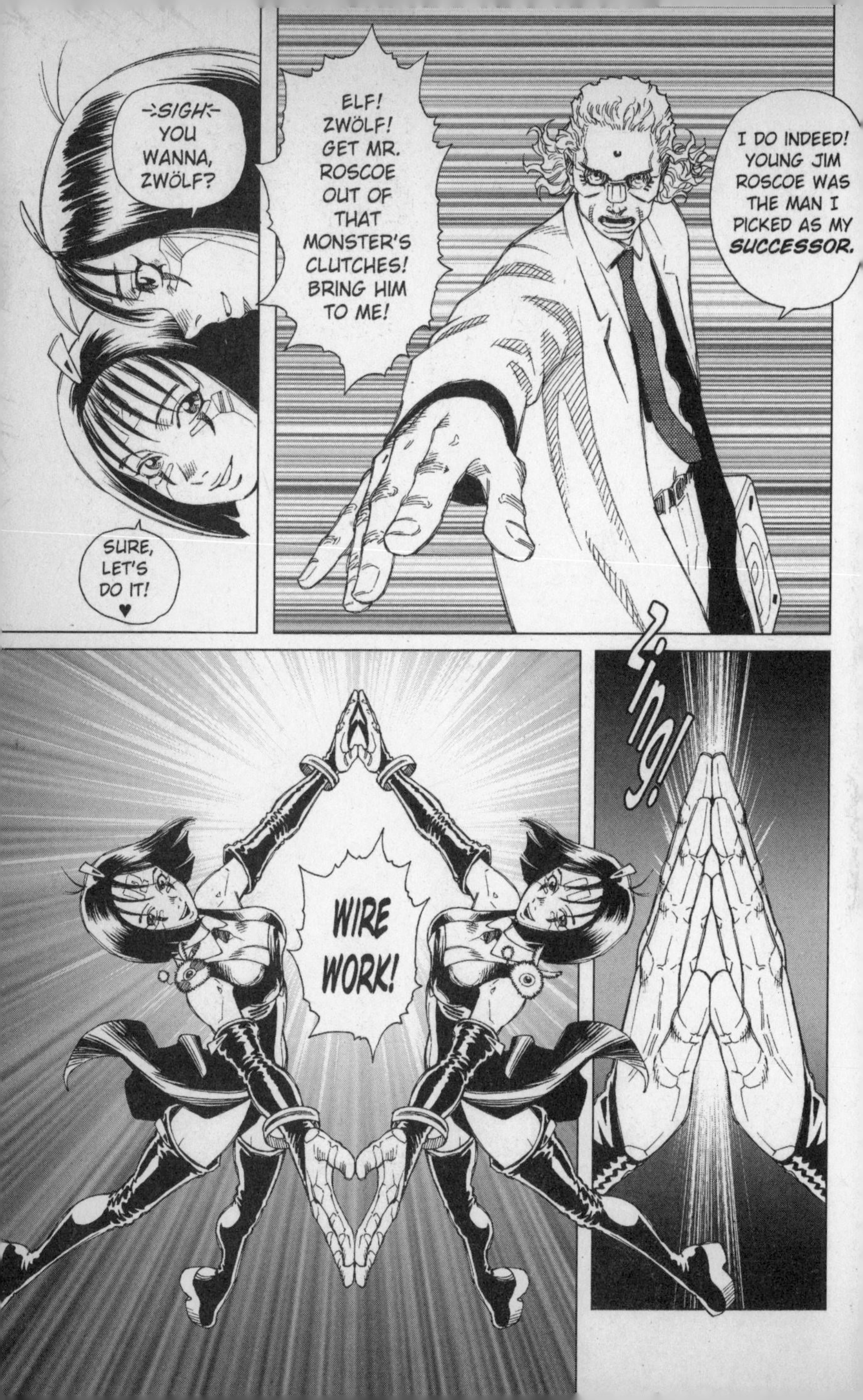
I DO INDEED! YOUNG JIM ROSCOE WAS THE MAN I PICKED AS MY SUCCESSOR.
ELF! ZWÖLF! GET MR. ROSCOE OUT OF THAT MONSTER'S CLUTCHES! BRING HIM TO ME!
-SIGH- YOU WANNA, ZWÖLF?
SURE, LET'S DO IT! ♥
Zing!
WIRE WORK!

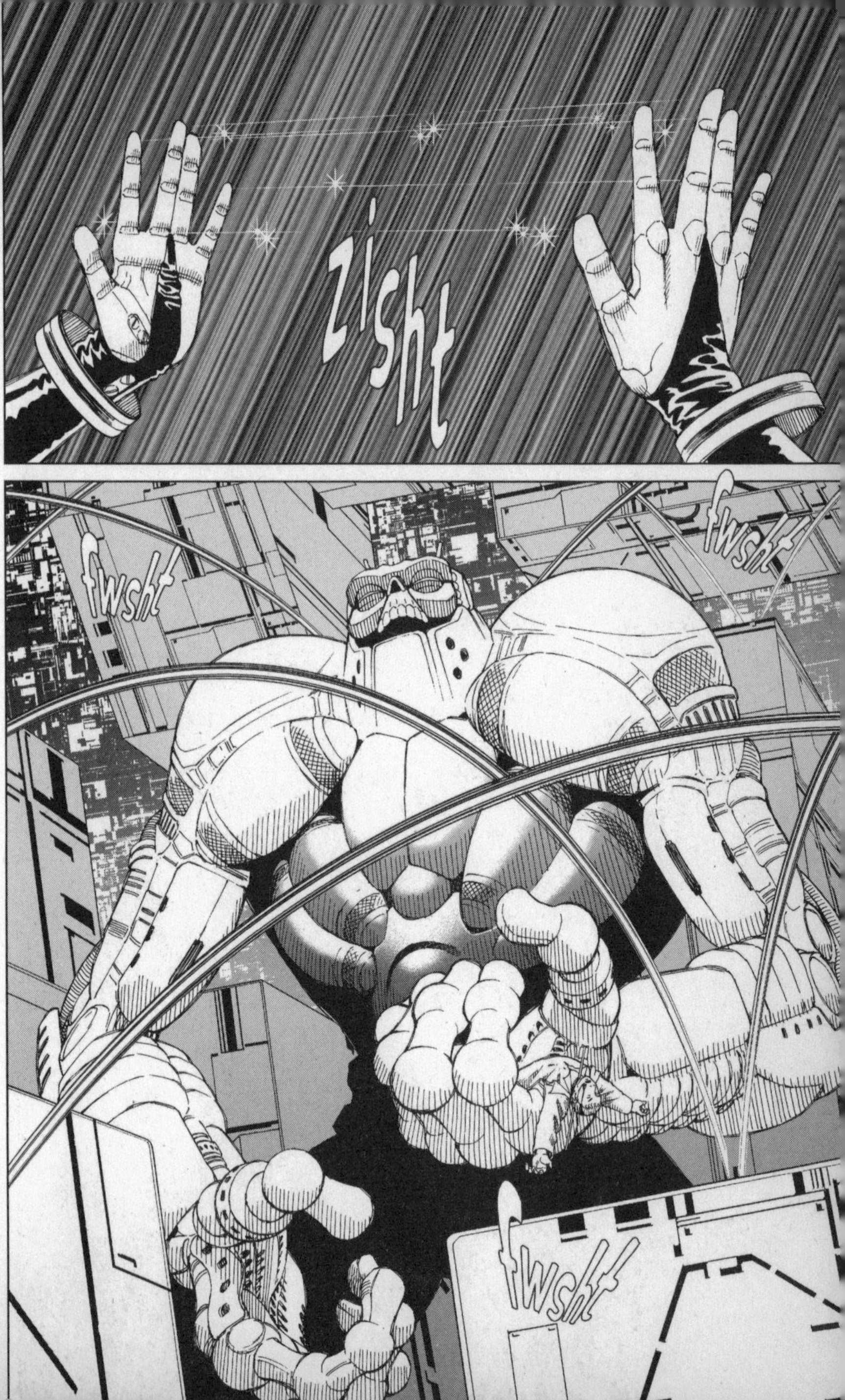
zisht
fwsht
fwsht
fwsht

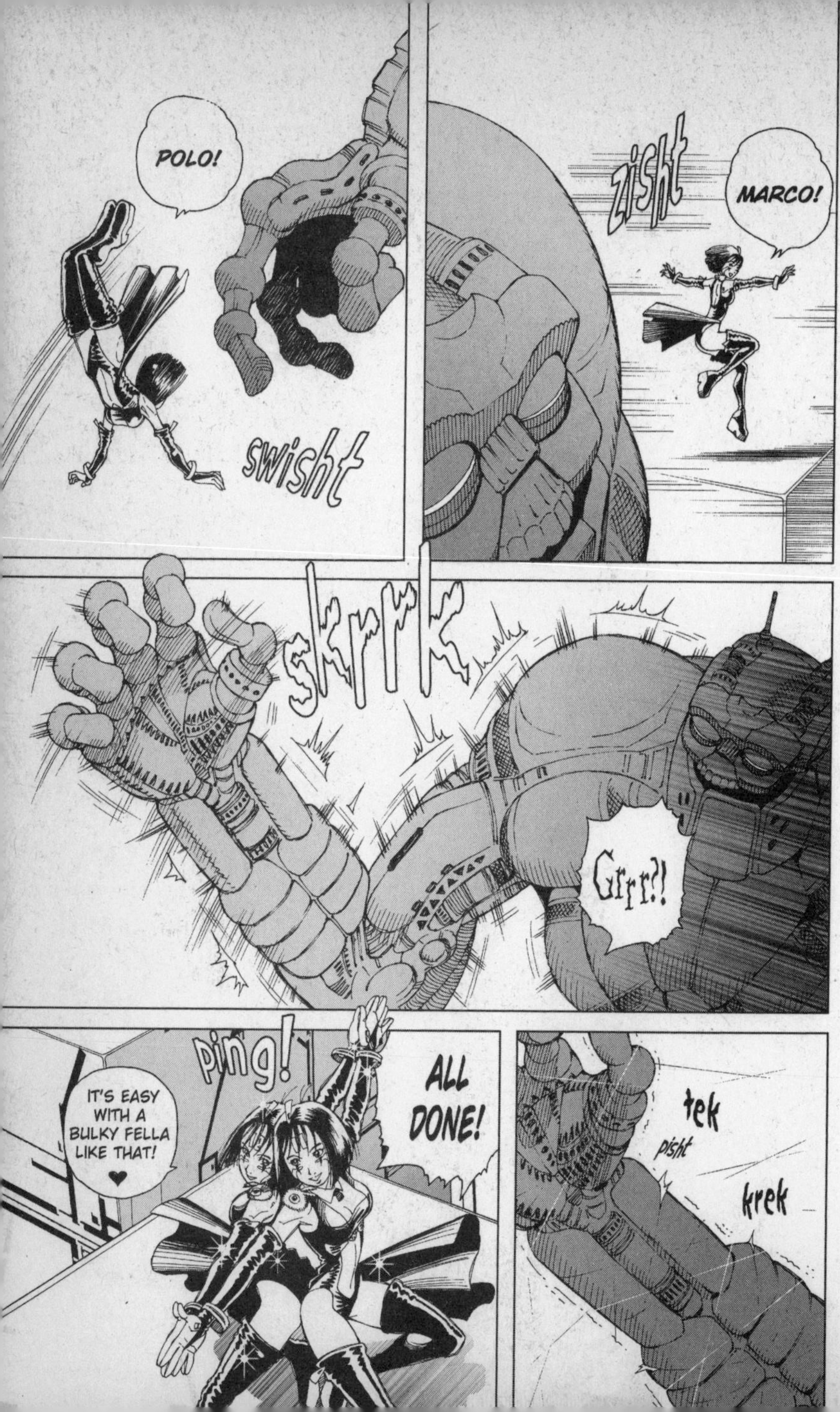
zisht
MARCO!
POLO!
swisht
skrrk
Grrr?!
tek
pisht
krek
ALL DONE!
ping!
IT'S EASY WITH A BULKY FELLA LIKE THAT! ♥

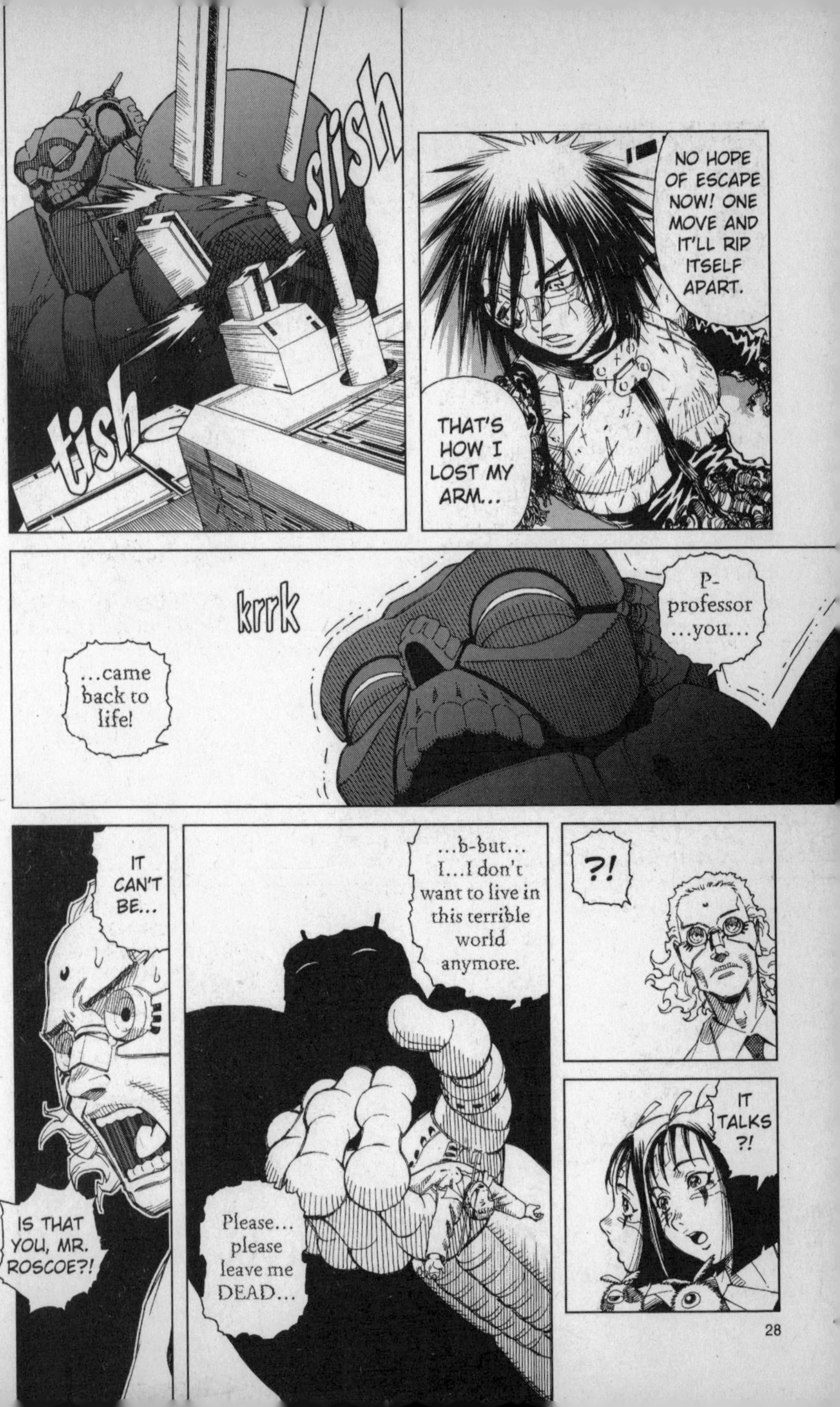
NO HOPE OF ESCAPE NOW! ONE MOVE AND IT'LL RIP ITSELF APART.
THAT'S HOW I LOST MY ARM...
slish
tish
P- professor ...you...
krrk
...came back to life!
?!
IT TALKS?!
...b-but... I...I don't want to live in this terrible world anymore.
Please... please leave me DEAD...
IT CAN'T BE...
IS THAT YOU, MR. ROSCOE?!

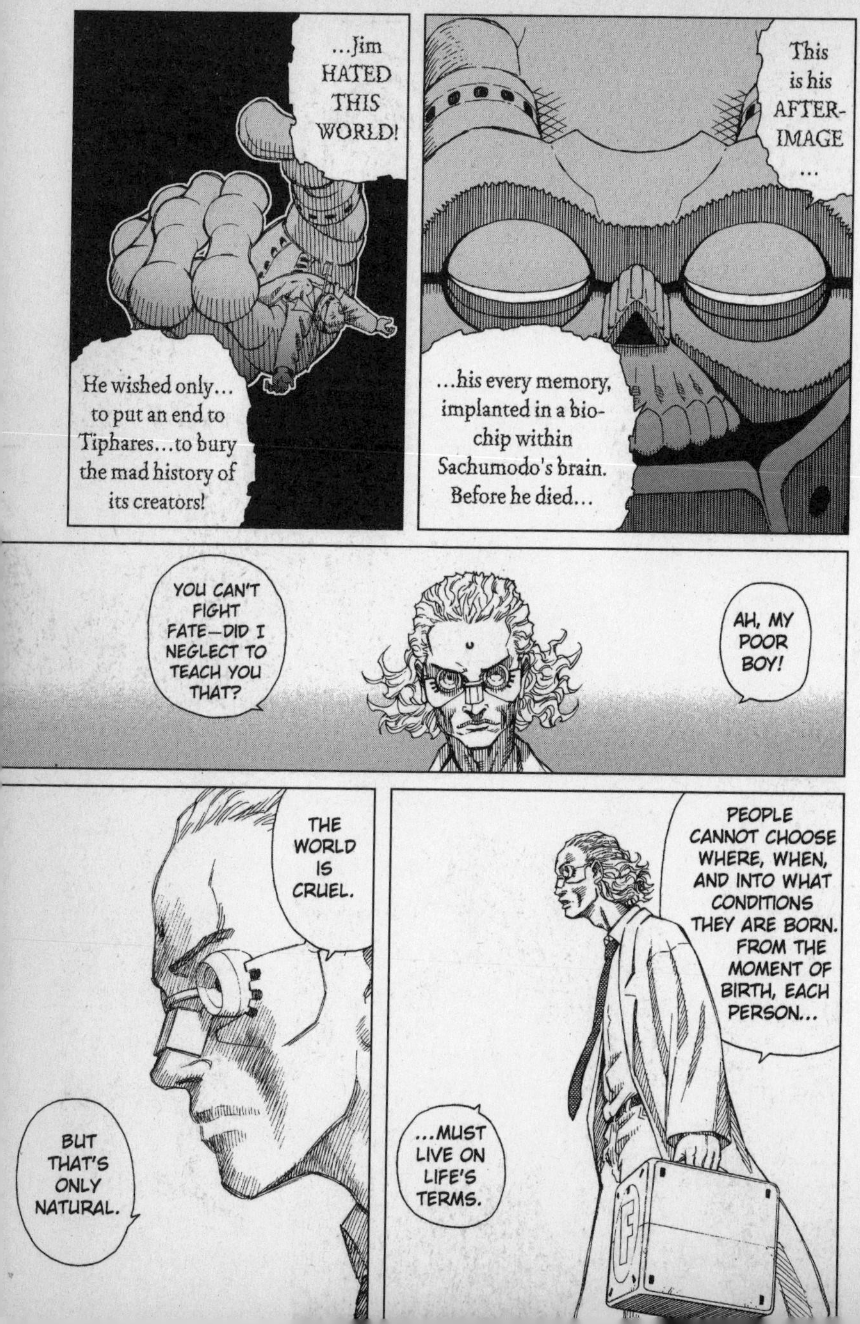
This is his AFTER-IMAGE...
...his every memory, implanted in a bio-chip within Sachumodo's brain. Before he died...
...Jim HATED THIS WORLD!
He wished only... to put an end to Tiphares...to bury the mad history of its creators!
AH, MY POOR BOY!
YOU CAN'T FIGHT FATE—DID I NEGLECT TO TEACH YOU THAT?
PEOPLE CANNOT CHOOSE WHERE, WHEN, AND INTO WHAT CONDITIONS THEY ARE BORN. FROM THE MOMENT OF BIRTH, EACH PERSON...
...MUST LIVE ON LIFE'S TERMS.
THE WORLD IS CRUEL.
BUT THAT'S ONLY NATURAL.

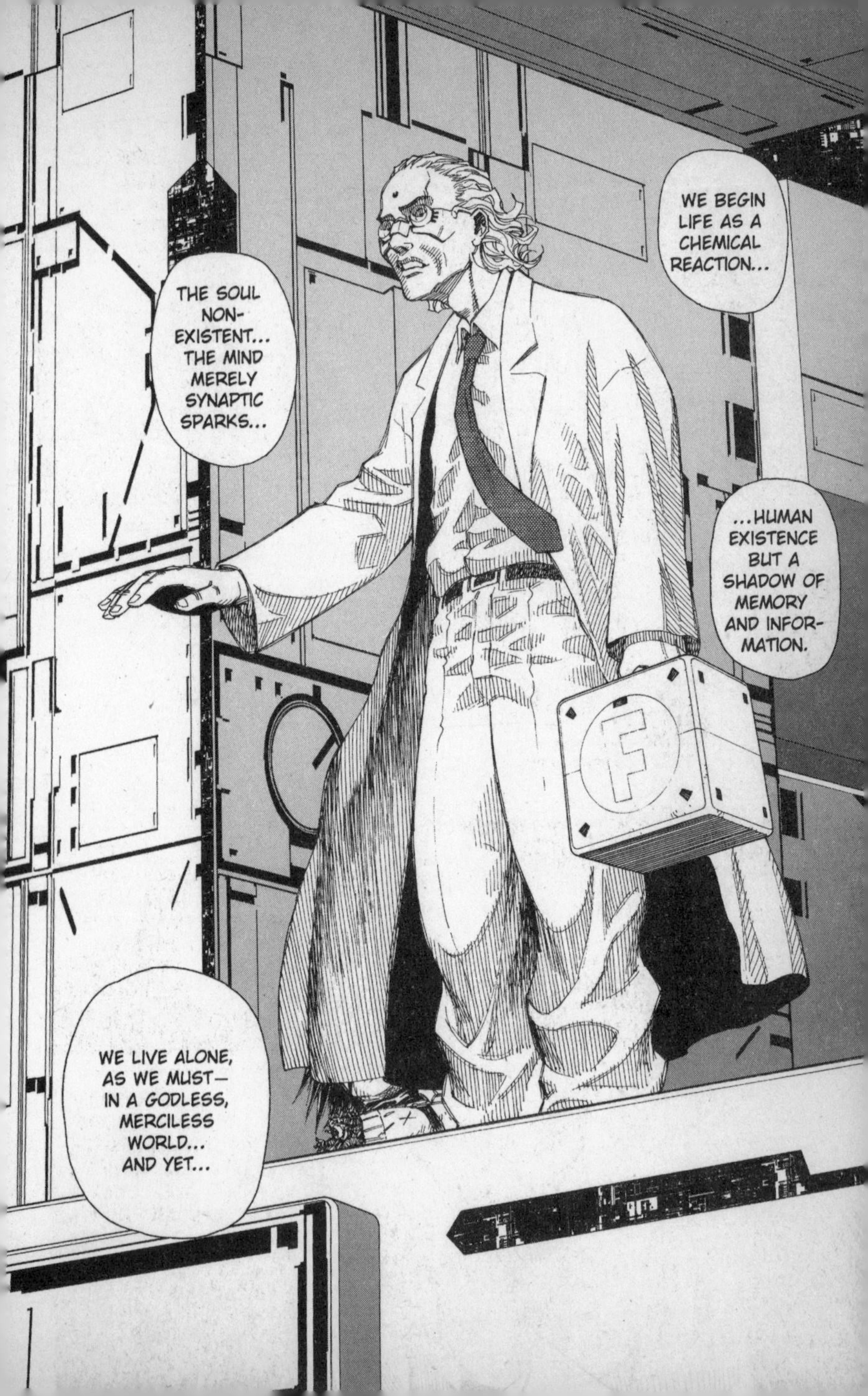
WE BEGIN LIFE AS A CHEMICAL REACTION...
THE SOUL NON-EXISTENT... THE MIND MERELY SYNAPTIC SPARKS...
...HUMAN EXISTENCE BUT A SHADOW OF MEMORY AND INFORMATION.
WE LIVE ALONE, AS WE MUST— IN A GODLESS, MERCILESS WORLD... AND YET...

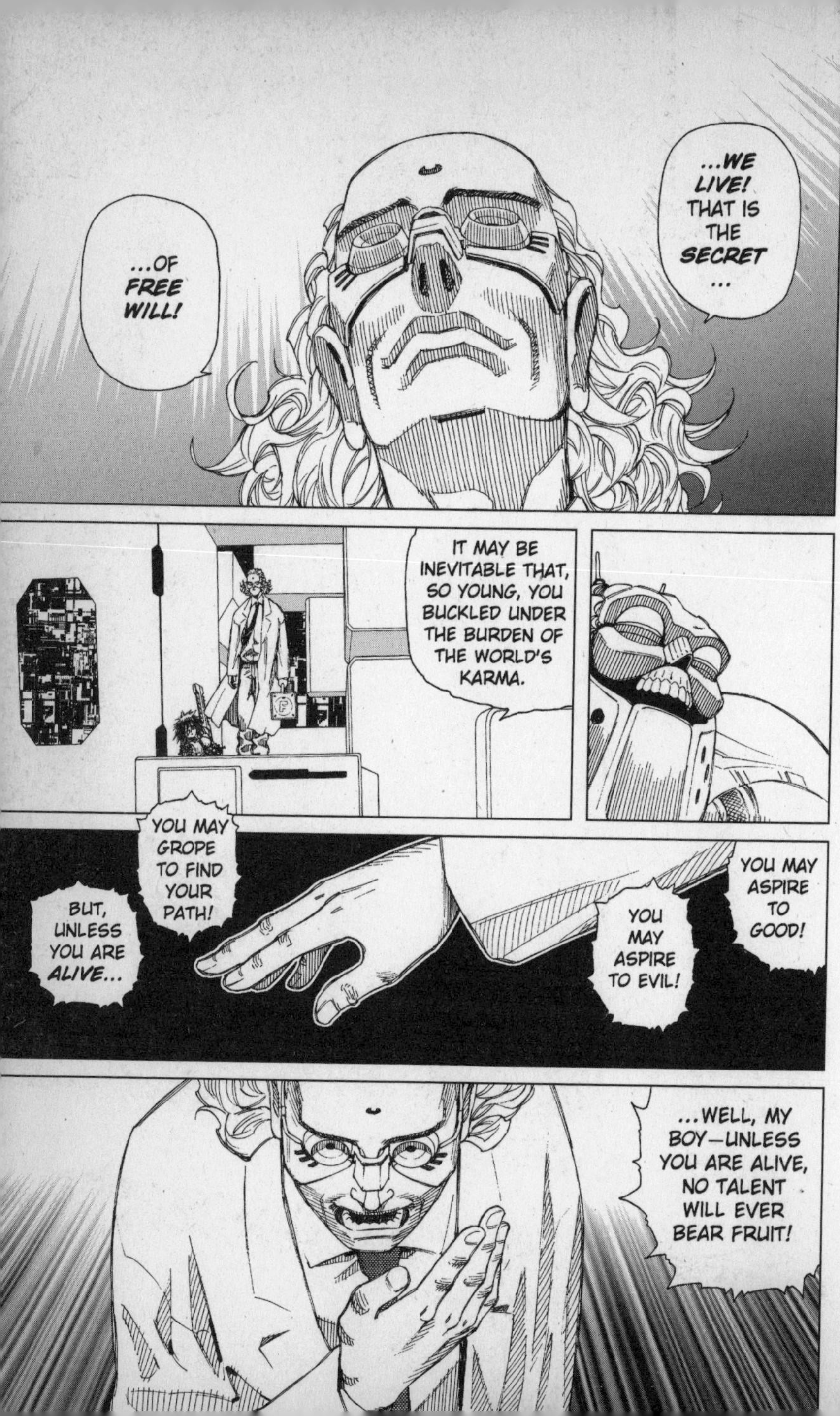
...WE LIVE! THAT IS THE SECRET ...
...OF FREE WILL!
IT MAY BE INEVITABLE THAT, SO YOUNG, YOU BUCKLED UNDER THE BURDEN OF THE WORLD'S KARMA.
YOU MAY ASPIRE TO GOOD!
YOU MAY ASPIRE TO EVIL!
YOU MAY GROPE TO FIND YOUR PATH!
BUT, UNLESS YOU ARE ALIVE...
...WELL, MY BOY—UNLESS YOU ARE ALIVE, NO TALENT WILL EVER BEAR FRUIT!

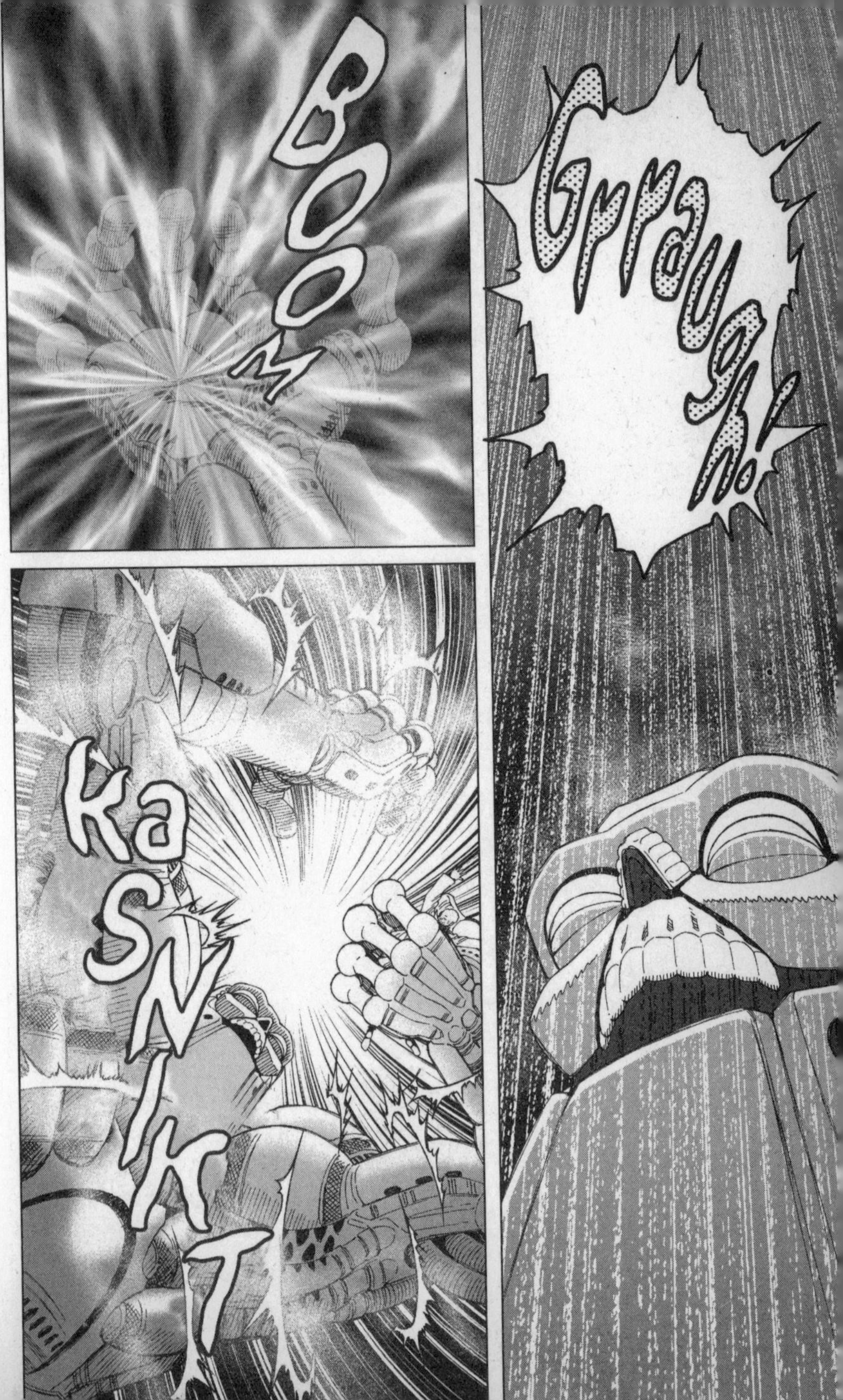
Grraugh!
BOOM
KaSNIKT

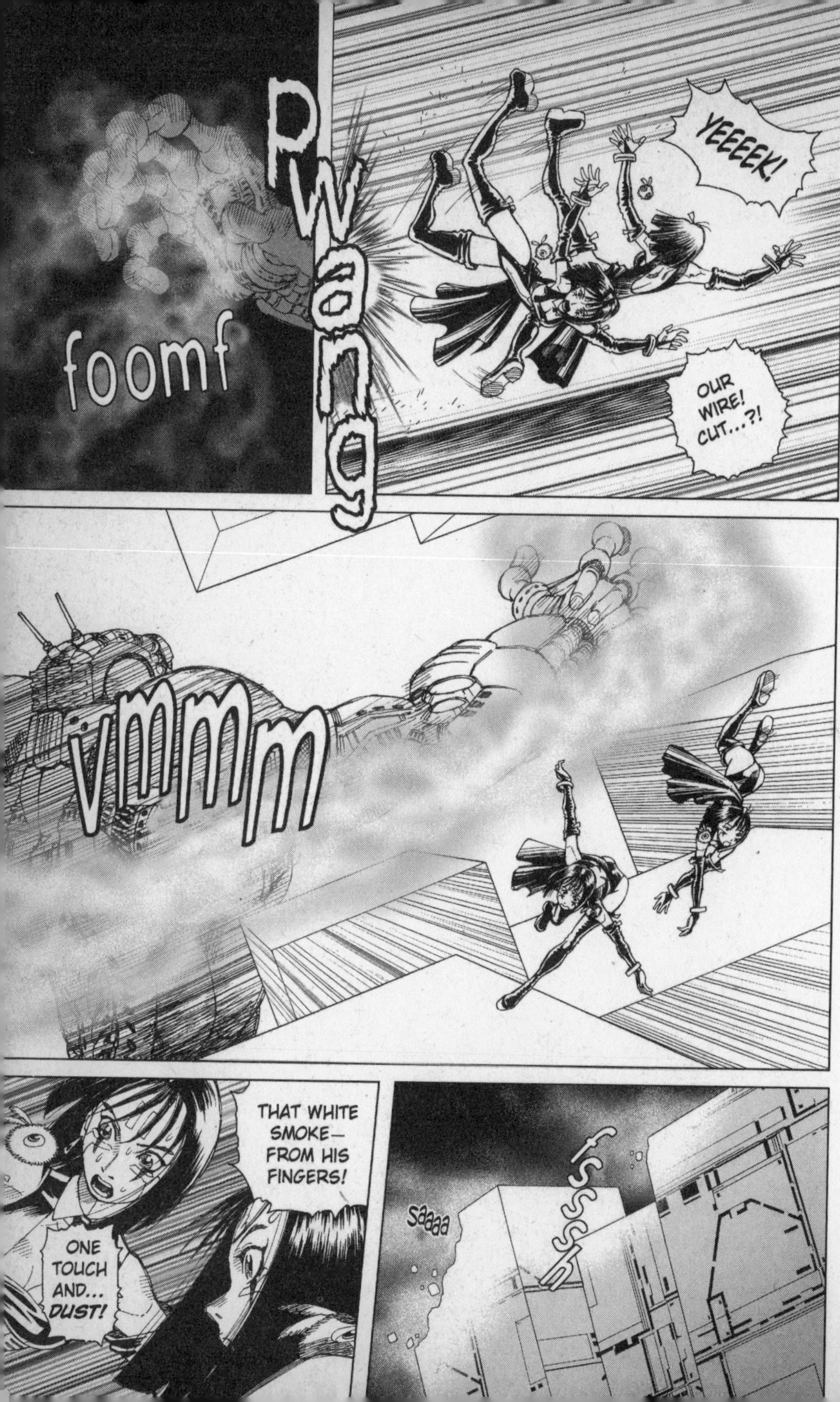
YEEEEK!
OUR WIRE! CUT...?!
Pwang
foomf
vmmm
fssh
saaaa
THAT WHITE SMOKE— FROM HIS FINGERS!
ONE TOUCH AND... *DUST!*

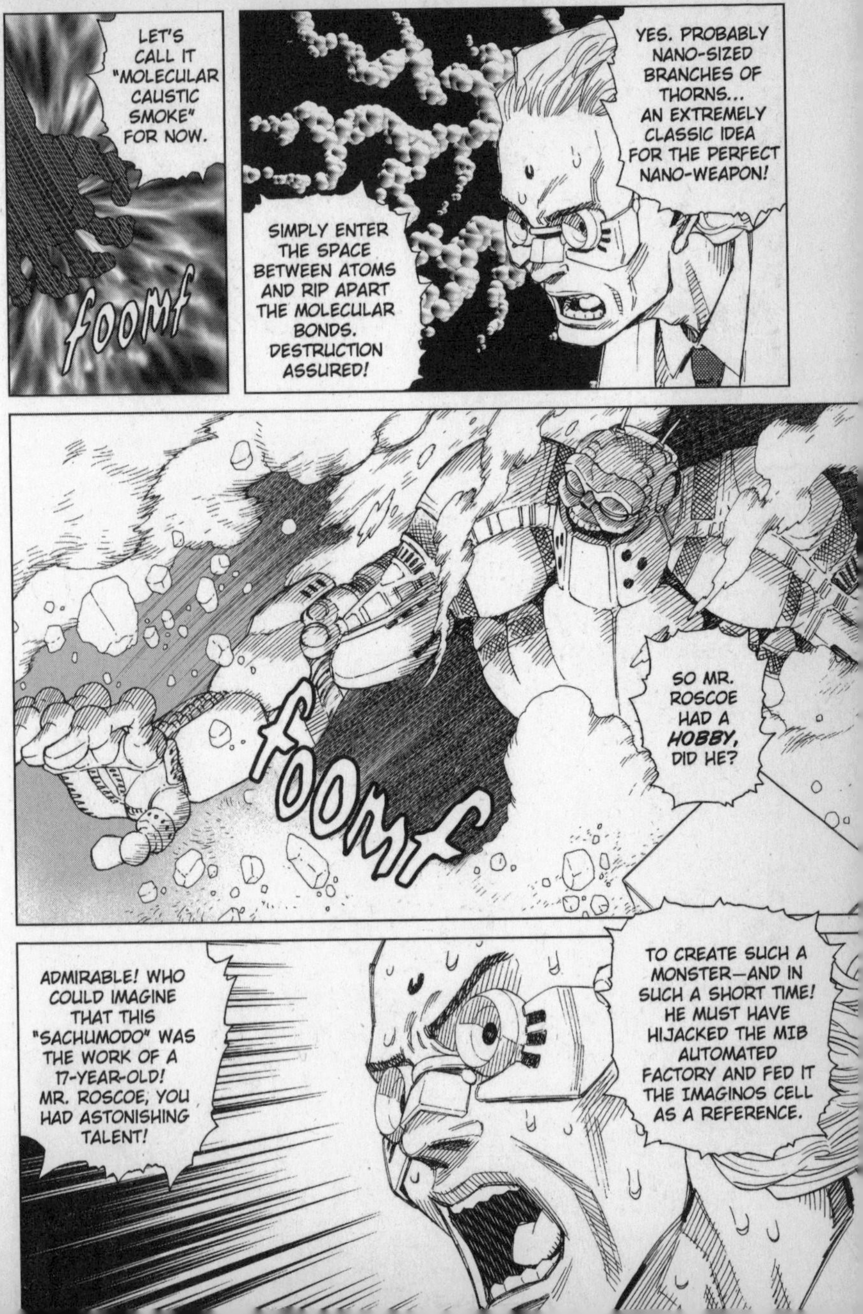
YES. PROBABLY NANO-SIZED BRANCHES OF THORNS... AN EXTREMELY CLASSIC IDEA FOR THE PERFECT NANO-WEAPON!
SIMPLY ENTER THE SPACE BETWEEN ATOMS AND RIP APART THE MOLECULAR BONDS. DESTRUCTION ASSURED!
LET'S CALL IT "MOLECULAR CAUSTIC SMOKE" FOR NOW.
foomf
SO MR. ROSCOE HAD A ***HOBBY***, DID HE?
foomf
TO CREATE SUCH A MONSTER—AND IN SUCH A SHORT TIME! HE MUST HAVE HIJACKED THE MIB AUTOMATED FACTORY AND FED IT THE IMAGINOS CELL AS A REFERENCE.
ADMIRABLE! WHO COULD IMAGINE THAT THIS "SACHUMODO" WAS THE WORK OF A 17-YEAR-OLD! MR. ROSCOE, YOU HAD ASTONISHING TALENT!

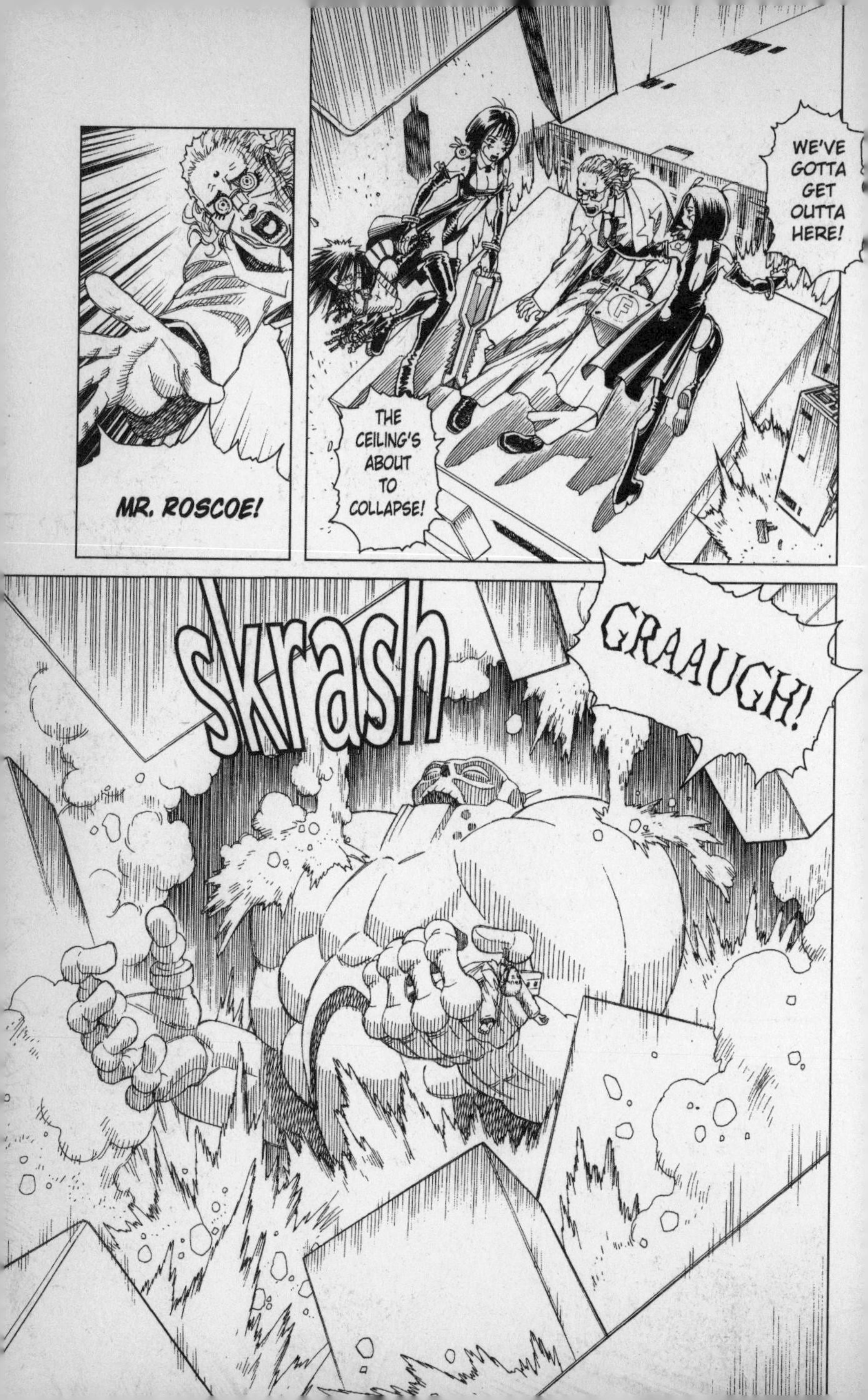
WE'VE GOTTA GET OUTTA HERE!
THE CEILING'S ABOUT TO COLLAPSE!
MR. ROSCOE!
GRAAUGH!
skrash

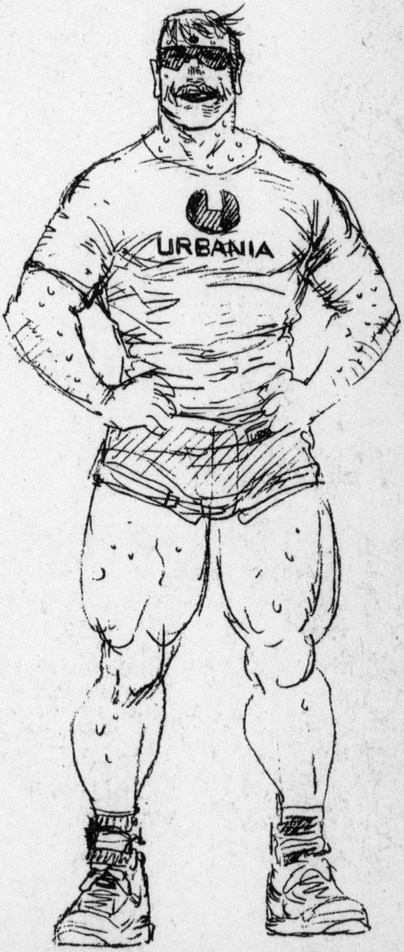
URBANIA

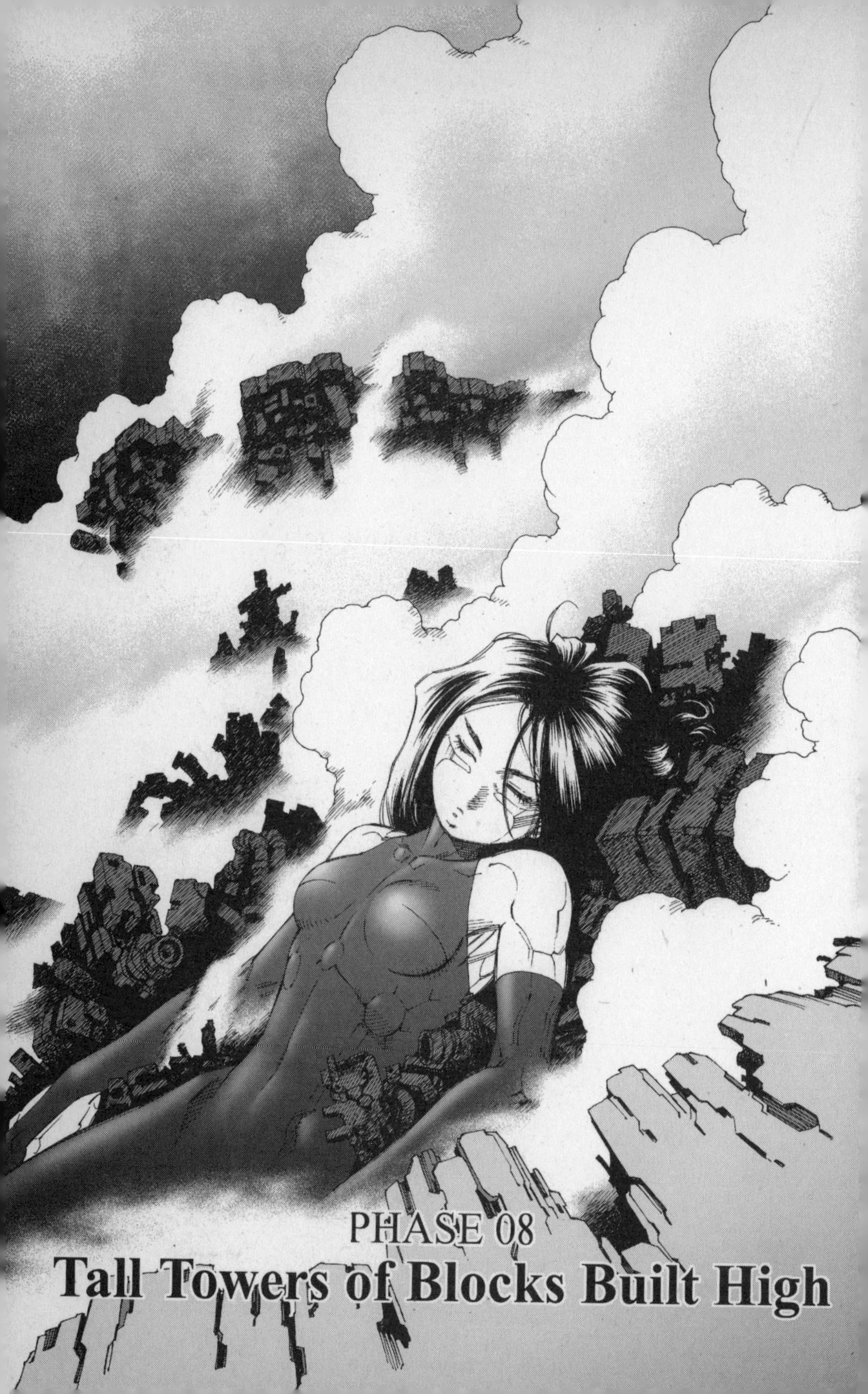

PHASE 08

Tall Towers of Blocks Built High

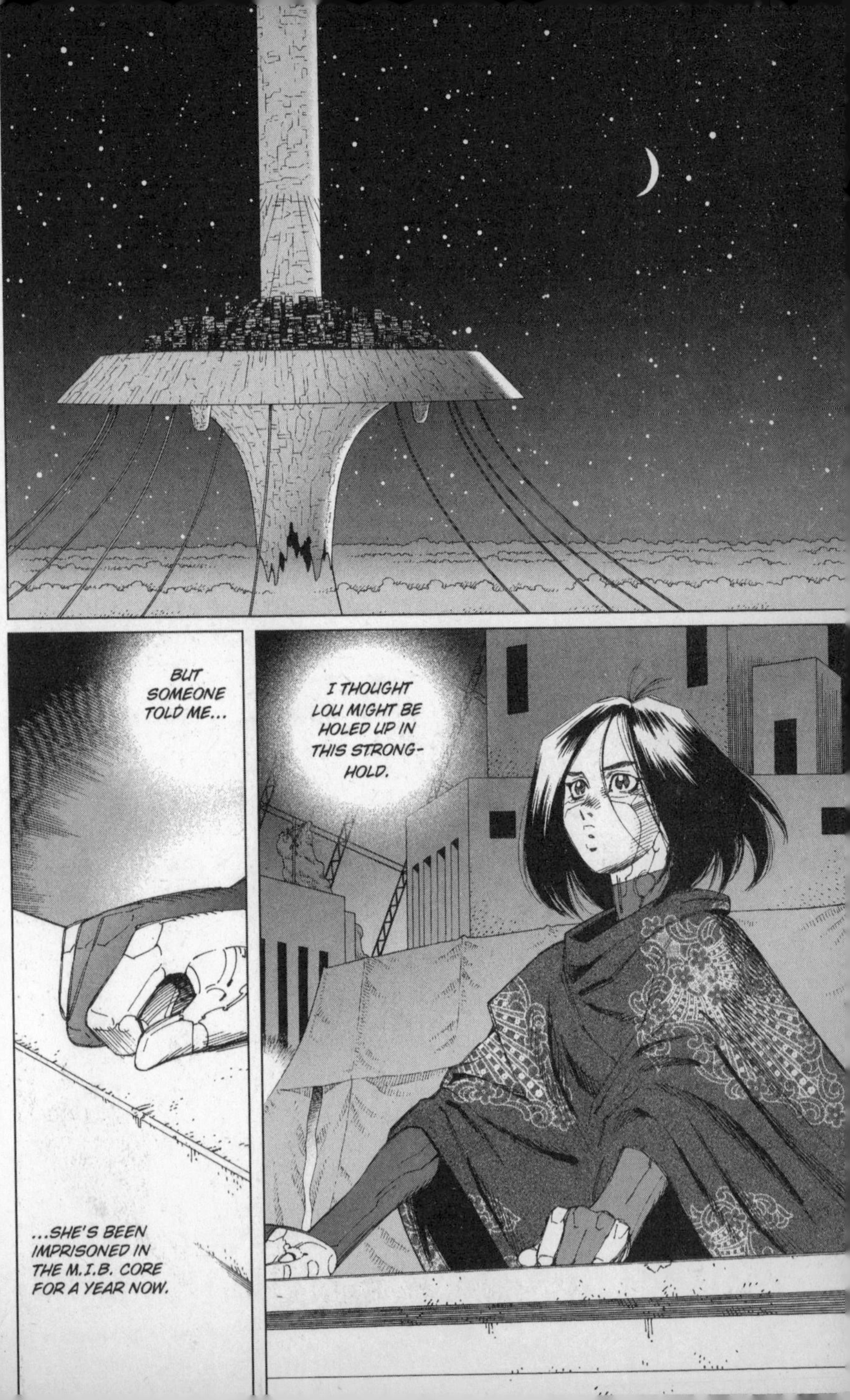
I THOUGHT LOU MIGHT BE HOLED UP IN THIS STRONG-HOLD.
BUT SOMEONE TOLD ME...
...SHE'S BEEN IMPRISONED IN THE M.I.B. CORE FOR A YEAR NOW.

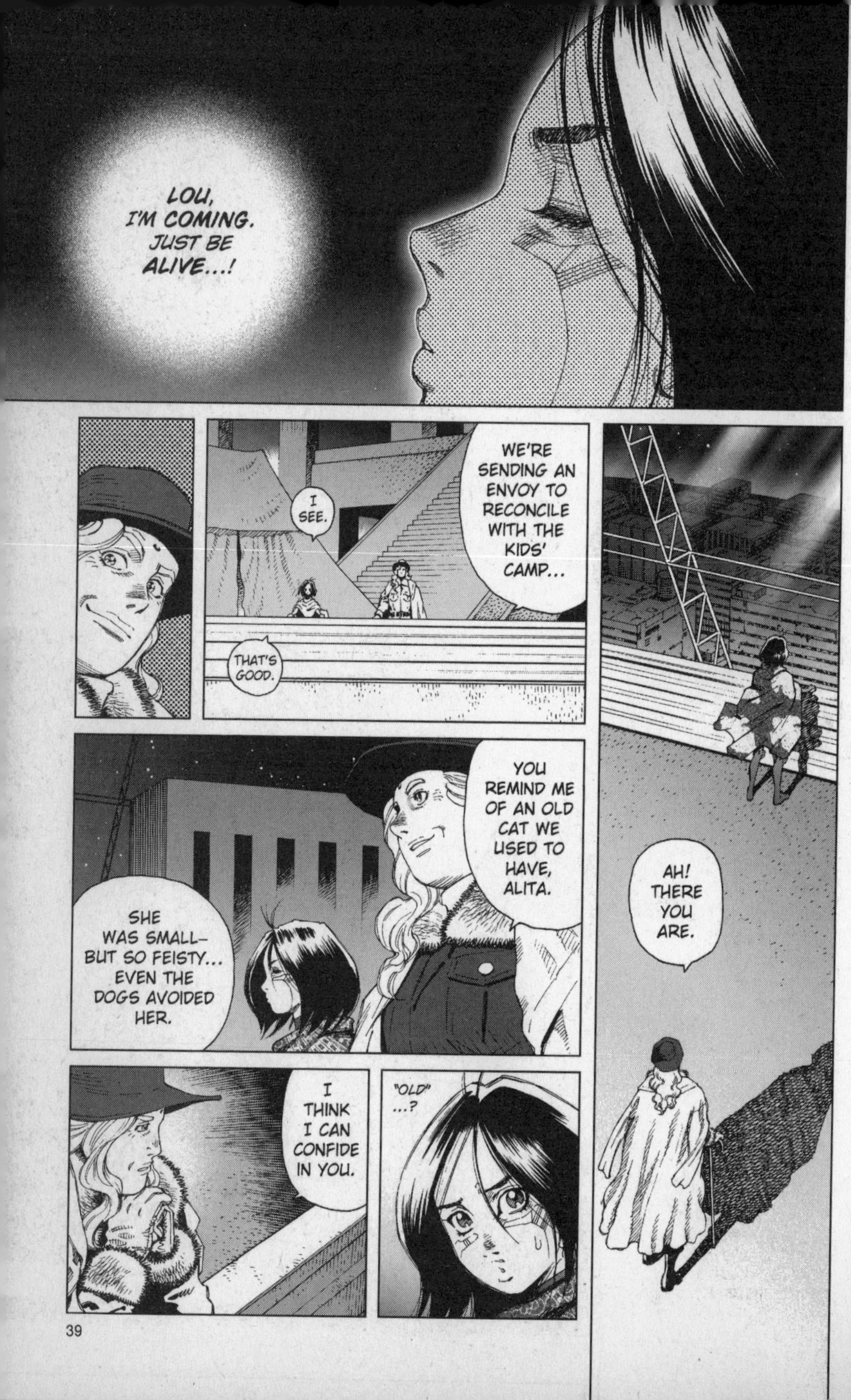
LOU, I'M COMING. JUST BE ALIVE...!
AH! THERE YOU ARE.
WE'RE SENDING AN ENVOY TO RECONCILE WITH THE KIDS' CAMP...
I SEE.
THAT'S GOOD.
YOU REMIND ME OF AN OLD CAT WE USED TO HAVE, ALITA.
SHE WAS SMALL— BUT SO FEISTY... EVEN THE DOGS AVOIDED HER.
"OLD" ...?
I THINK I CAN CONFIDE IN YOU.

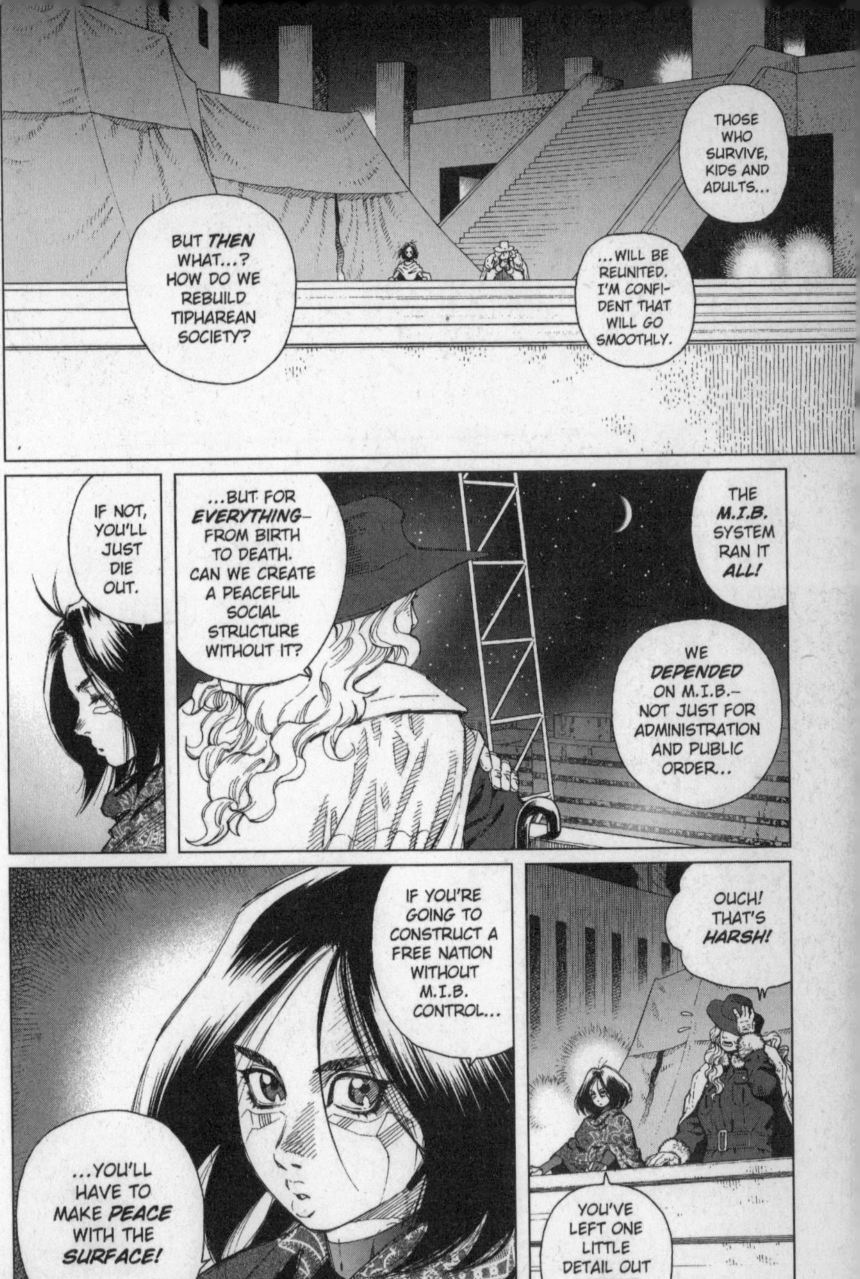
THOSE WHO SURVIVE, KIDS AND ADULTS...
...WILL BE REUNITED. I'M CONFIDENT THAT WILL GO SMOOTHLY.
BUT THEN WHAT...? HOW DO WE REBUILD TIPHAREAN SOCIETY?
THE M.I.B. SYSTEM RAN IT ALL!
WE DEPENDED ON M.I.B.– NOT JUST FOR ADMINISTRATION AND PUBLIC ORDER...
...BUT FOR EVERYTHING– FROM BIRTH TO DEATH. CAN WE CREATE A PEACEFUL SOCIAL STRUCTURE WITHOUT IT?
IF NOT, YOU'LL JUST DIE OUT.
OUCH! THAT'S HARSH!
YOU'VE LEFT ONE LITTLE DETAIL OUT OF YOUR PLANS...
IF YOU'RE GOING TO CONSTRUCT A FREE NATION WITHOUT M.I.B. CONTROL...
...YOU'LL HAVE TO MAKE PEACE WITH THE SURFACE!

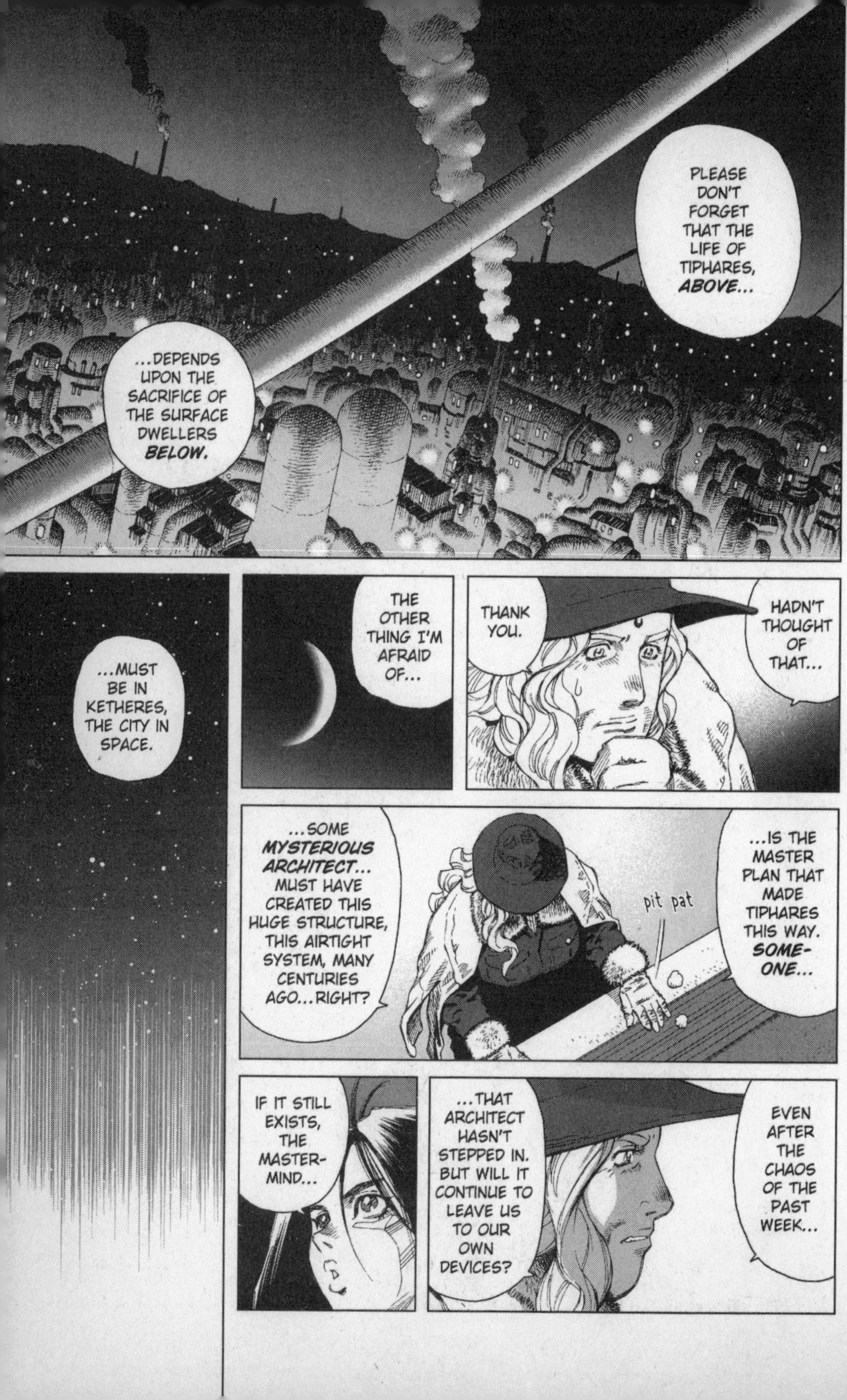
PLEASE DON'T FORGET THAT THE LIFE OF TIPHARES, ABOVE...
...DEPENDS UPON THE SACRIFICE OF THE SURFACE DWELLERS BELOW.
HADN'T THOUGHT OF THAT...
THANK YOU.
THE OTHER THING I'M AFRAID OF...
...IS THE MASTER PLAN THAT MADE TIPHARES THIS WAY. SOME-ONE...
pit pat
...SOME MYSTERIOUS ARCHITECT... MUST HAVE CREATED THIS HUGE STRUCTURE, THIS AIRTIGHT SYSTEM, MANY CENTURIES AGO... RIGHT?
EVEN AFTER THE CHAOS OF THE PAST WEEK...
...THAT ARCHITECT HASN'T STEPPED IN. BUT WILL IT CONTINUE TO LEAVE US TO OUR OWN DEVICES?
IF IT STILL EXISTS, THE MASTER-MIND...
...MUST BE IN KETHERES, THE CITY IN SPACE.

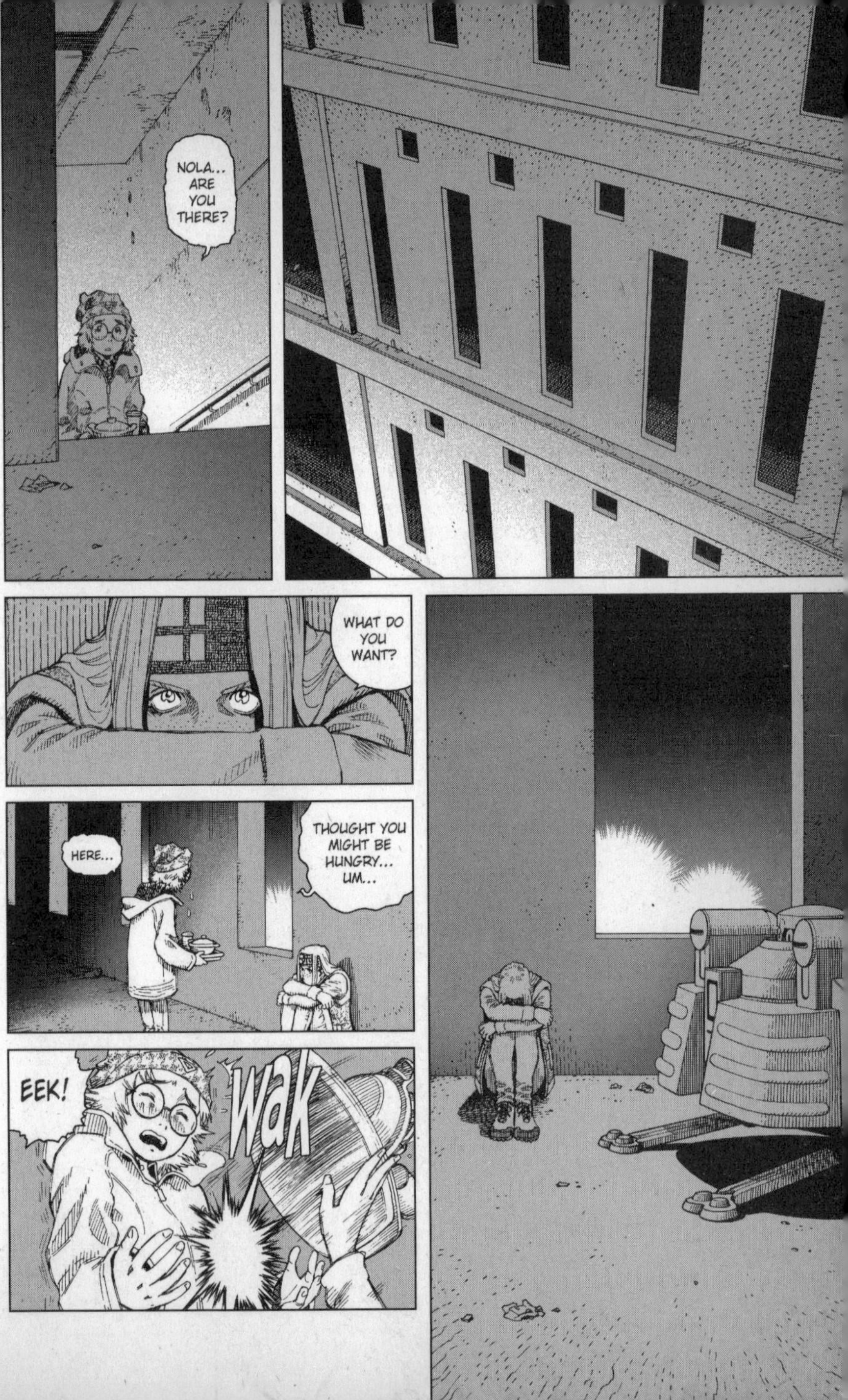
NOLA... ARE YOU THERE?
WHAT DO YOU WANT?
THOUGHT YOU MIGHT BE HUNGRY... UM...
HERE...
wak
EEK!

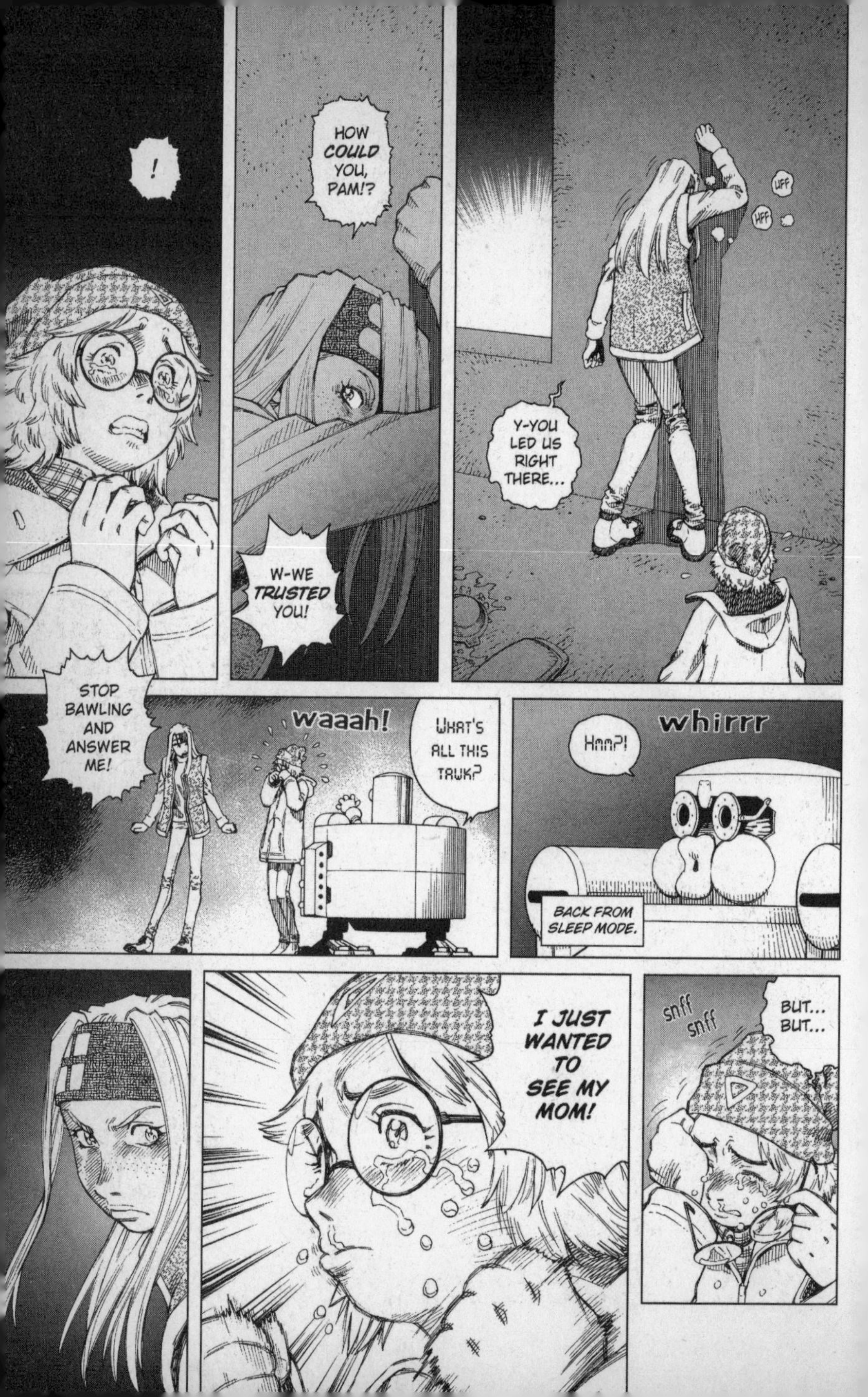

UFF
HFF
Y-YOU LED US RIGHT THERE...
HOW COULD YOU, PAM!?
W-WE TRUSTED YOU!
!
whirrr
Hmm?!
BACK FROM SLEEP MODE.
WHAT'S ALL THIS TAWK?
waaah!
STOP BAWLING AND ANSWER ME!
BUT... BUT...
snff
snff
I JUST WANTED TO SEE MY MOM!

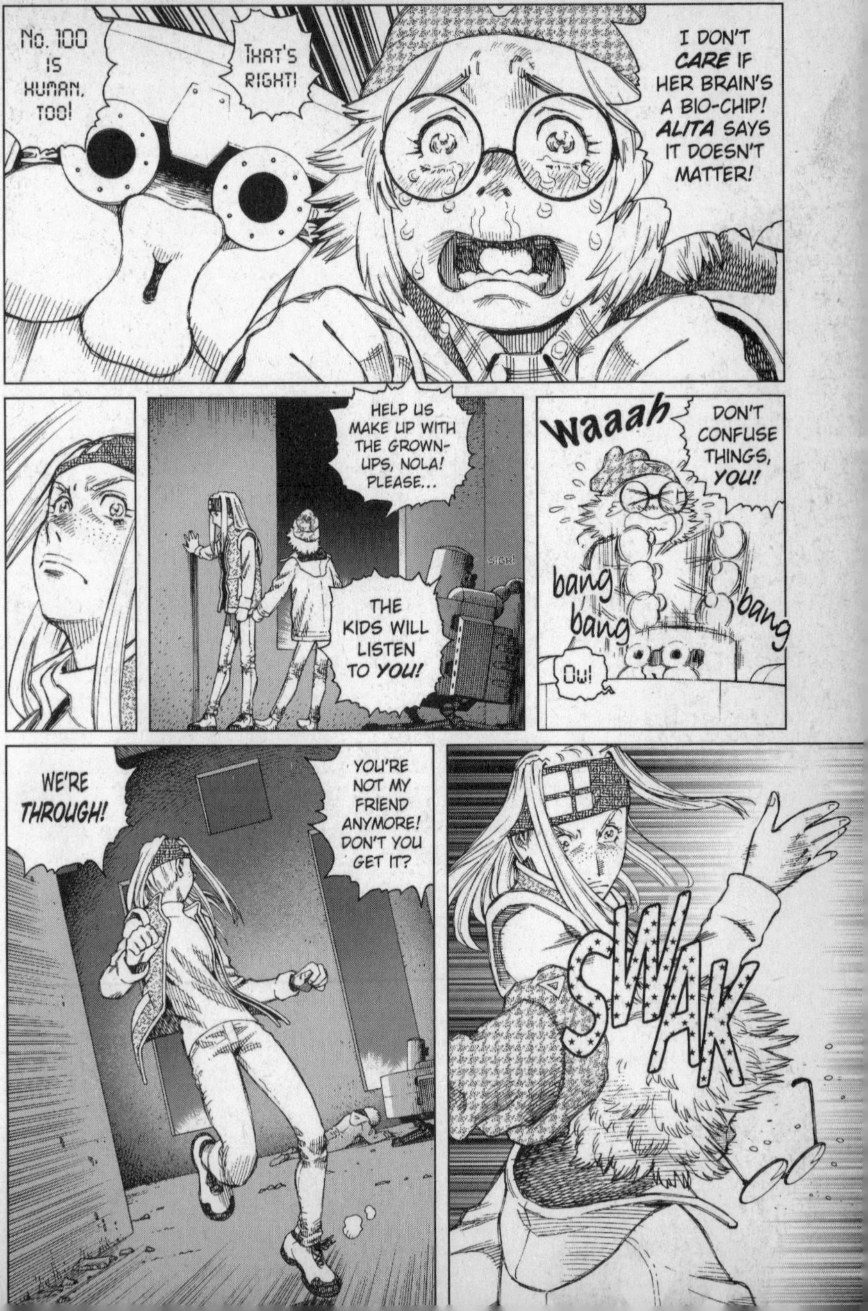
I DON'T CARE IF HER BRAIN'S A BIO-CHIP! ALITA SAYS IT DOESN'T MATTER!
THAT'S RIGHT!
No. 100 IS HUMAN, TOO!
Waaah
DON'T CONFUSE THINGS, YOU!
bang
bang
bang
Ow!
HELP US MAKE UP WITH THE GROWN-UPS, NOLA! PLEASE...
SIGH
THE KIDS WILL LISTEN TO YOU!
SWAK
YOU'RE NOT MY FRIEND ANYMORE! DON'T YOU GET IT?
WE'RE THROUGH!

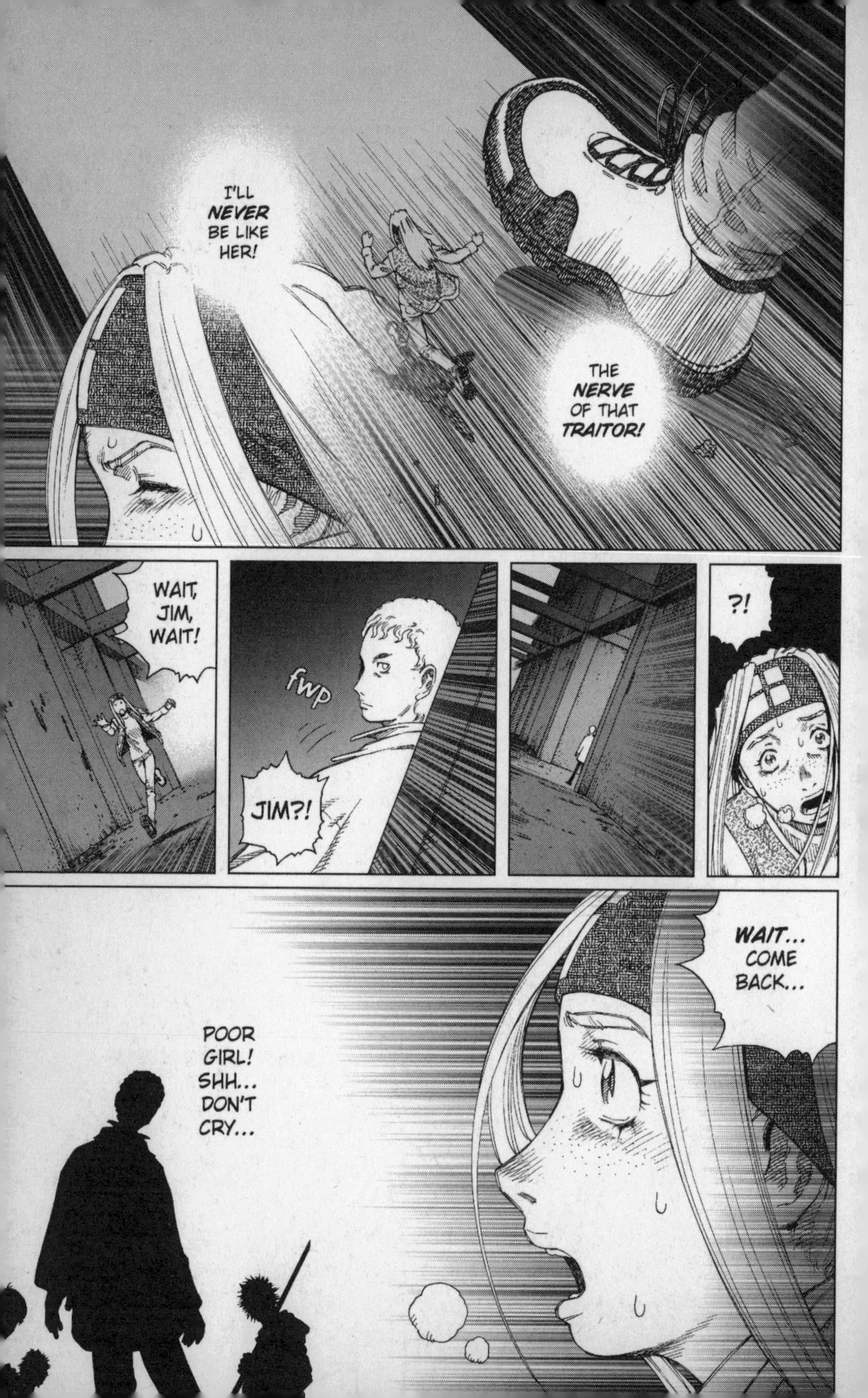
THE NERVE OF THAT TRAITOR!
I'LL NEVER BE LIKE HER!
?!
fwp
JIM?!
WAIT, JIM, WAIT!
WAIT... COME BACK...
POOR GIRL! SHH... DON'T CRY...

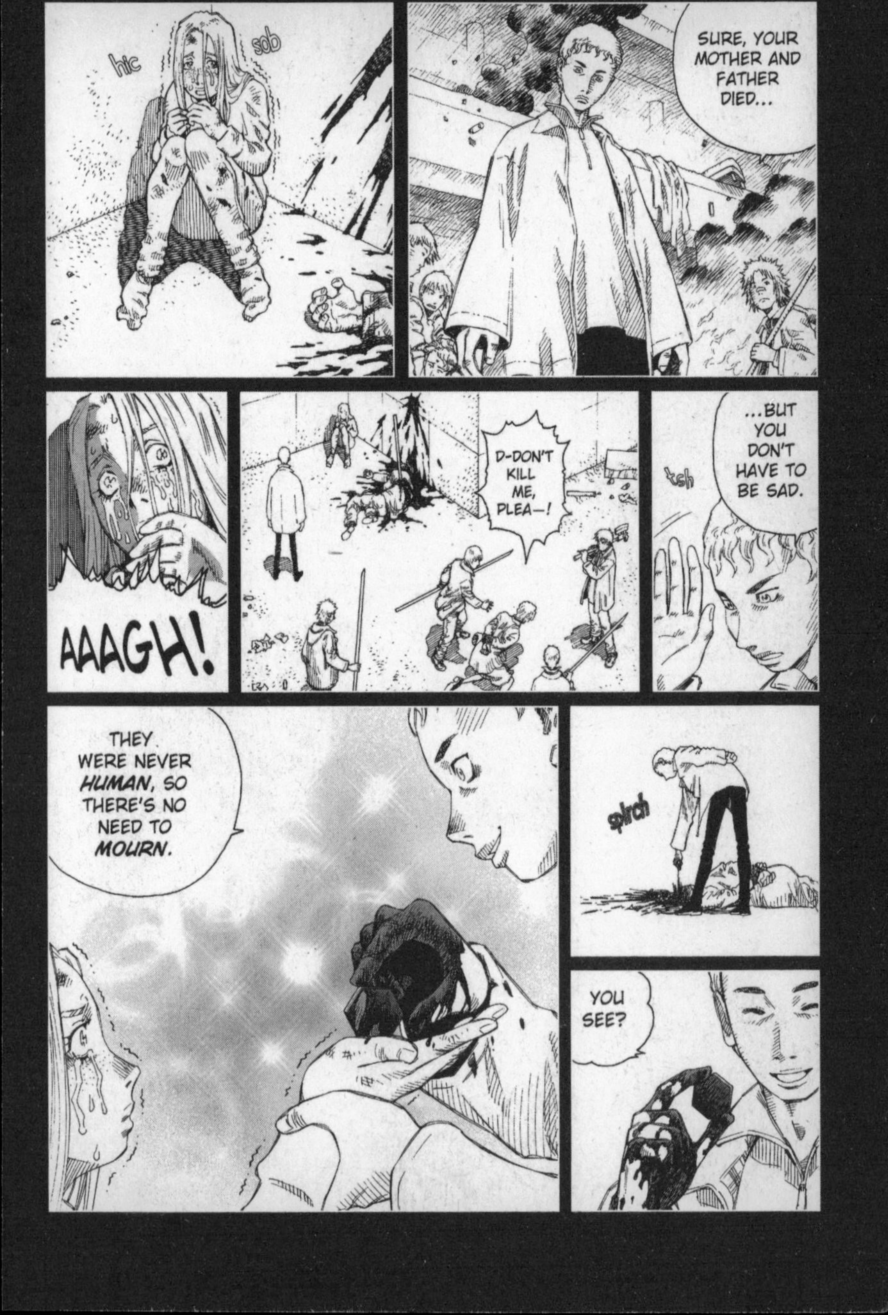

SURE, YOUR MOTHER AND FATHER DIED...
sob
hic
tsh
...BUT YOU DON'T HAVE TO BE SAD.
D-DON'T KILL ME, PLEA—!
AAAGH!
splrch
YOU SEE?
THEY WERE NEVER *HUMAN*, SO THERE'S NO NEED TO *MOURN*.

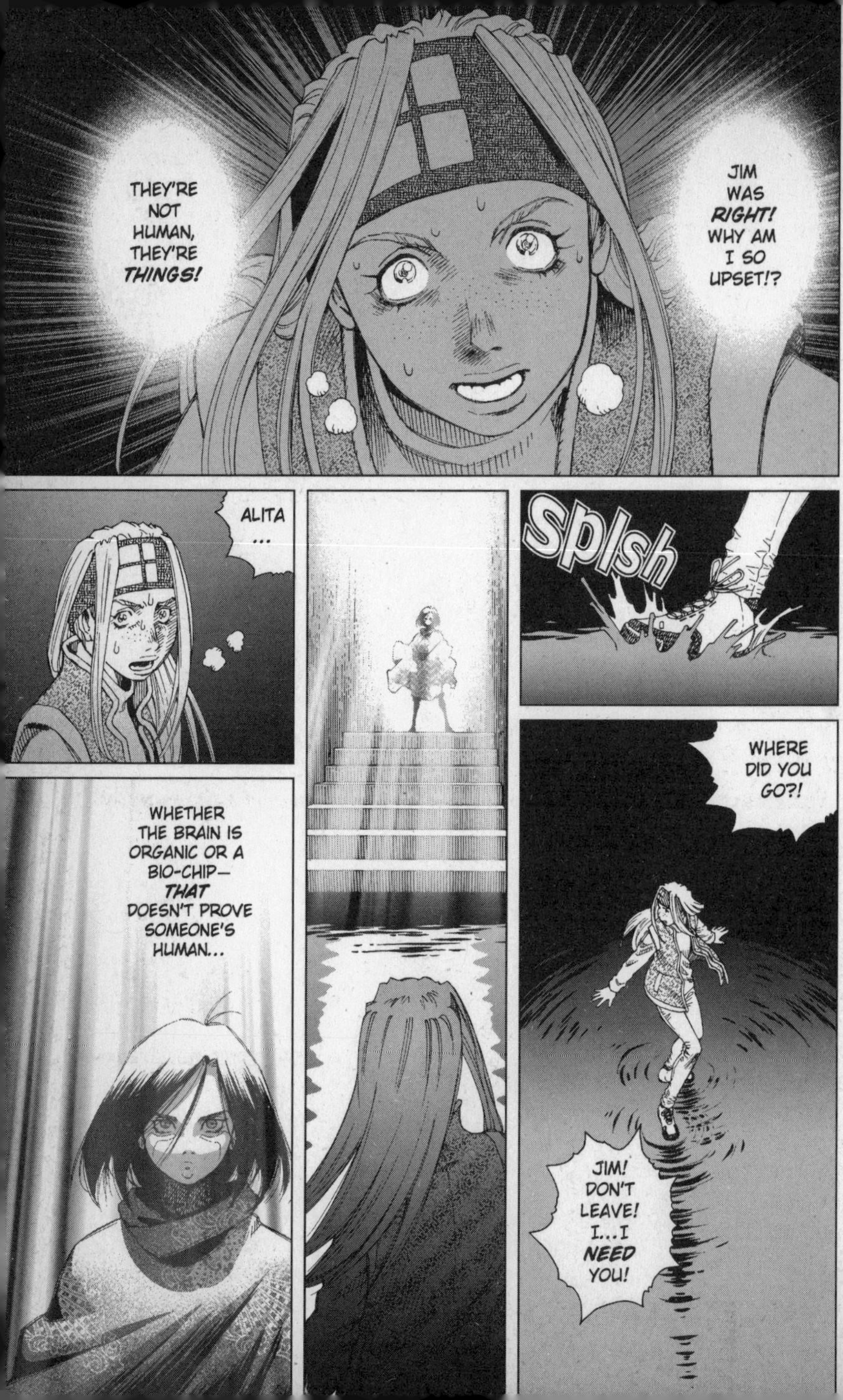
JIM WAS RIGHT! WHY AM I SO UPSET!?
THEY'RE NOT HUMAN, THEY'RE THINGS!
Splsh
WHERE DID YOU GO?!
JIM! DON'T LEAVE! I...I NEED YOU!
ALITA...
WHETHER THE BRAIN IS ORGANIC OR A BIO-CHIP— THAT DOESN'T PROVE SOMEONE'S HUMAN...

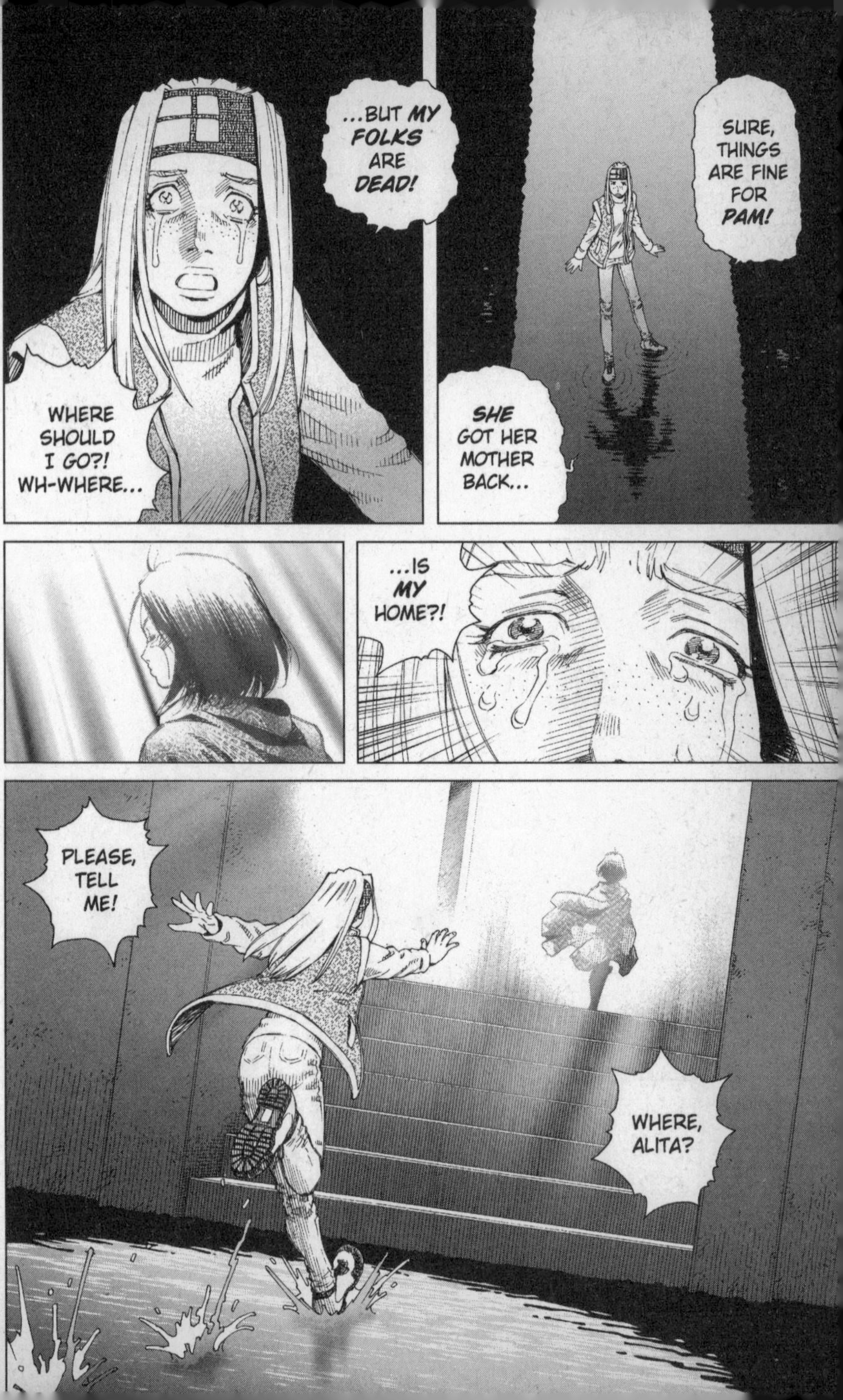
SURE, THINGS ARE FINE FOR PAM!
SHE GOT HER MOTHER BACK...
...BUT MY FOLKS ARE DEAD!
WHERE SHOULD I GO?! WH-WHERE...
...IS MY HOME?!
PLEASE, TELL ME!
WHERE, ALITA?

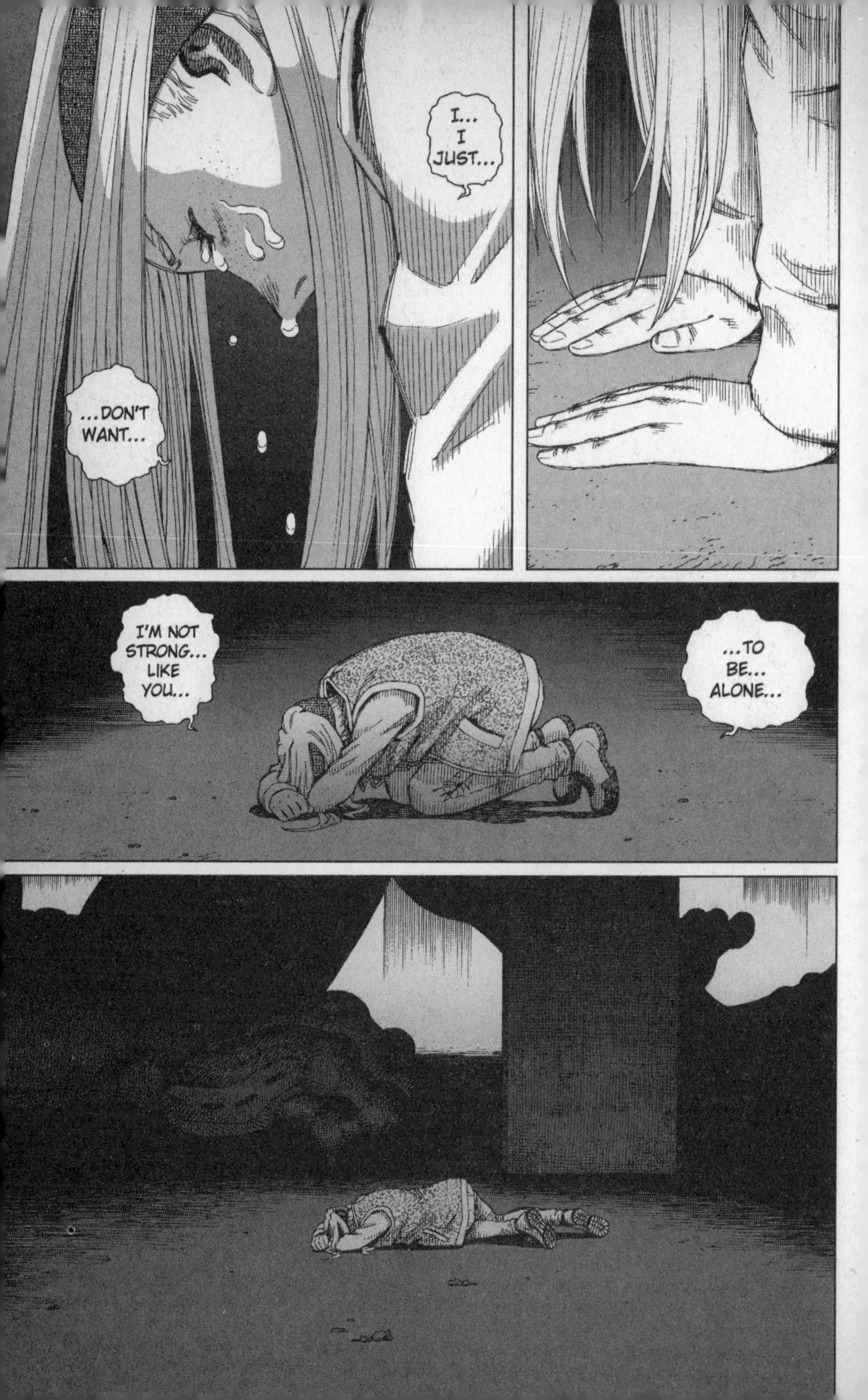
I... I JUST...
...DON'T WANT...
...TO BE... ALONE...
I'M NOT STRONG... LIKE YOU...

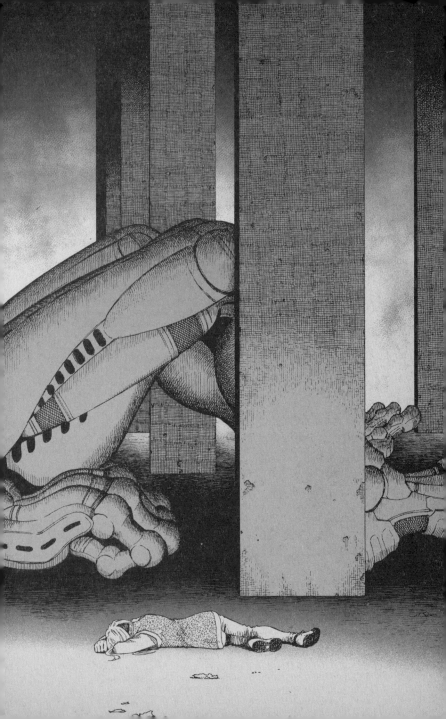

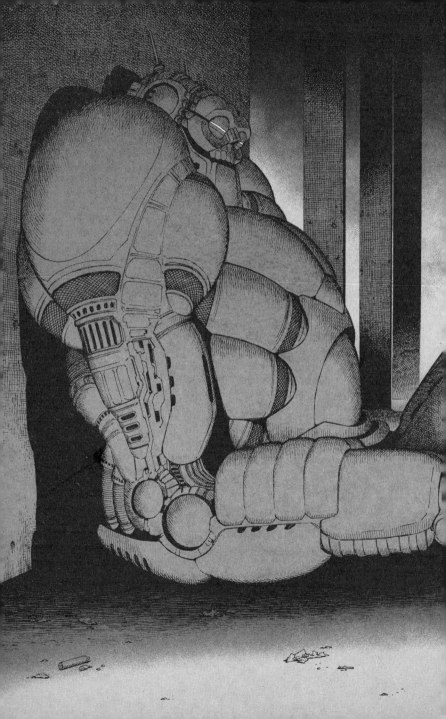

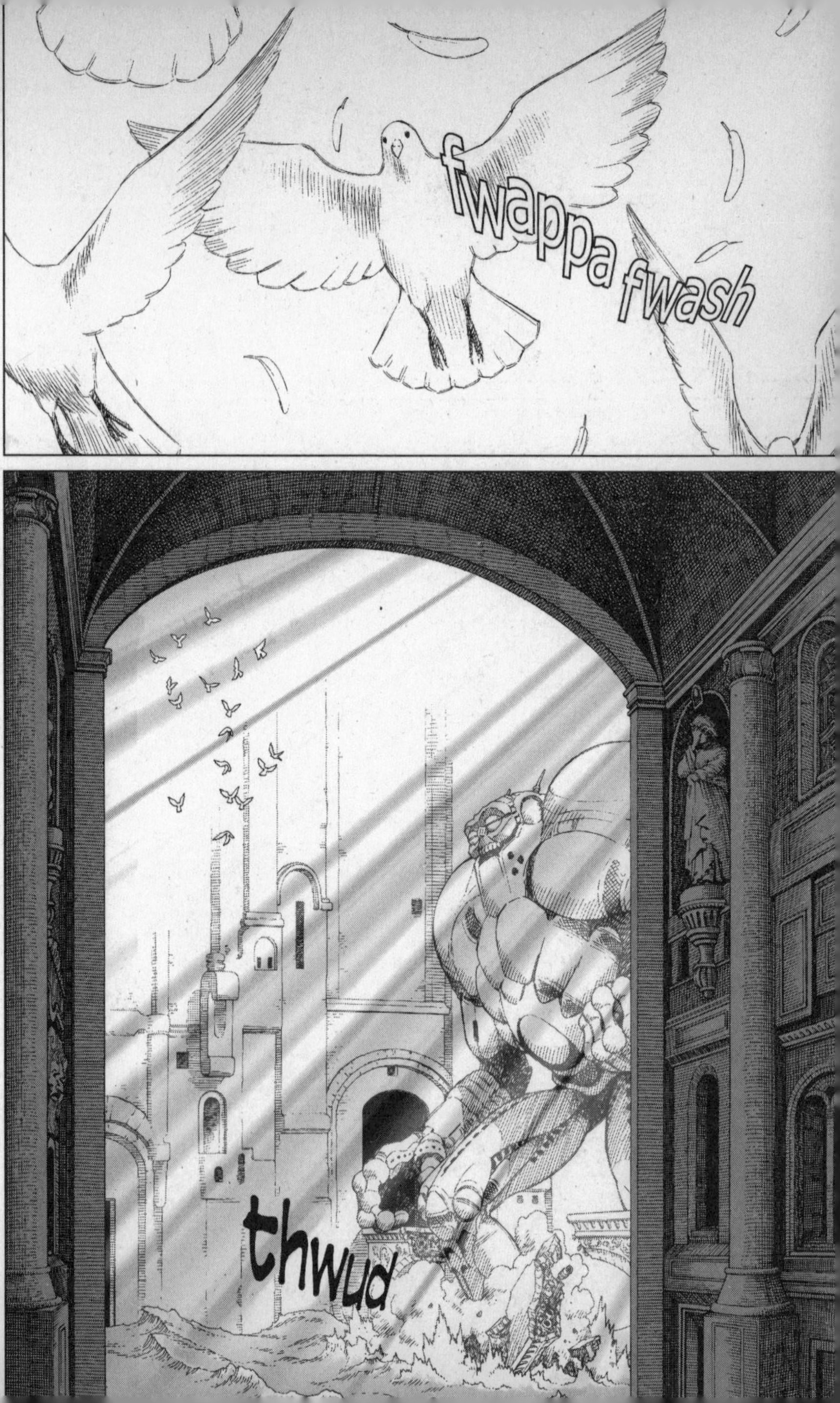
fwappa fwash
thwud

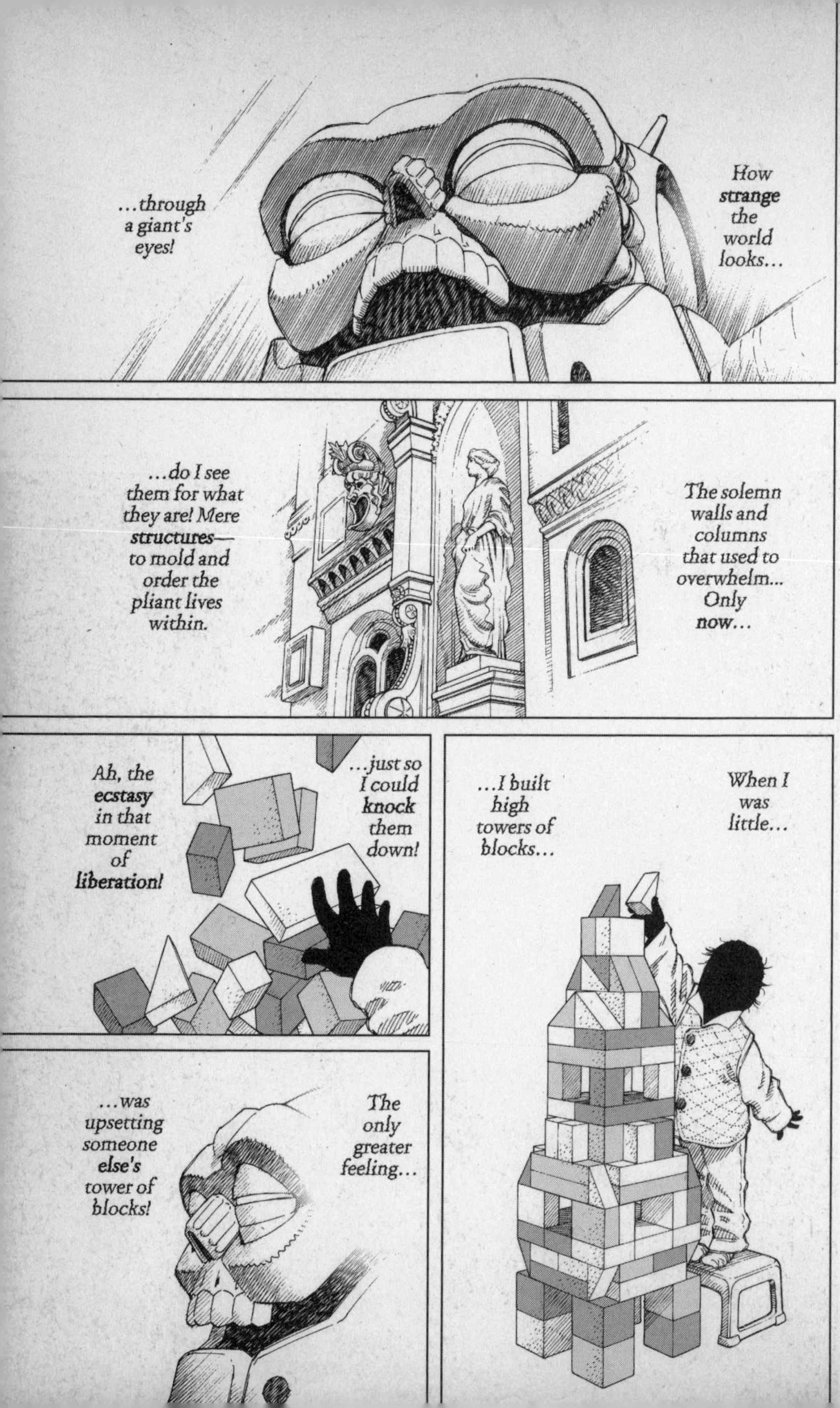
How strange the world looks...
...through a giant's eyes!
The solemn walls and columns that used to overwhelm... Only now...
...do I see them for what they are! Mere structures— to mold and order the pliant lives within.
When I was little...
...I built high towers of blocks...
...just so I could knock them down!
Ah, the ecstasy in that moment of liberation!
The only greater feeling...
...was upsetting someone else's tower of blocks!

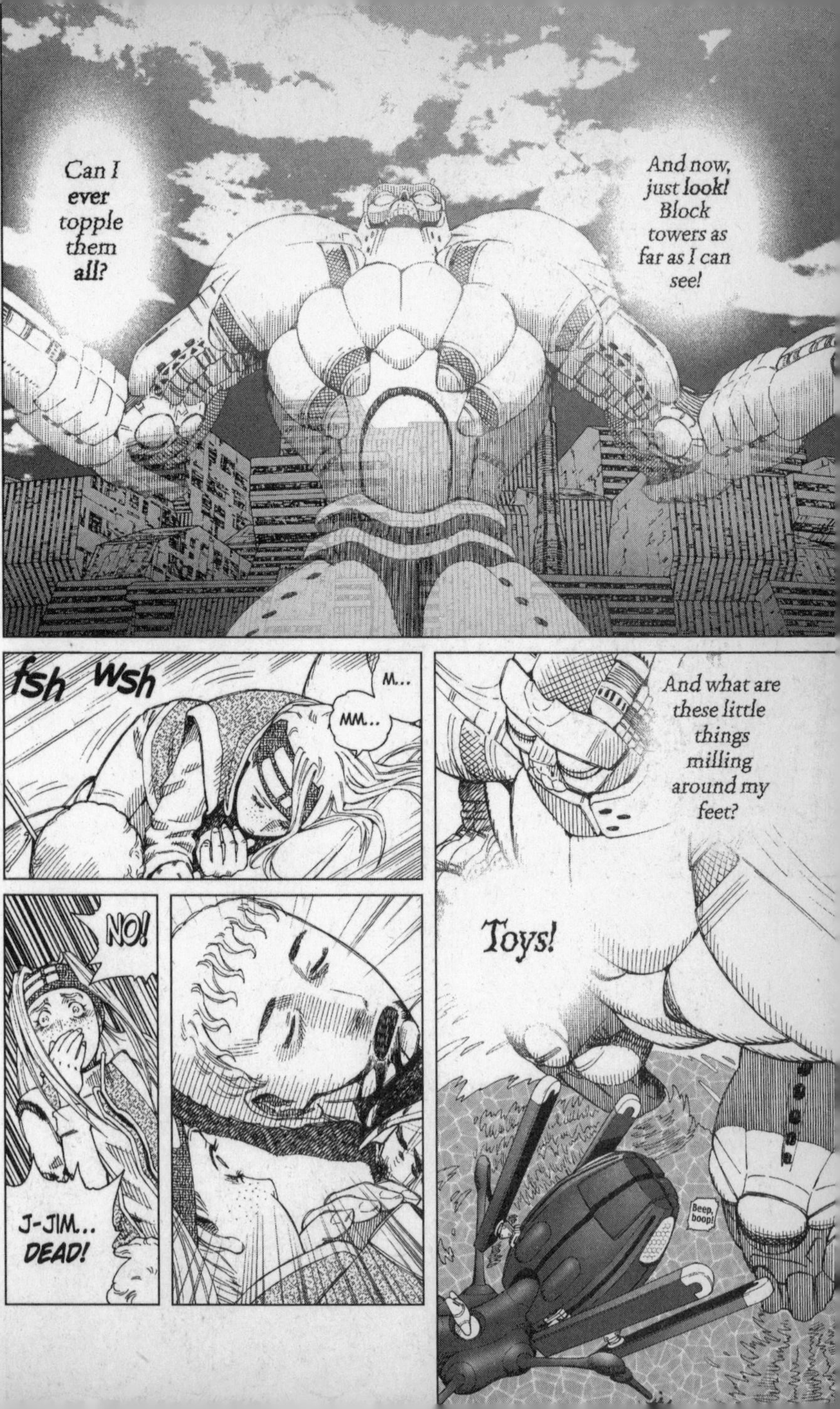
And now, just look! Block towers as far as I can see!
Can I ever topple them all?
And what are these little things milling around my feet?
M...
MM...
fsh
wsh
Toys!
Beep, boop!
NO!
J-JIM.. DEAD!

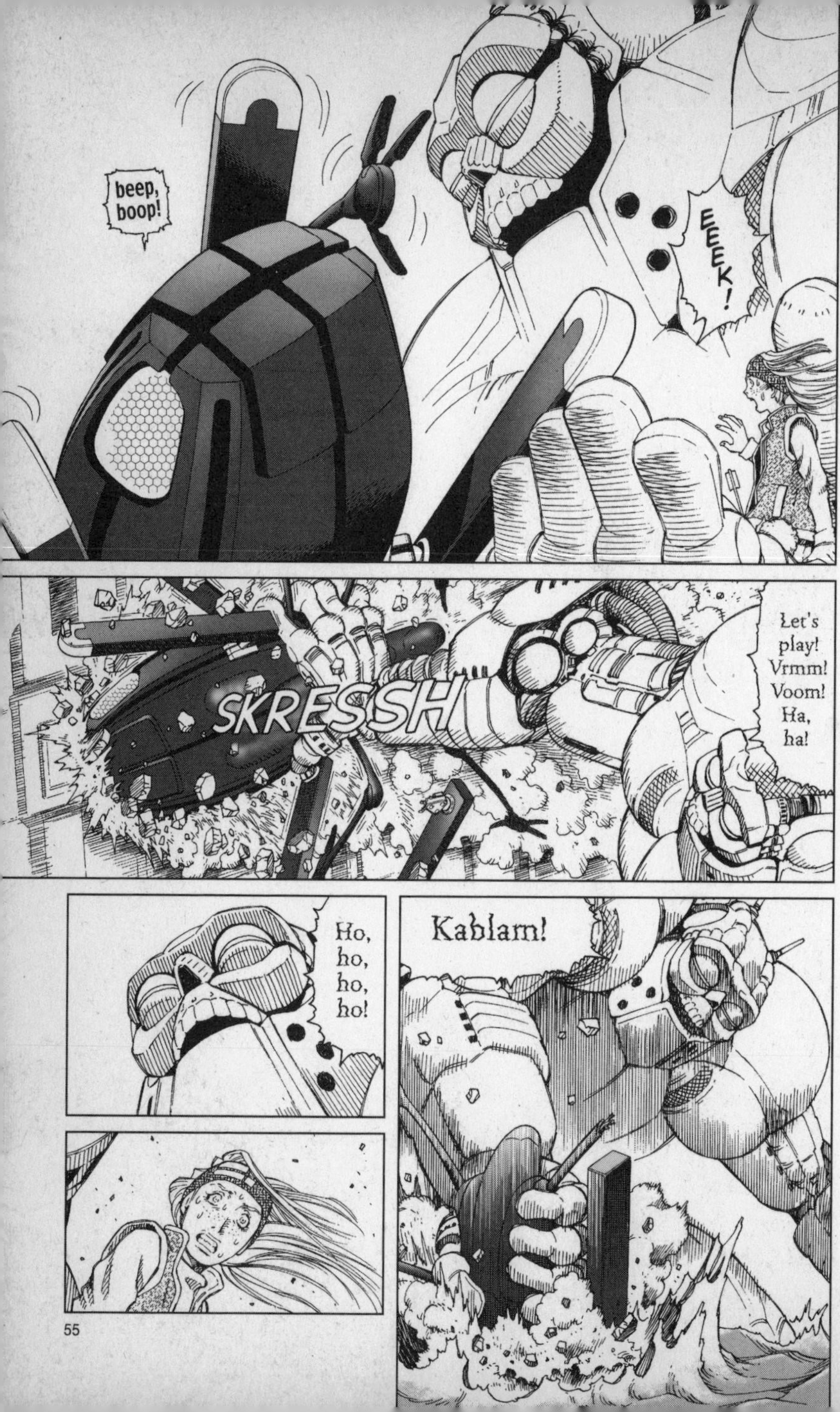

EEEK!
beep, boop!
Let's play! Vrmm! Voom! Ha, ha!
SKRESSH
Kablam!
Ho, ho, ho, ho!

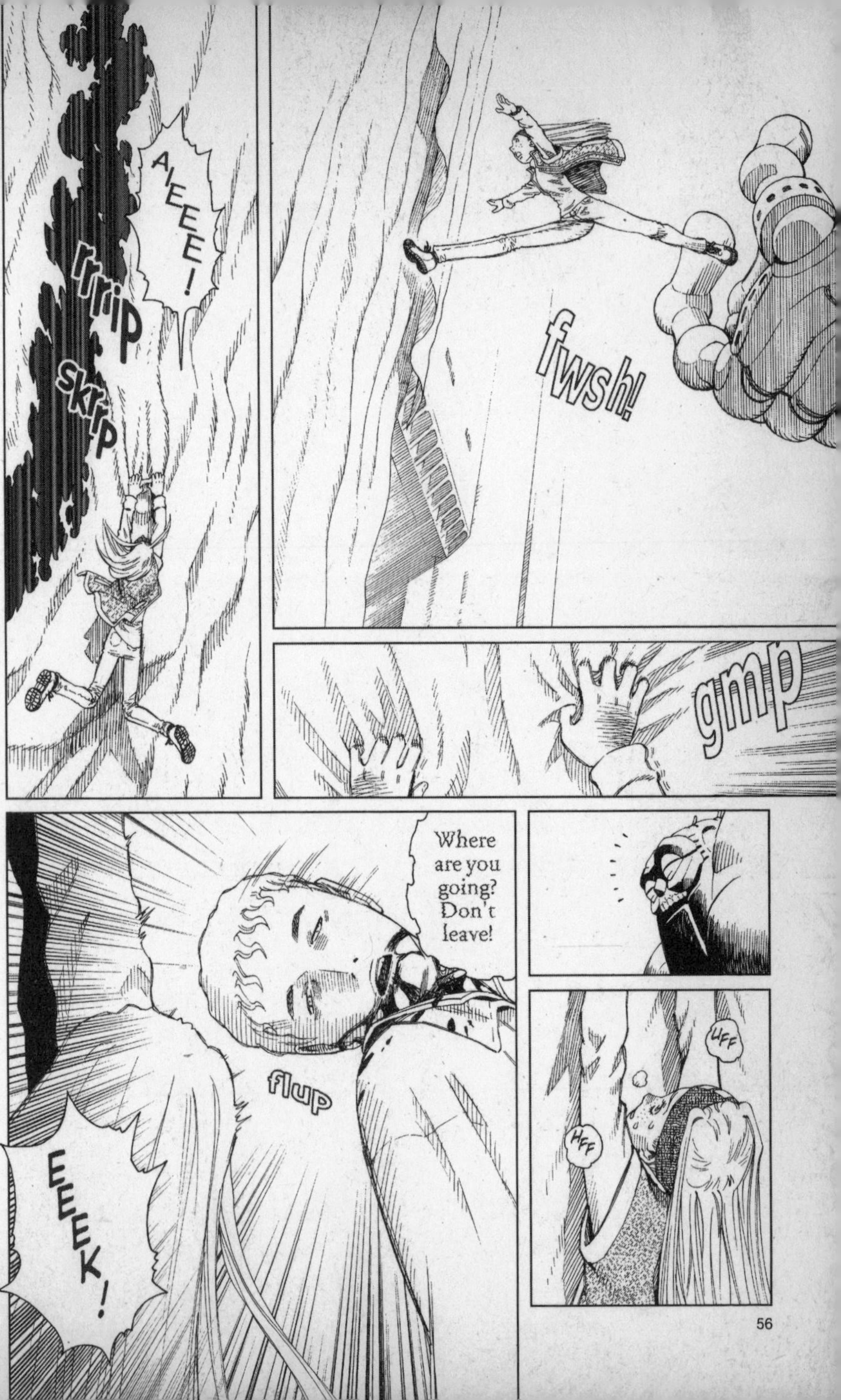
fwsh!
gmp
AIEEE!
rrrip
skrrip
UFF
HFF
Where are you going? Don't leave!
flup
EEEK!

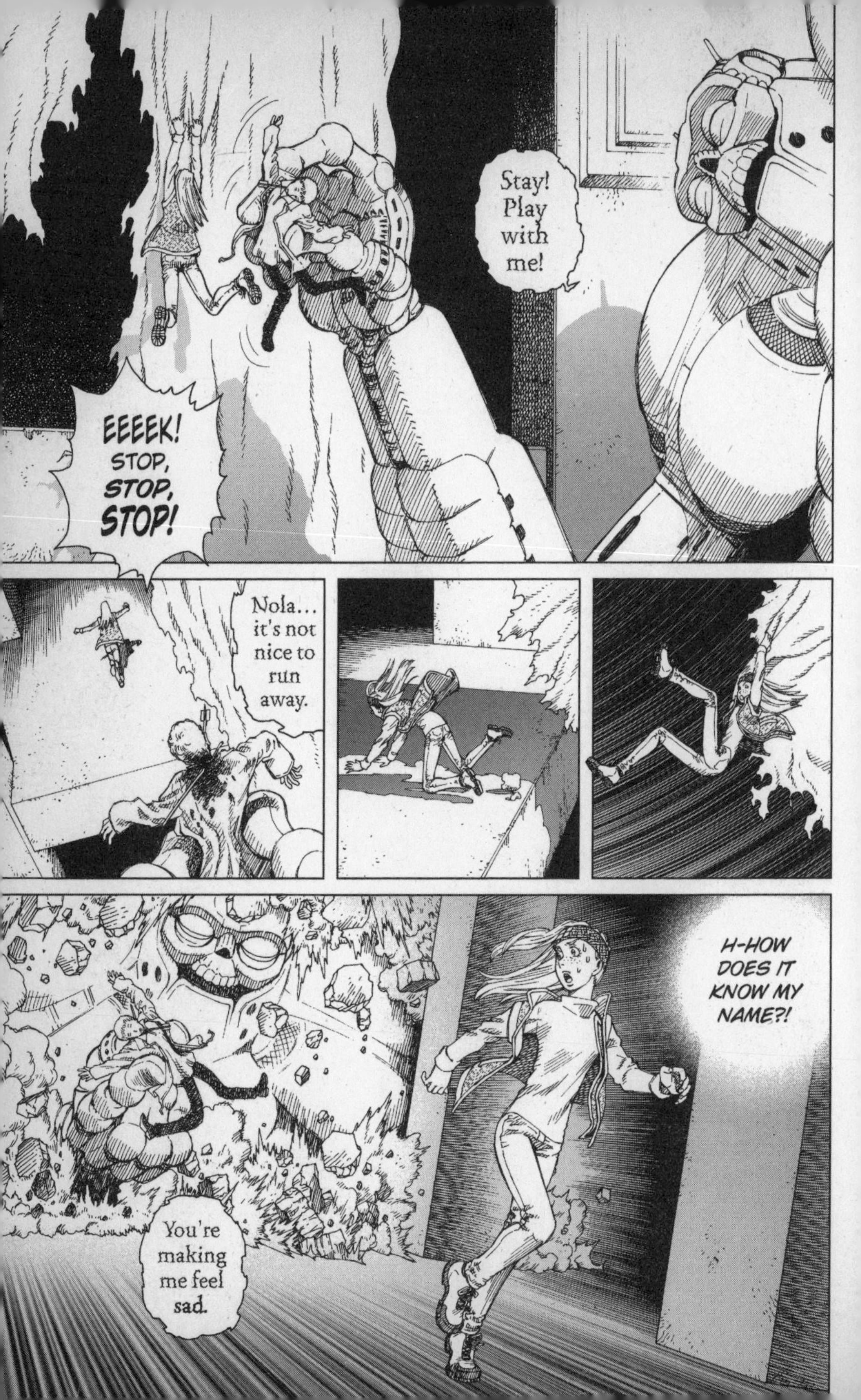
Stay! Play with me!
EEEEK! STOP, STOP, STOP!
Nola... it's not nice to run away.
H-HOW DOES IT KNOW MY NAME?!
You're making me feel sad.

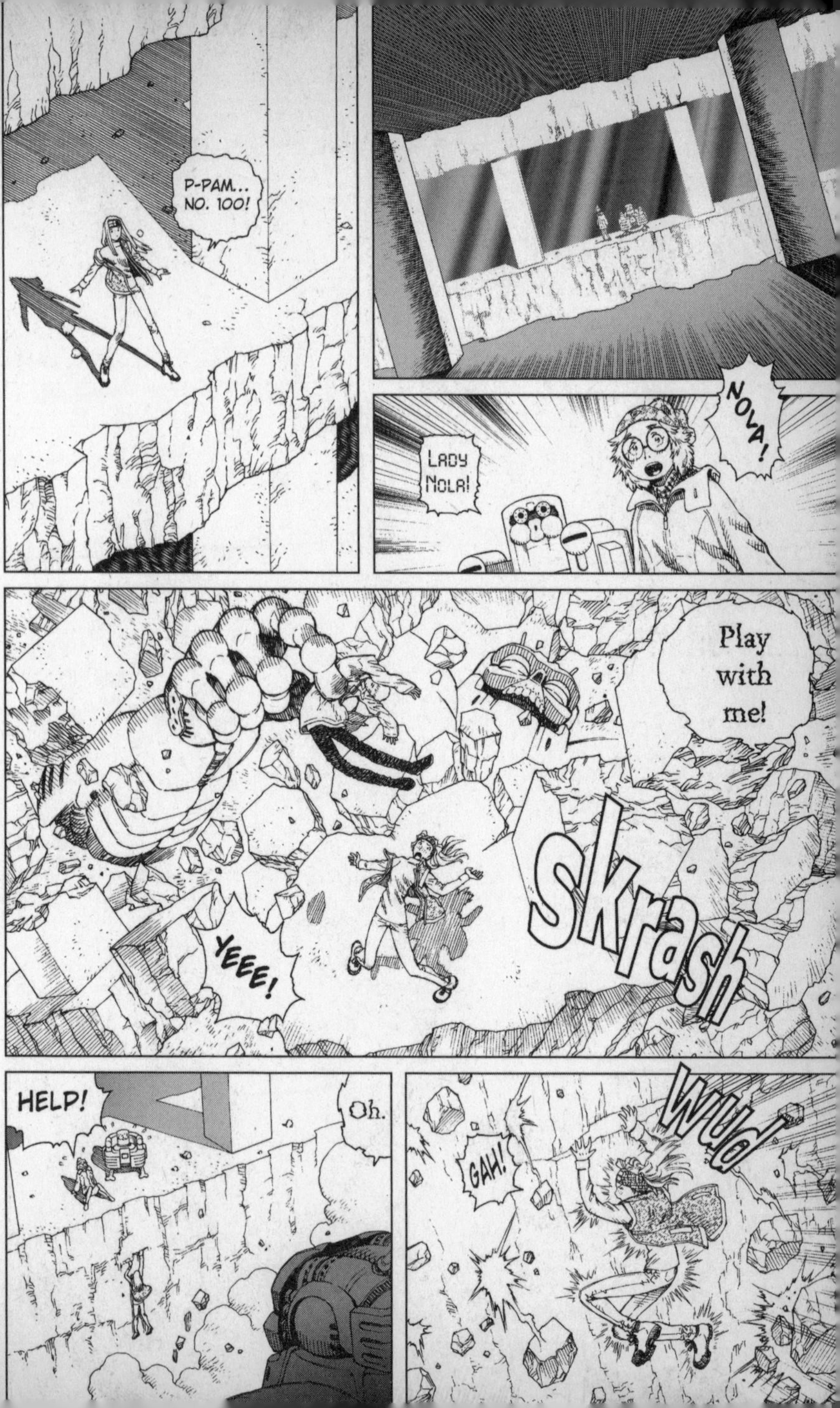
NOVA!
LADY NOLA!
P-PAM... NO. 100!
Play with me!
SKRASH
YEEE!
WUD
GAH!
Oh.
HELP!

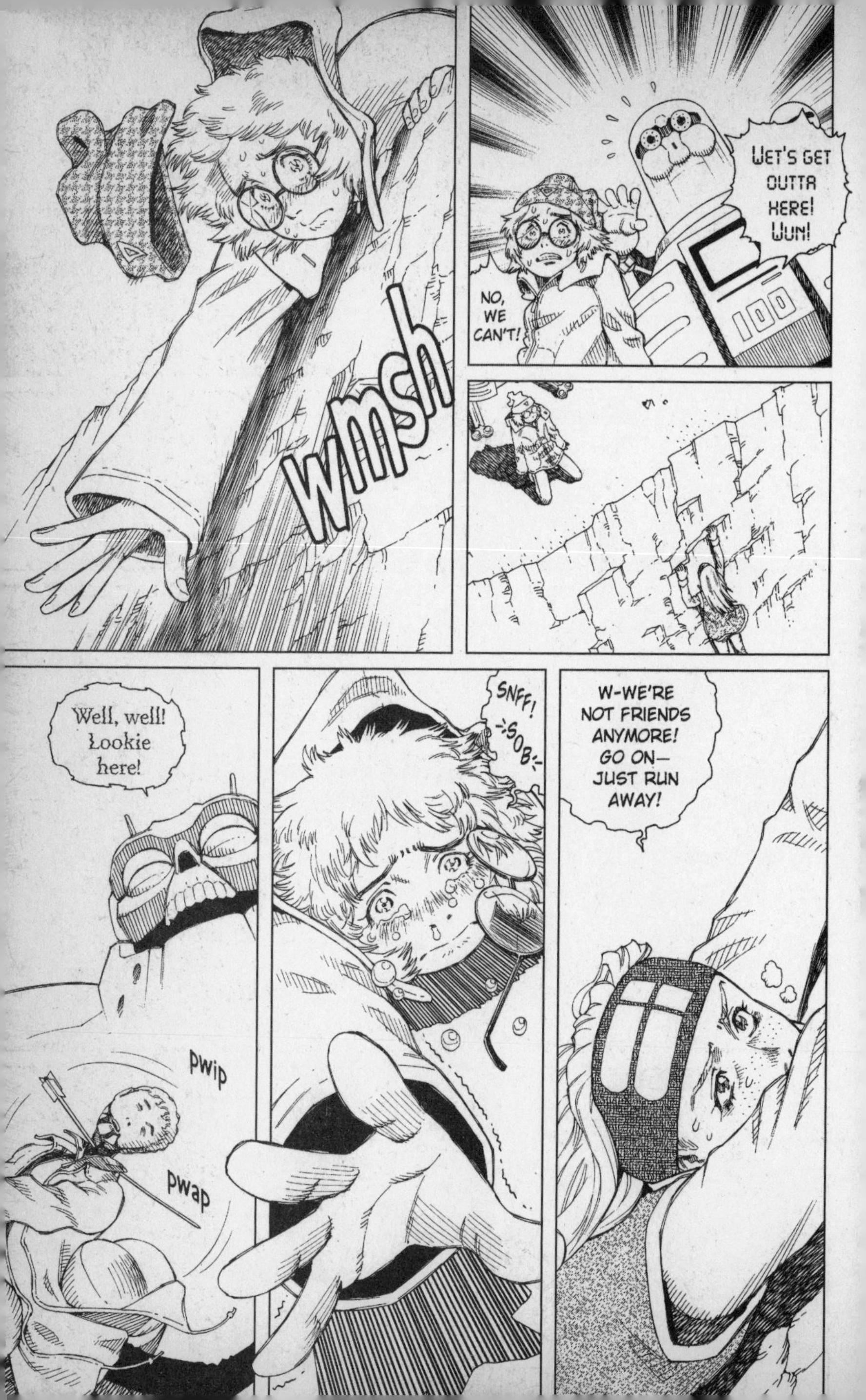
WET'S GET OUTTA HERE! WUN!
NO, WE CAN'T!
wmsh
W-WE'RE NOT FRIENDS ANYMORE! GO ON— JUST RUN AWAY!
SNFF!
SOB
Well, well! Lookie here!
pwip
pwap

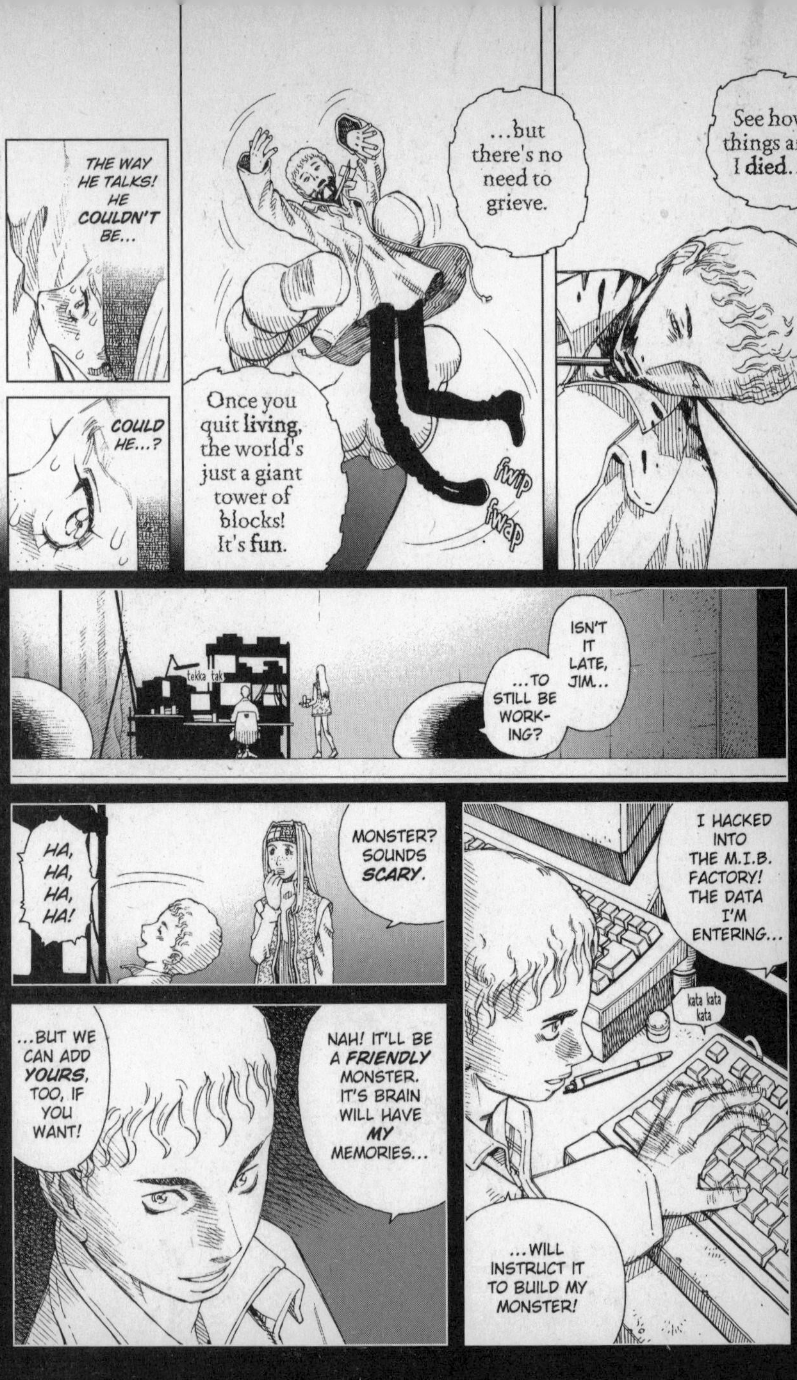
See how things are? I died...
...but there's no need to grieve.
Once you quit living, the world's just a giant tower of blocks! It's fun.
fwip
fwap
THE WAY HE TALKS! HE COULDN'T BE...
COULD HE...?
ISN'T IT LATE, JIM...
...TO STILL BE WORKING?
tekka tak
I HACKED INTO THE M.I.B. FACTORY! THE DATA I'M ENTERING...
kata kata kata
...WILL INSTRUCT IT TO BUILD MY MONSTER!
MONSTER? SOUNDS SCARY.
HA, HA, HA, HA!
NAH! IT'LL BE A FRIENDLY MONSTER. IT'S BRAIN WILL HAVE MY MEMORIES...
...BUT WE CAN ADD YOURS, TOO, IF YOU WANT!

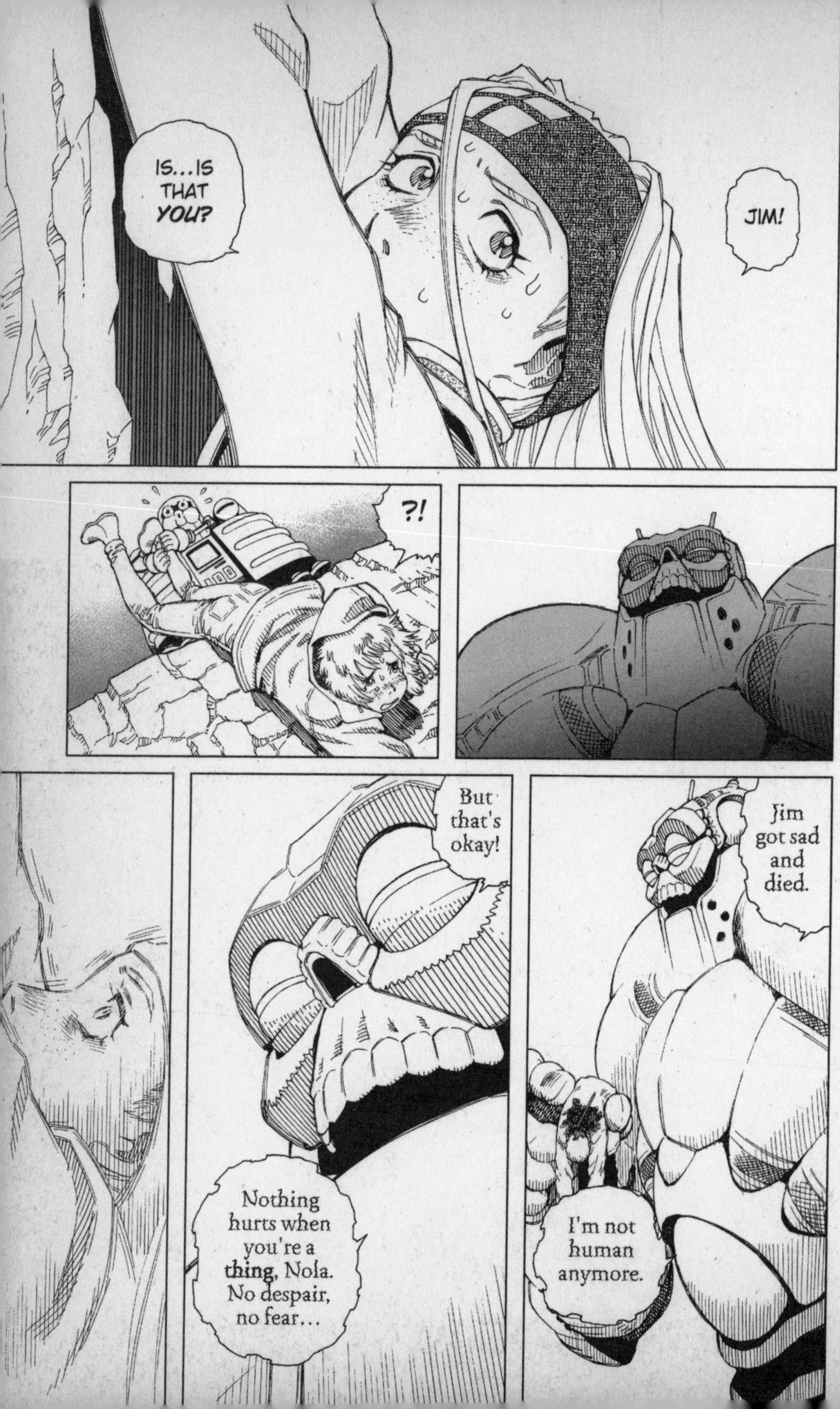
JIM!
IS...IS THAT YOU?
?!
Jim got sad and died.
I'm not human anymore.
But that's okay!
Nothing hurts when you're a thing, Nola. No despair, no fear...

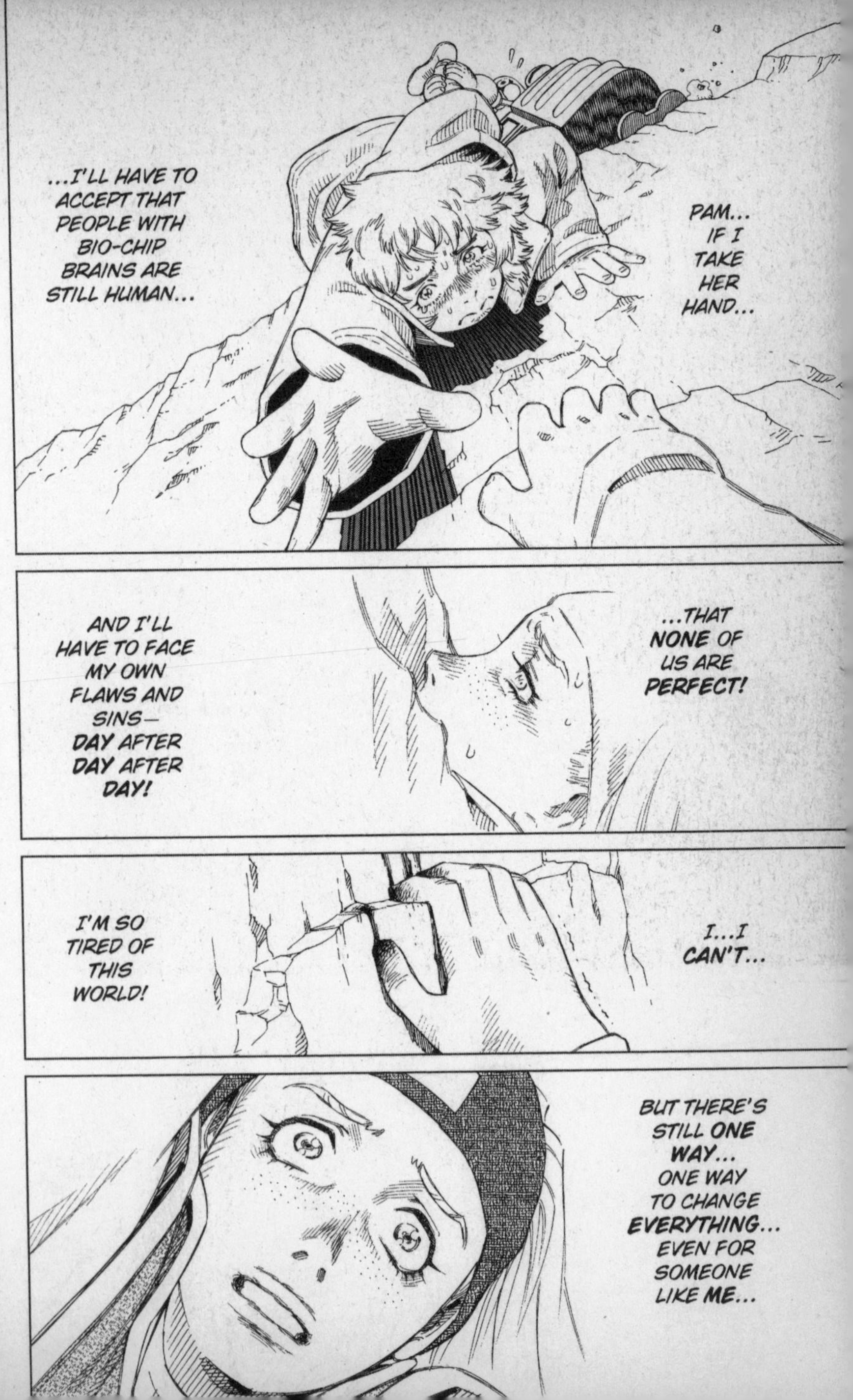
PAM... IF I TAKE HER HAND...
...I'LL HAVE TO ACCEPT THAT PEOPLE WITH BIO-CHIP BRAINS ARE STILL HUMAN...
...THAT NONE OF US ARE PERFECT!
AND I'LL HAVE TO FACE MY OWN FLAWS AND SINS— DAY AFTER DAY AFTER DAY!
I...I CAN'T...
I'M SO TIRED OF THIS WORLD!
BUT THERE'S STILL ONE WAY... ONE WAY TO CHANGE EVERYTHING... EVEN FOR SOMEONE LIKE ME...

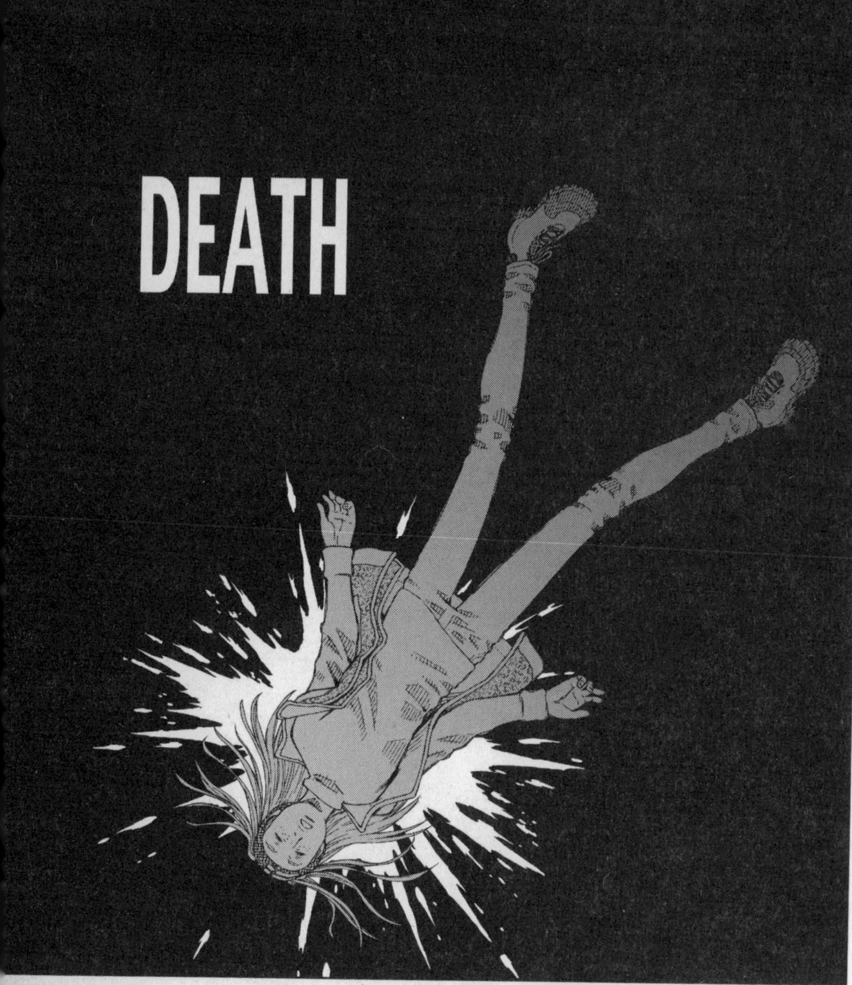
DEATH
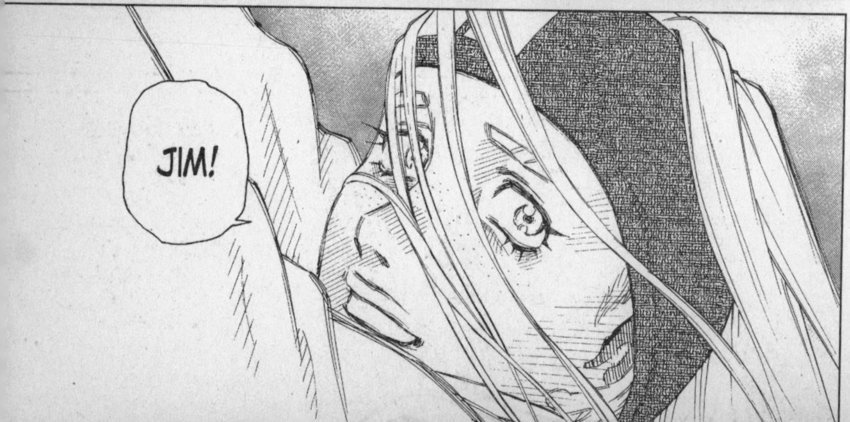
JIM!

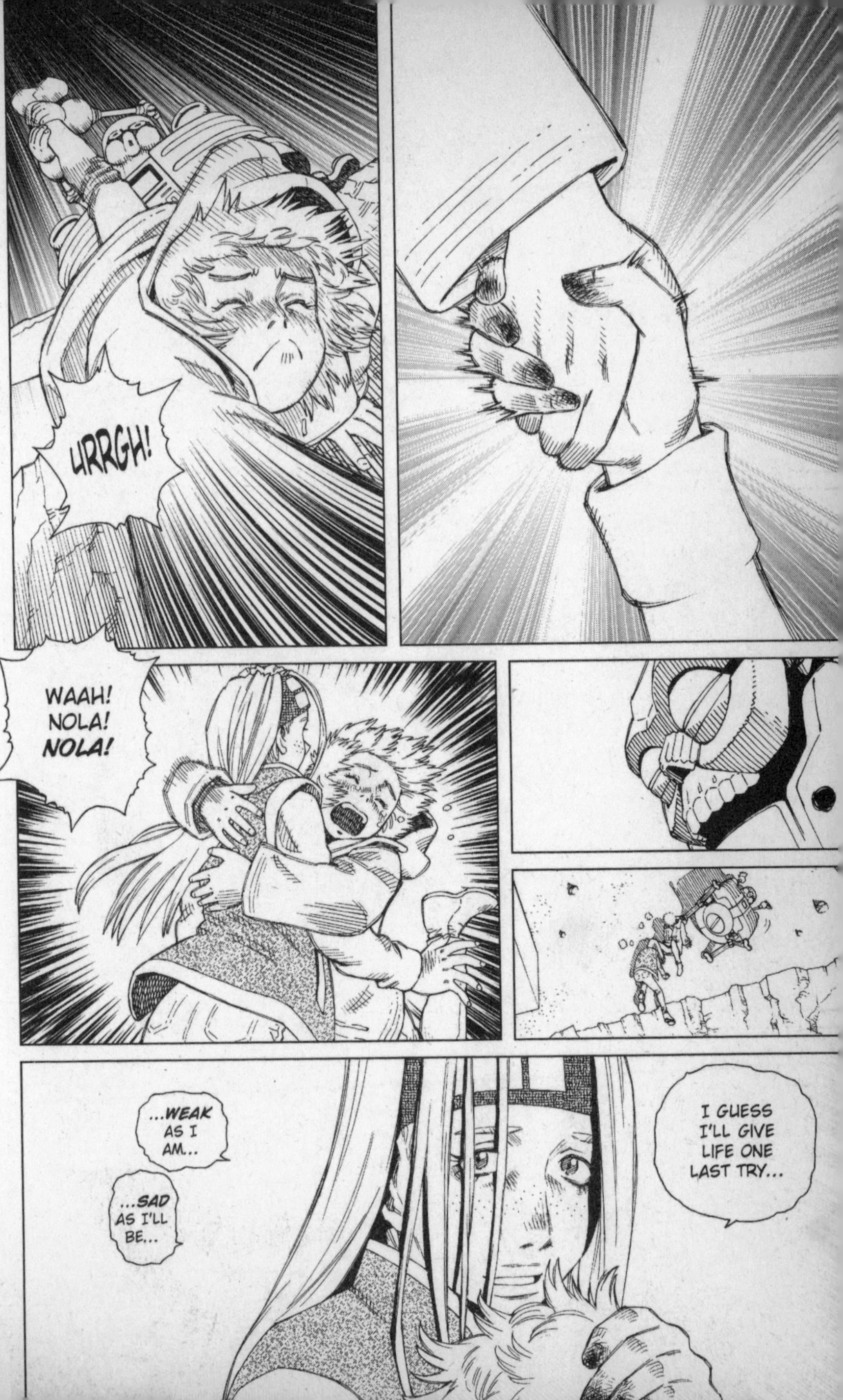
URRGH!
WAAH! NOLA! **NOLA!**
I GUESS I'LL GIVE LIFE ONE LAST TRY...
...**WEAK** AS I AM...
...**SAD** AS I'LL BE...

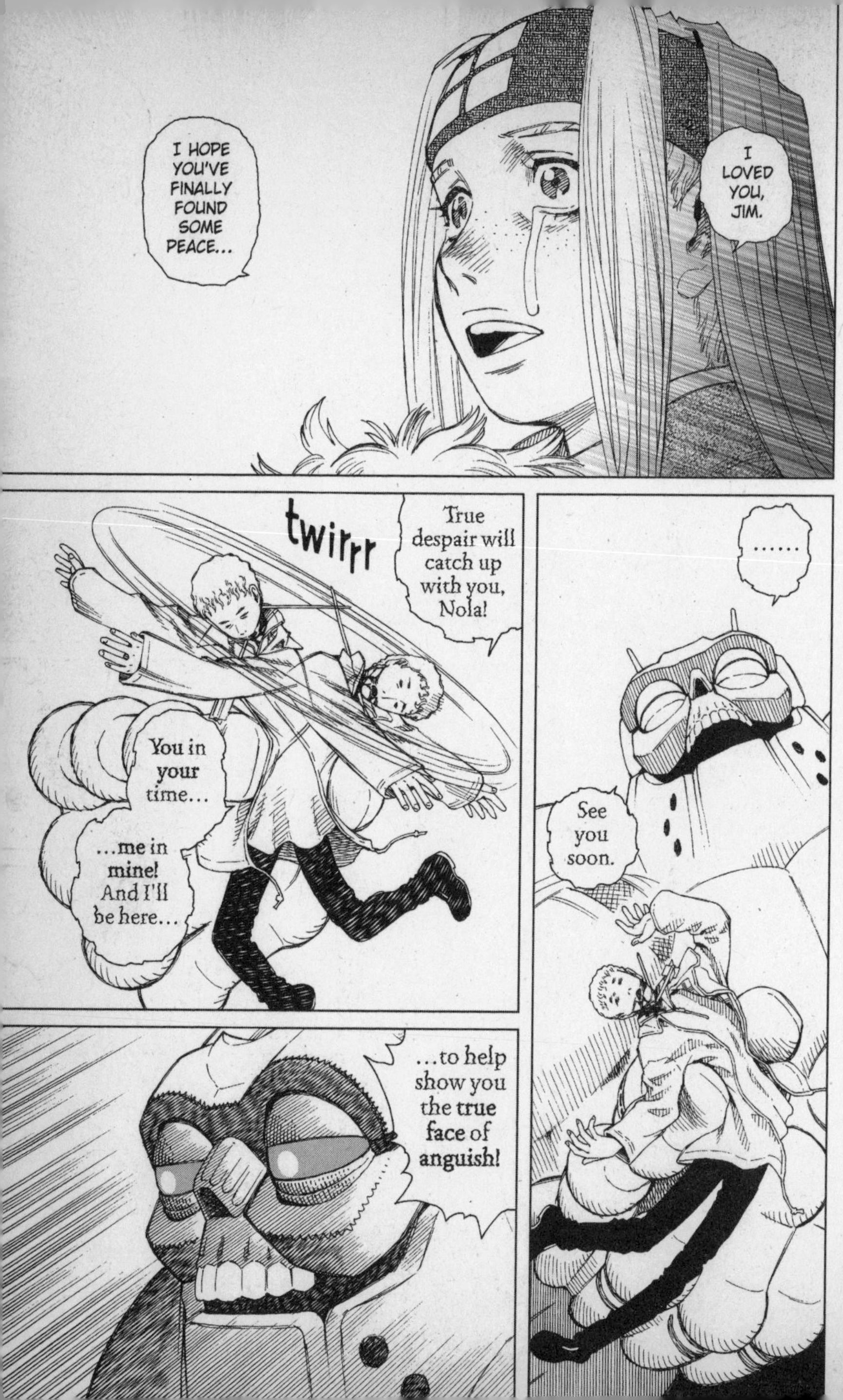
I LOVED YOU, JIM.
I HOPE YOU'VE FINALLY FOUND SOME PEACE...
......
See you soon.
True despair will catch up with you, Nola!
twirrr
You in your time...
...me in mine! And I'll be here...
...to help show you the true face of anguish!

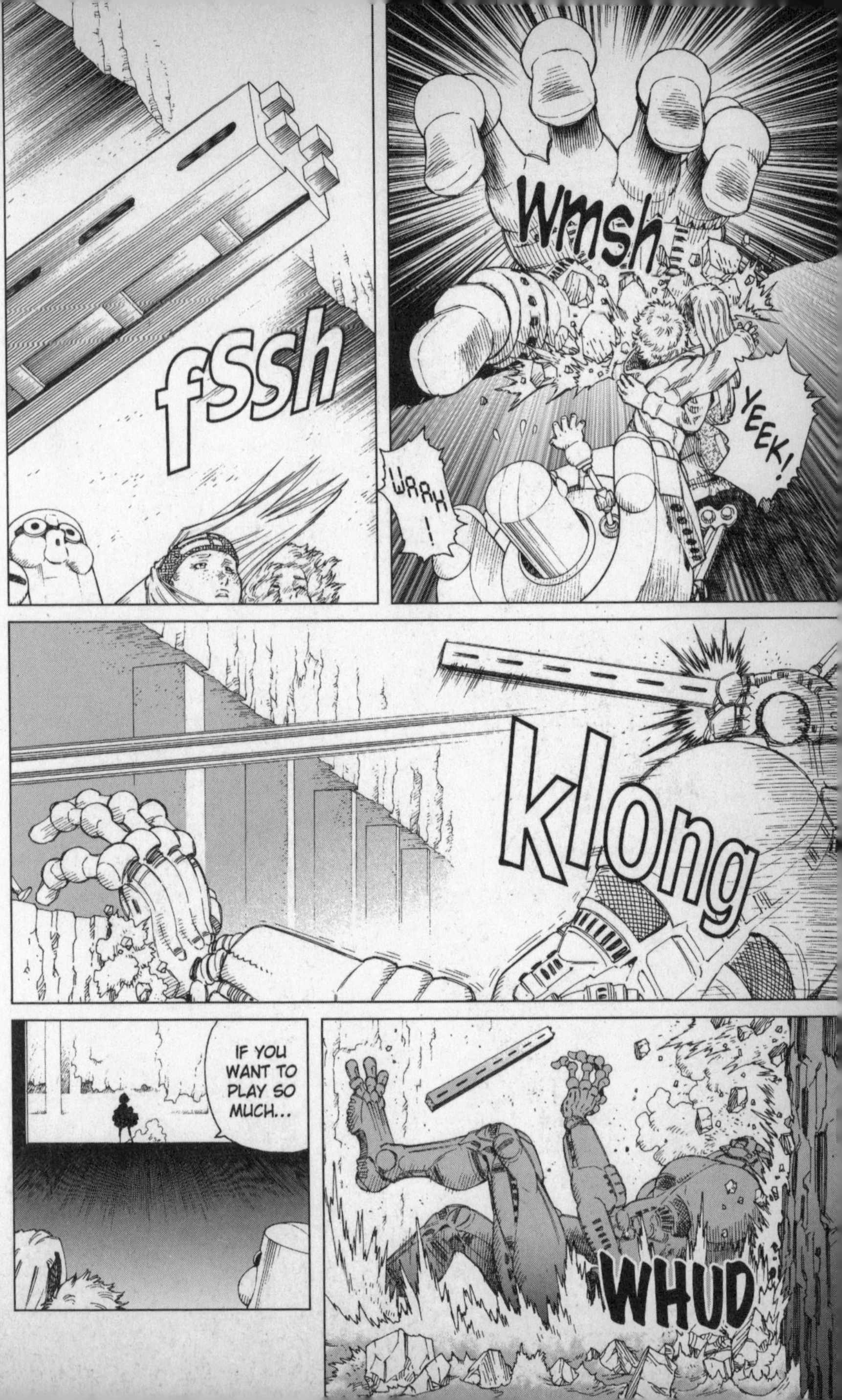
wmsh
YEEK!
WRAAH!
fssh
klong
WHUD
IF YOU WANT TO PLAY SO MUCH...

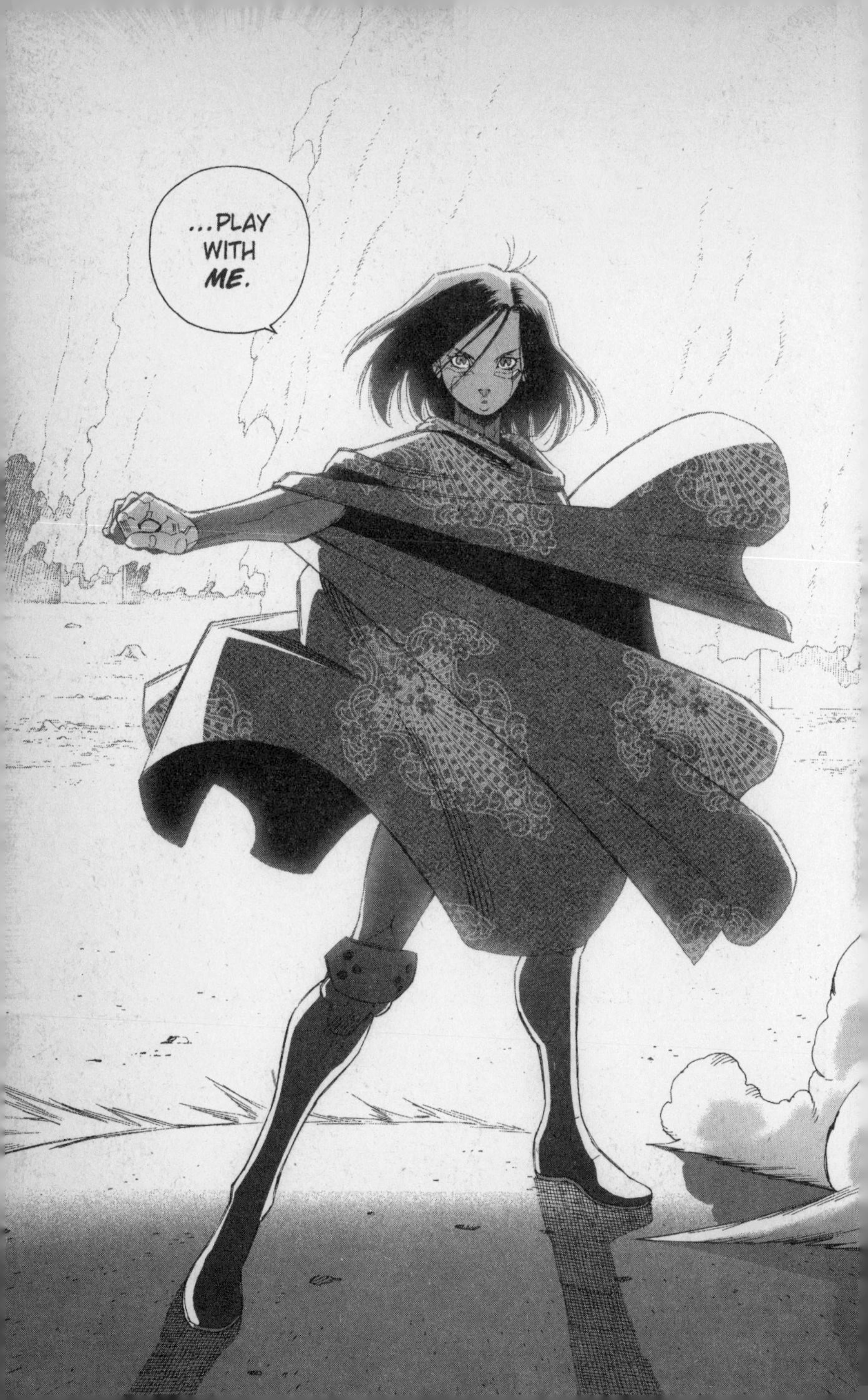
...PLAY WITH ME.

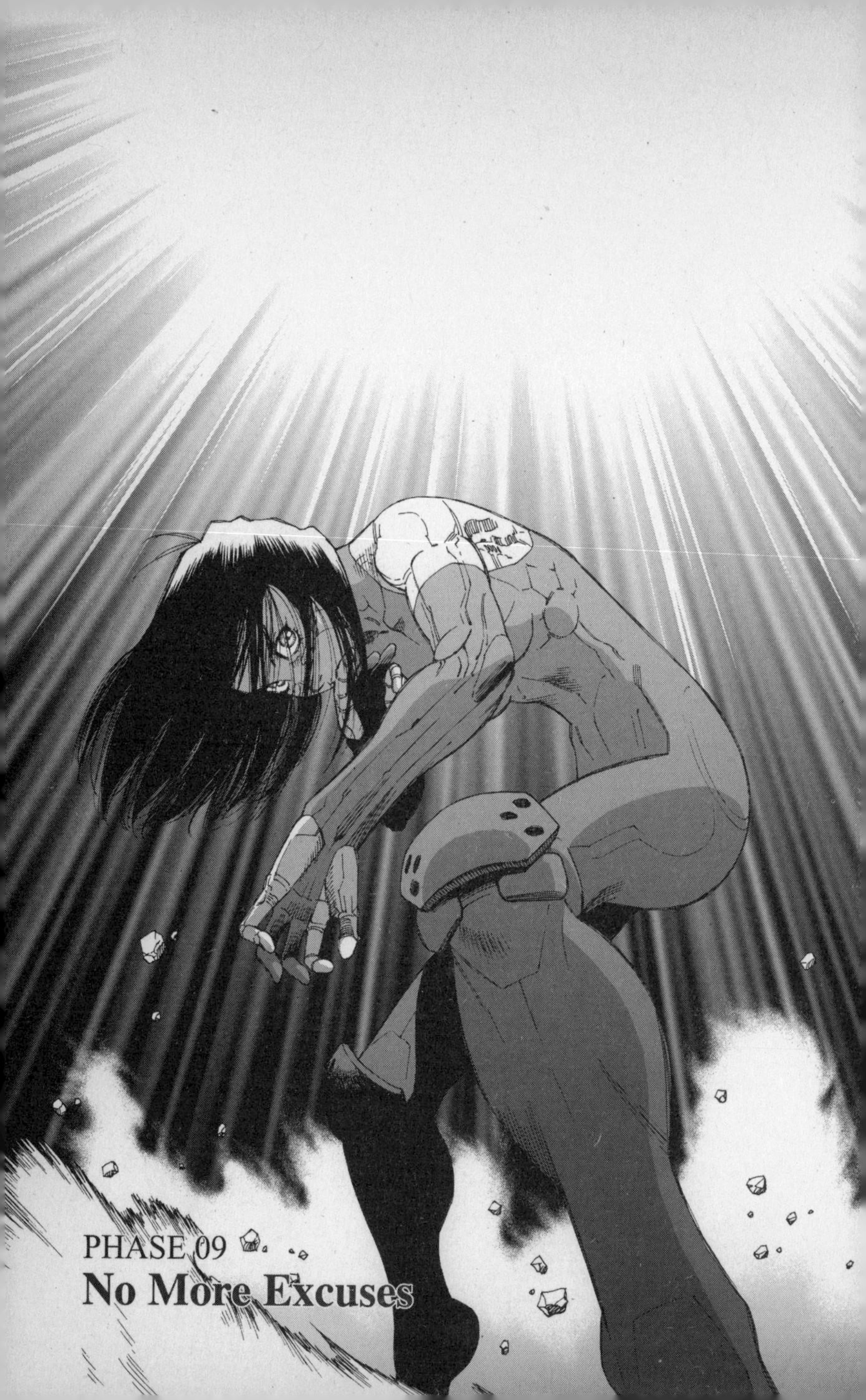
PHASE 09
No More Excuses

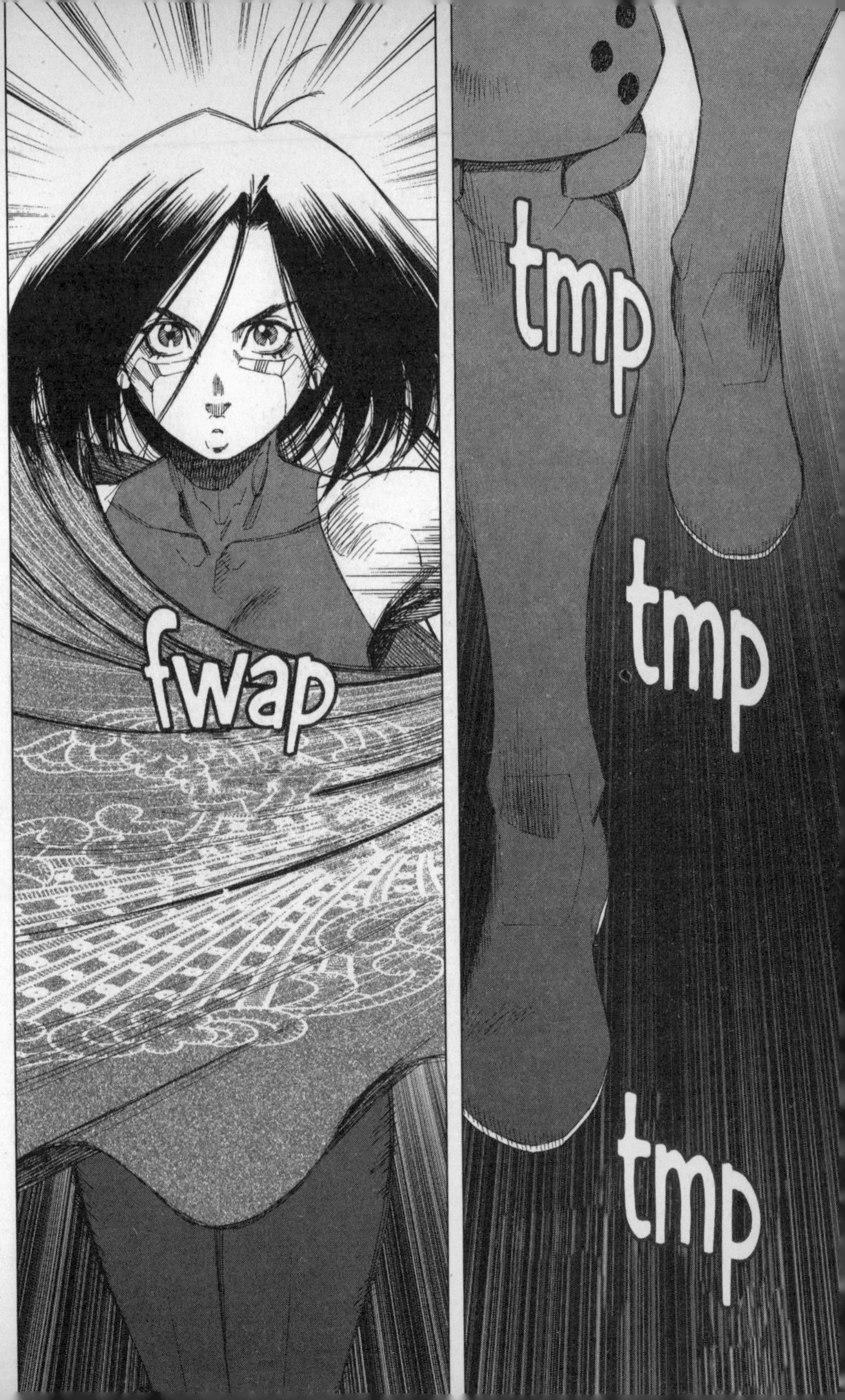
tmp
tmp
tmp
fwap

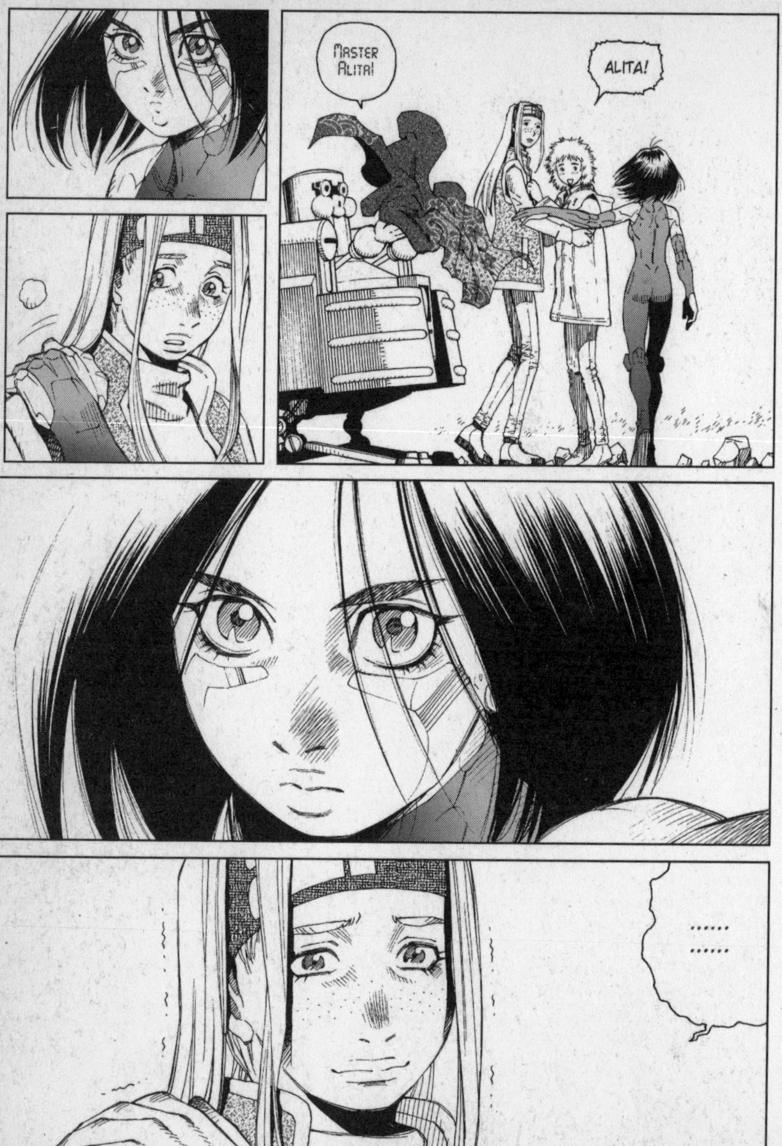
ALITA!
MASTER ALITA!
......
......

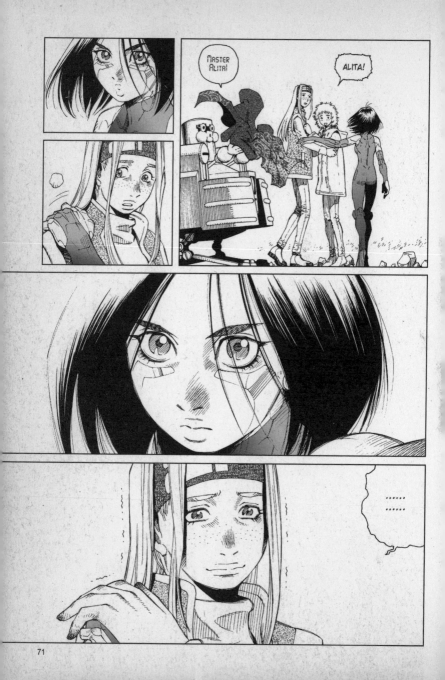

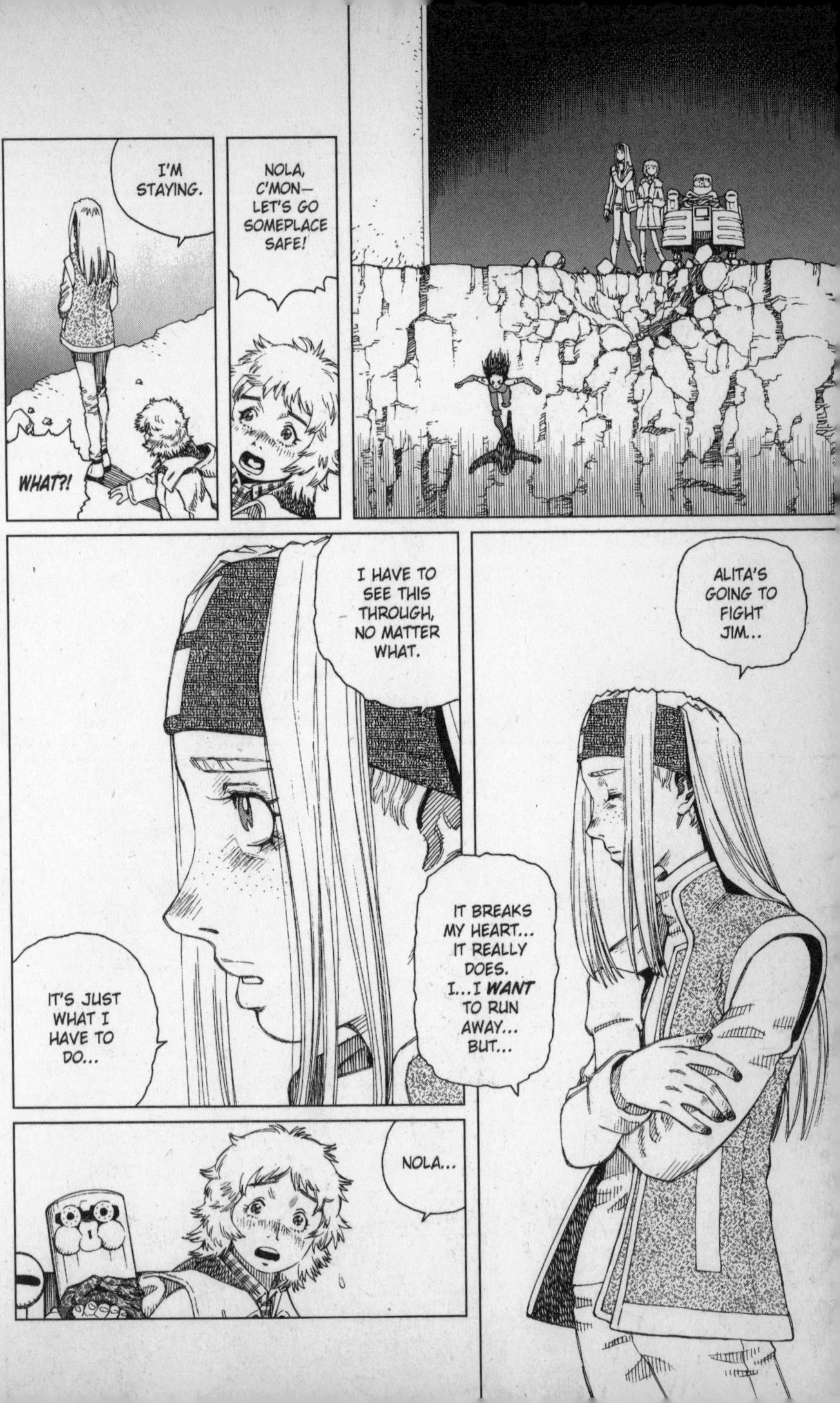
NOLA, C'MON— LET'S GO SOMEPLACE SAFE!
I'M STAYING.
WHAT?!
ALITA'S GOING TO FIGHT JIM...
IT BREAKS MY HEART... IT REALLY DOES. I...I *WANT* TO RUN AWAY... BUT...
I HAVE TO SEE THIS THROUGH, NO MATTER WHAT.
IT'S JUST WHAT I HAVE TO DO...
NOLA...

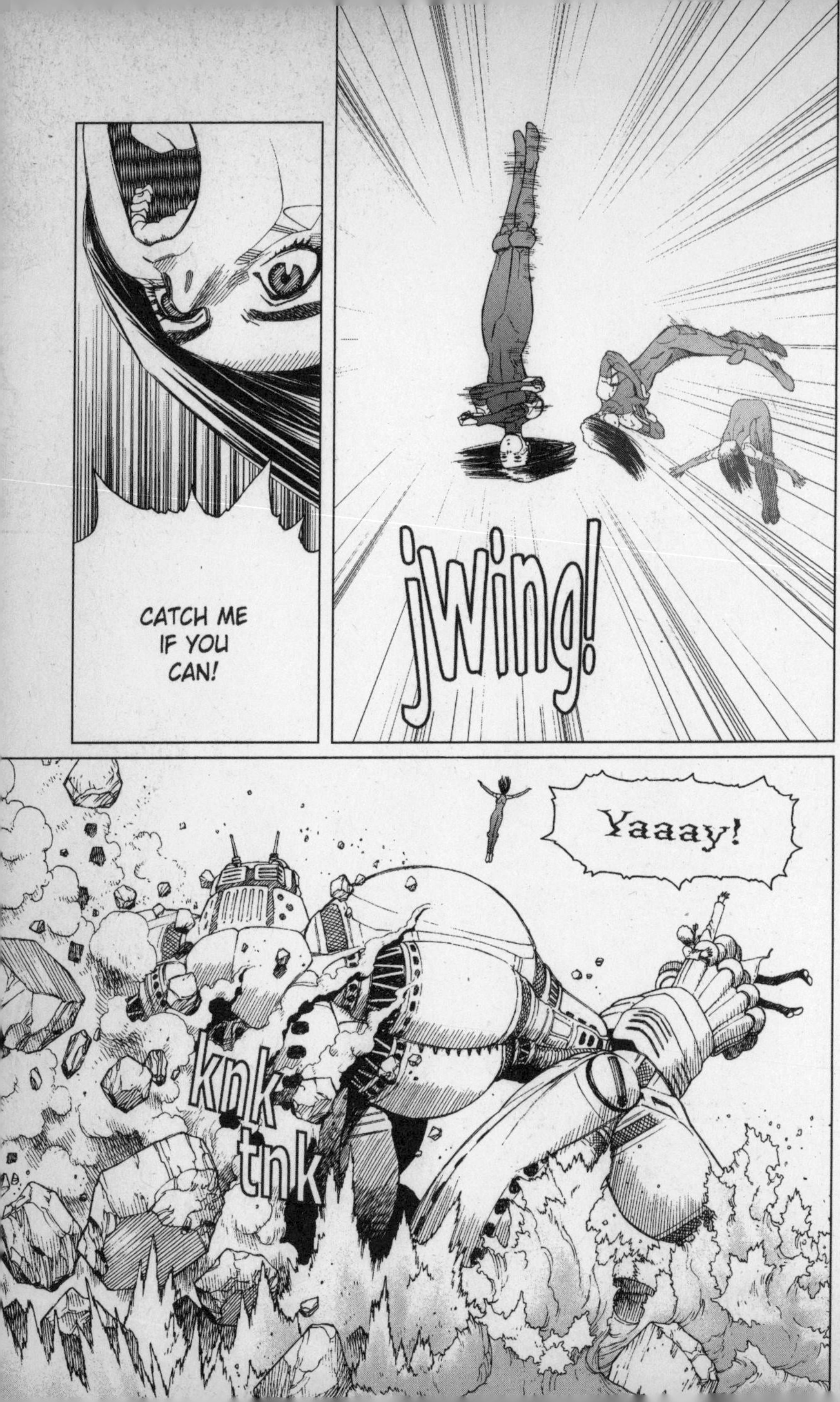
¡WING!
CATCH ME IF YOU CAN!
Yaaay!
knk
tnk

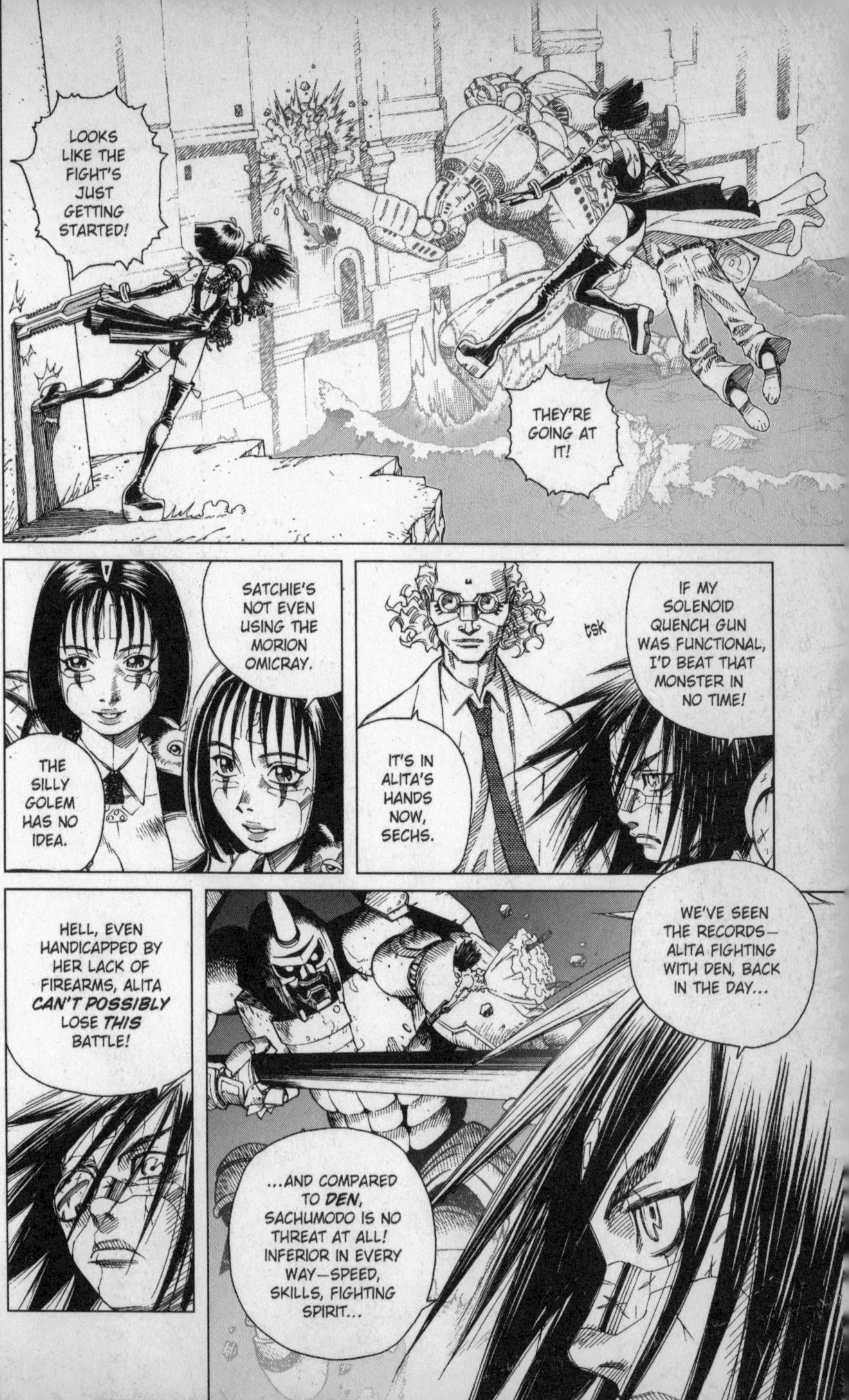
LOOKS LIKE THE FIGHT'S JUST GETTING STARTED!
THEY'RE GOING AT IT!
IF MY SOLENOID QUENCH GUN WAS FUNCTIONAL, I'D BEAT THAT MONSTER IN NO TIME!
tsk
IT'S IN ALITA'S HANDS NOW, SECHS.
SATCHIE'S NOT EVEN USING THE MORION OMICRAY.
THE SILLY GOLEM HAS NO IDEA.
WE'VE SEEN THE RECORDS—ALITA FIGHTING WITH DEN, BACK IN THE DAY...
...AND COMPARED TO *DEN*, SACHUMODO IS NO THREAT AT ALL! INFERIOR IN EVERY WAY—SPEED, SKILLS, FIGHTING SPIRIT...
HELL, EVEN HANDICAPPED BY HER LACK OF FIREARMS, ALITA *CAN'T POSSIBLY* LOSE *THIS* BATTLE!

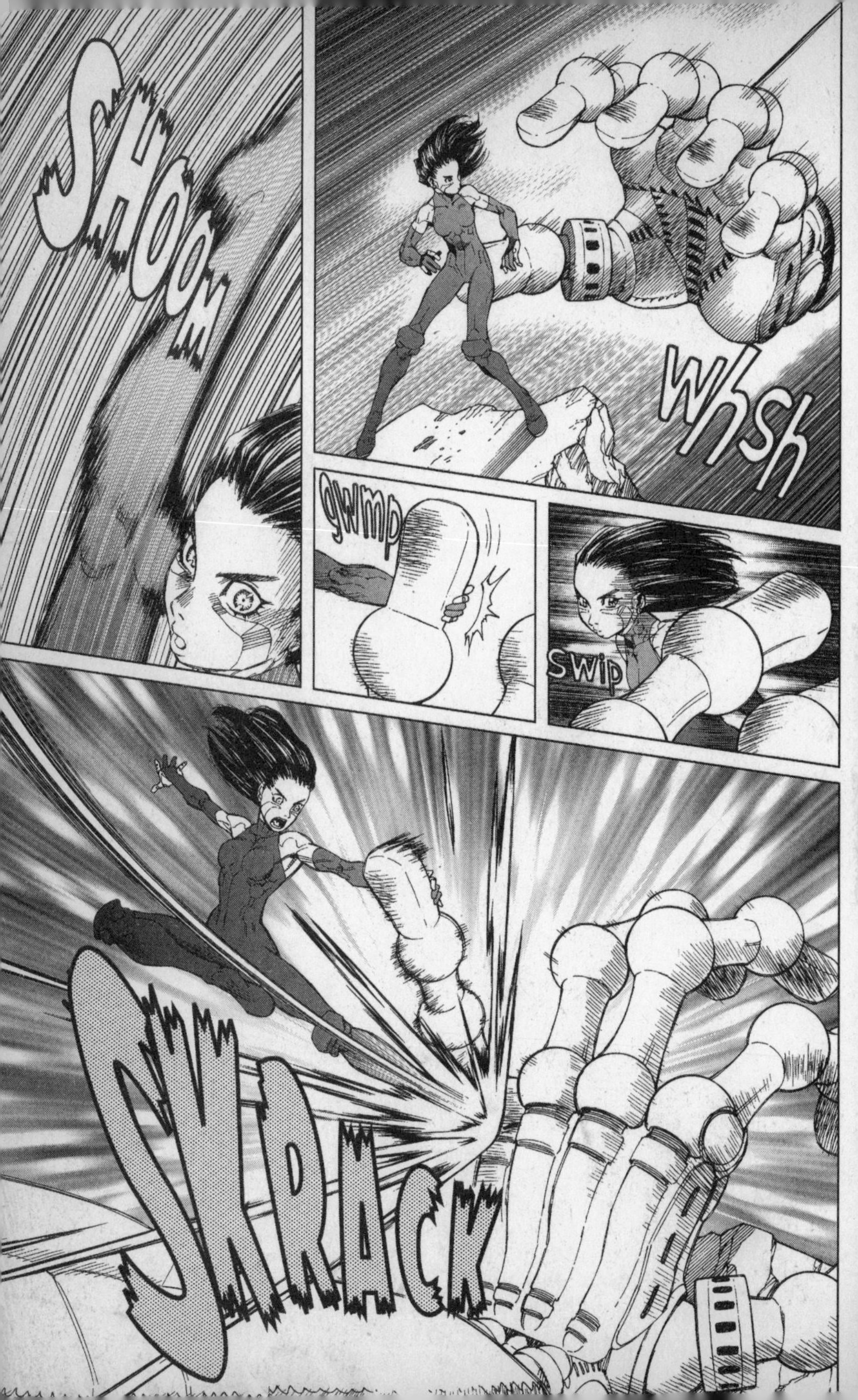
whsh
swip
gwmp
SHOOM
SHRACK

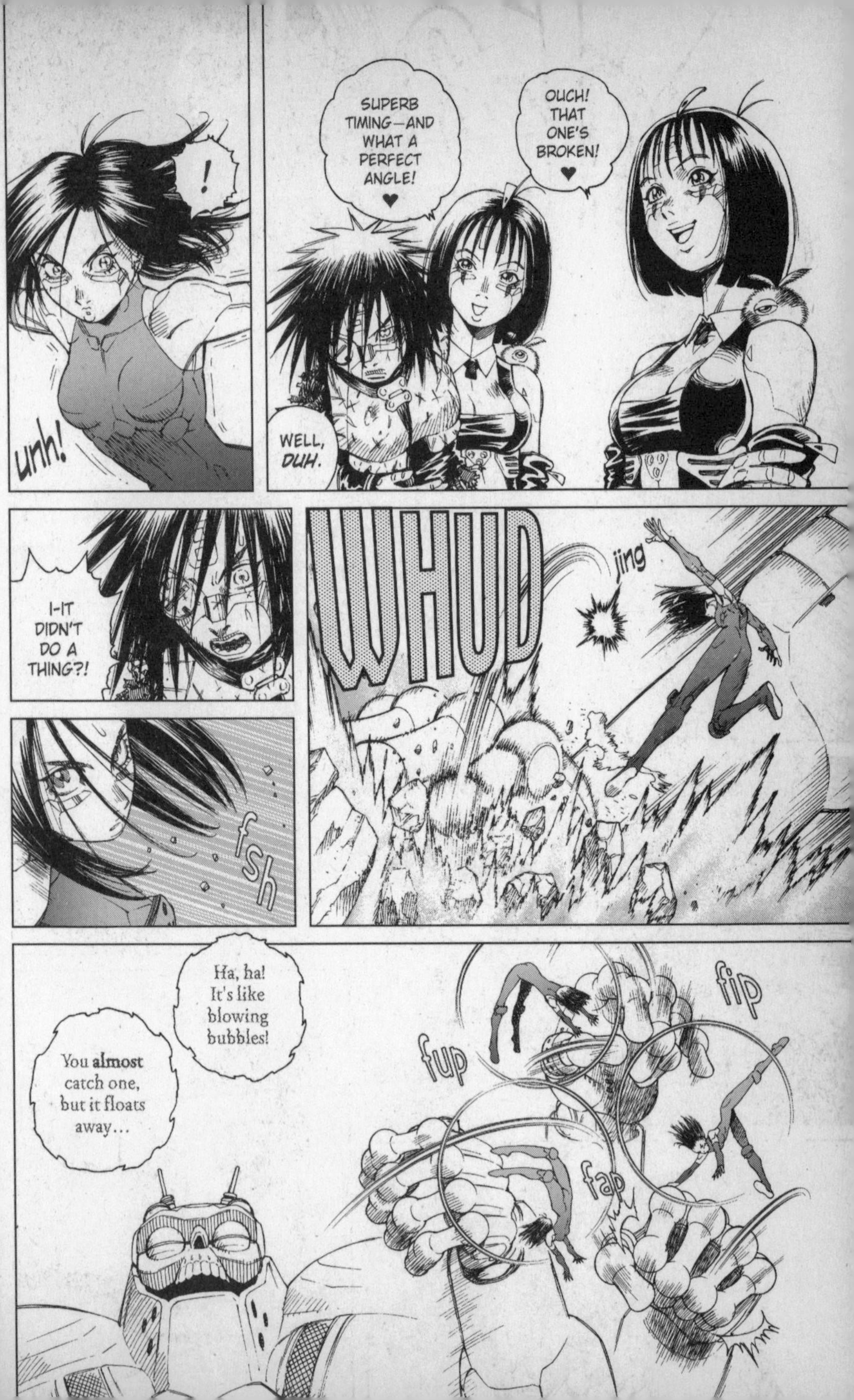
OUCH! THAT ONE'S BROKEN! ♥
SUPERB TIMING—AND WHAT A PERFECT ANGLE! ♥
WELL, DUH.
!
unh!
WHUD
jing
I-IT DIDN'T DO A THING?!
fsh
Ha, ha! It's like blowing bubbles!
You **almost** catch one, but it floats away…
fip
fup
fap

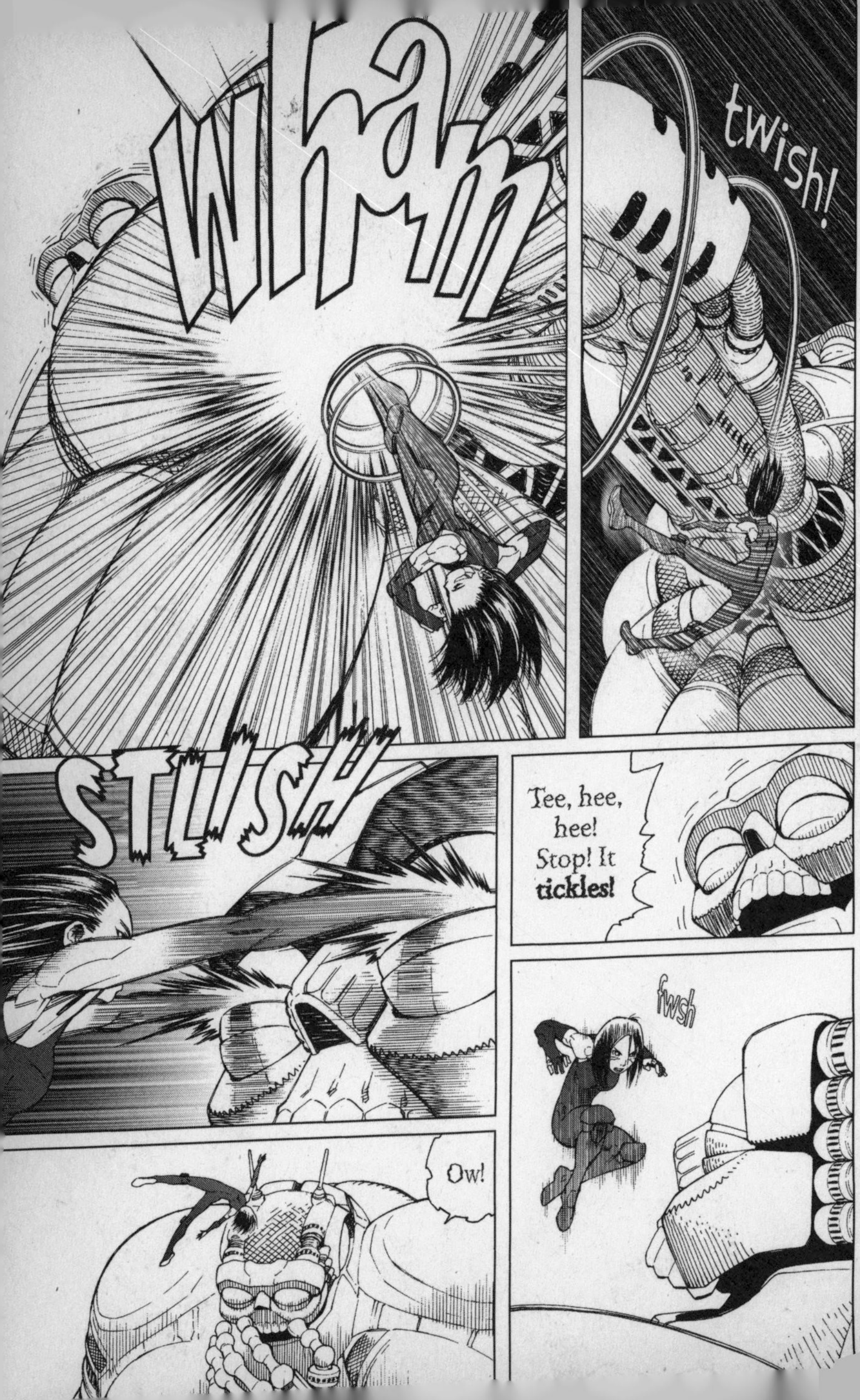
twish!
Wham
Tee, hee, hee! Stop! It **tickles!**
STLISH
fwsh
Ow!

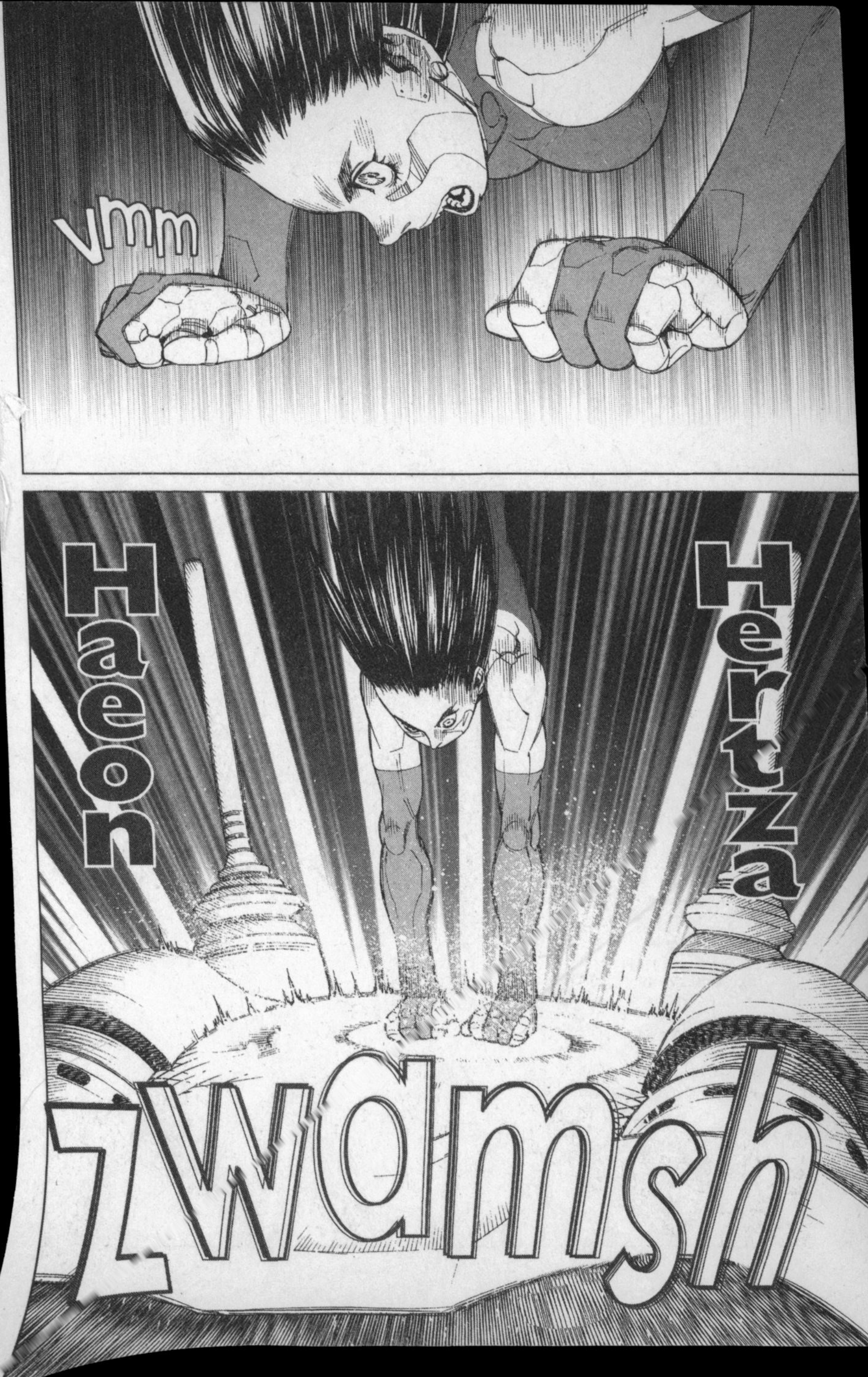
Vmm
Hertza
Haeon
zwamsh

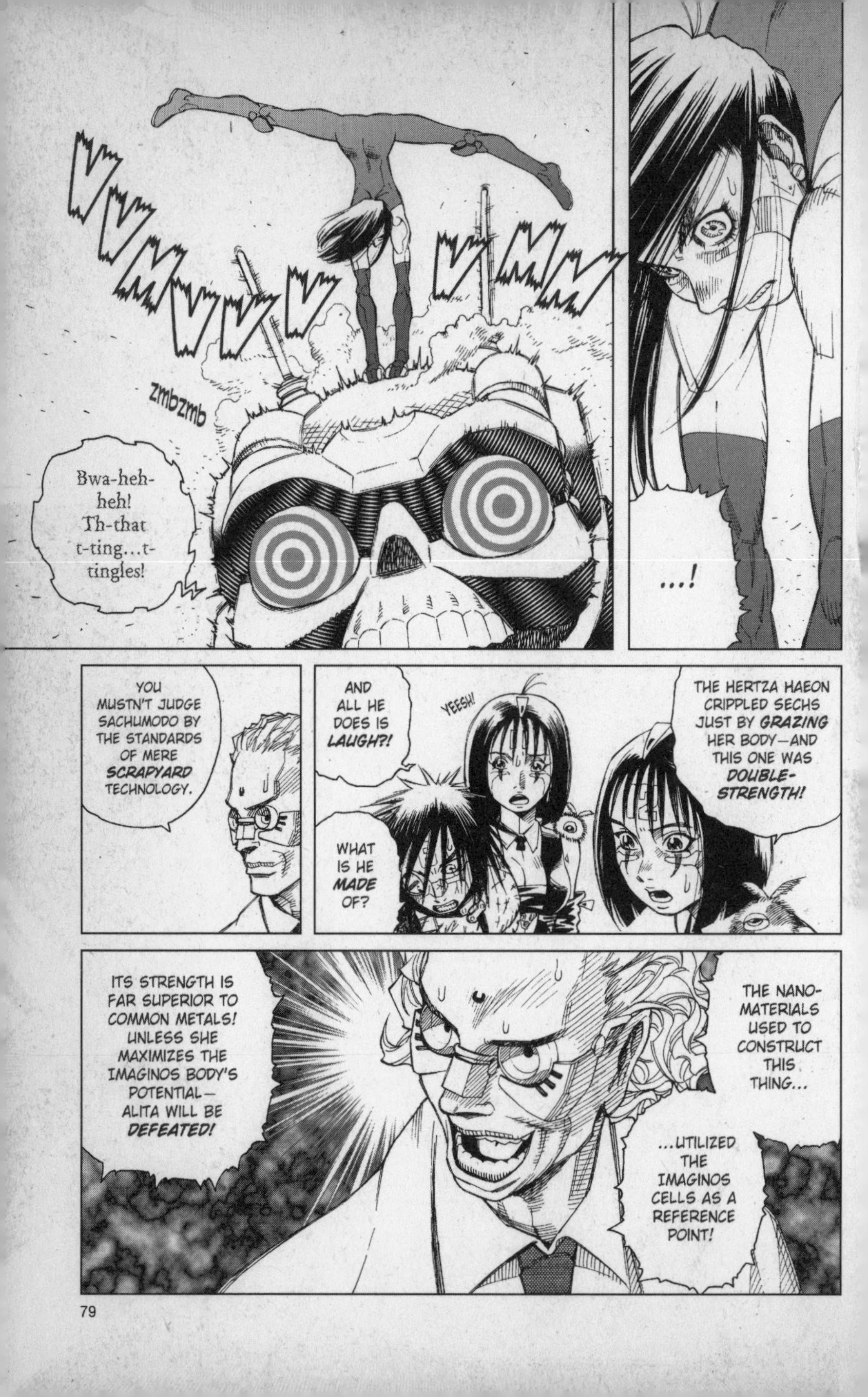
...!
VVMVVV VMMM
zmbzmb
Bwa-heh-heh! Th-that t-ting...t-tingles!
THE HERTZA HAEON CRIPPLED SECHS JUST BY GRAZING HER BODY—AND THIS ONE WAS DOUBLE-STRENGTH!
AND ALL HE DOES IS LAUGH?!
YEESH!
WHAT IS HE MADE OF?
YOU MUSTN'T JUDGE SACHUMODO BY THE STANDARDS OF MERE SCRAPYARD TECHNOLOGY.
THE NANO-MATERIALS USED TO CONSTRUCT THIS THING...
...UTILIZED THE IMAGINOS CELLS AS A REFERENCE POINT!
ITS STRENGTH IS FAR SUPERIOR TO COMMON METALS! UNLESS SHE MAXIMIZES THE IMAGINOS BODY'S POTENTIAL—ALITA WILL BE DEFEATED!

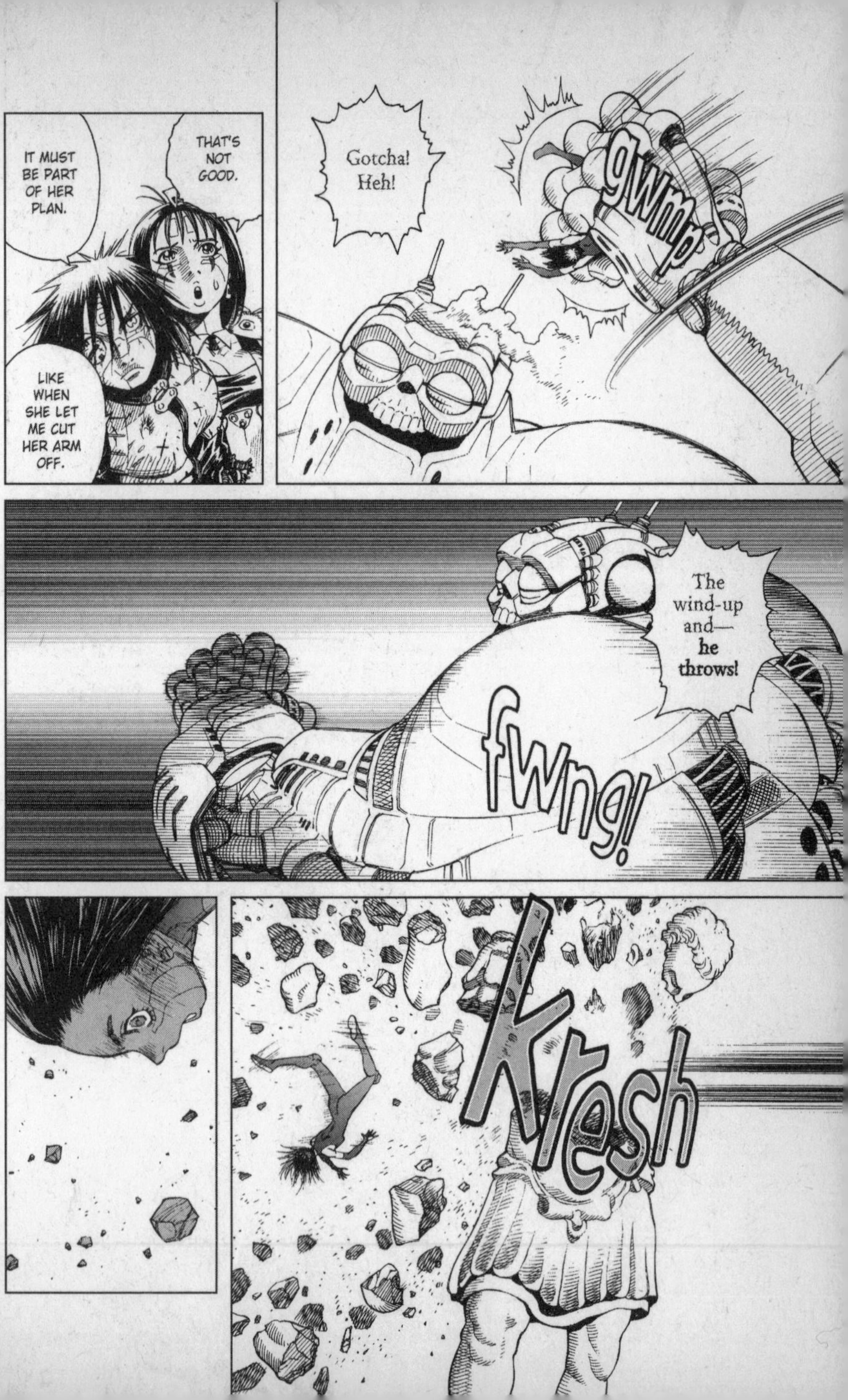
Gotcha! Heh!
gwmp
THAT'S NOT GOOD.
IT MUST BE PART OF HER PLAN.
LIKE WHEN SHE LET ME CUT HER ARM OFF.
The wind-up and— **he throws!**
fwng!
Kresh

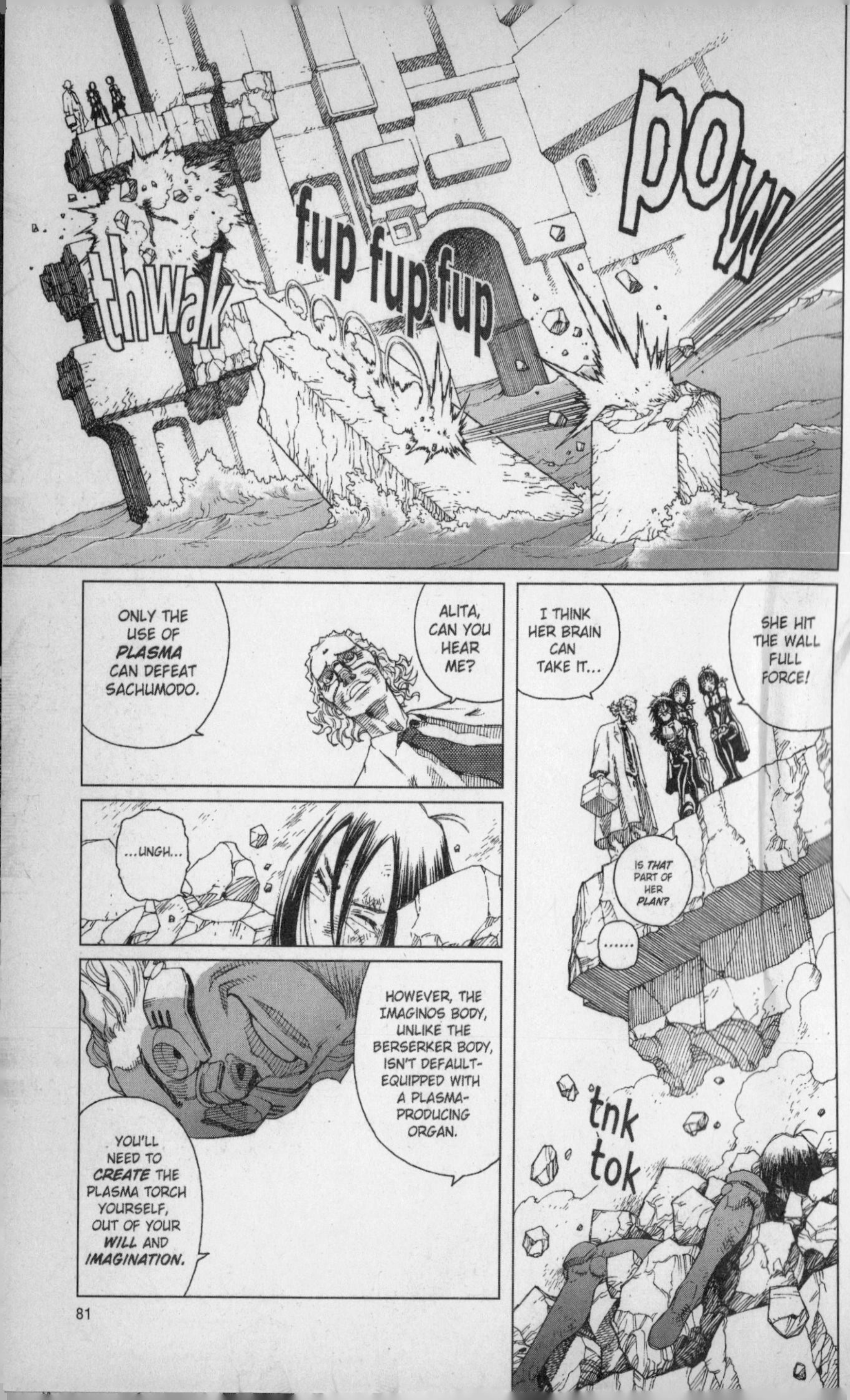
pow
fup fup fup
thwak
SHE HIT THE WALL FULL FORCE!
I THINK HER BRAIN CAN TAKE IT...
IS THAT PART OF HER PLAN?
......
tnk tok
ALITA, CAN YOU HEAR ME?
ONLY THE USE OF PLASMA CAN DEFEAT SACHUMODO.
...UNGH...
HOWEVER, THE IMAGINOS BODY, UNLIKE THE BERSERKER BODY, ISN'T DEFAULT-EQUIPPED WITH A PLASMA-PRODUCING ORGAN.
YOU'LL NEED TO CREATE THE PLASMA TORCH YOURSELF, OUT OF YOUR WILL AND IMAGINATION.

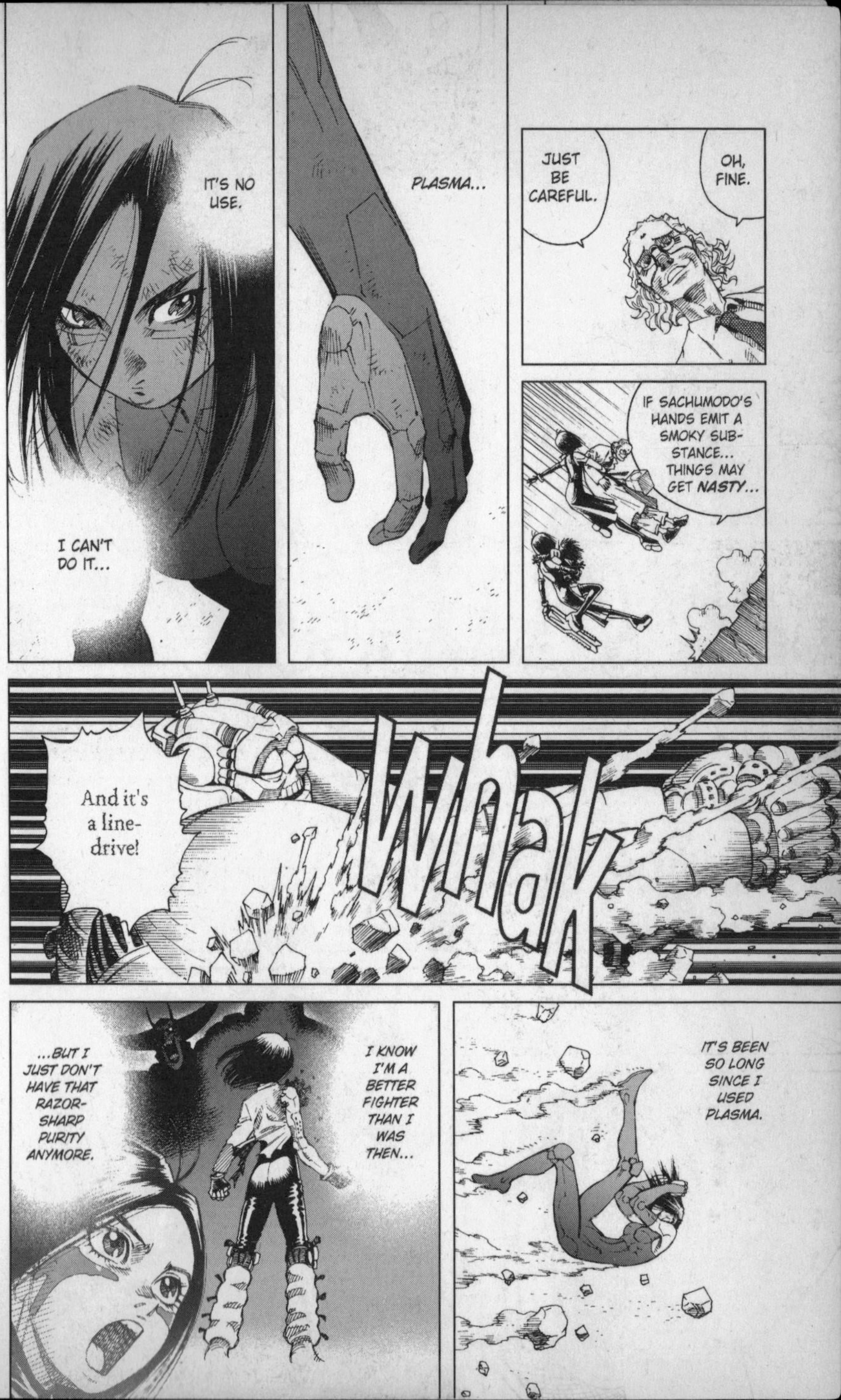
OH, FINE.
JUST BE CAREFUL.
IF SACHUMODO'S HANDS EMIT A SMOKY SUBSTANCE... THINGS MAY GET **NASTY**...
PLASMA...
IT'S NO USE.
I CAN'T DO IT...
Whak
And it's a line-drive!
IT'S BEEN SO LONG SINCE I USED PLASMA.
I KNOW I'M A BETTER FIGHTER THAN I WAS THEN...
...BUT I JUST DON'T HAVE THAT RAZOR-SHARP PURITY ANYMORE.

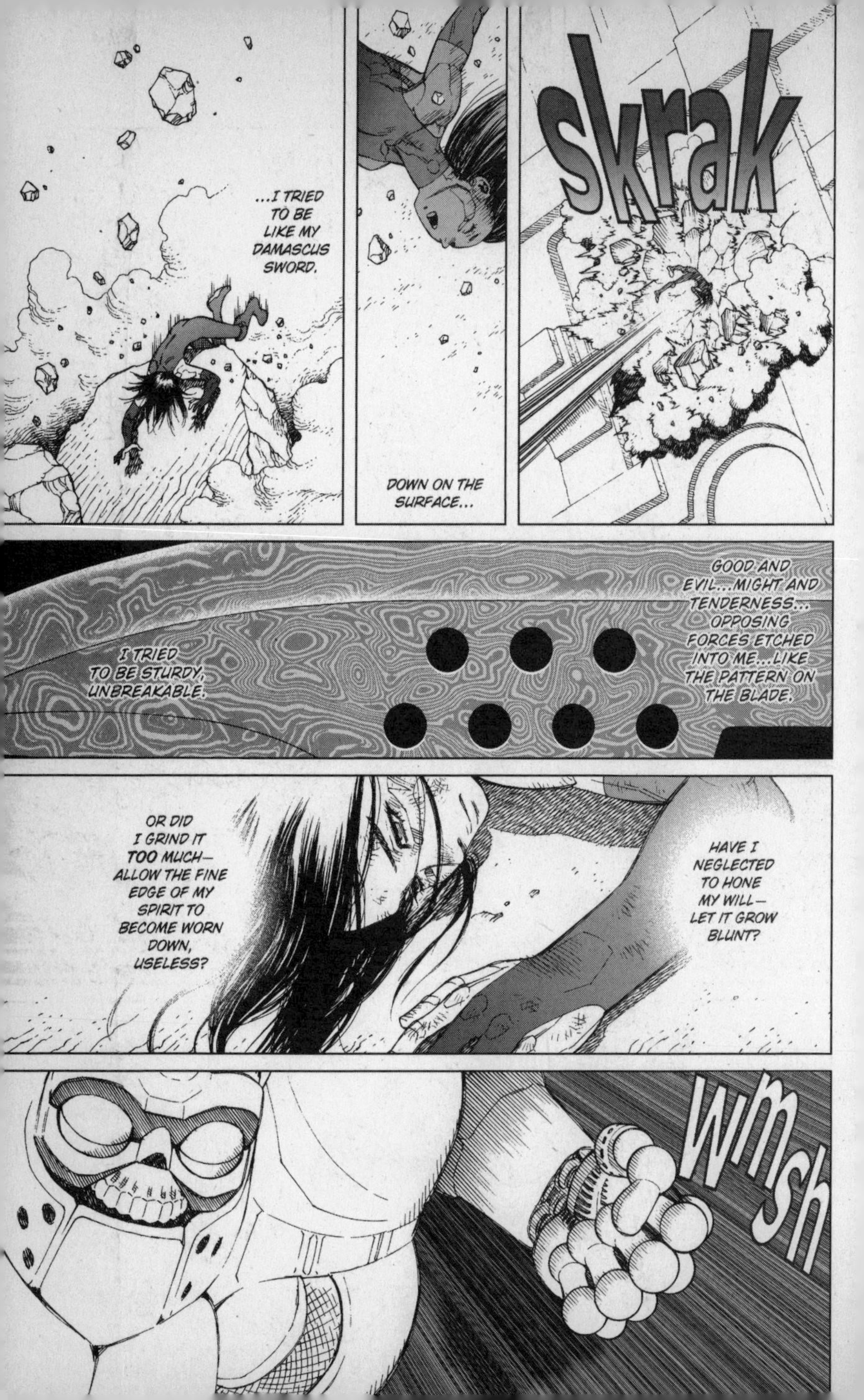
skrak
DOWN ON THE SURFACE...
...I TRIED TO BE LIKE MY DAMASCUS SWORD.
GOOD AND EVIL...MIGHT AND TENDERNESS... OPPOSING FORCES ETCHED INTO ME...LIKE THE PATTERN ON THE BLADE.
I TRIED TO BE STURDY, UNBREAKABLE.
HAVE I NEGLECTED TO HONE MY WILL— LET IT GROW BLUNT?
OR DID I GRIND IT TOO MUCH— ALLOW THE FINE EDGE OF MY SPIRIT TO BECOME WORN DOWN, USELESS?
wmsh

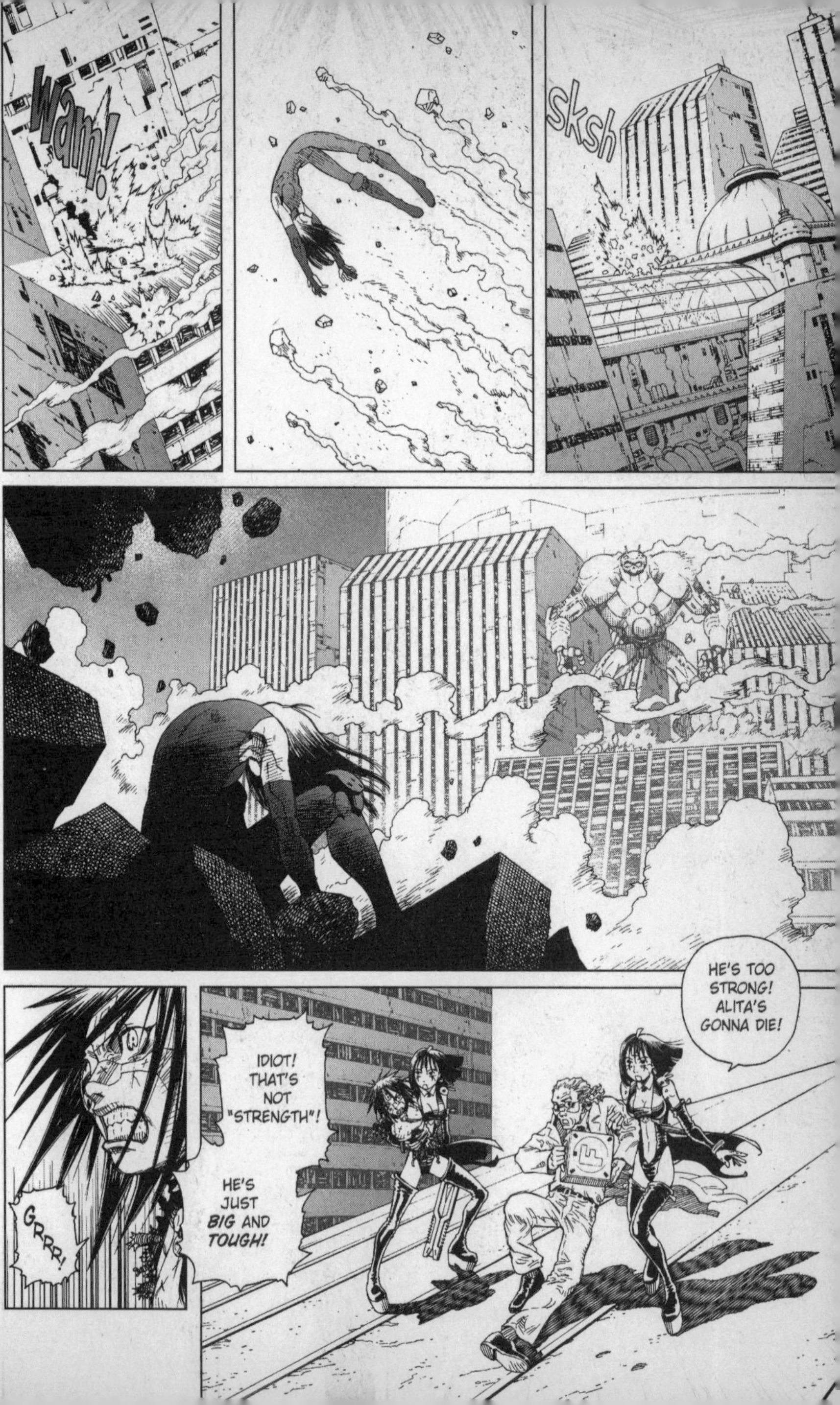
sksh
WAM!
HE'S TOO STRONG! ALITA'S GONNA DIE!
IDIOT! THAT'S NOT "STRENGTH"!
HE'S JUST BIG AND TOUGH!
GRRR!

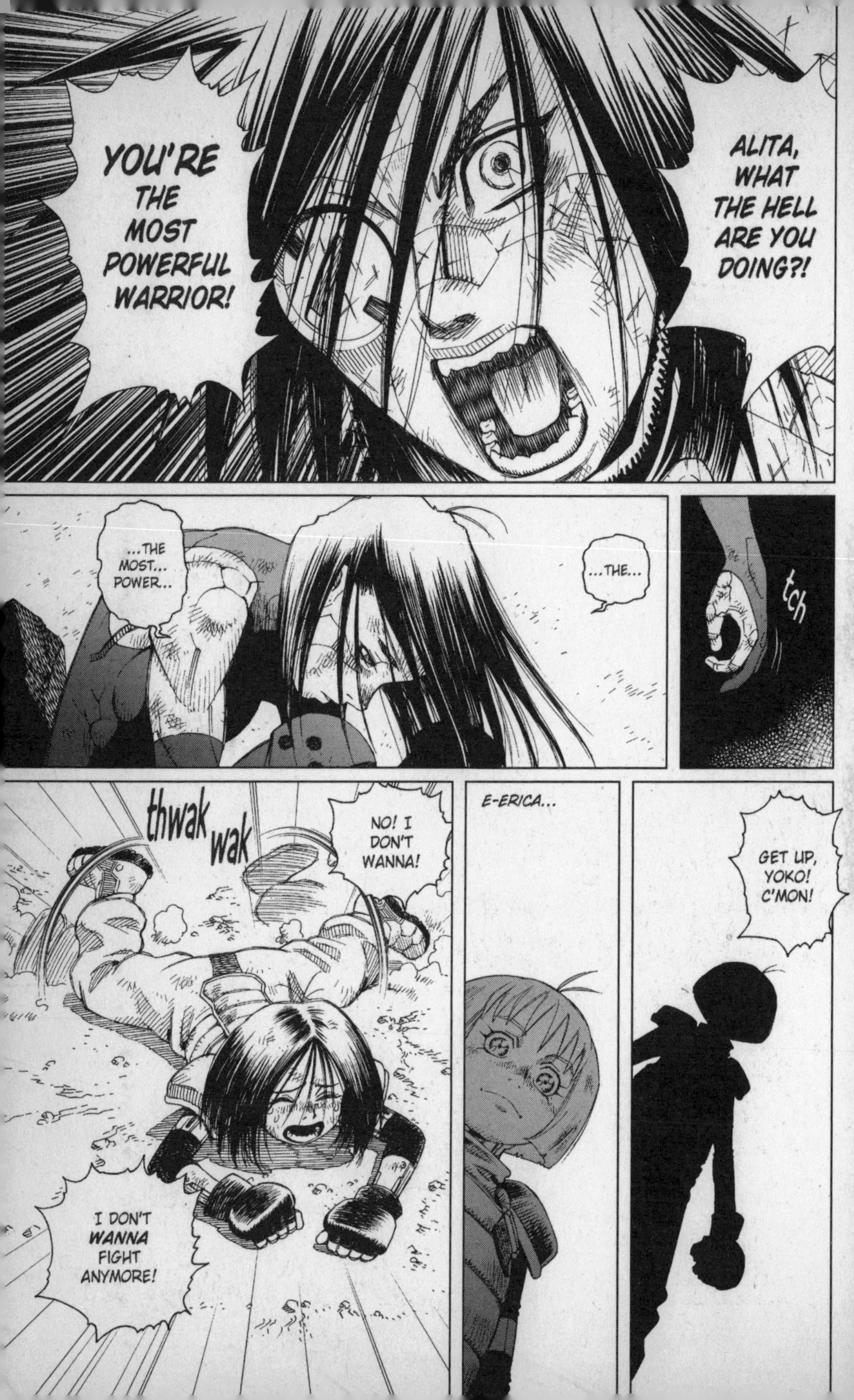
ALITA, WHAT THE HELL ARE YOU DOING?!
YOU'RE THE MOST POWERFUL WARRIOR!
tch
...THE...
...THE MOST... POWER...
GET UP, YOKO! C'MON!
E-ERICA...
NO! I DON'T WANNA!
thwak wak
I DON'T WANNA FIGHT ANYMORE!

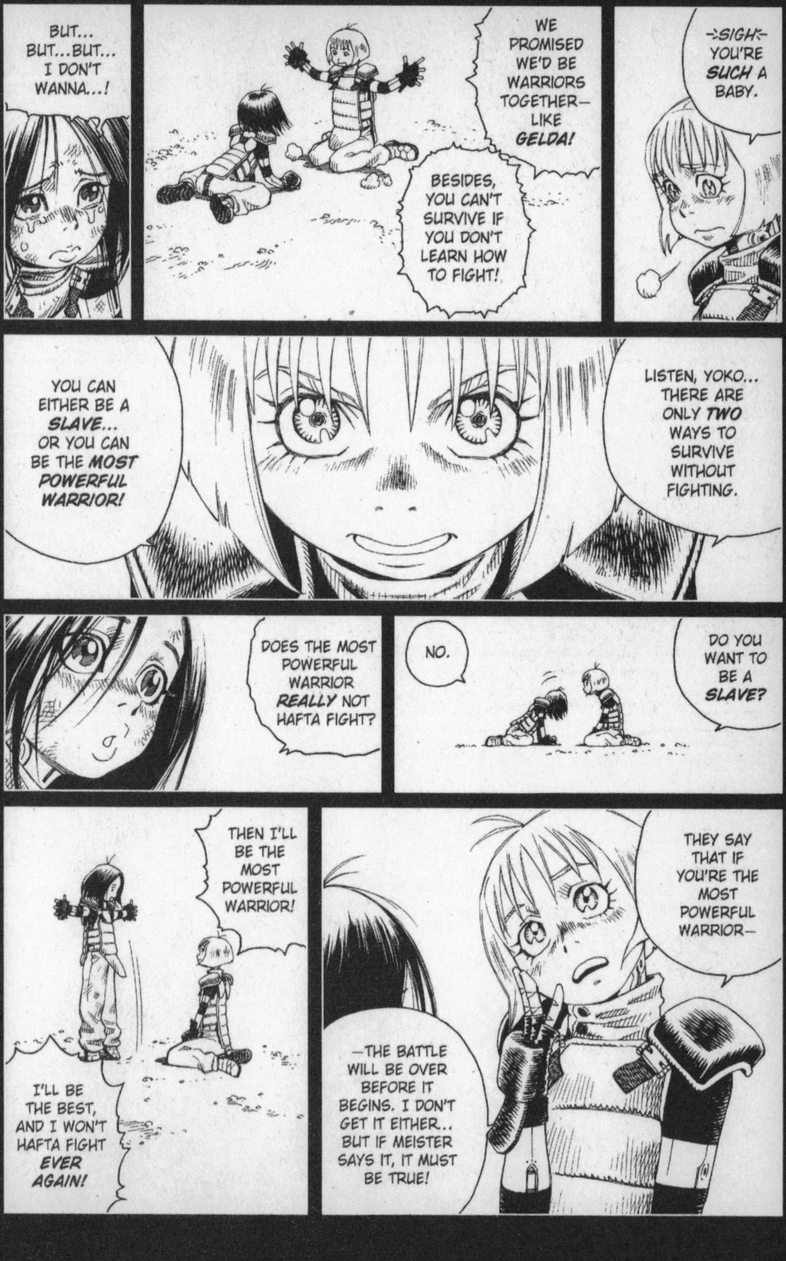
~SIGH~ YOU'RE SUCH A BABY.
WE PROMISED WE'D BE WARRIORS TOGETHER— LIKE GELDA!
BESIDES, YOU CAN'T SURVIVE IF YOU DON'T LEARN HOW TO FIGHT!
BUT... BUT...BUT... I DON'T WANNA...!
LISTEN, YOKO... THERE ARE ONLY TWO WAYS TO SURVIVE WITHOUT FIGHTING.
YOU CAN EITHER BE A SLAVE... OR YOU CAN BE THE MOST POWERFUL WARRIOR!
DO YOU WANT TO BE A SLAVE?
NO.
DOES THE MOST POWERFUL WARRIOR REALLY NOT HAFTA FIGHT?
THEY SAY THAT IF YOU'RE THE MOST POWERFUL WARRIOR—
—THE BATTLE WILL BE OVER BEFORE IT BEGINS. I DON'T GET IT EITHER.. BUT IF MEISTER SAYS IT, IT MUST BE TRUE!
THEN I'LL BE THE MOST POWERFUL WARRIOR!
I'LL BE THE BEST, AND I WON'T HAFTA FIGHT EVER AGAIN!

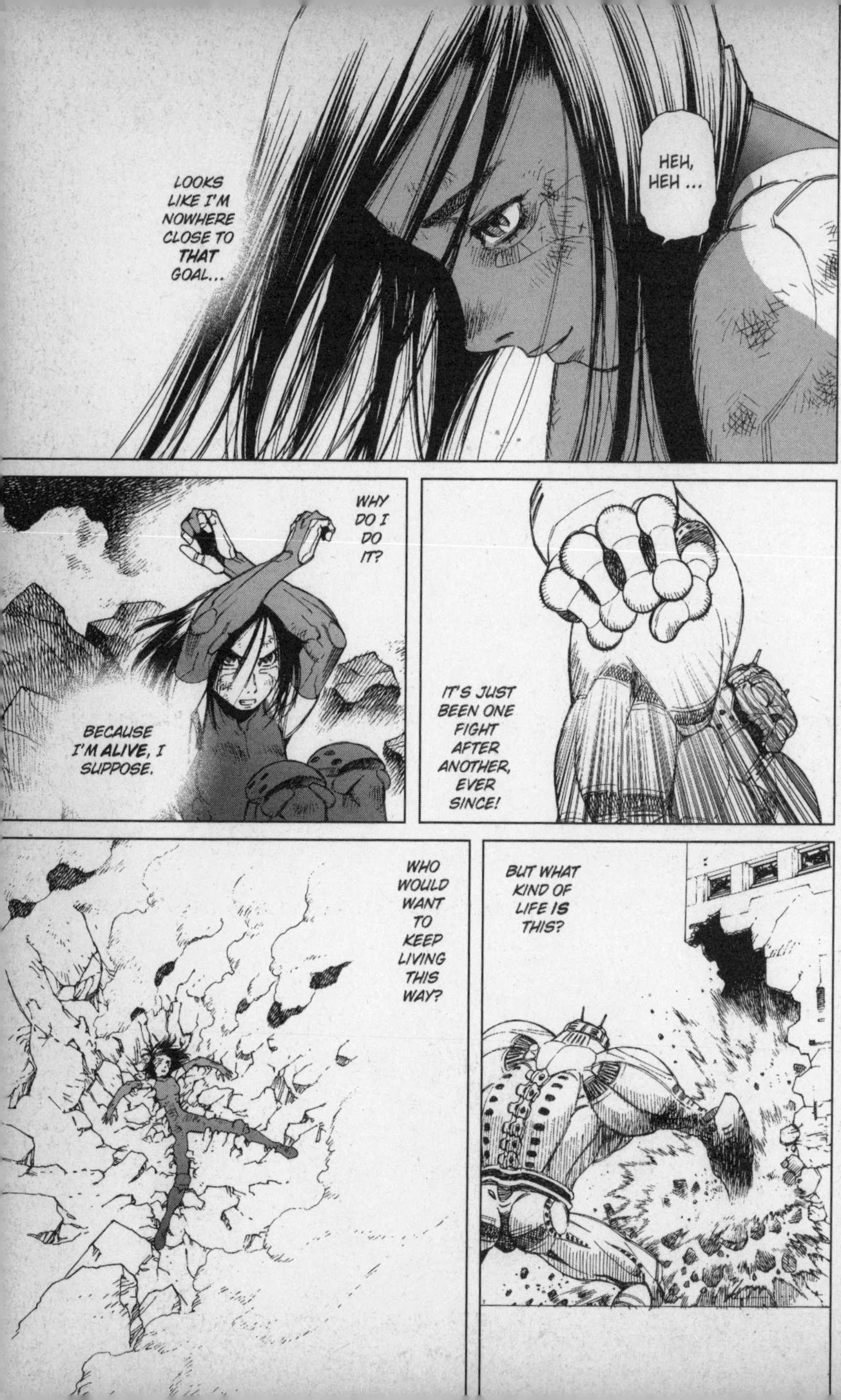
HEH, HEH ...
LOOKS LIKE I'M NOWHERE CLOSE TO THAT GOAL...
IT'S JUST BEEN ONE FIGHT AFTER ANOTHER, EVER SINCE!
WHY DO I DO IT?
BECAUSE I'M ALIVE, I SUPPOSE.
BUT WHAT KIND OF LIFE IS THIS?
WHO WOULD WANT TO KEEP LIVING THIS WAY?

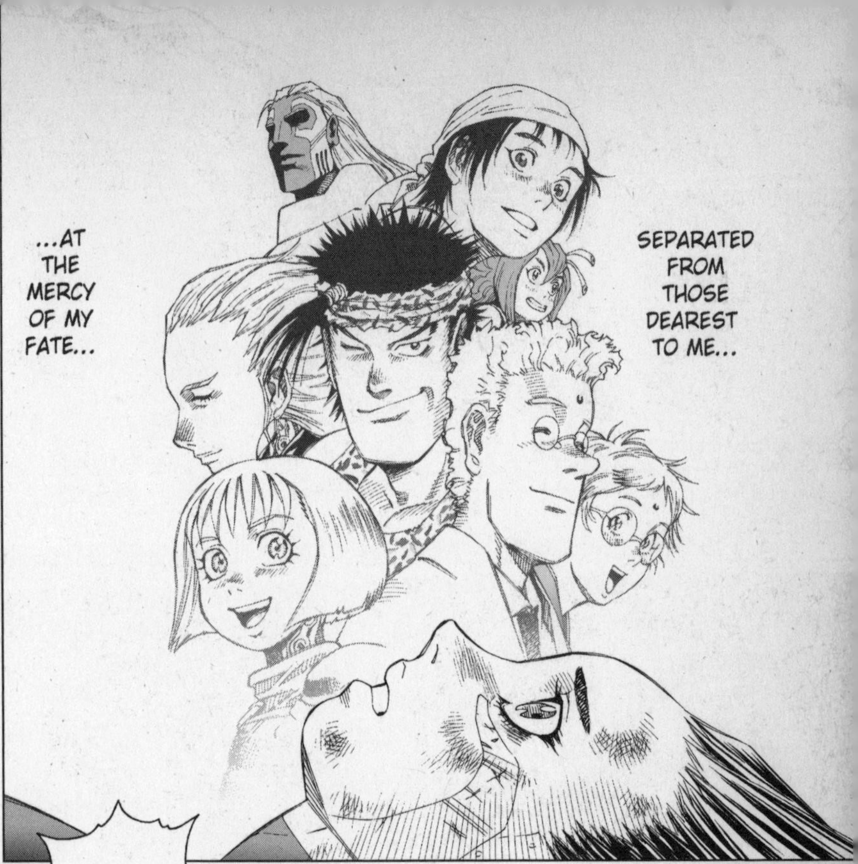
SEPARATED FROM THOSE DEAREST TO ME...
...AT THE MERCY OF MY FATE...
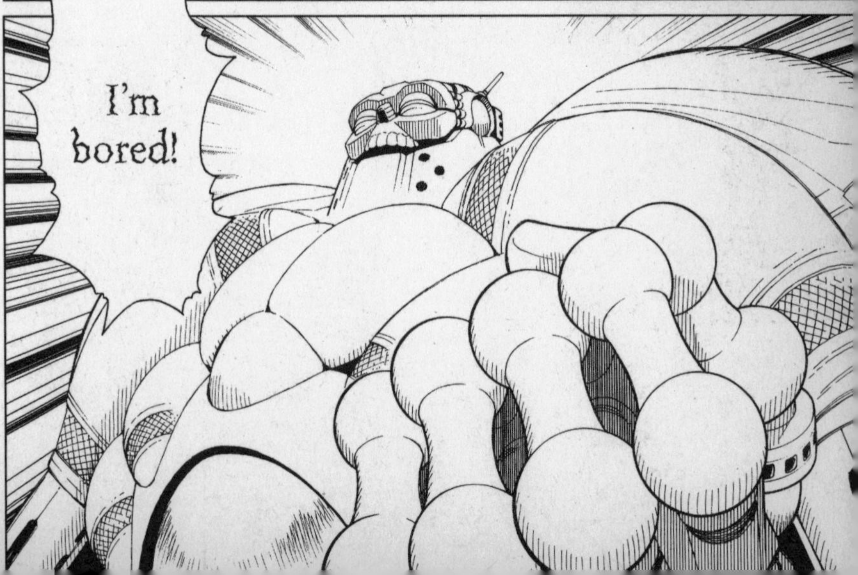
I'm bored!

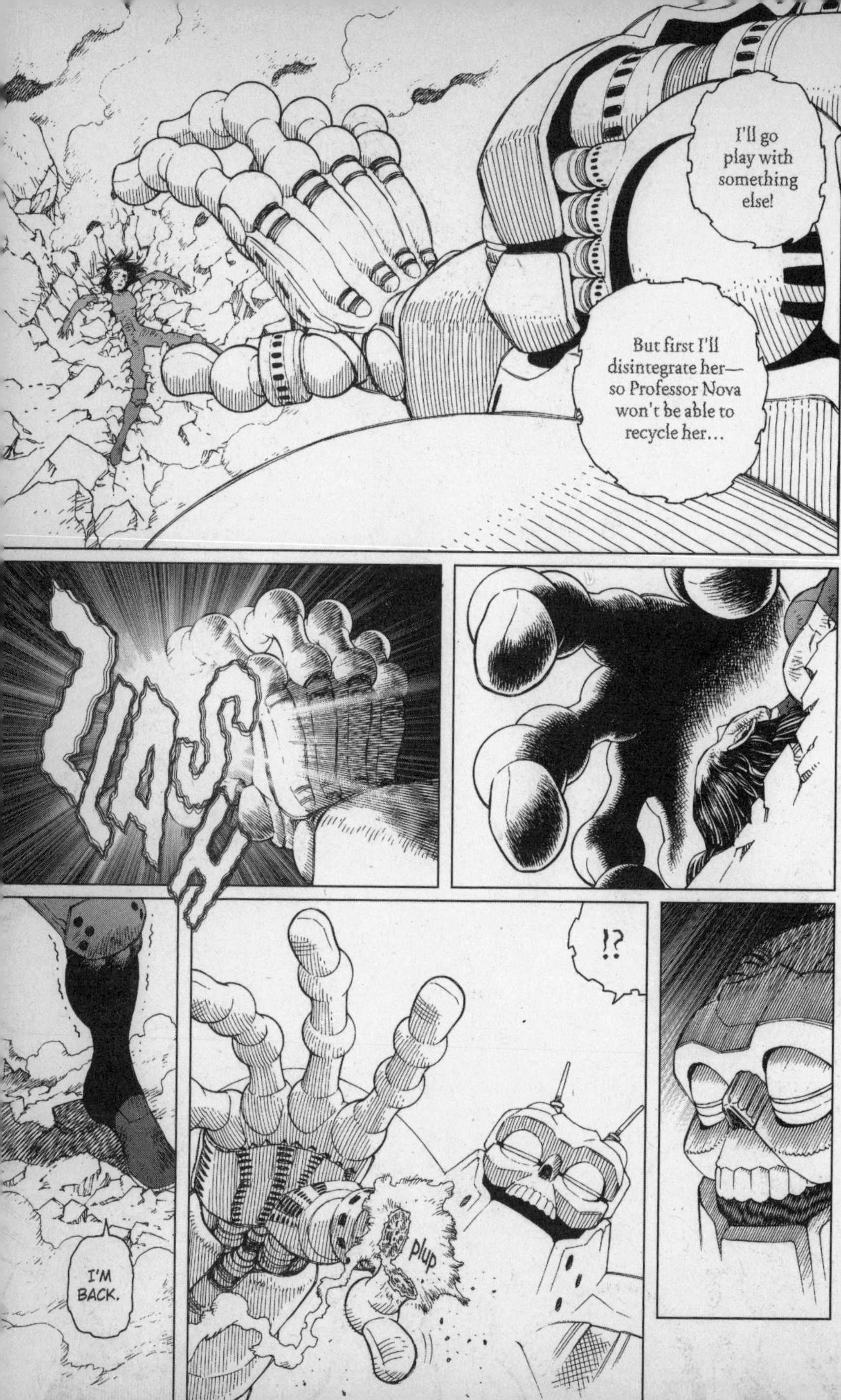
I'll go play with something else!
But first I'll disintegrate her—so Professor Nova won't be able to recycle her...
!?
plup
I'M BACK.

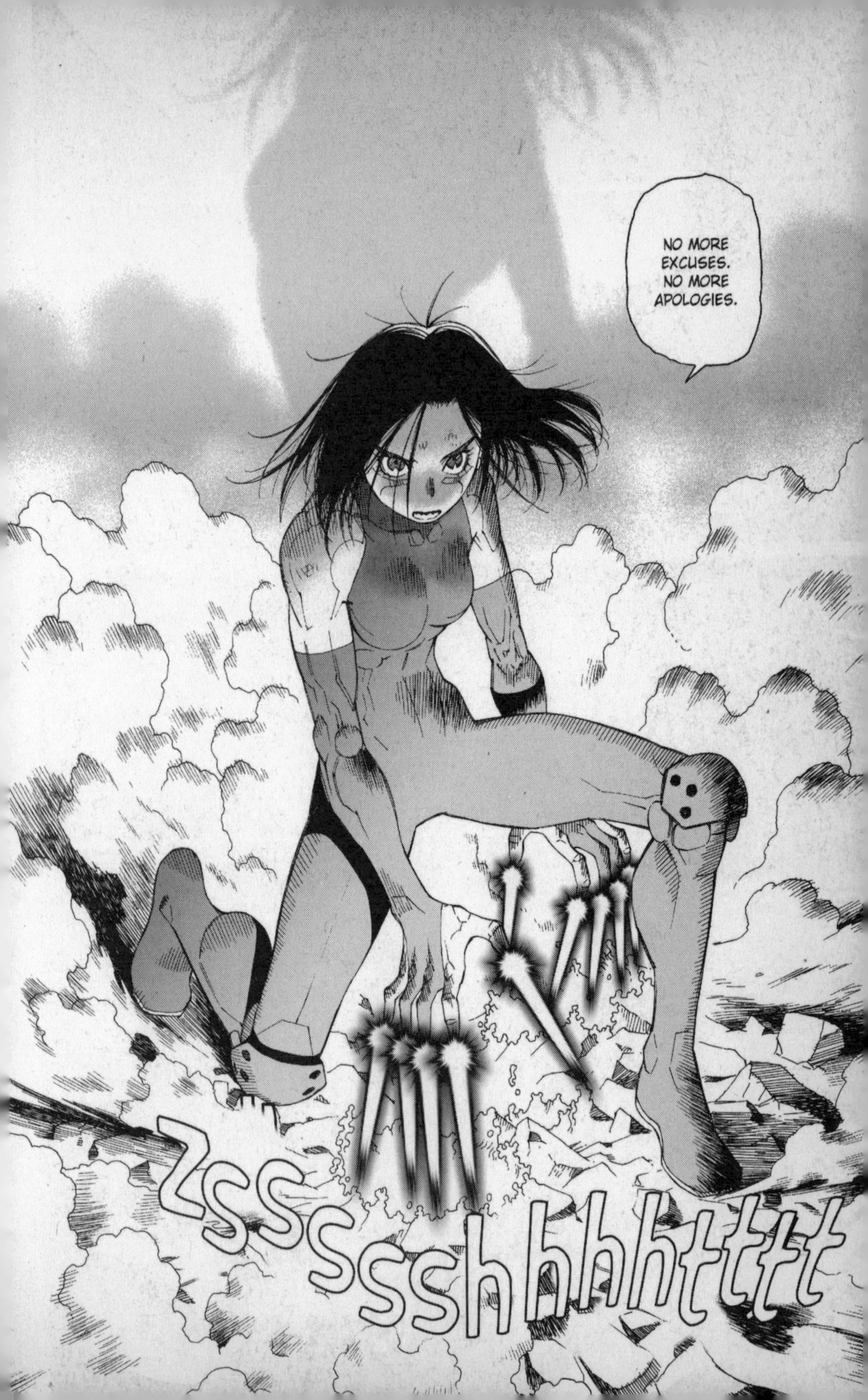
NO MORE EXCUSES. NO MORE APOLOGIES.
ZSSSSSHHHTTTT

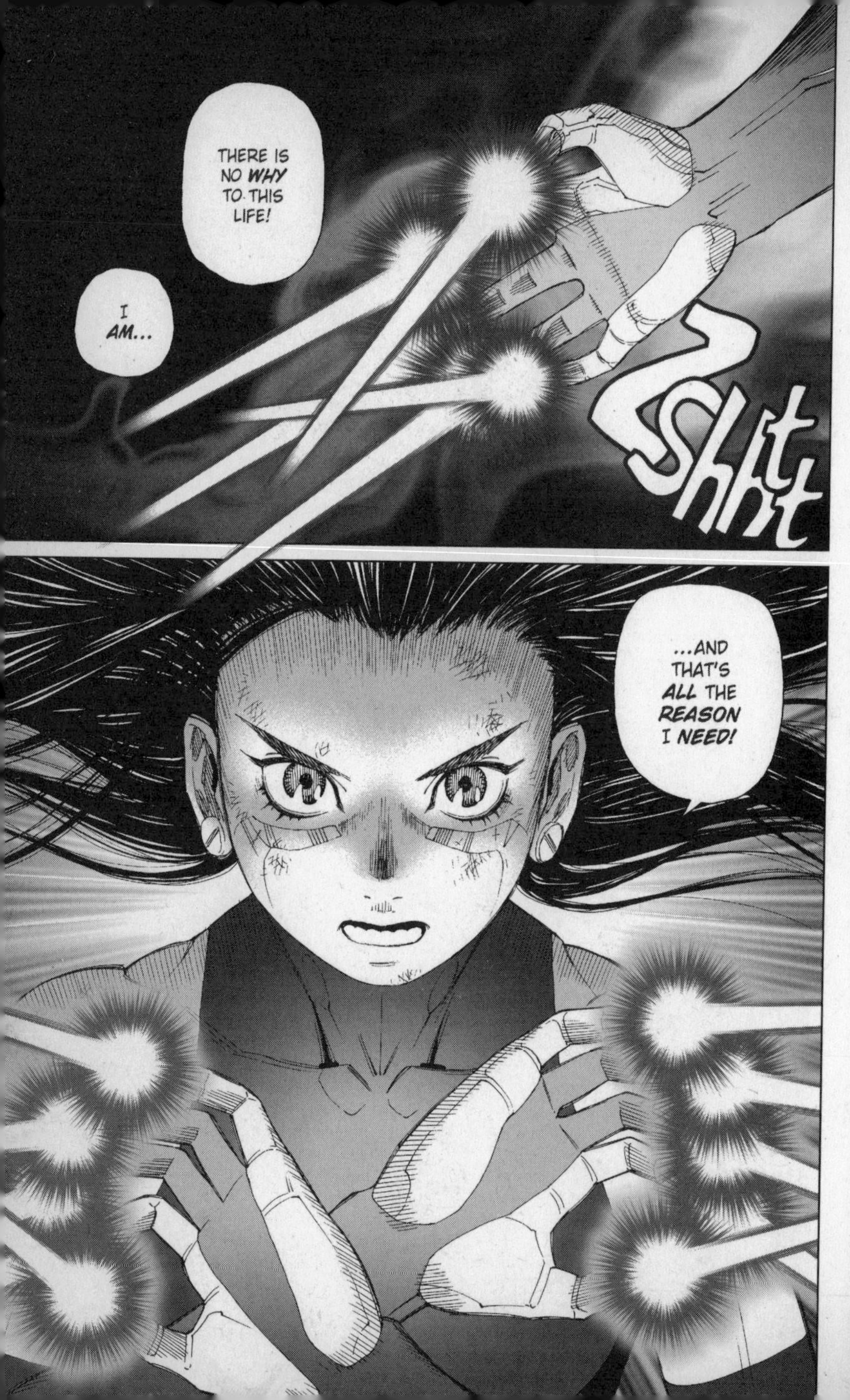
THERE IS NO WHY TO THIS LIFE!
I AM...
SHHT
...AND THAT'S ALL THE REASON I NEED!

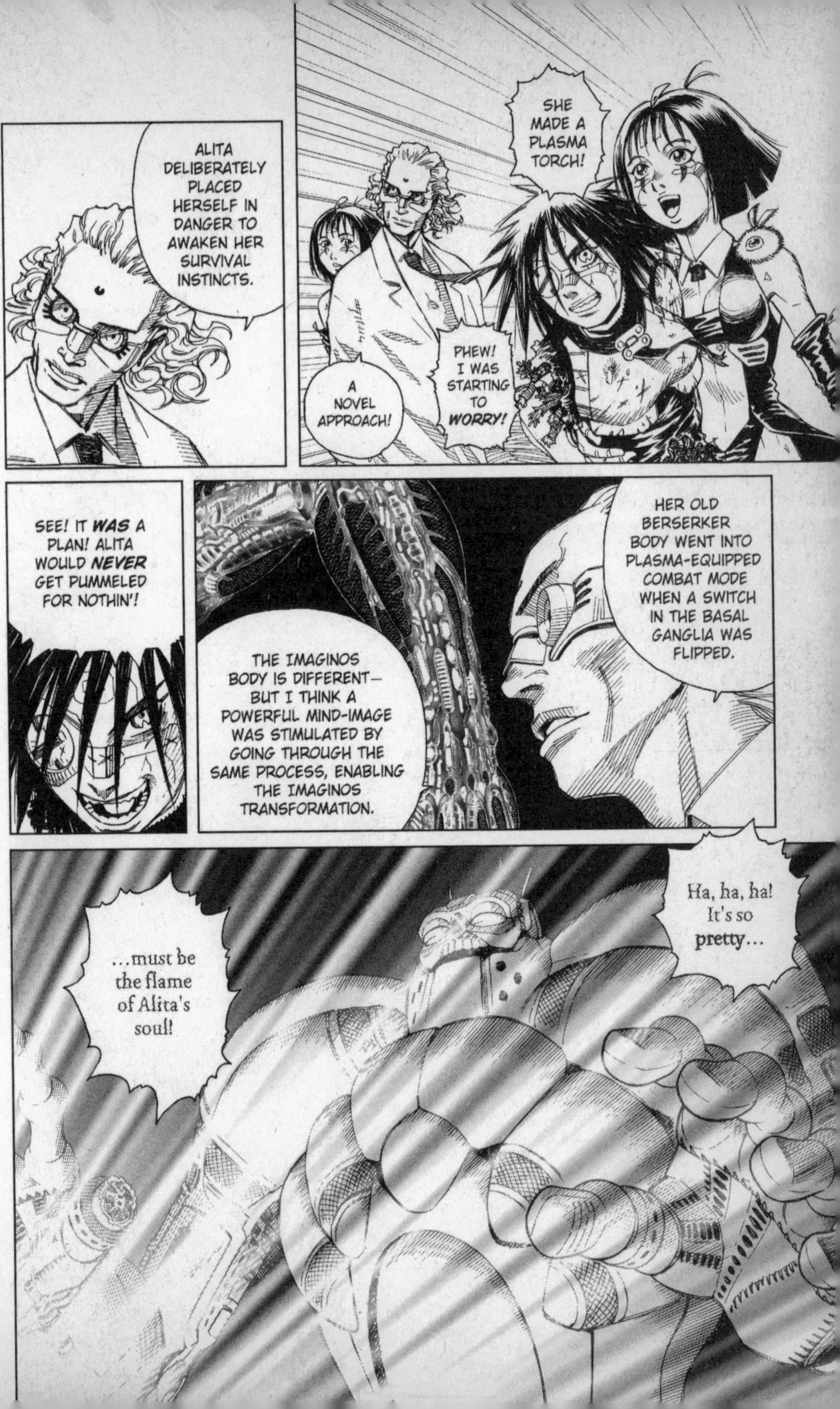
SHE MADE A PLASMA TORCH!
PHEW! I WAS STARTING TO **WORRY!**
A NOVEL APPROACH!
ALITA DELIBERATELY PLACED HERSELF IN DANGER TO AWAKEN HER SURVIVAL INSTINCTS.
HER OLD BERSERKER BODY WENT INTO PLASMA-EQUIPPED COMBAT MODE WHEN A SWITCH IN THE BASAL GANGLIA WAS FLIPPED.
THE IMAGINOS BODY IS DIFFERENT— BUT I THINK A POWERFUL MIND-IMAGE WAS STIMULATED BY GOING THROUGH THE SAME PROCESS, ENABLING THE IMAGINOS TRANSFORMATION.
SEE! IT **WAS** A PLAN! ALITA WOULD **NEVER** GET PUMMELED FOR NOTHIN'!
Ha, ha, ha! It's so **pretty**...
...must be the flame of Alita's soul!

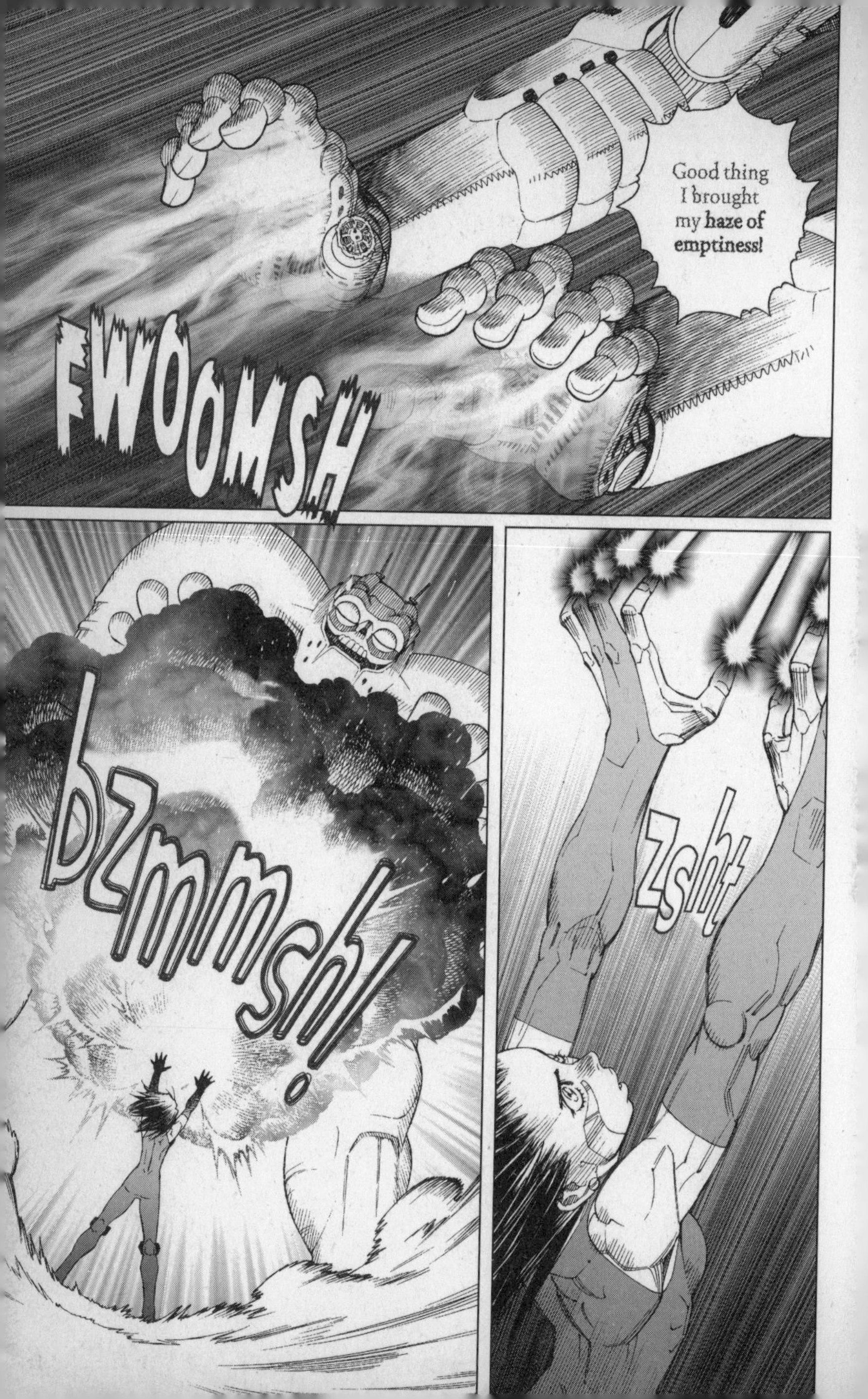
Good thing I brought my **haze of emptiness!**
FWOOMSH
zsht
bzmmsh!

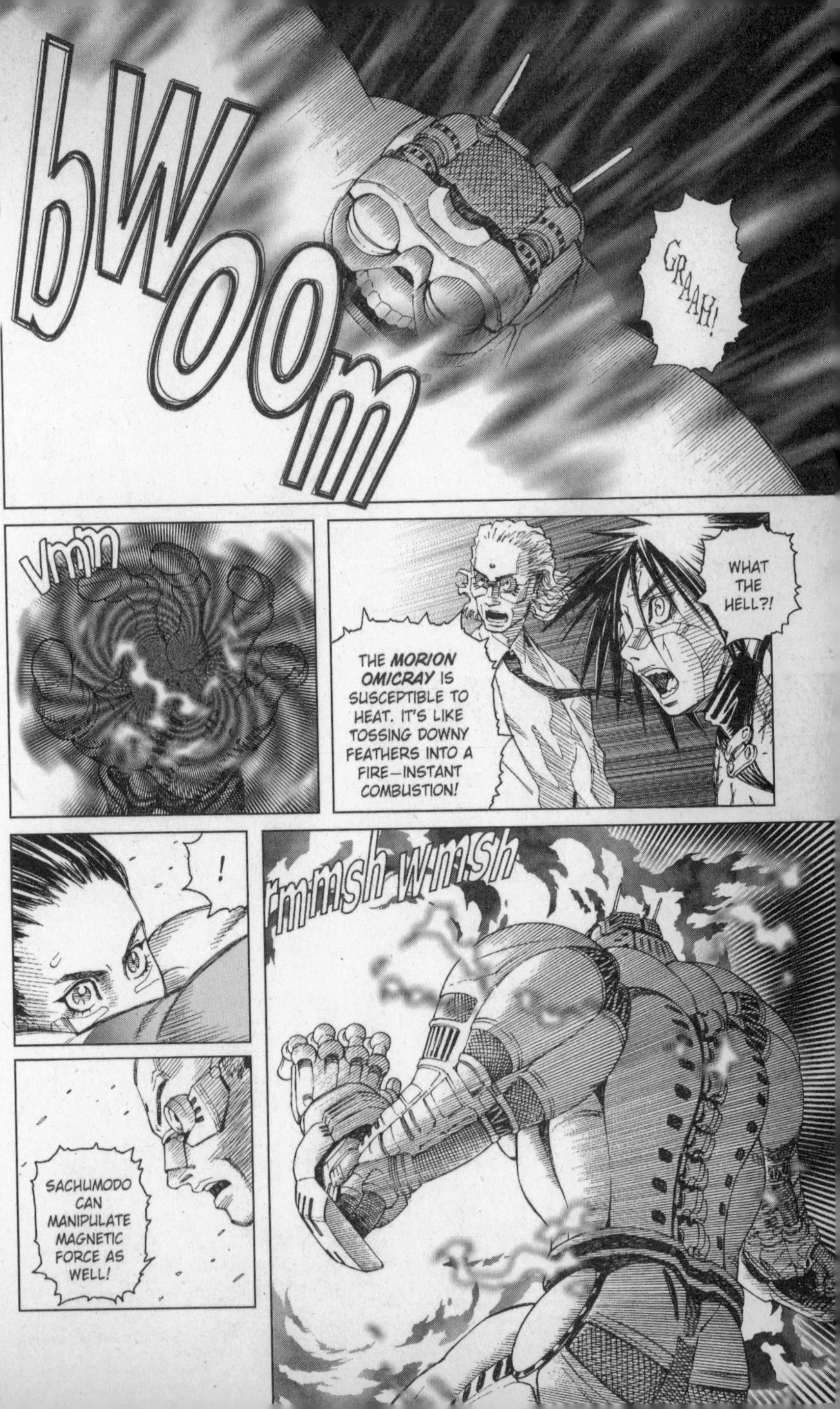
GRAAAH!
bwooom
WHAT THE HELL?!
THE ***MORION OMICRAY*** IS SUSCEPTIBLE TO HEAT. IT'S LIKE TOSSING DOWNY FEATHERS INTO A FIRE—INSTANT COMBUSTION!
vmm
rmmsh wmsh
!
SACHUMODO CAN MANIPULATE MAGNETIC FORCE AS WELL!

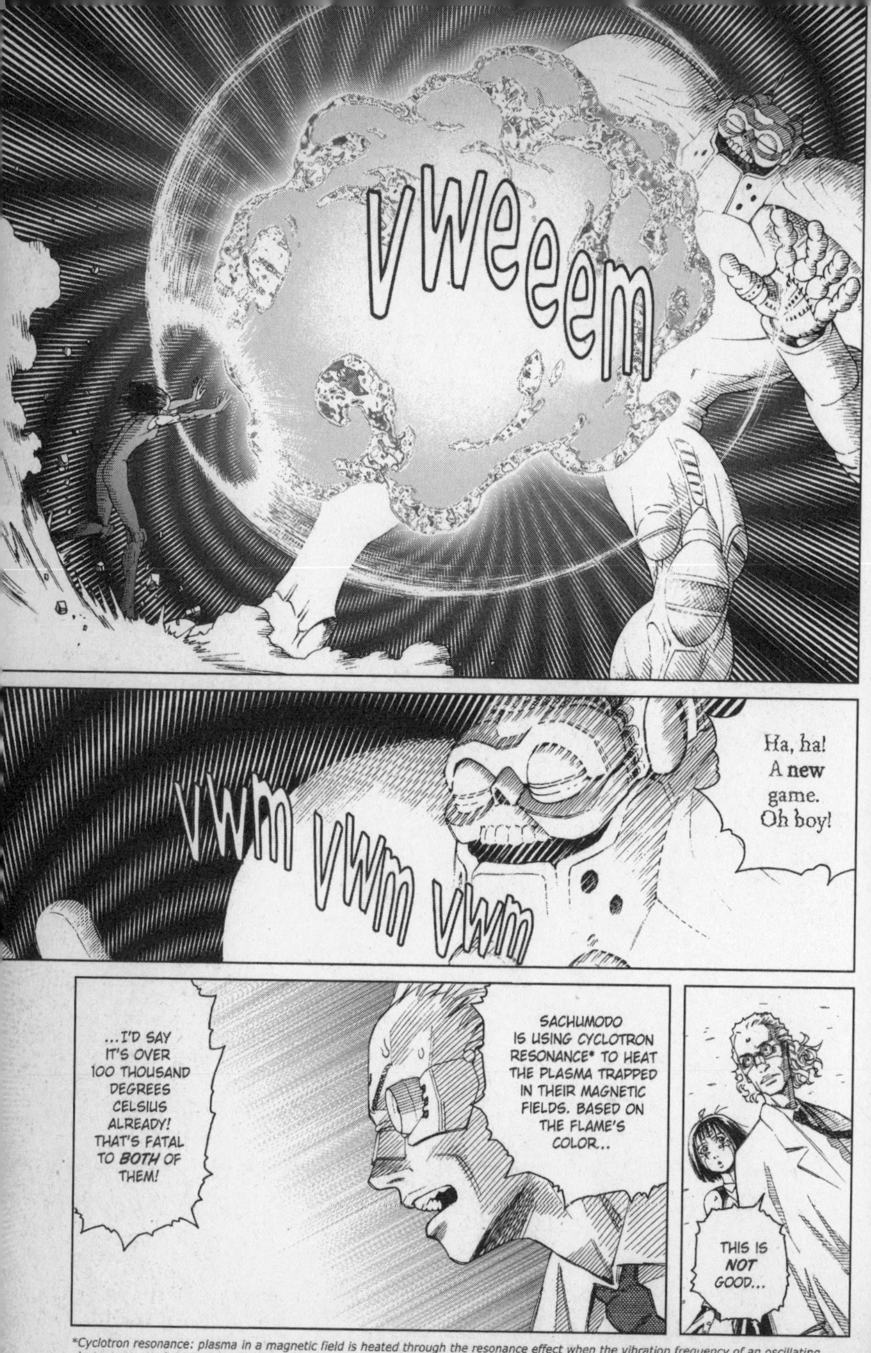
vWeeem
Ha, ha! A **new** game. Oh boy!
vwm vwm vwm
THIS IS ***NOT*** GOOD...
SACHUMODO IS USING CYCLOTRON RESONANCE* TO HEAT THE PLASMA TRAPPED IN THEIR MAGNETIC FIELDS. BASED ON THE FLAME'S COLOR..
...I'D SAY IT'S OVER 100 THOUSAND DEGREES CELSIUS ALREADY! THAT'S FATAL TO ***BOTH*** OF THEM!

*Cyclotron resonance: plasma in a magnetic field is heated through the resonance effect when the vibration frequency of an oscillating electromagnetic field matches the gyro-frequency of the charged particles in the plasma. This effect is known as Ion Cyclotron Resonance Heating, and enables the generation of superheated plasma over 100 million degrees Celsius of temperature.

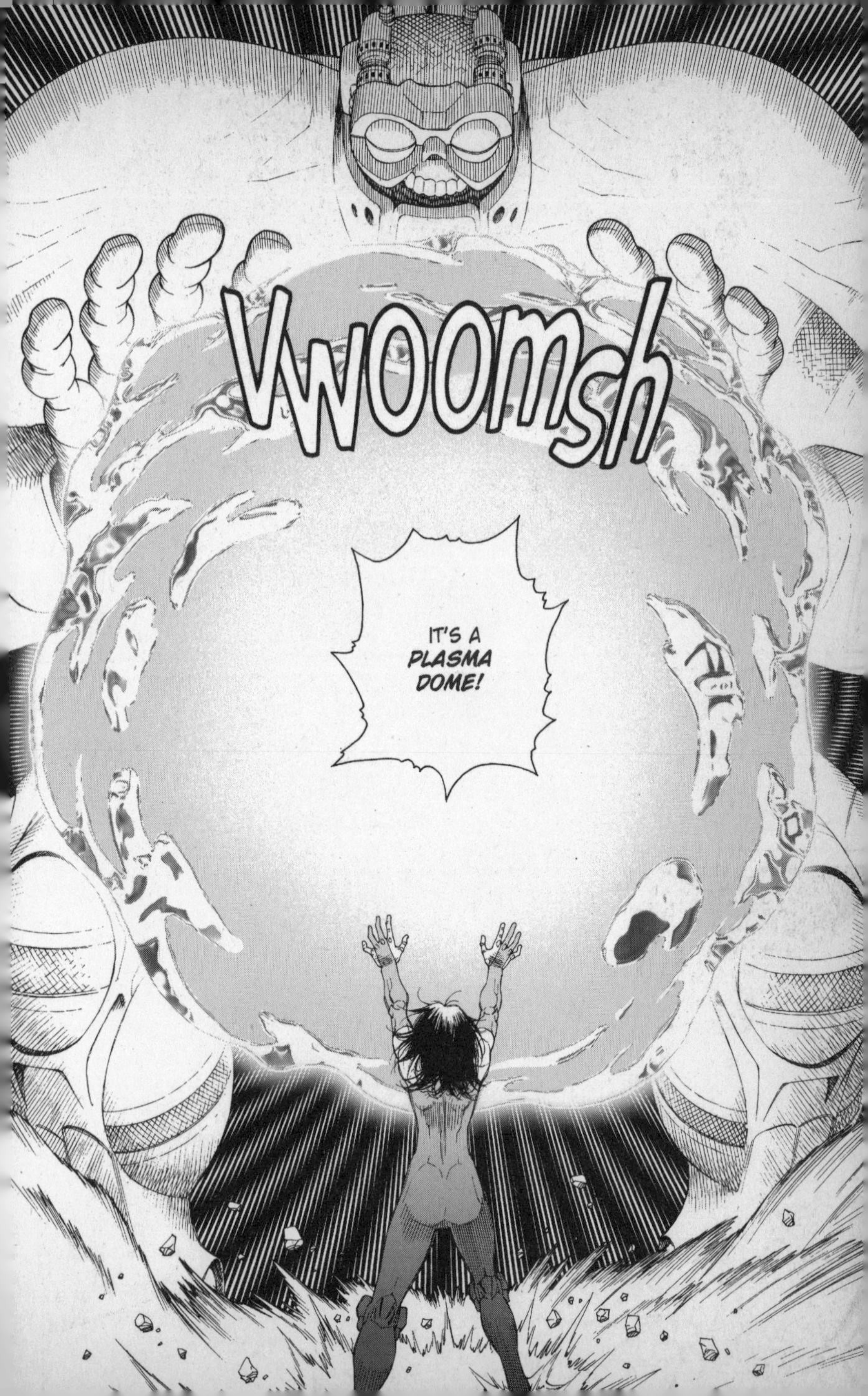
VWOOMSH
IT'S A PLASMA DOME!

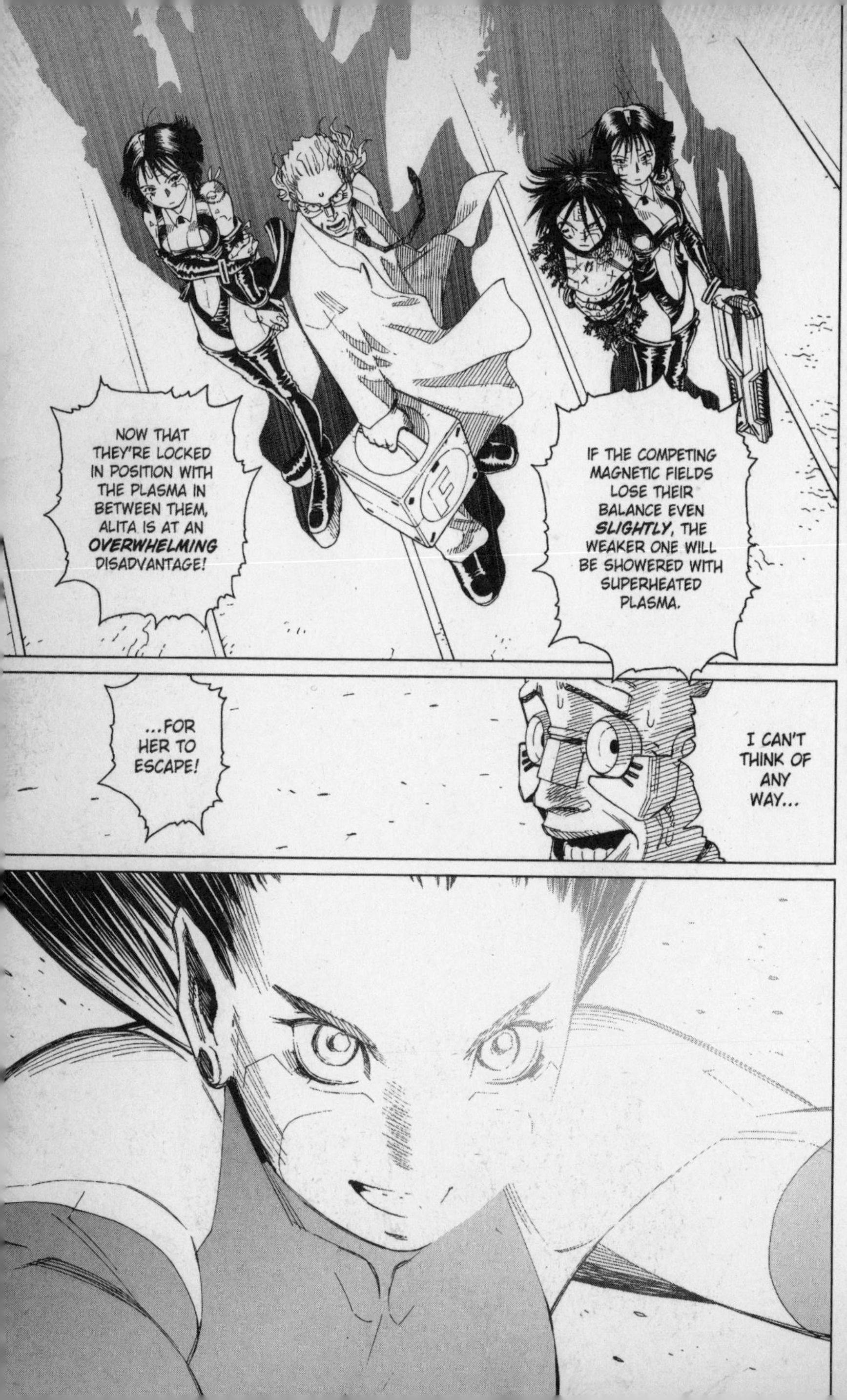
IF THE COMPETING MAGNETIC FIELDS LOSE THEIR BALANCE EVEN SLIGHTLY, THE WEAKER ONE WILL BE SHOWERED WITH SUPERHEATED PLASMA.
NOW THAT THEY'RE LOCKED IN POSITION WITH THE PLASMA IN BETWEEN THEM, ALITA IS AT AN OVERWHELMING DISADVANTAGE!
I CAN'T THINK OF ANY WAY...
...FOR HER TO ESCAPE!

PHASE 10
A Song From Long Ago

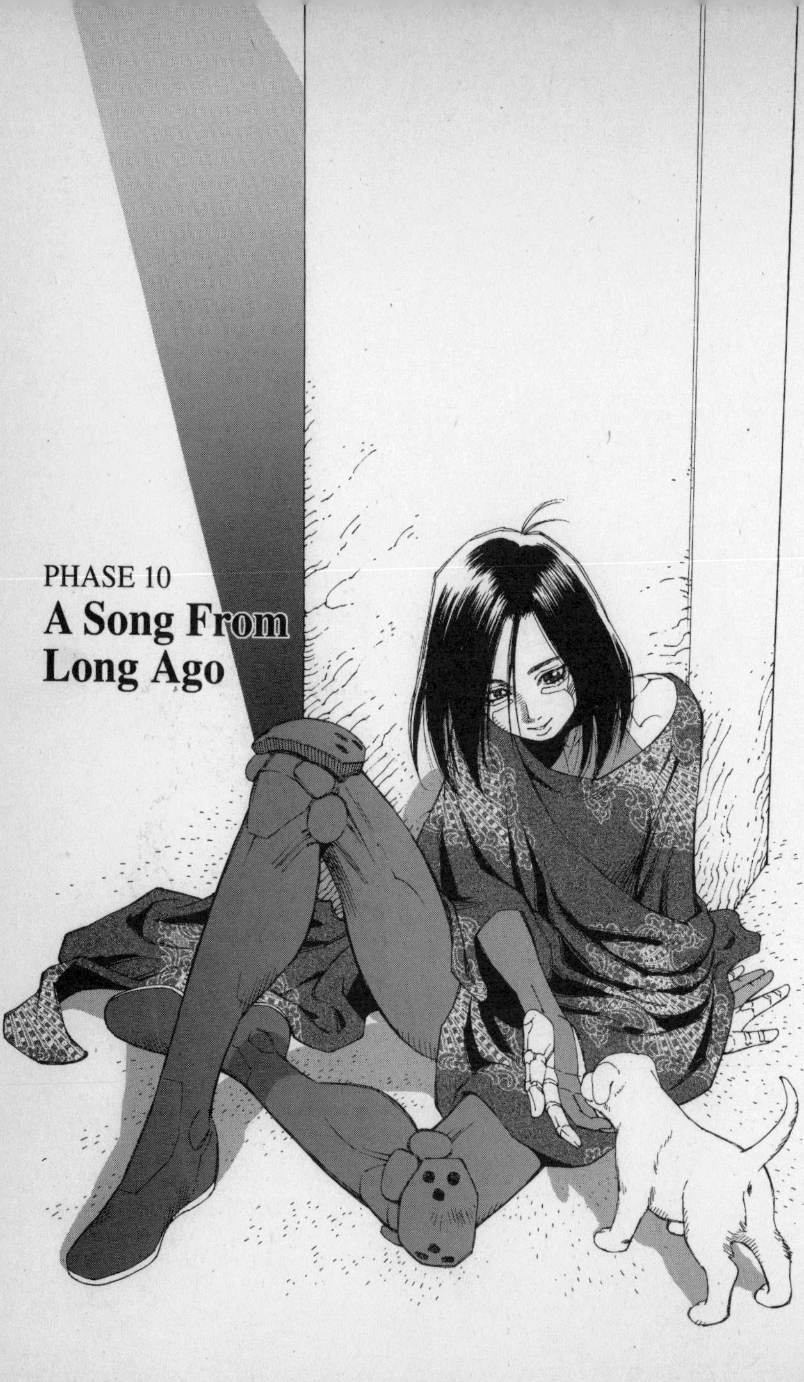

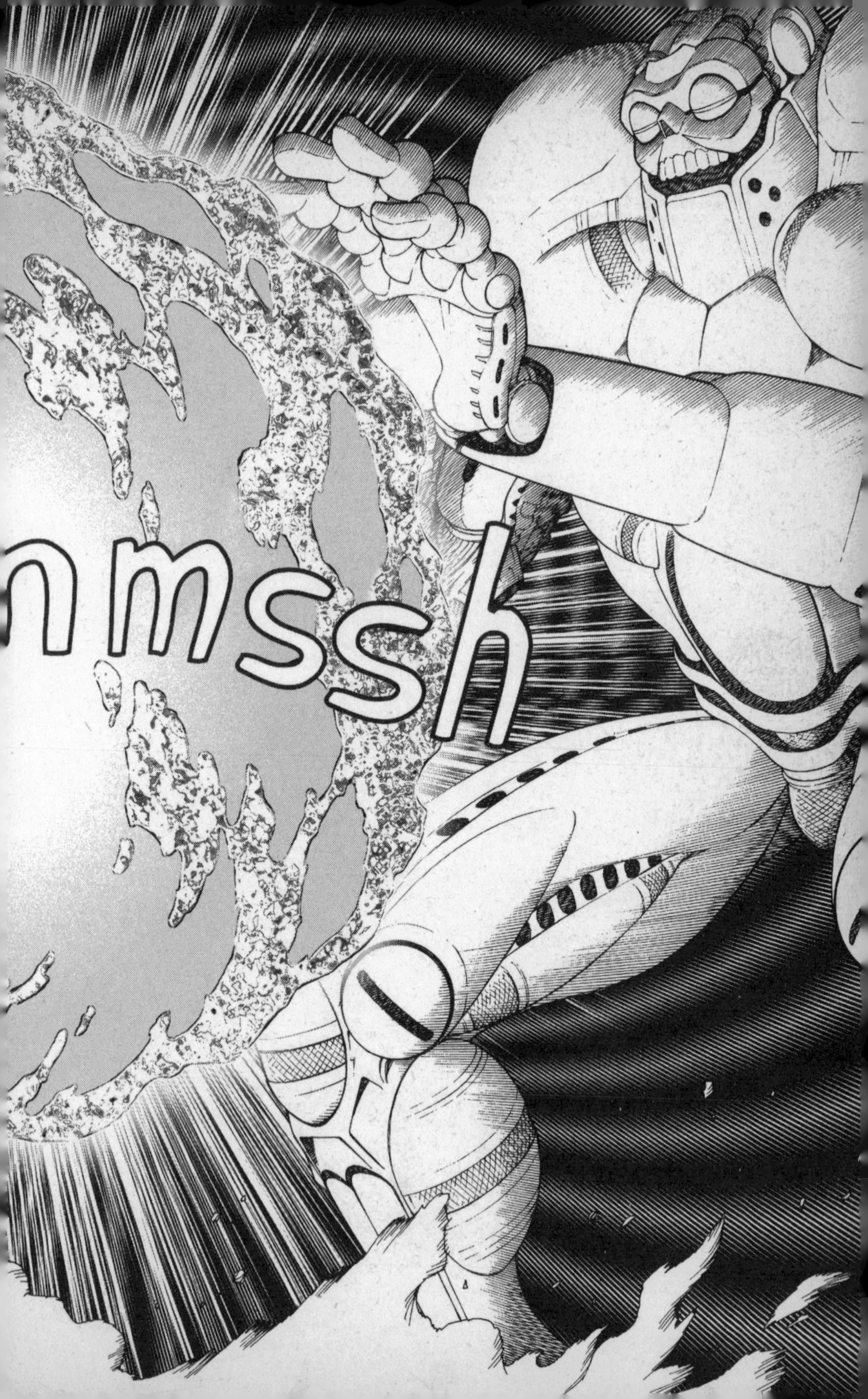
nmssh

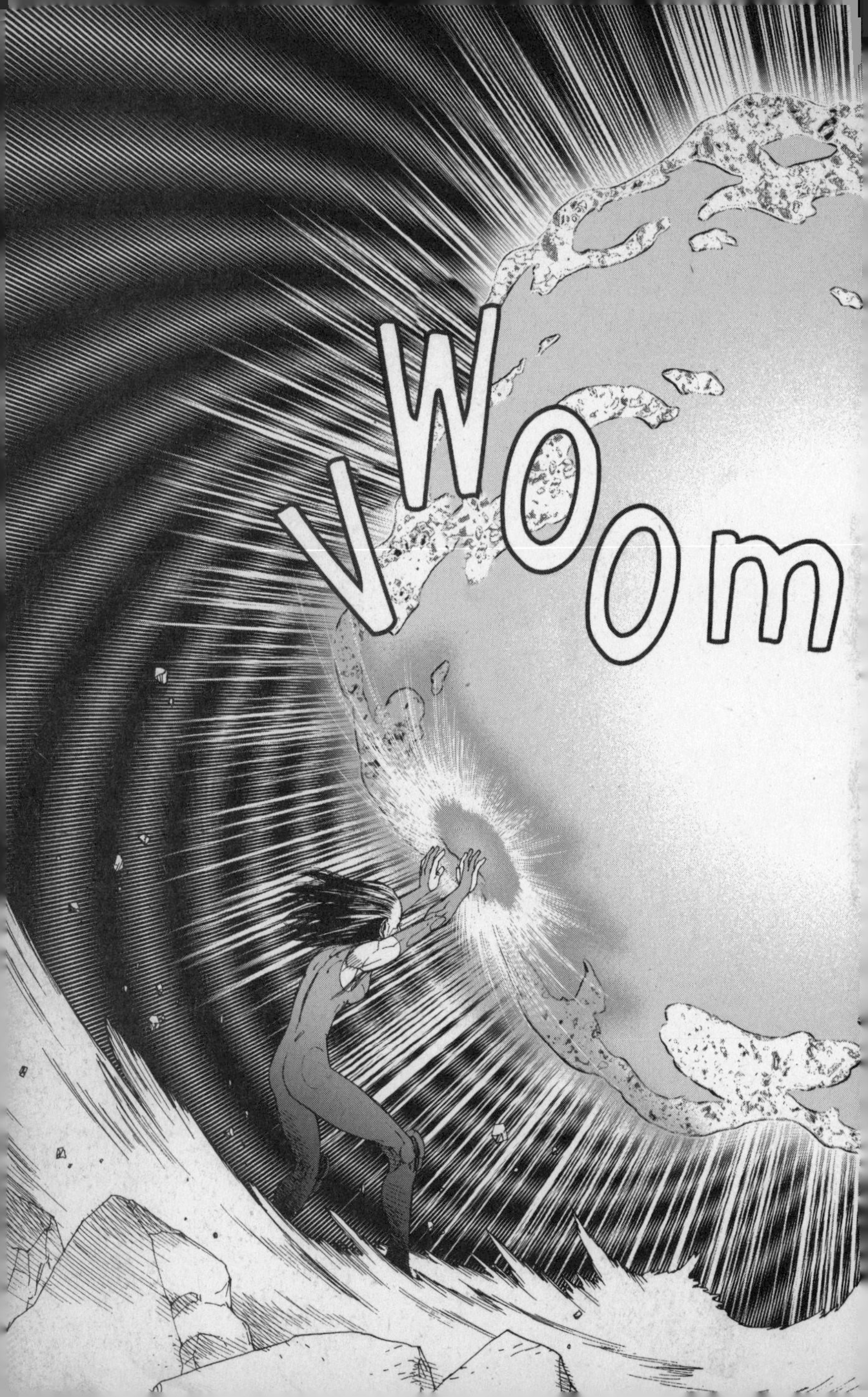
VWOOm

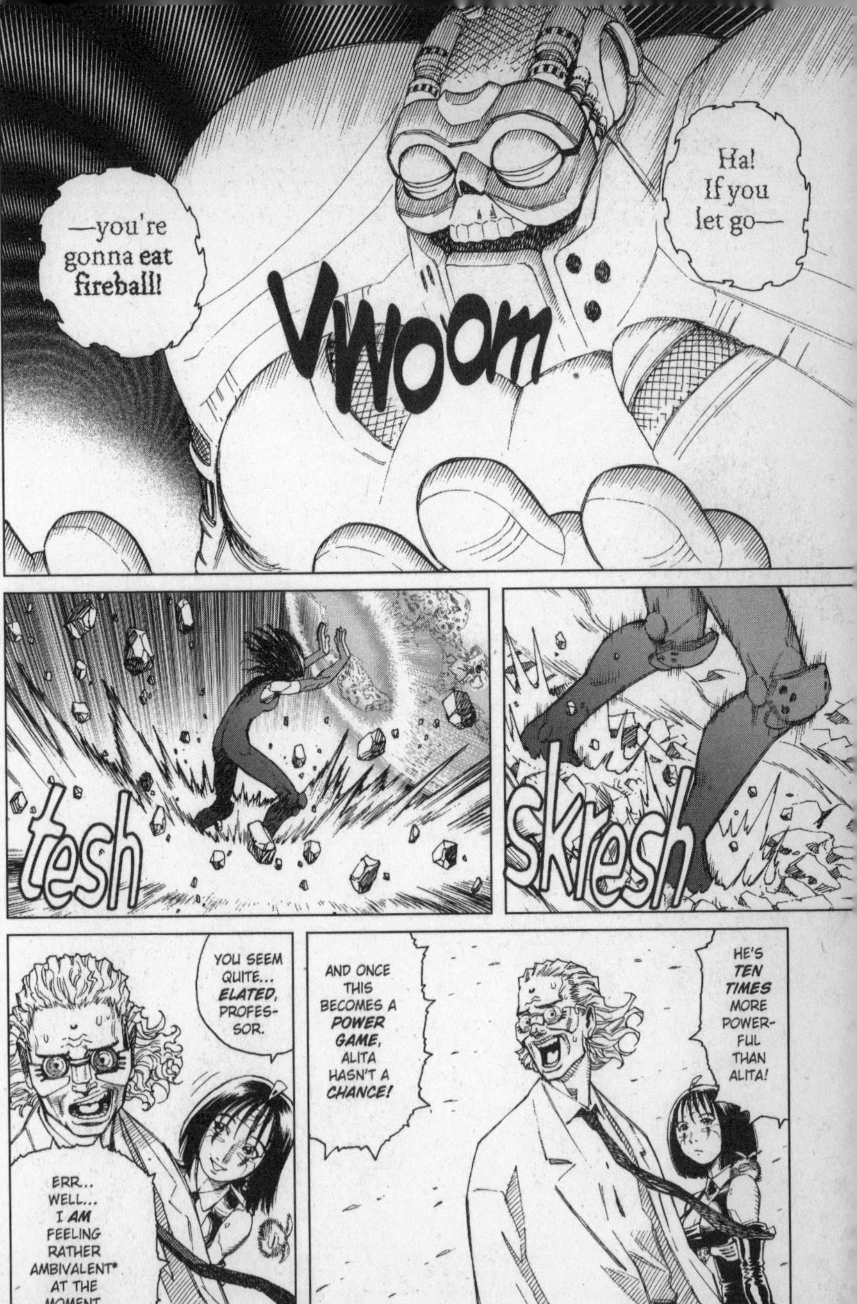
Ha! If you let go—
—you're gonna eat fireball!
Vwoom
skresh
tesh
HE'S TEN TIMES MORE POWERFUL THAN ALITA!
AND ONCE THIS BECOMES A POWER GAME, ALITA HASN'T A CHANCE!
YOU SEEM QUITE... ELATED, PROFESSOR.
ERR... WELL... I AM FEELING RATHER AMBIVALENT* AT THE MOMENT.

*Ambivalence: simultaneous and contradictory feelings toward the same object that can lead to psychological "splitting," in which a subject separates irreconcilable parts of his/her personality.

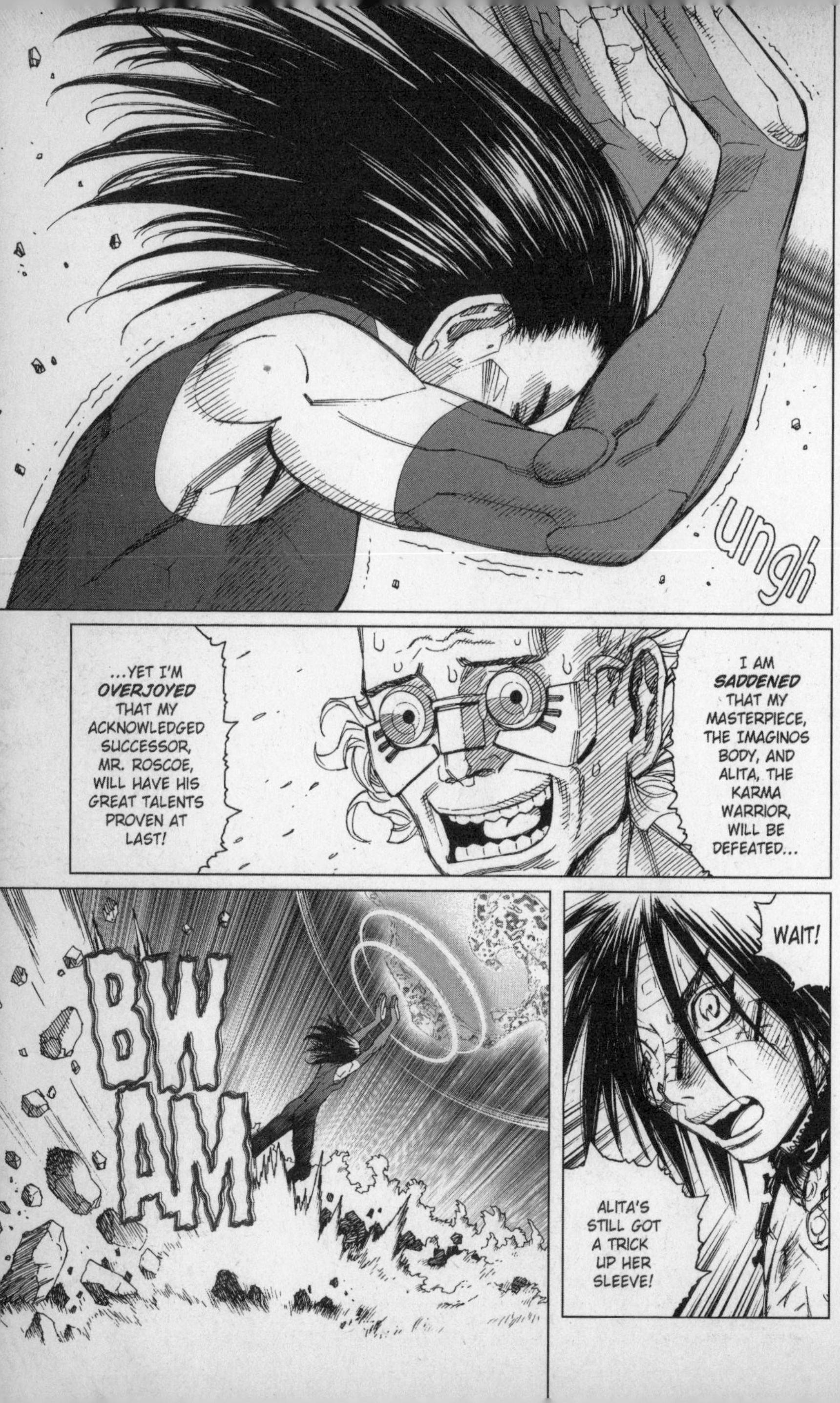
ungh
I AM ***SADDENED*** THAT MY MASTERPIECE, THE IMAGINOS BODY, AND ALITA, THE KARMA WARRIOR, WILL BE DEFEATED...
...YET I'M ***OVERJOYED*** THAT MY ACKNOWLEDGED SUCCESSOR, MR. ROSCOE, WILL HAVE HIS GREAT TALENTS PROVEN AT LAST!
WAIT!
ALITA'S STILL GOT A TRICK UP HER SLEEVE!
BWAM

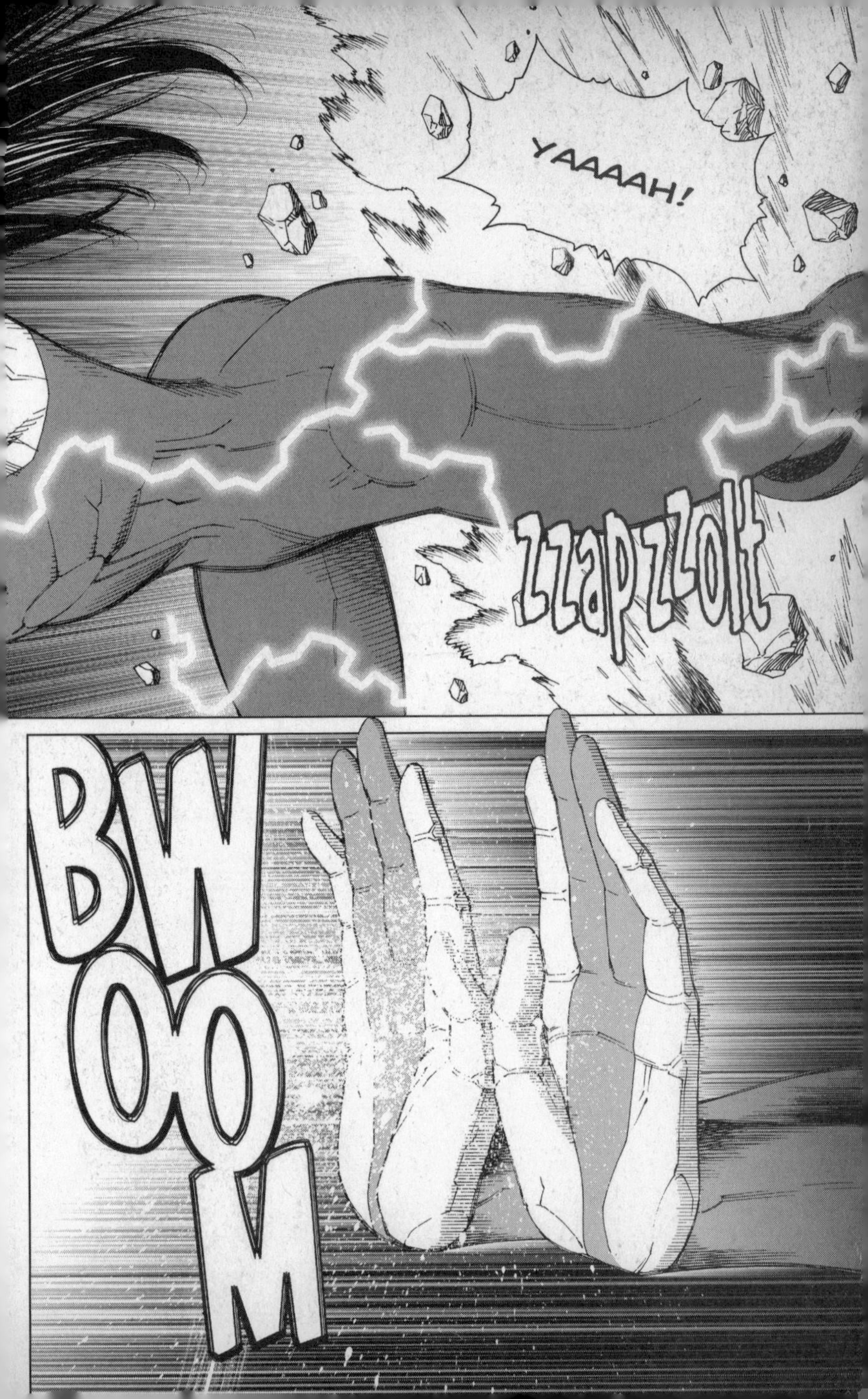
YAAAAH!
ZZAPZZOLT
BWOOM

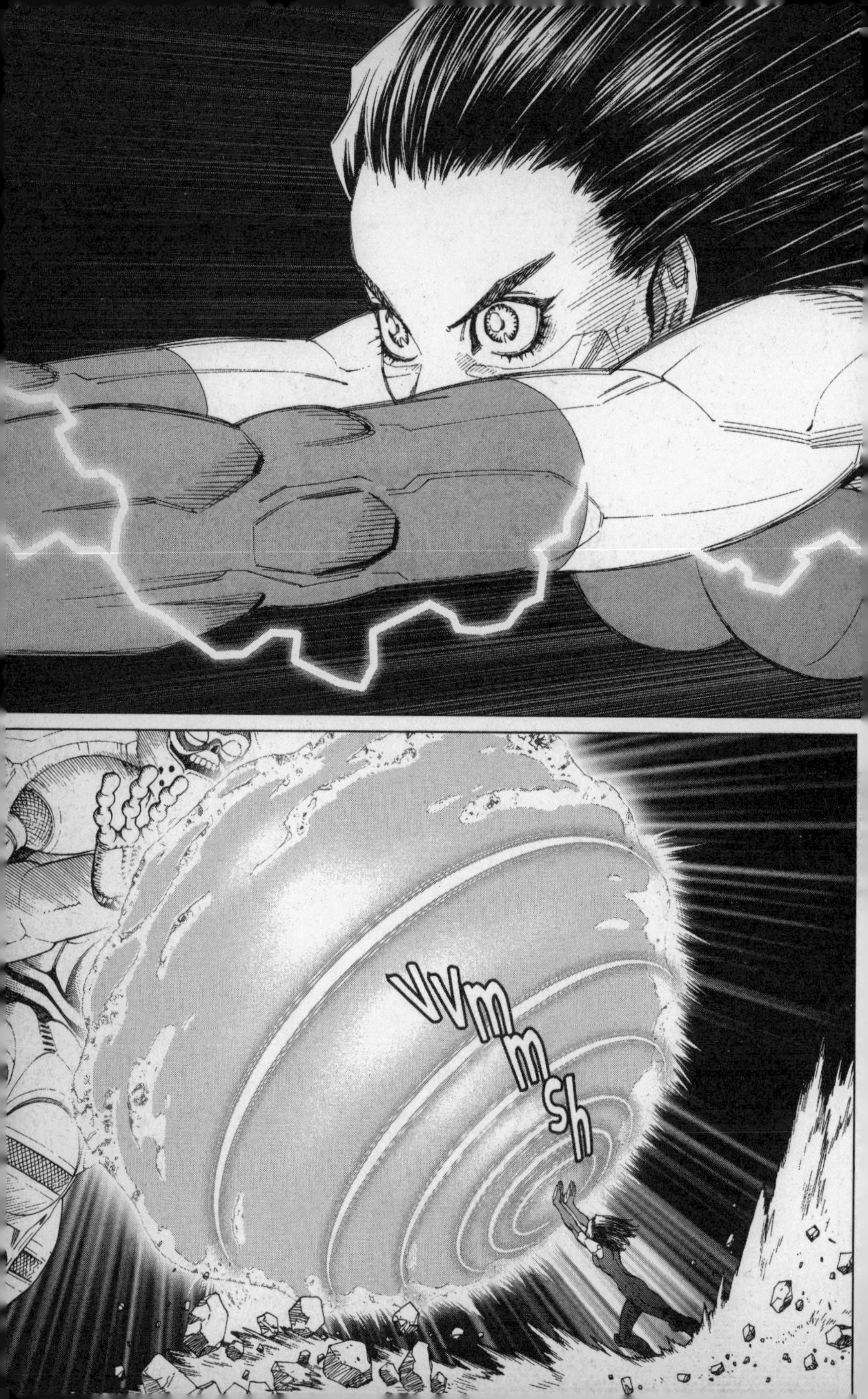
VVMMSH

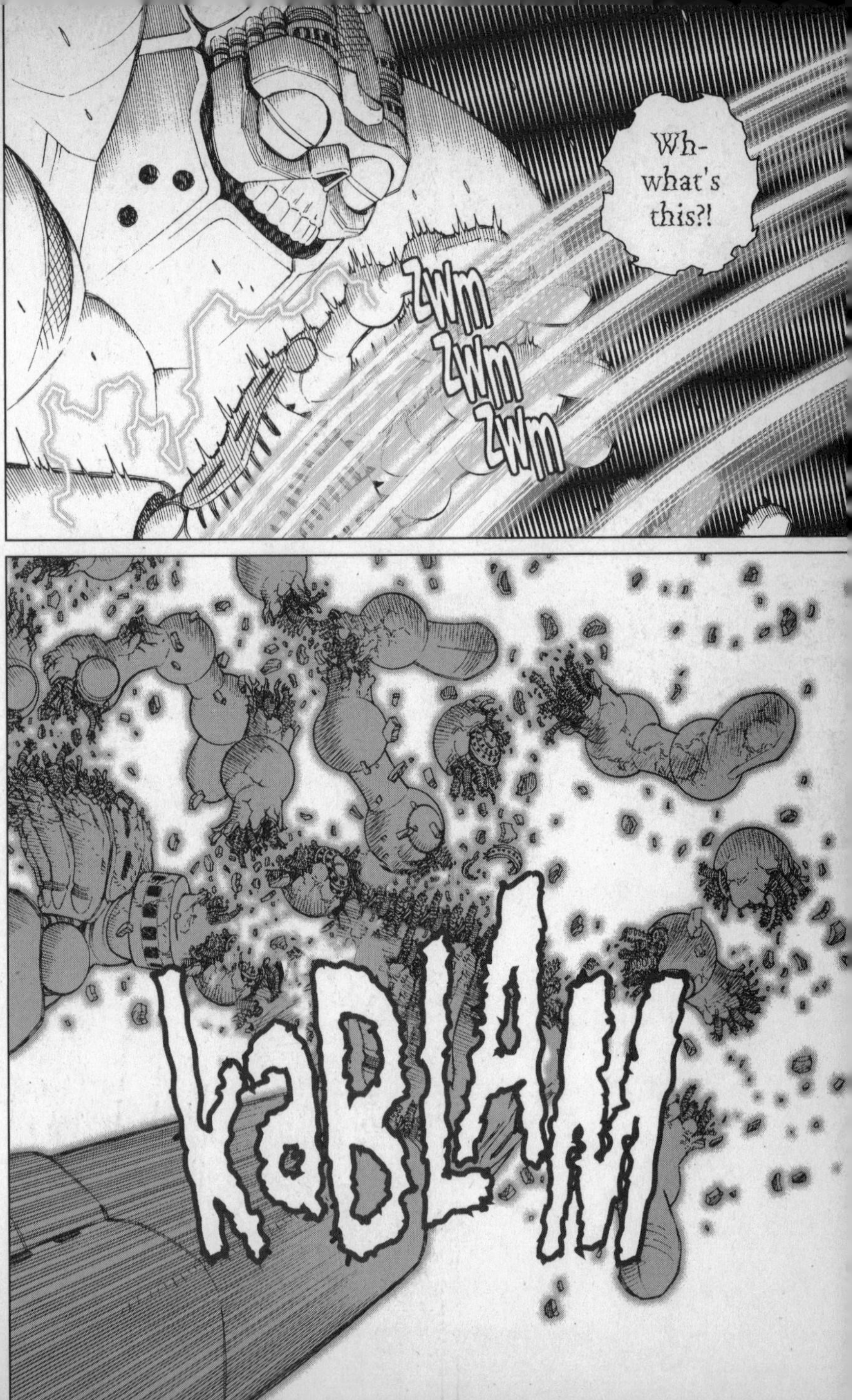
Wh-
what's
this?!
ZWm
ZWm
ZWm
KaBLAM

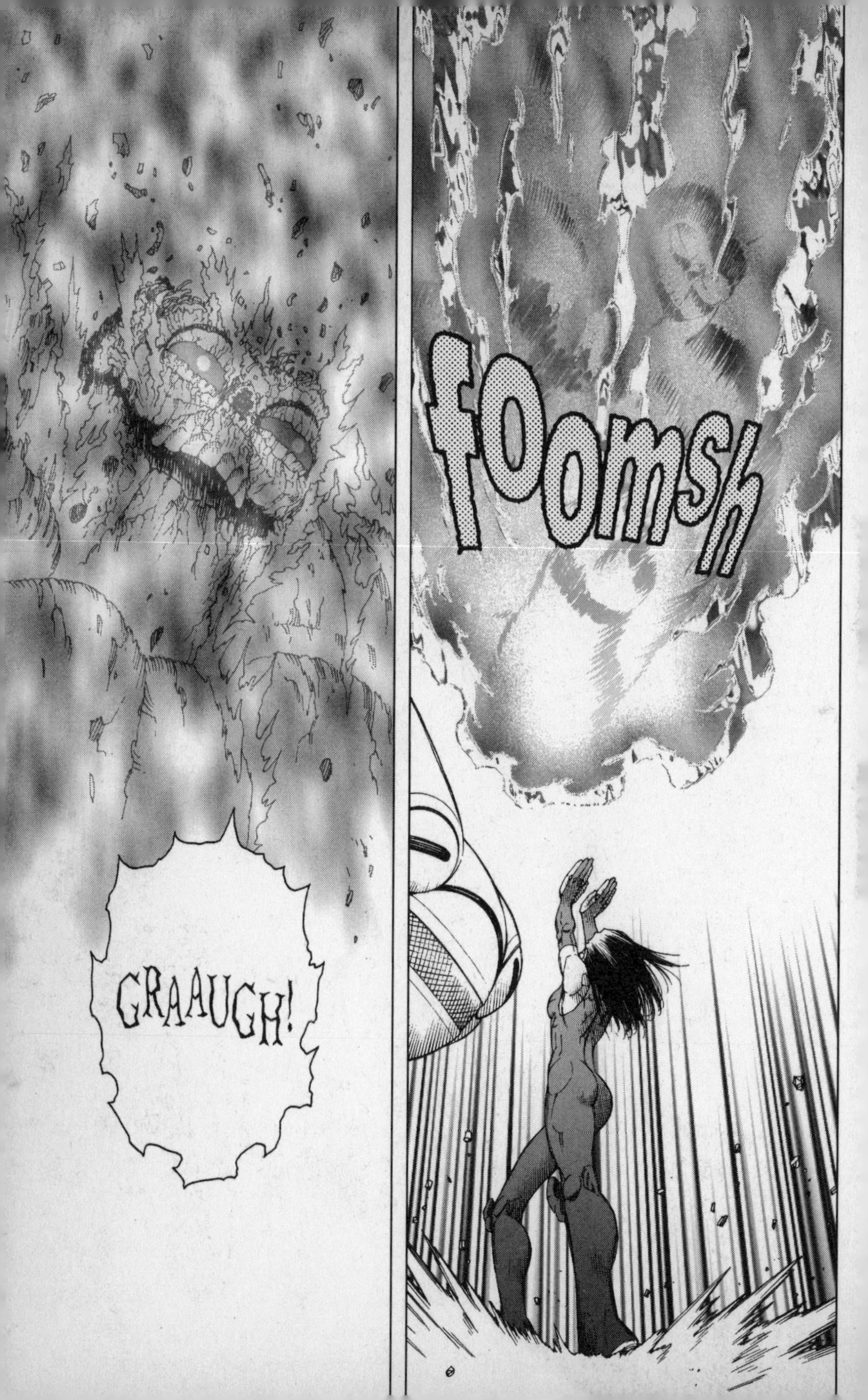
fOOMSh
GRAAUGH!

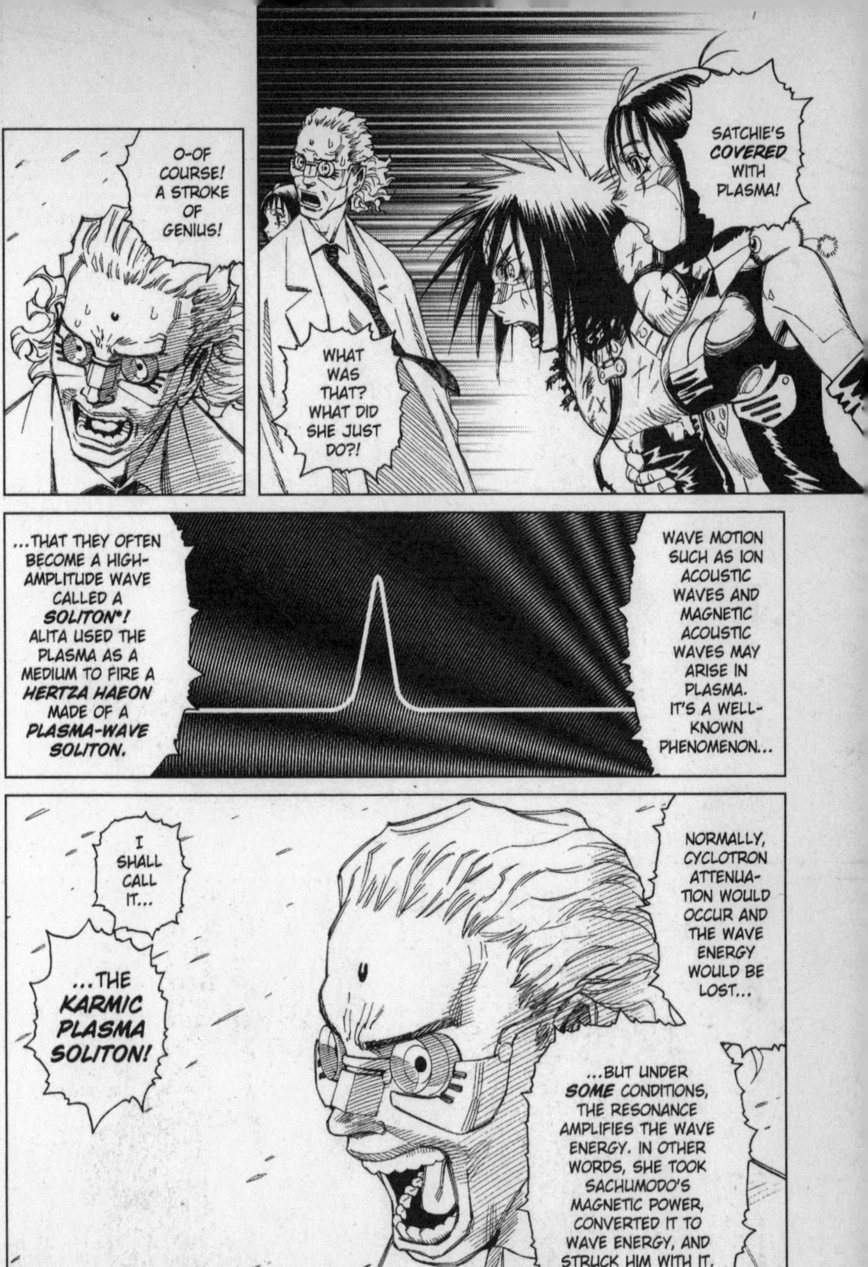
SATCHIE'S COVERED WITH PLASMA!
WHAT WAS THAT? WHAT DID SHE JUST DO?!
O-OF COURSE! A STROKE OF GENIUS!
WAVE MOTION SUCH AS ION ACOUSTIC WAVES AND MAGNETIC ACOUSTIC WAVES MAY ARISE IN PLASMA. IT'S A WELL-KNOWN PHENOMENON...
...THAT THEY OFTEN BECOME A HIGH-AMPLITUDE WAVE CALLED A SOLITON*! ALITA USED THE PLASMA AS A MEDIUM TO FIRE A HERTZA HAEON MADE OF A PLASMA-WAVE SOLITON.
NORMALLY, CYCLOTRON ATTENUATION WOULD OCCUR AND THE WAVE ENERGY WOULD BE LOST...
...BUT UNDER SOME CONDITIONS, THE RESONANCE AMPLIFIES THE WAVE ENERGY. IN OTHER WORDS, SHE TOOK SACHUMODO'S MAGNETIC POWER, CONVERTED IT TO WAVE ENERGY, AND STRUCK HIM WITH IT.
I SHALL CALL IT...
...THE KARMIC PLASMA SOLITON!

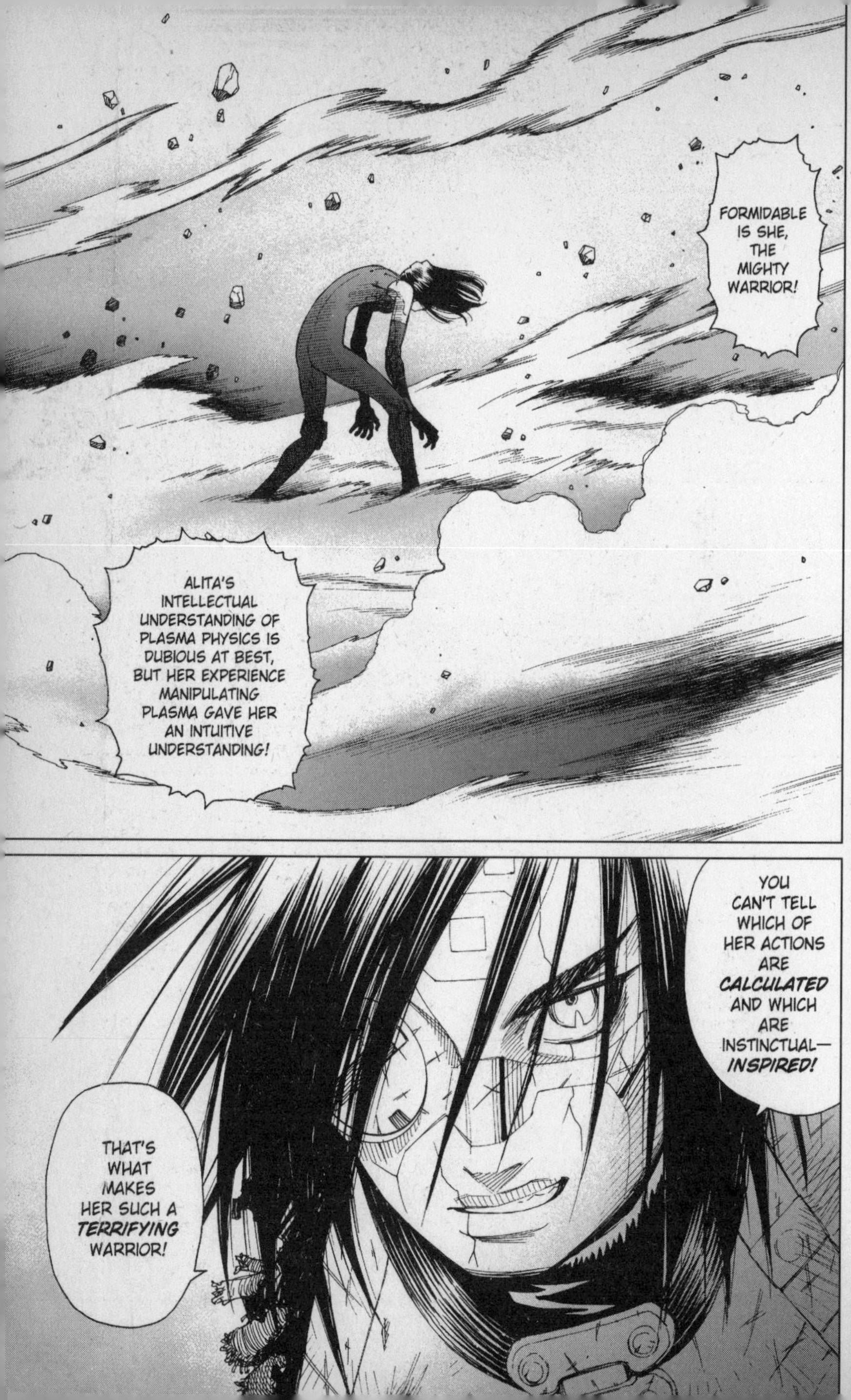
FORMIDABLE IS SHE, THE MIGHTY WARRIOR!
ALITA'S INTELLECTUAL UNDERSTANDING OF PLASMA PHYSICS IS DUBIOUS AT BEST, BUT HER EXPERIENCE MANIPULATING PLASMA GAVE HER AN INTUITIVE UNDERSTANDING!
YOU CAN'T TELL WHICH OF HER ACTIONS ARE ***CALCULATED*** AND WHICH ARE INSTINCTUAL— ***INSPIRED!***
THAT'S WHAT MAKES HER SUCH A ***TERRIFYING*** WARRIOR!

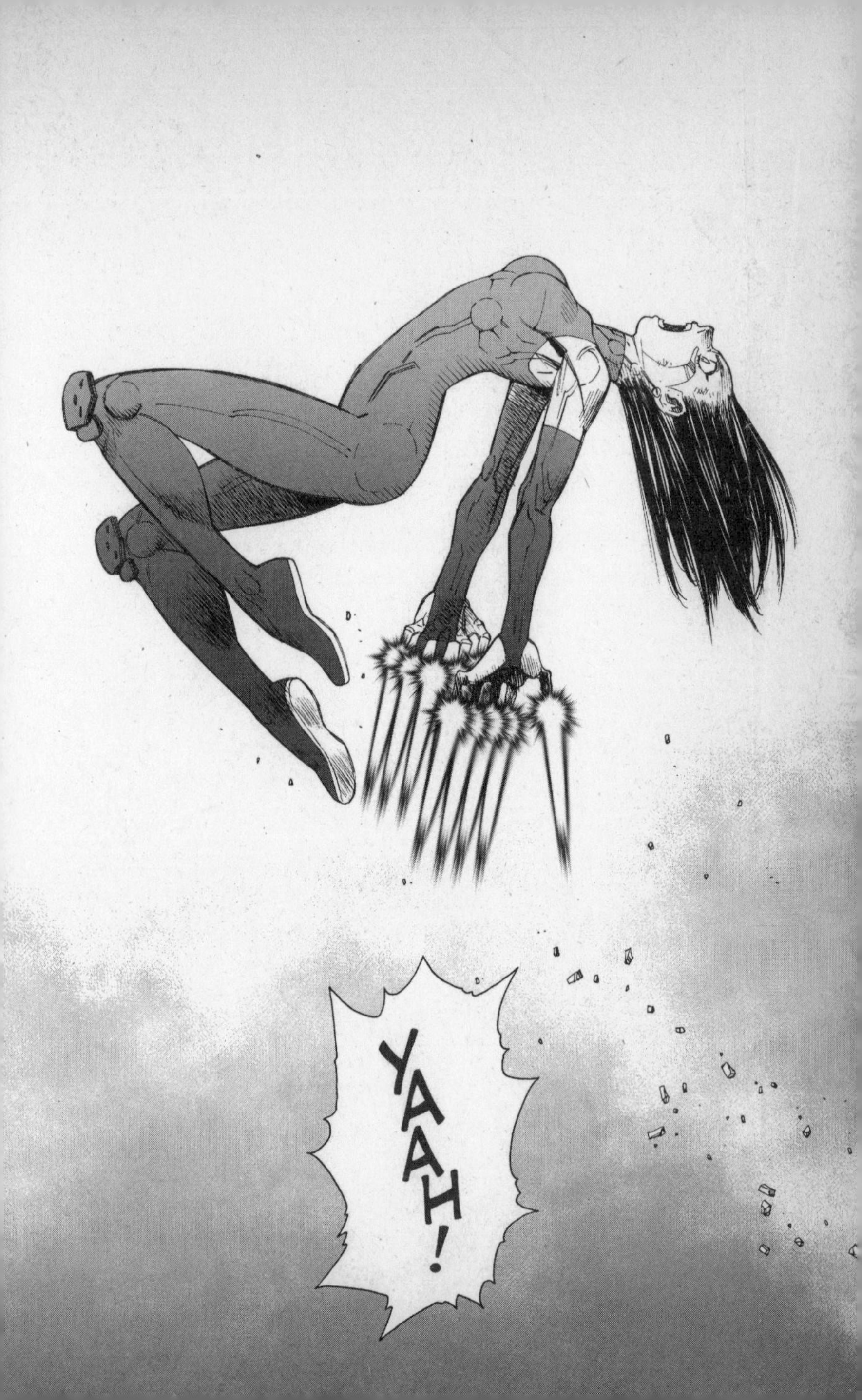
YAAH!

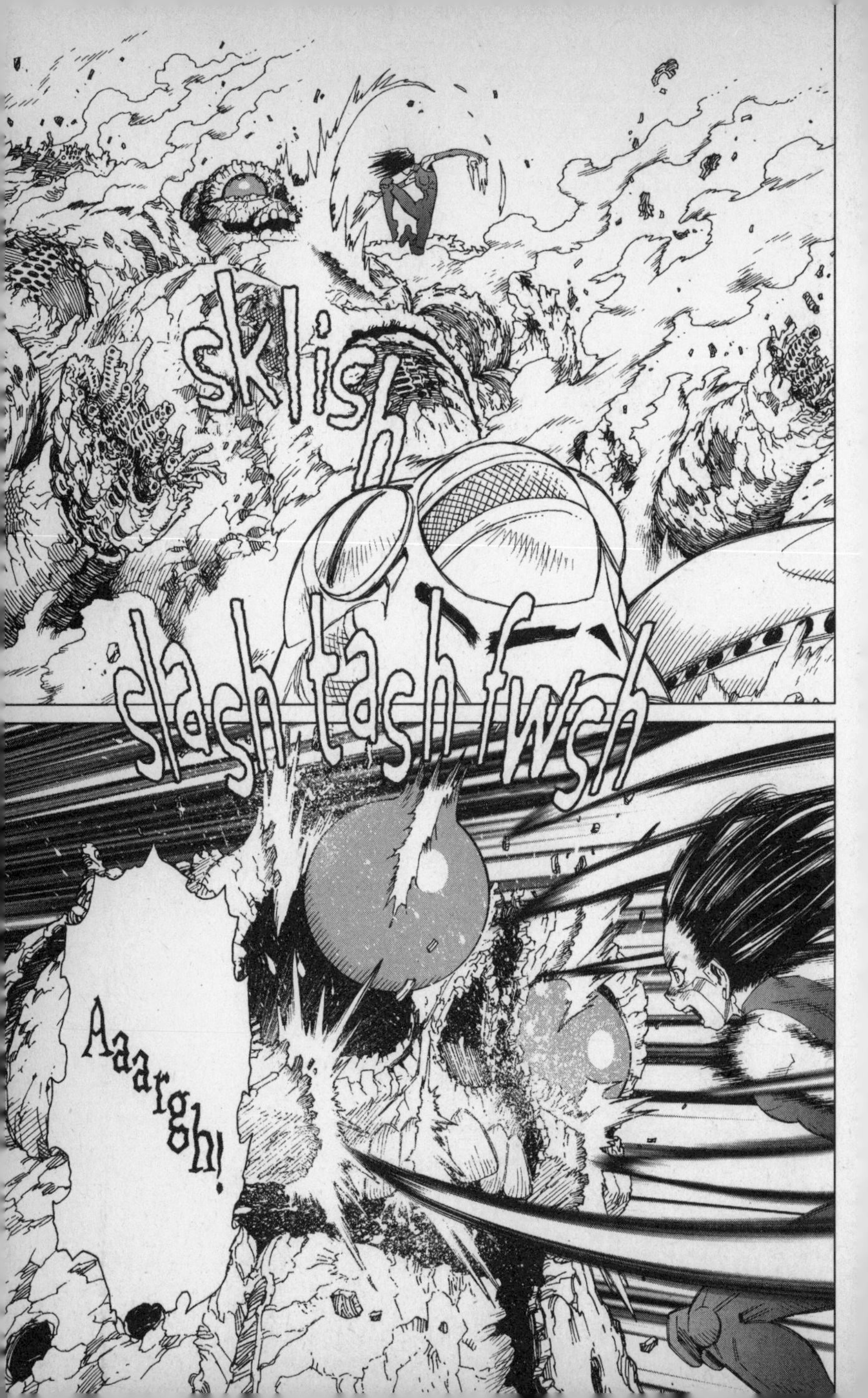
sklish
slash tash fwsh
Aaargh!

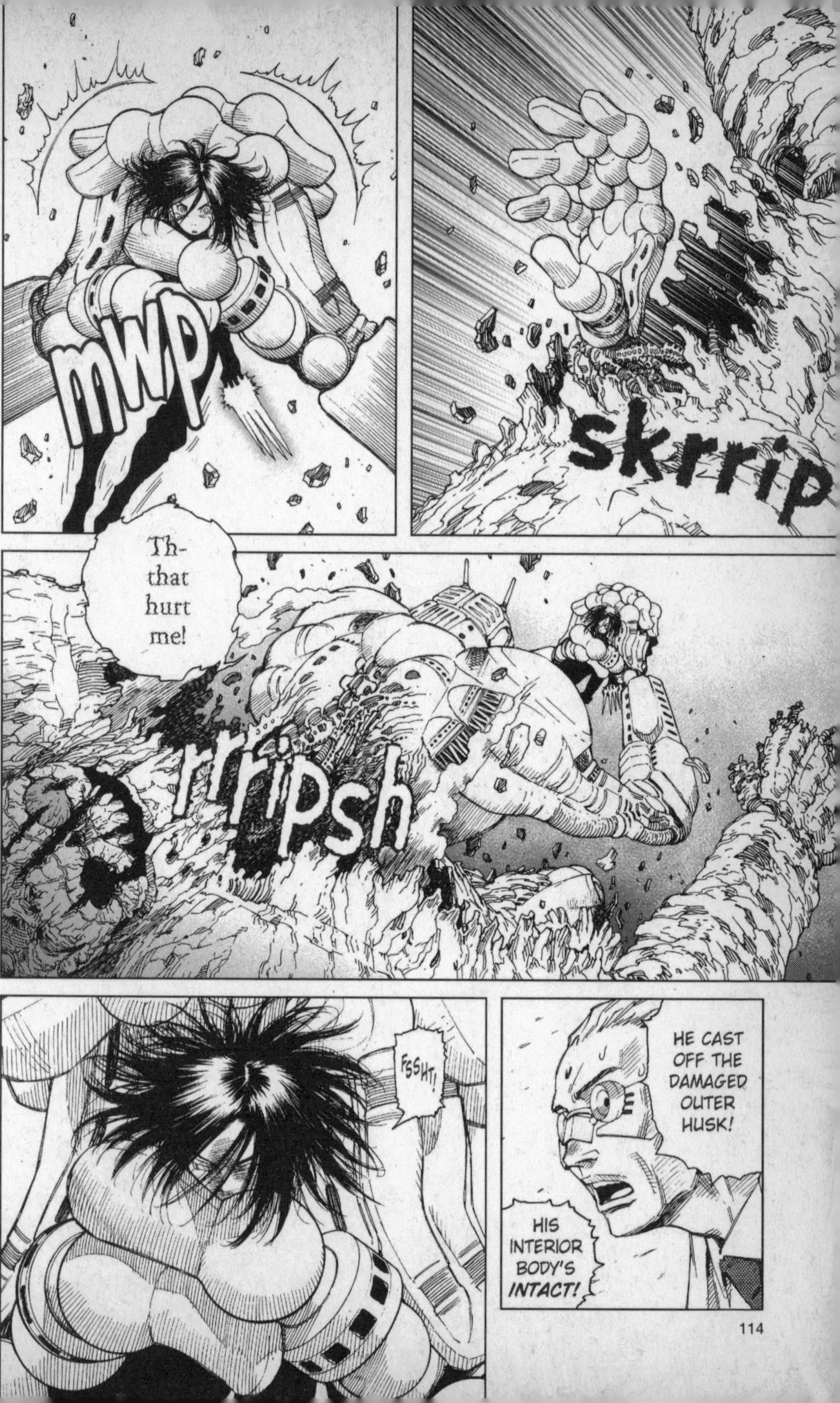
mwp
skrrip
Th-that hurt me!
rrripsh
FSSHT!
HE CAST OFF THE DAMAGED OUTER HUSK!
HIS INTERIOR BODY'S INTACT!

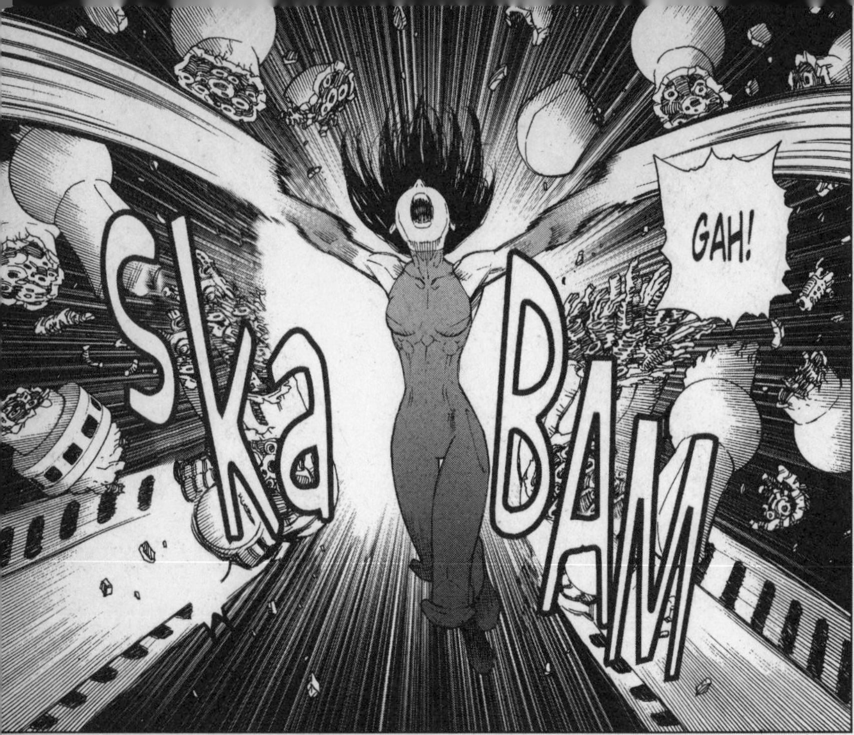
GAH!
SKABAM
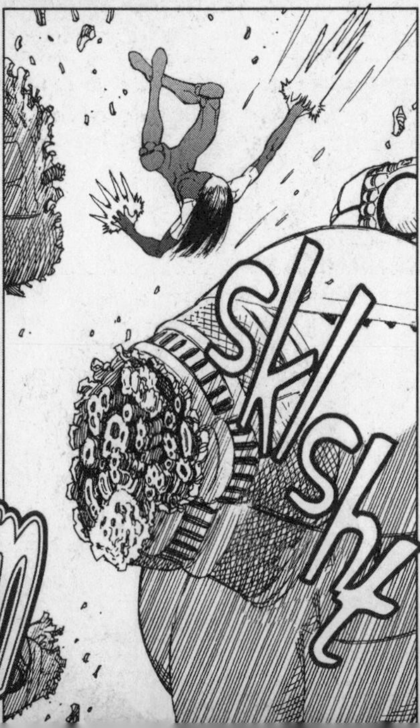
SKLSHT
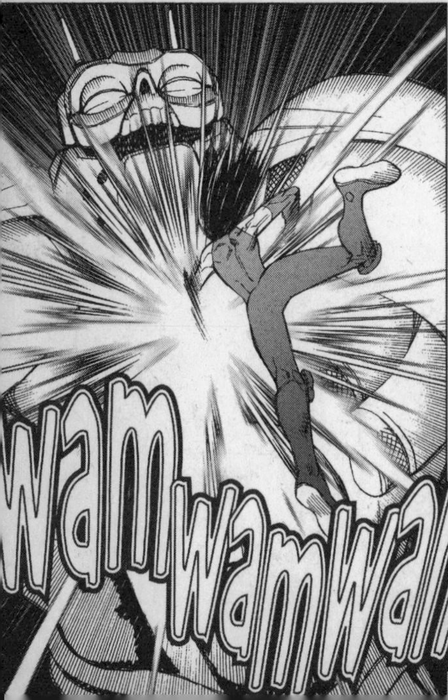
WAMWAMWAM

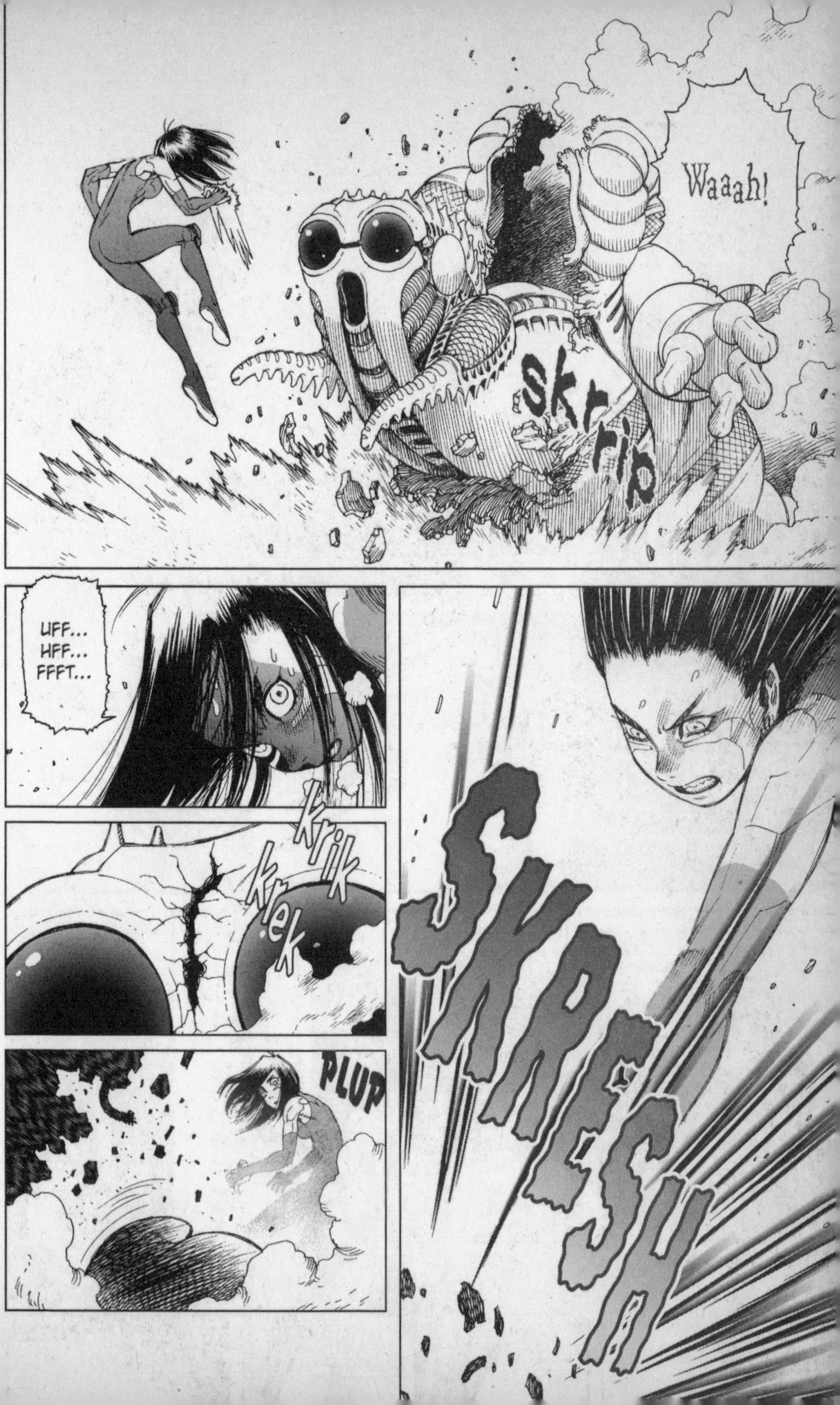
Waaah!
skrrip
SKRESH
UFF... HFF... FFFT...
krik
krek
PLUP

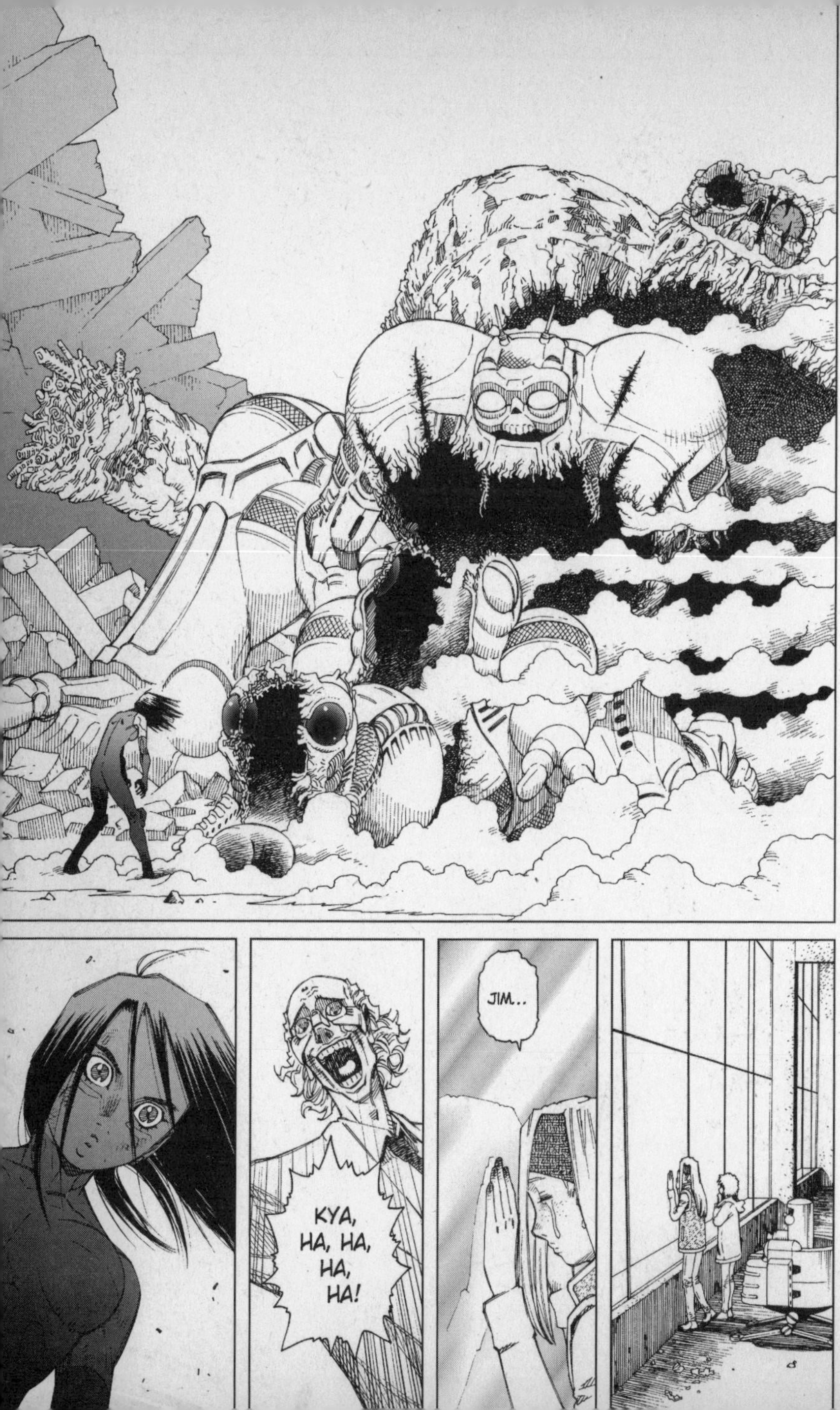
JIM...
KYA, HA, HA, HA, HA!

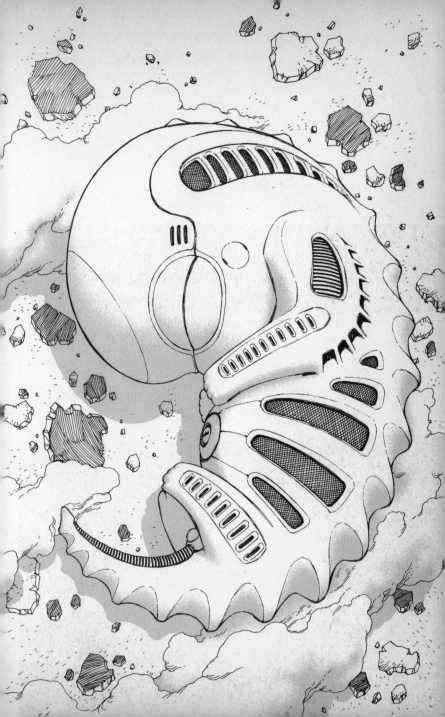

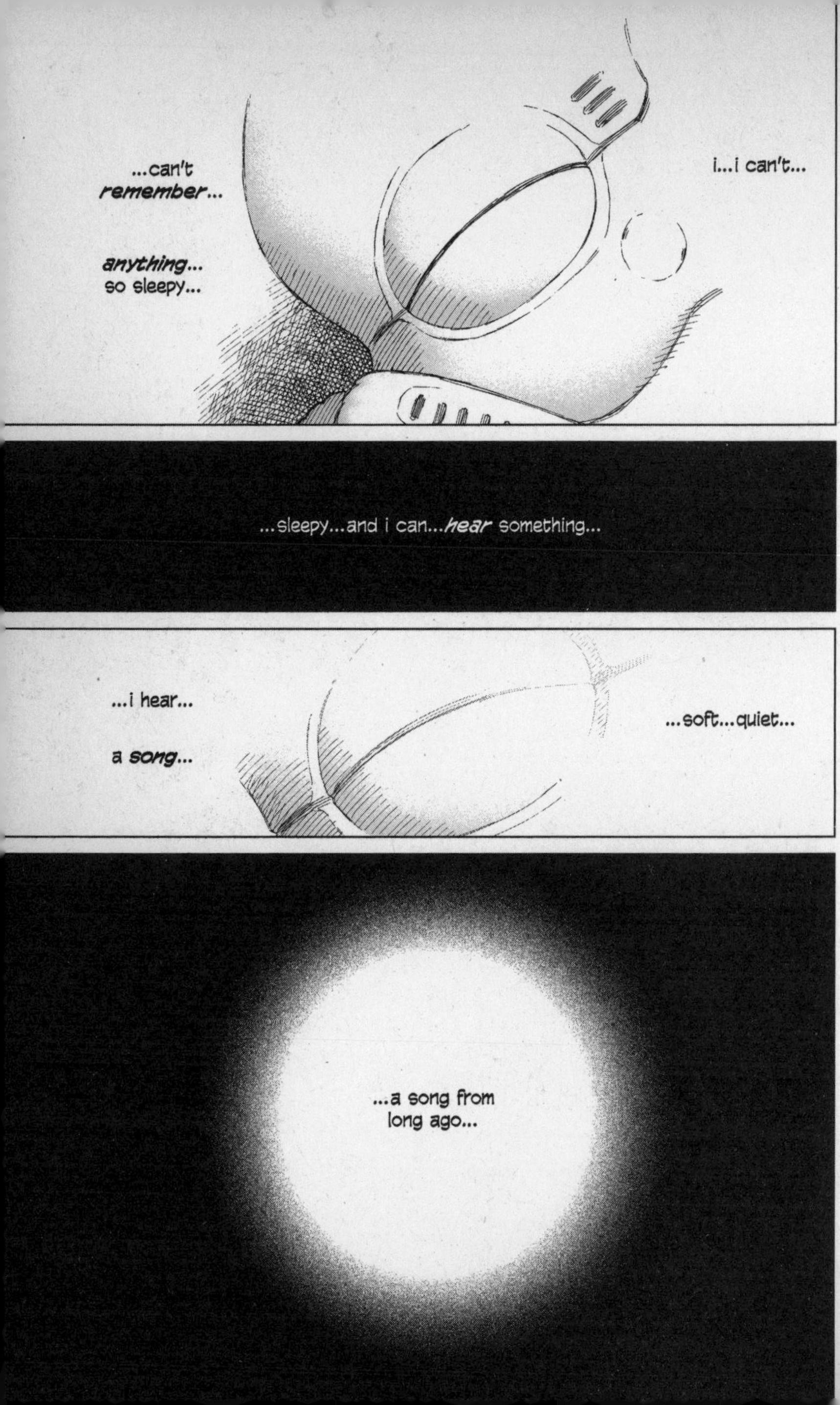
i...i can't...
...can't *remember*...
anything... so sleepy...
...sleepy...and i can...*hear* something...
...soft...quiet...
...i hear...
a *song*...
...a song from long ago...

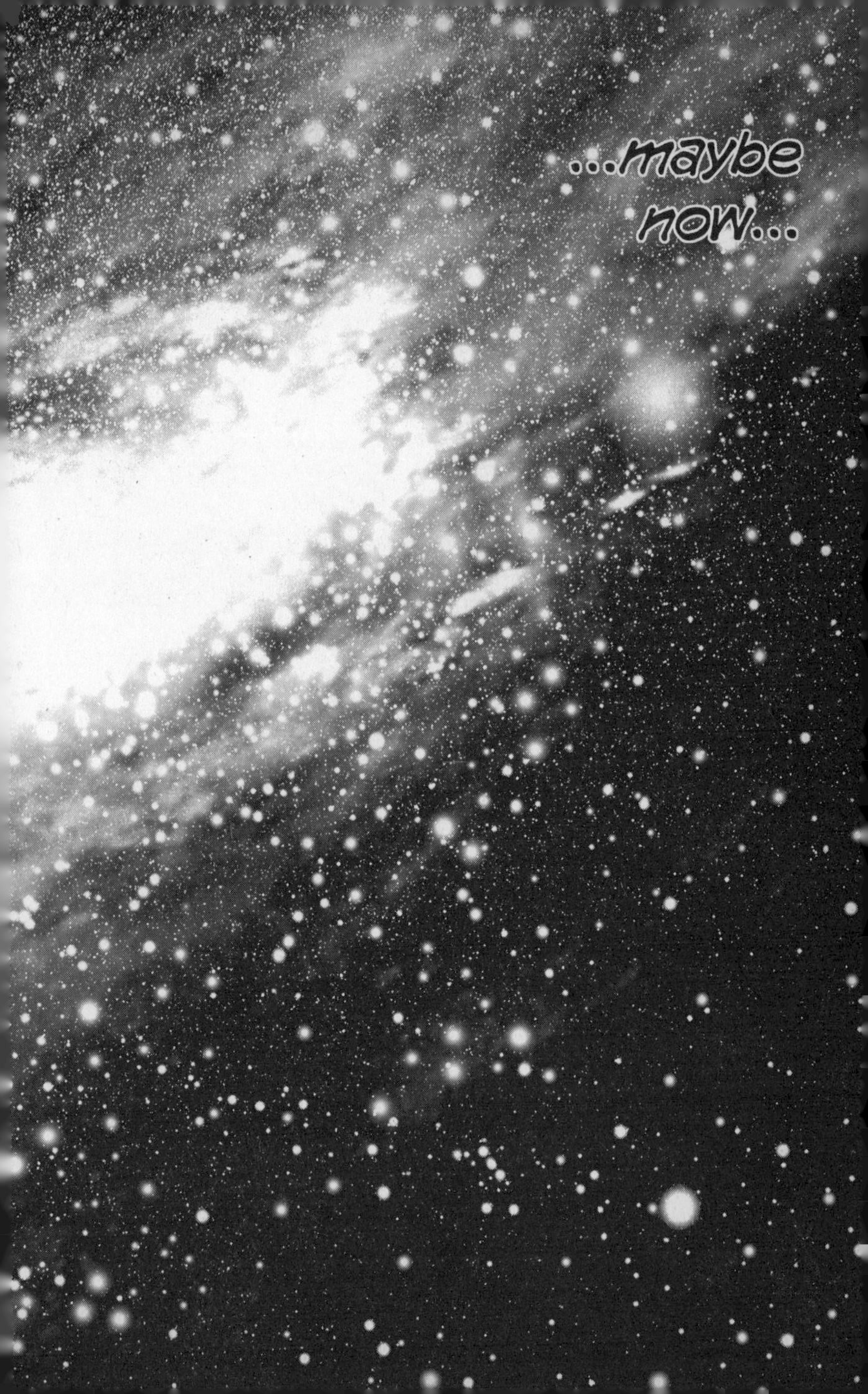
...maybe now...

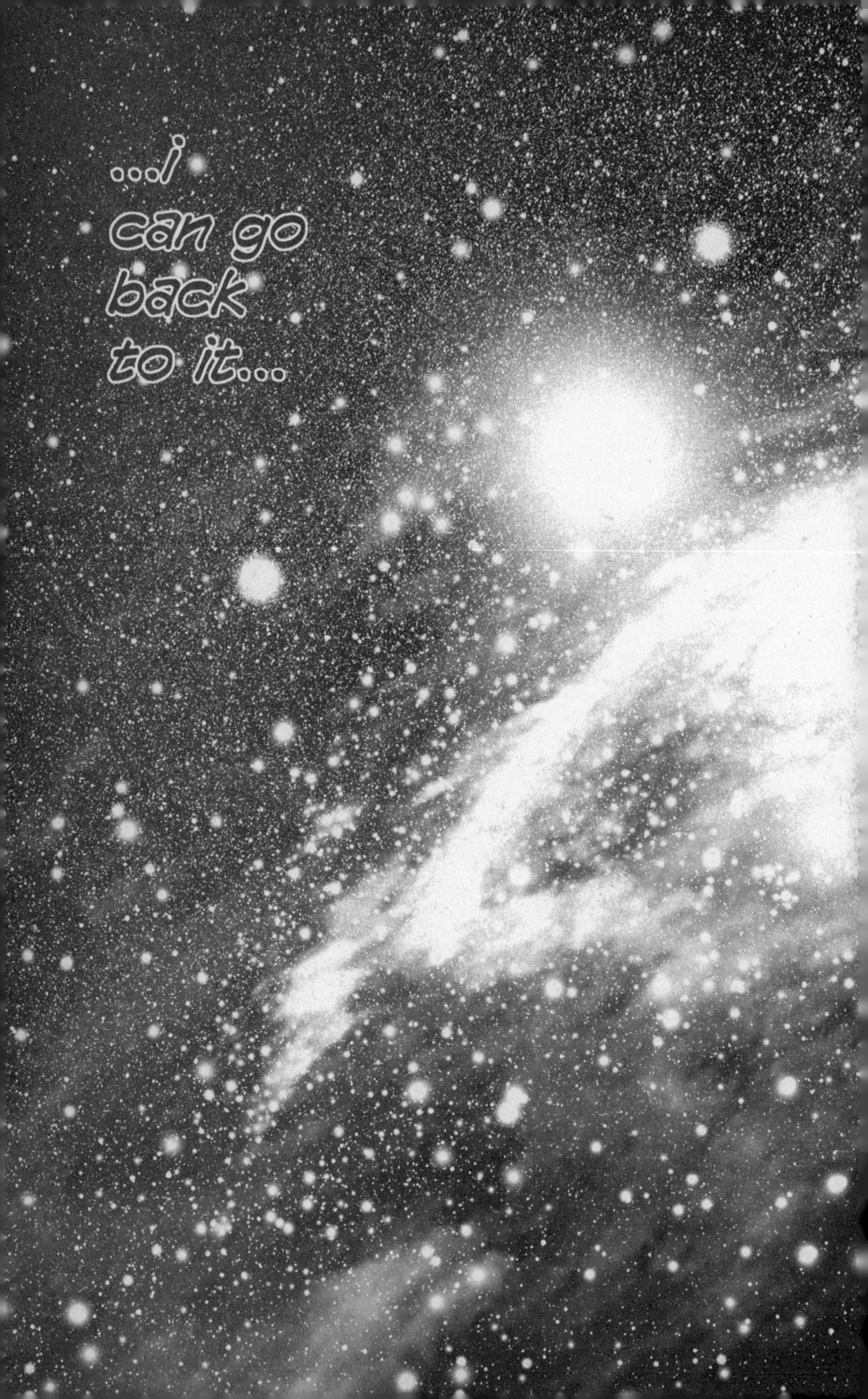
...i
can go
back
to it...

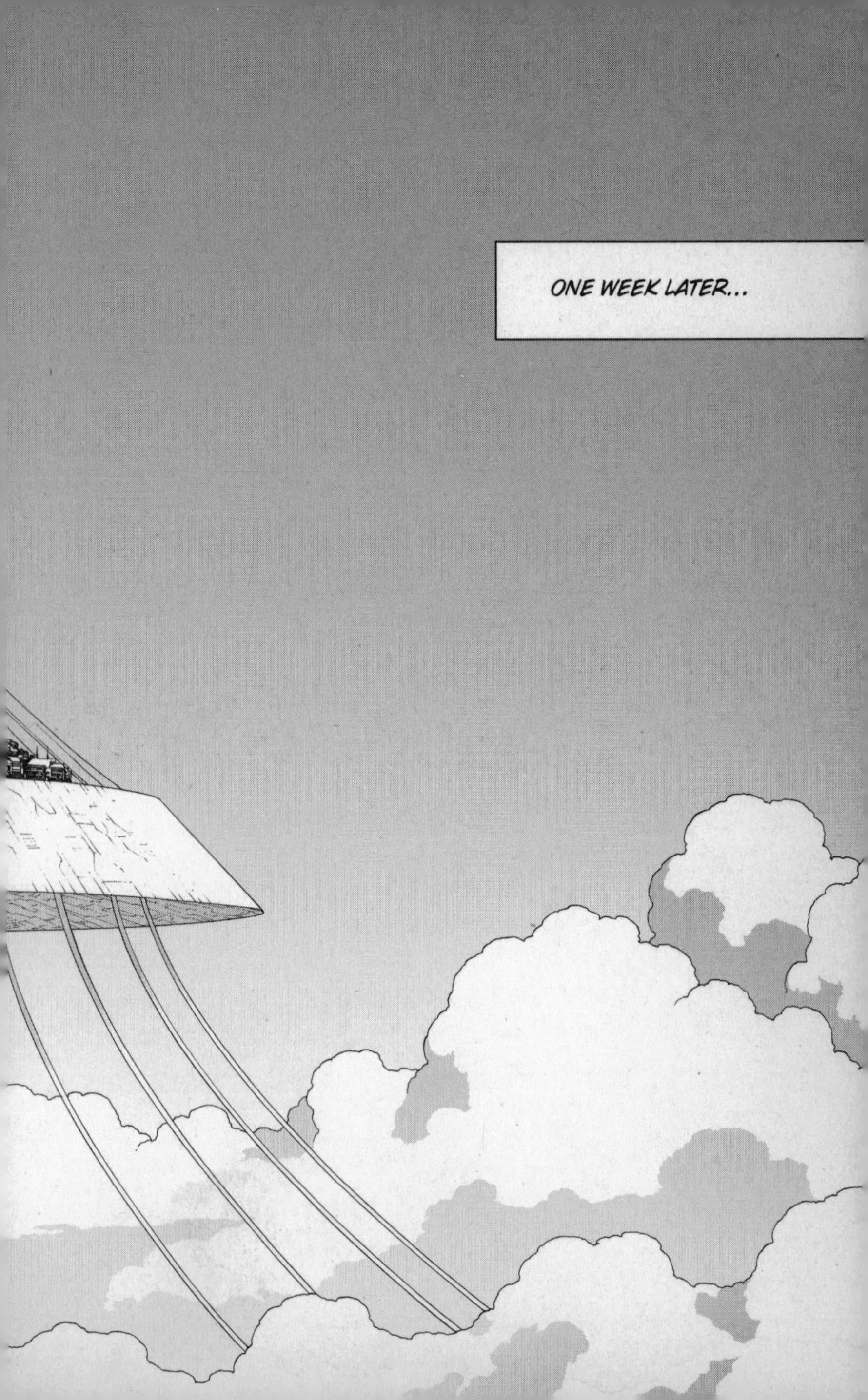
ONE WEEK LATER...

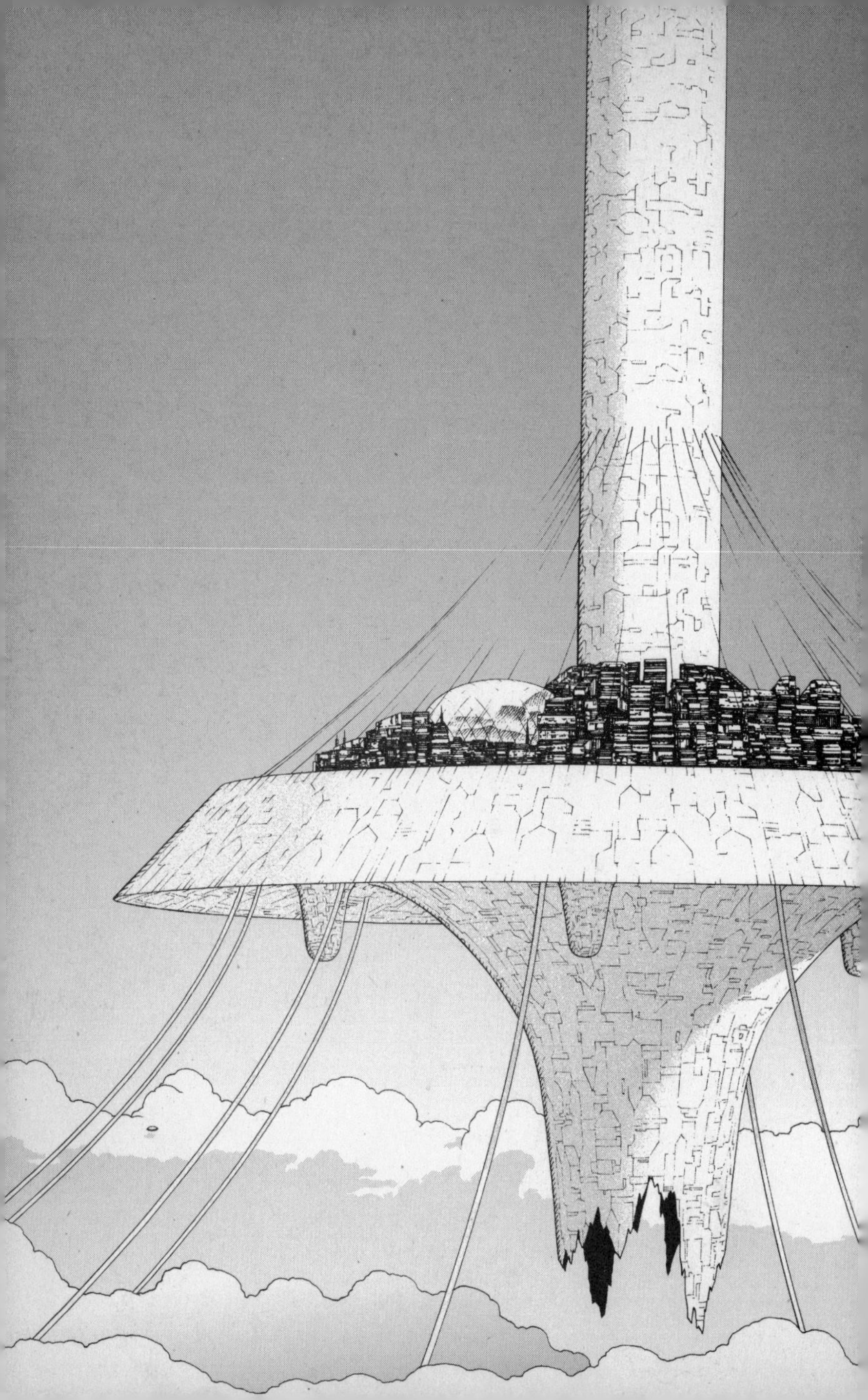

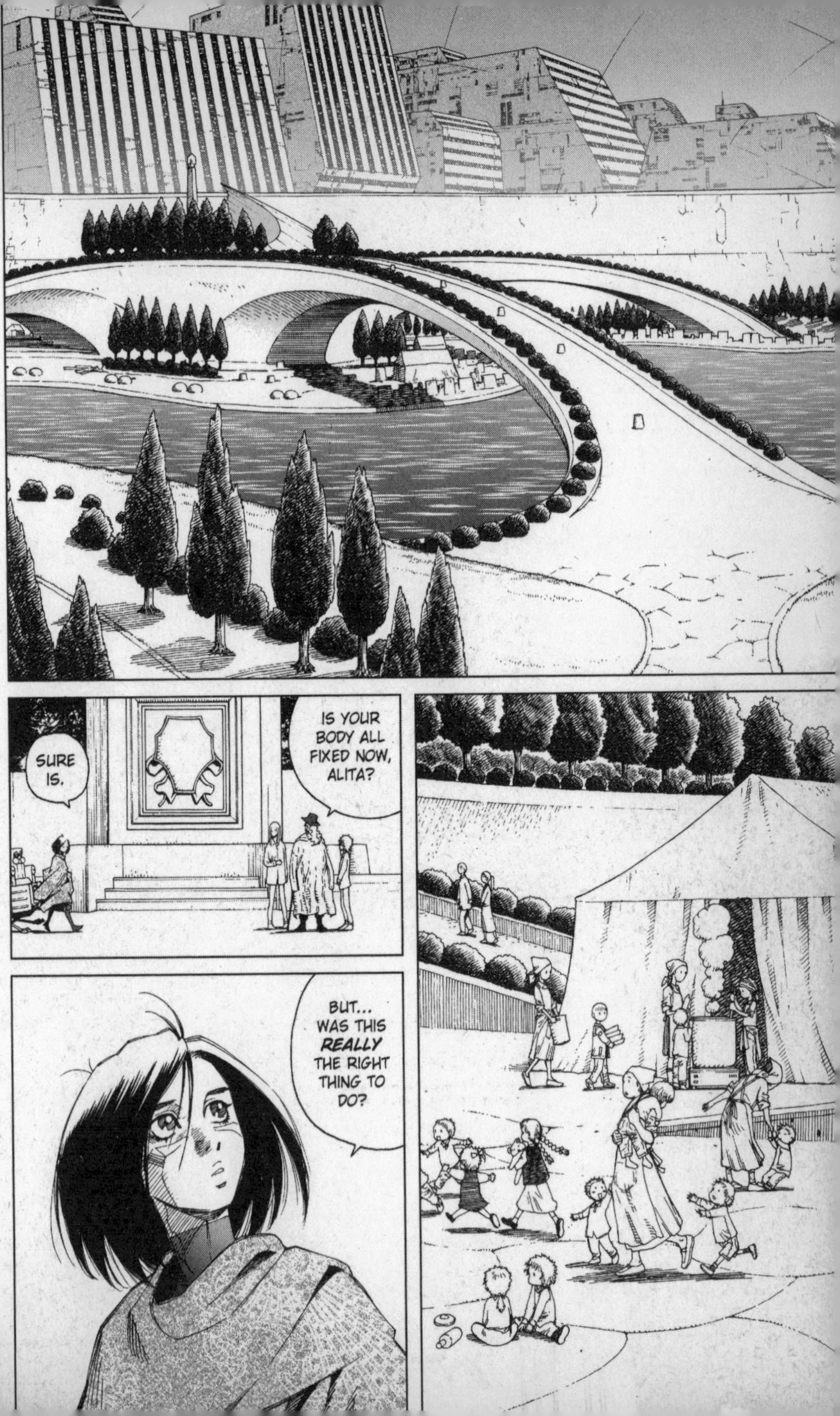
IS YOUR BODY ALL FIXED NOW, ALITA?
SURE IS.
BUT... WAS THIS *REALLY* THE RIGHT THING TO DO?

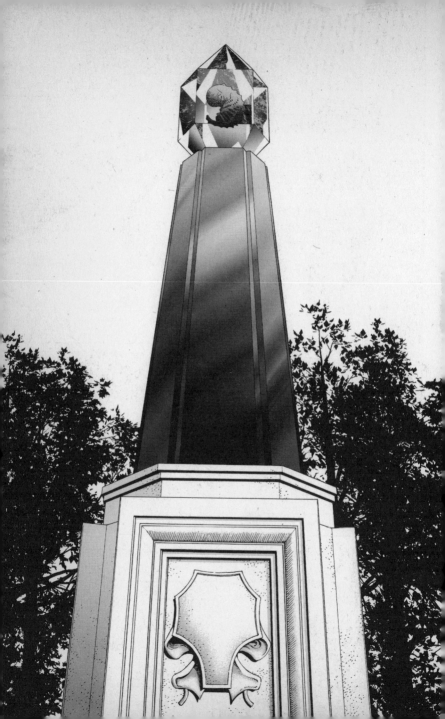

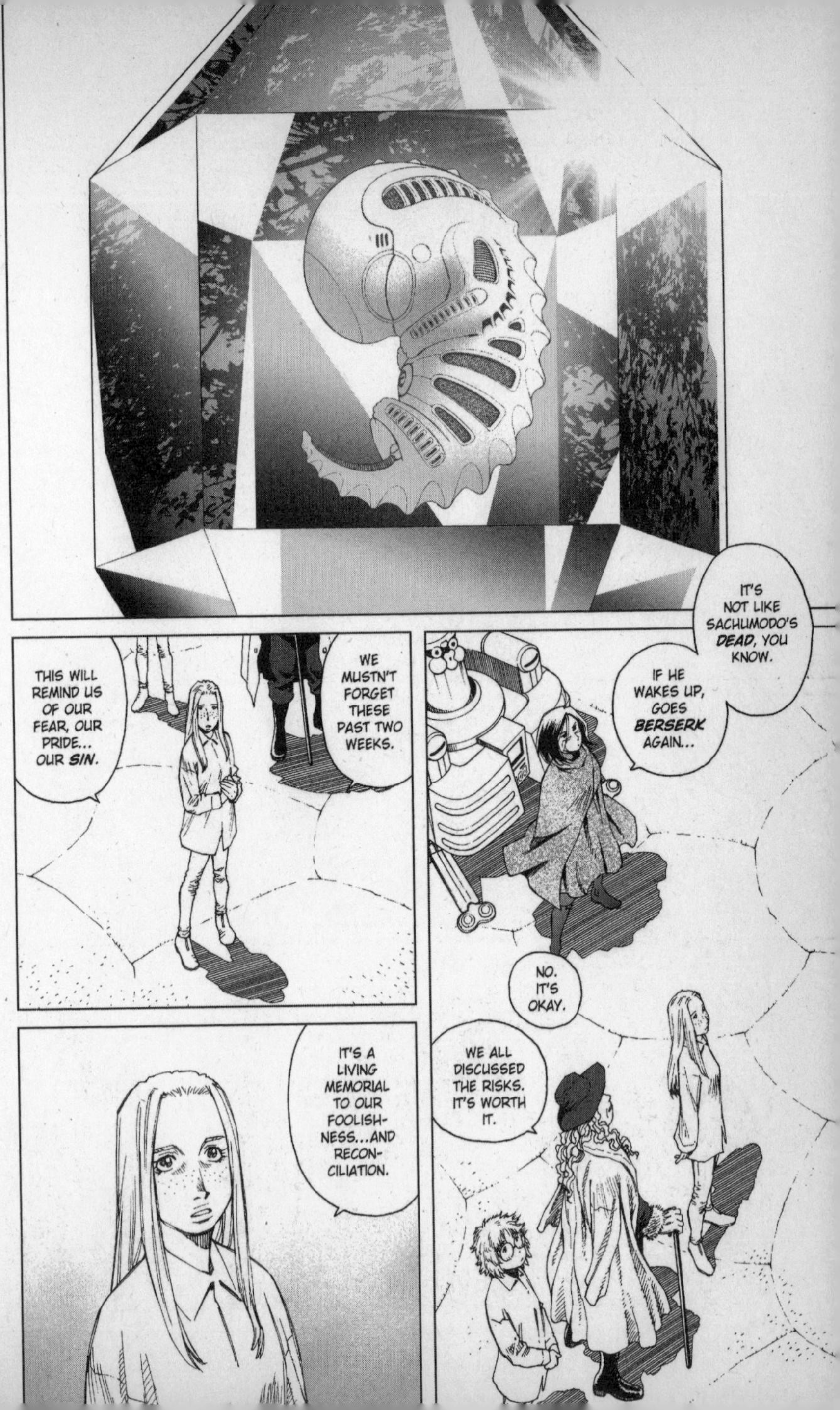
IT'S NOT LIKE SACHUMODO'S **DEAD**, YOU KNOW.
IF HE WAKES UP, GOES **BERSERK** AGAIN...
NO. IT'S OKAY.
WE ALL DISCUSSED THE RISKS. IT'S WORTH IT.
WE MUSTN'T FORGET THESE PAST TWO WEEKS.
THIS WILL REMIND US OF OUR FEAR, OUR PRIDE... OUR **SIN**.
IT'S A LIVING MEMORIAL TO OUR FOOLISHNESS...AND RECONCILIATION.

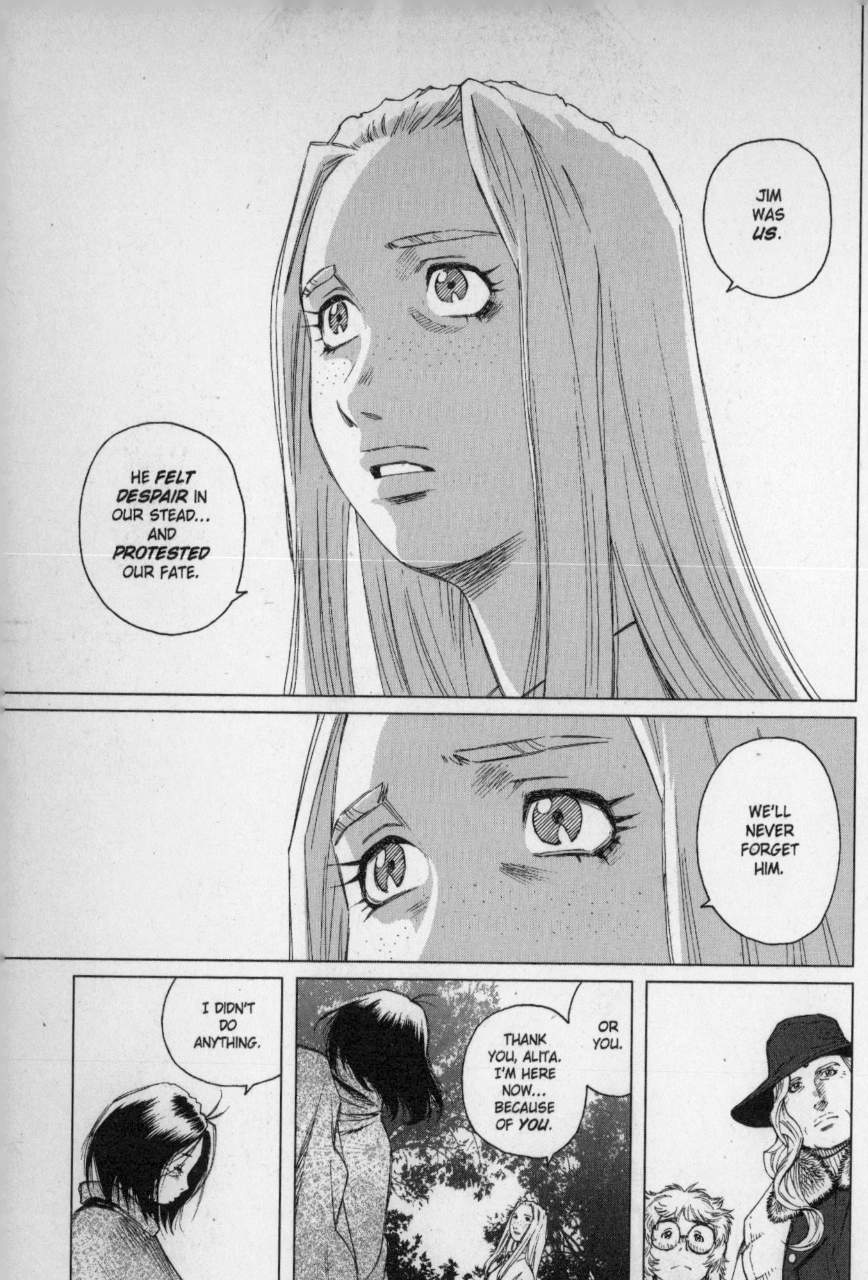
JIM WAS US.
HE FELT DESPAIR IN OUR STEAD... AND PROTESTED OUR FATE.
WE'LL NEVER FORGET HIM.
OR YOU.
THANK YOU, ALITA. I'M HERE NOW... BECAUSE OF YOU.
I DIDN'T DO ANYTHING.

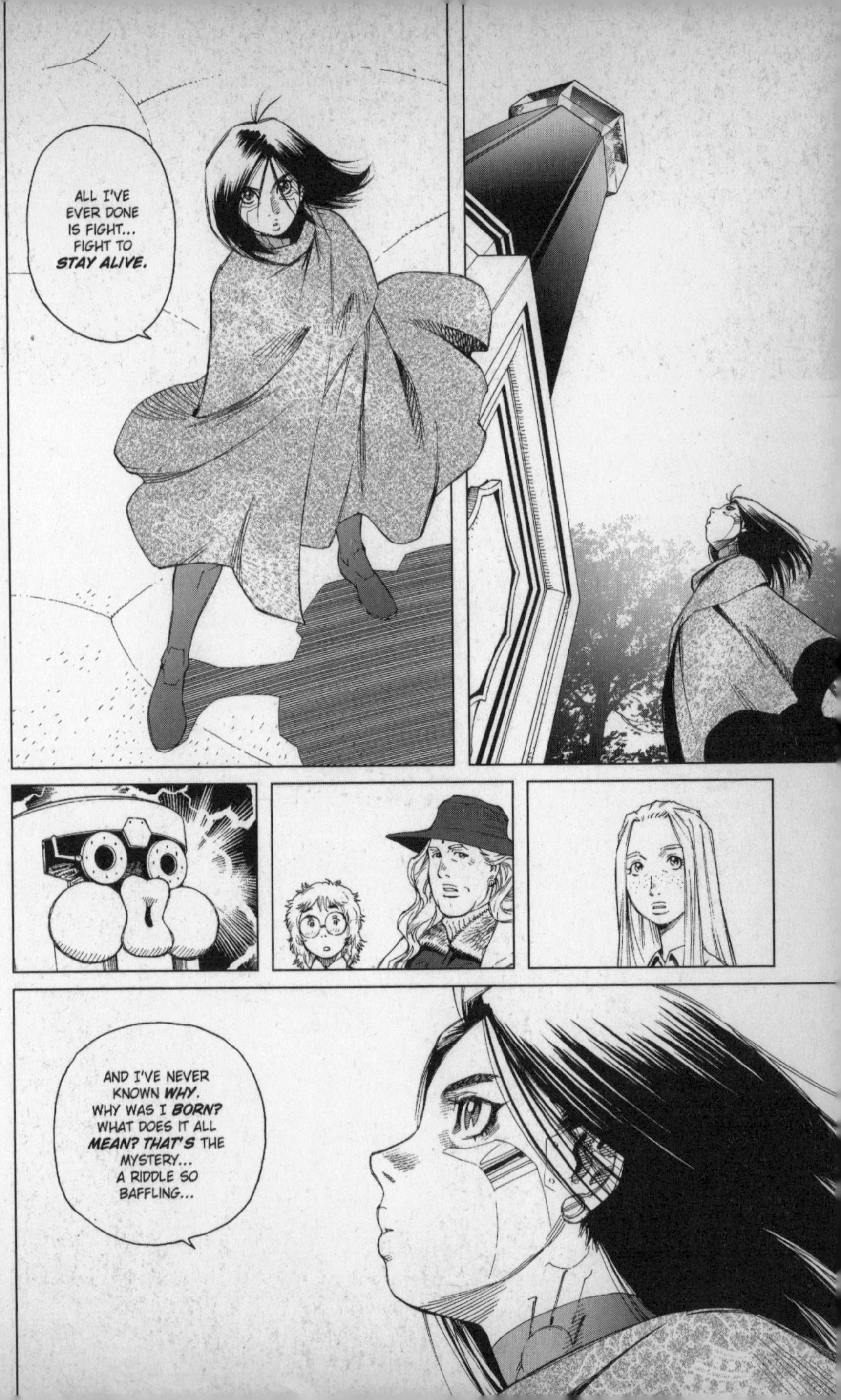
ALL I'VE EVER DONE IS FIGHT... FIGHT TO **STAY ALIVE.**
AND I'VE NEVER KNOWN **WHY**. WHY WAS I **BORN?** WHAT DOES IT ALL **MEAN? THAT'S** THE MYSTERY... A RIDDLE SO BAFFLING...

...THAT MOST ARE AFRAID TO EVEN ASK IT.
FOR TO LIVE WITH SUCH A PROFOUND PUZZLE...
...IS TO DIE PERPLEXED...
...TO END OUR LIVES AS WE BEGAN THEM—SEEKERS ON A HOPELESS QUEST!
LIFE'S GRAND ENIGMA IS A *CURSE* TO THOSE WHO SEEK ANSWERS...
...BUT A *BLESSING* TO THOSE WHO TAKE ACTION. FOR NO ONE CAN EVER CONQUER OUR THIRST TO KNOW THE TRUTH!

大童子

ミマンジ

タイジ

PHASE 11

Even So…

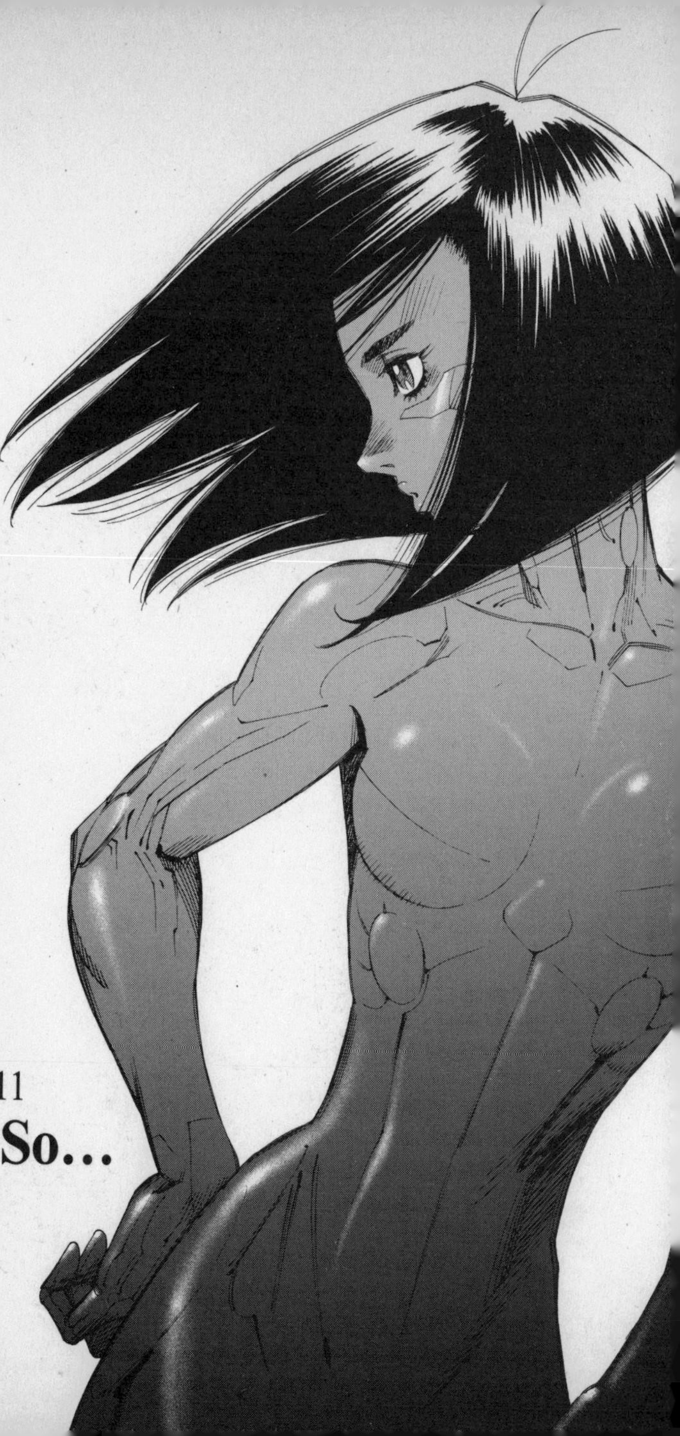

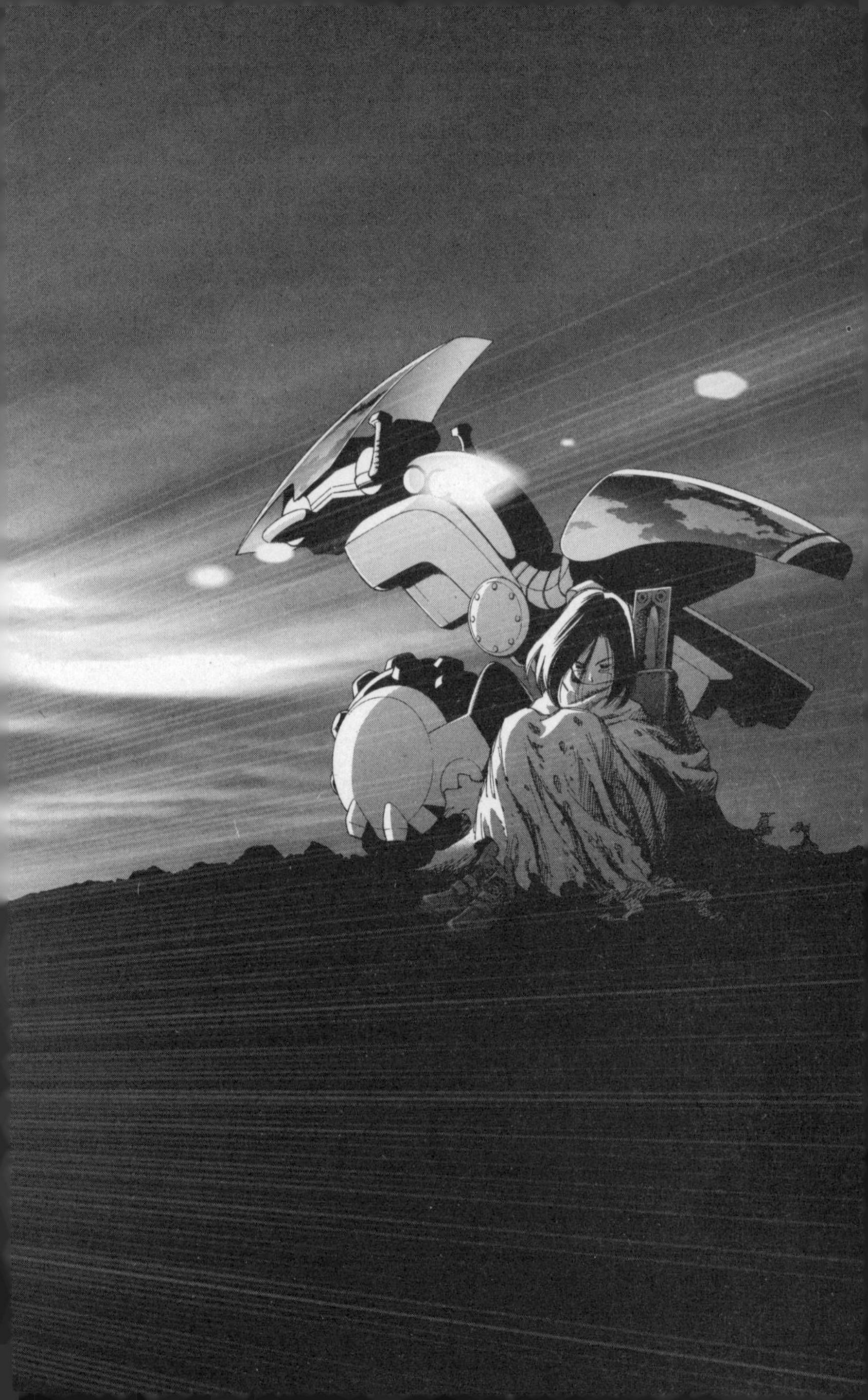

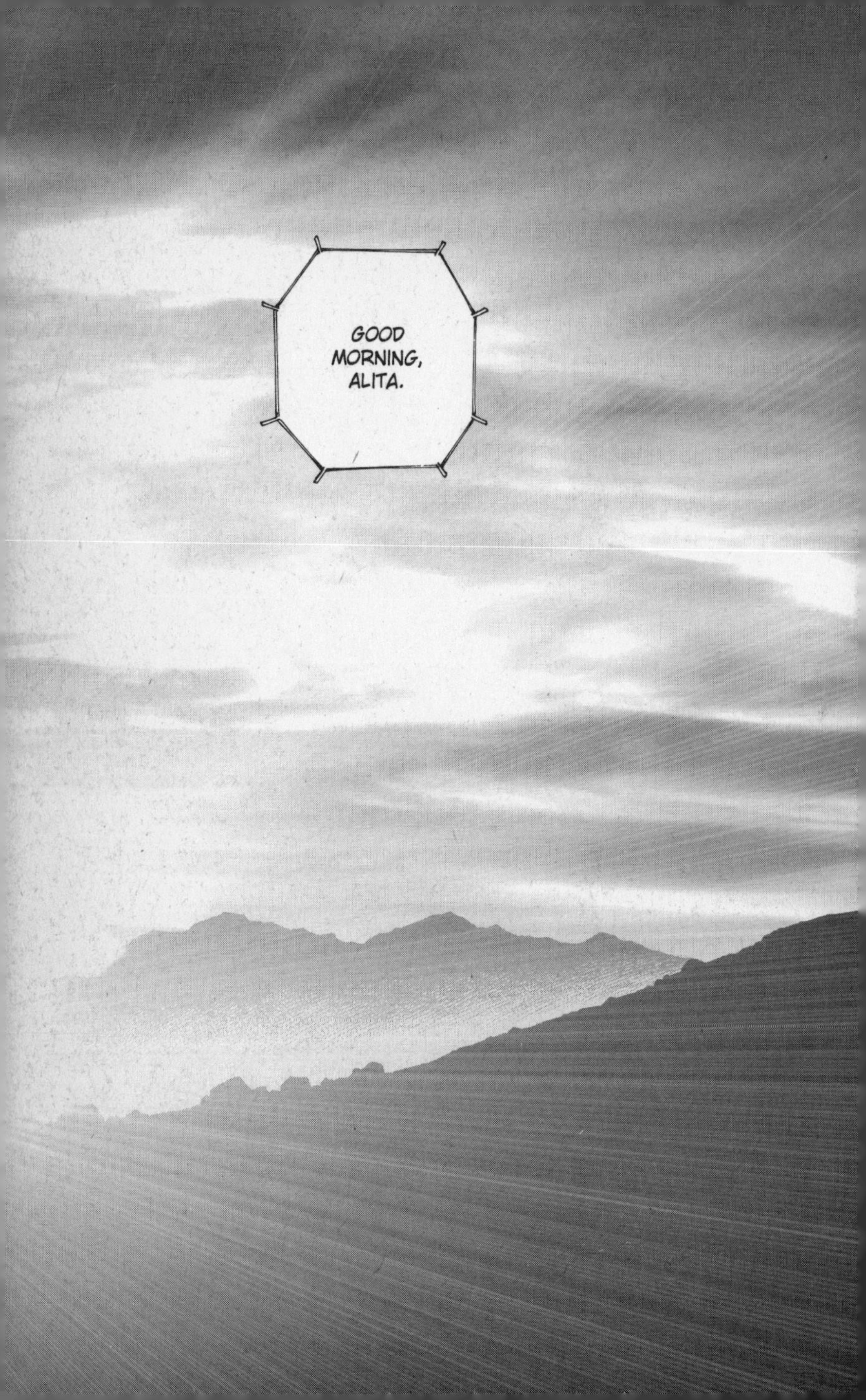
GOOD MORNING, ALITA.

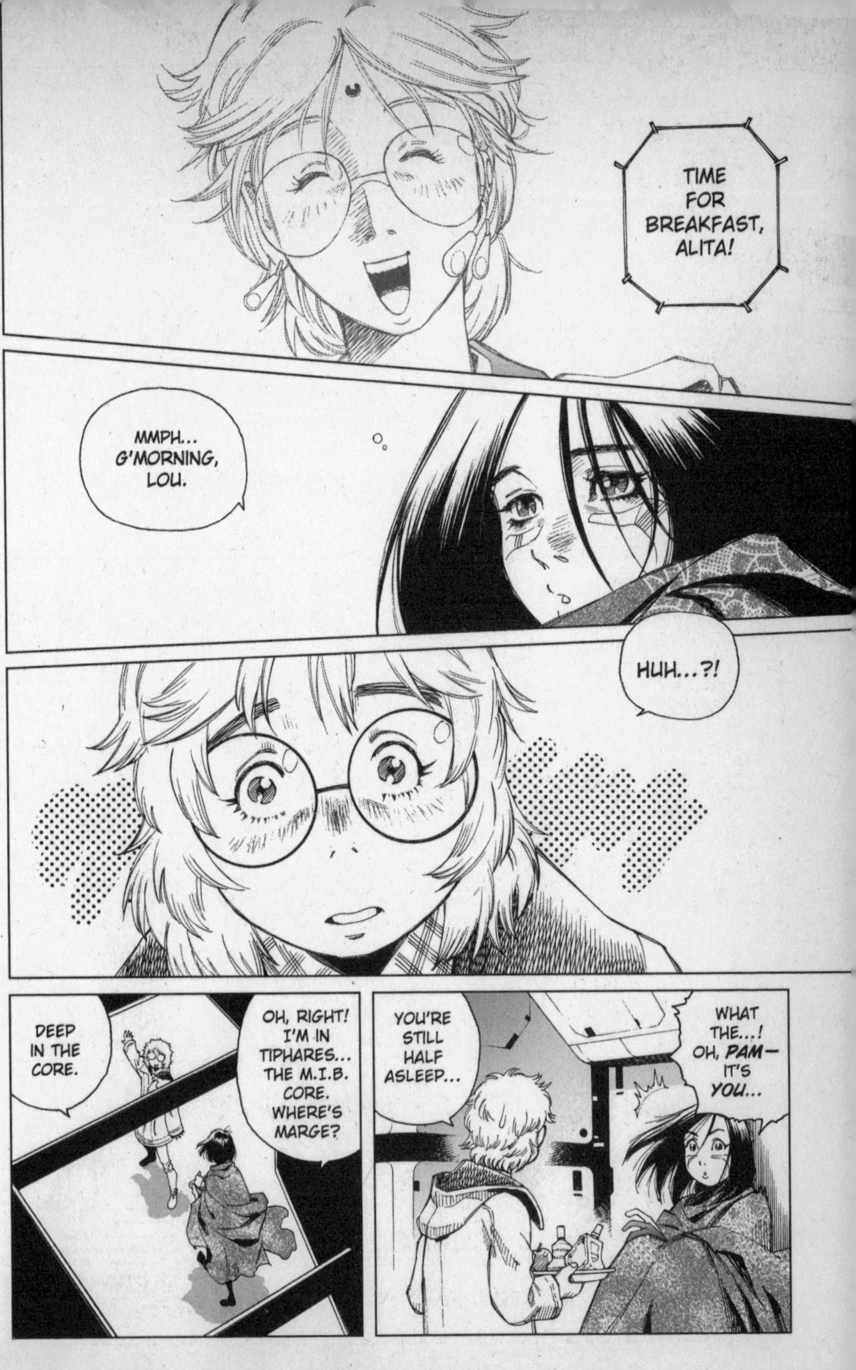
TIME FOR BREAKFAST, ALITA!
MMPH... G'MORNING, LOU.
HUH...?!
WHAT THE...! OH, PAM— IT'S YOU...
YOU'RE STILL HALF ASLEEP...
OH, RIGHT! I'M IN TIPHARES... THE M.I.B. CORE. WHERE'S MARGE?
DEEP IN THE CORE.

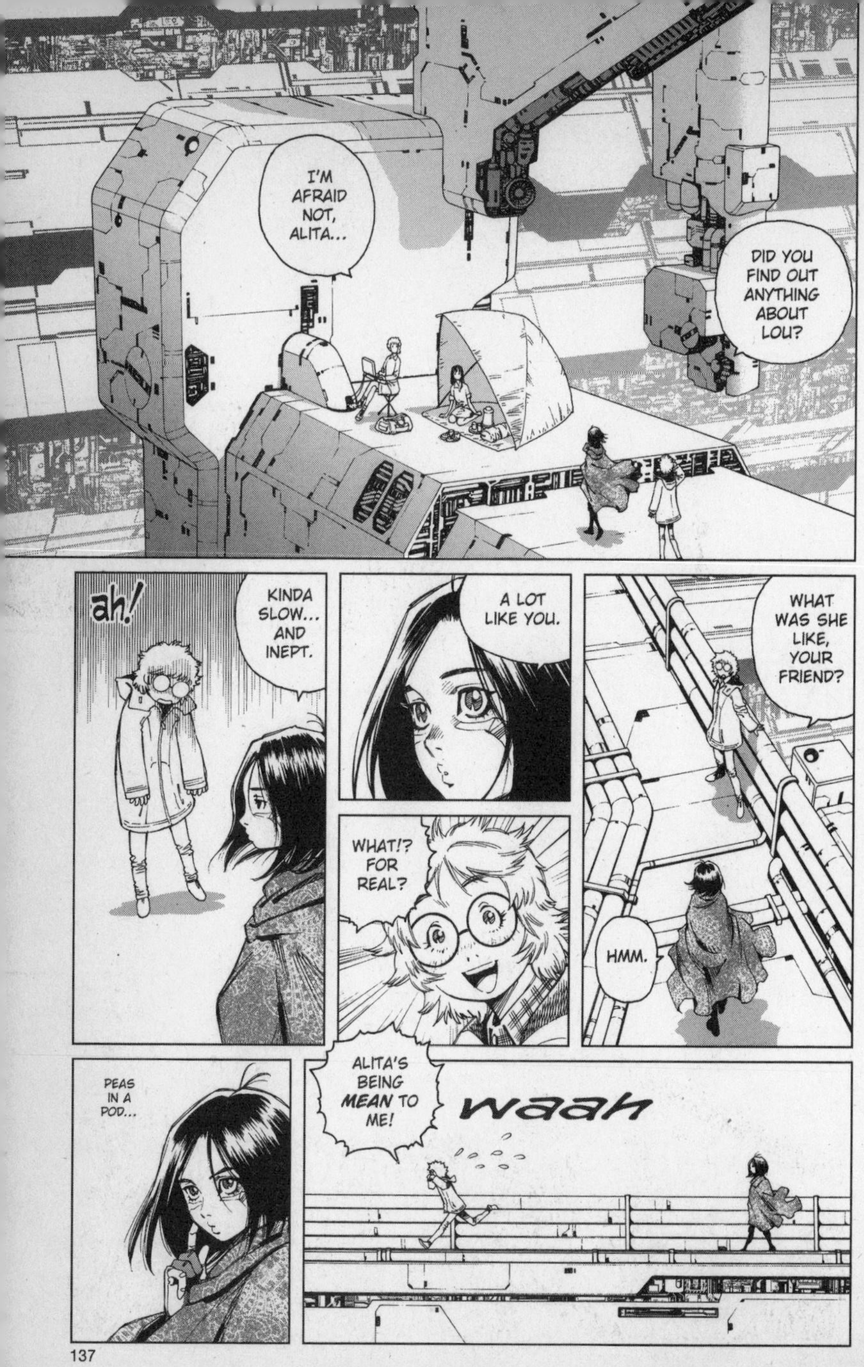
DID YOU FIND OUT ANYTHING ABOUT LOU?
I'M AFRAID NOT, ALITA...
WHAT WAS SHE LIKE, YOUR FRIEND?
HMM.
A LOT LIKE YOU.
WHAT!? FOR REAL?
KINDA SLOW... AND INEPT.
ah!
ALITA'S BEING *MEAN* TO ME!
waah
PEAS IN A POD...

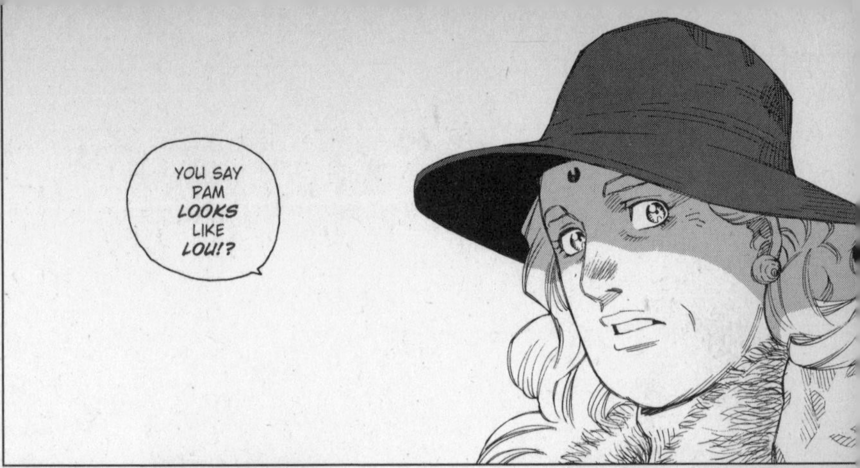
YOU SAY PAM LOOKS LIKE LOU!?

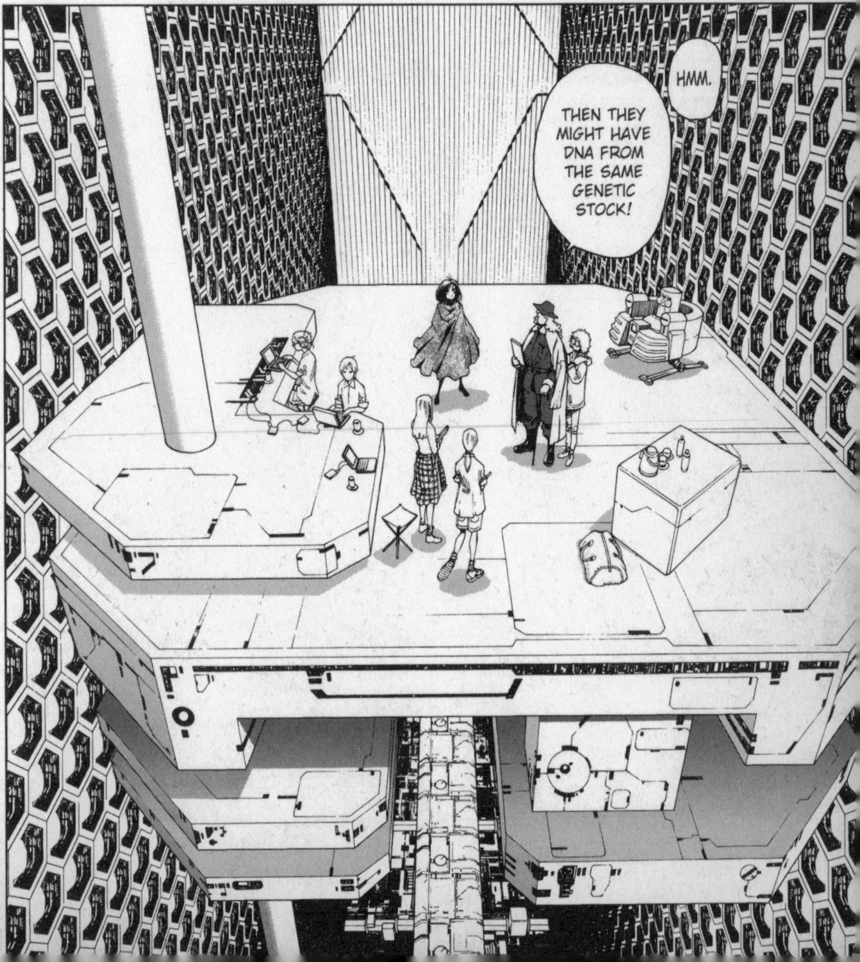
HMM.
THEN THEY MIGHT HAVE DNA FROM THE SAME GENETIC STOCK!

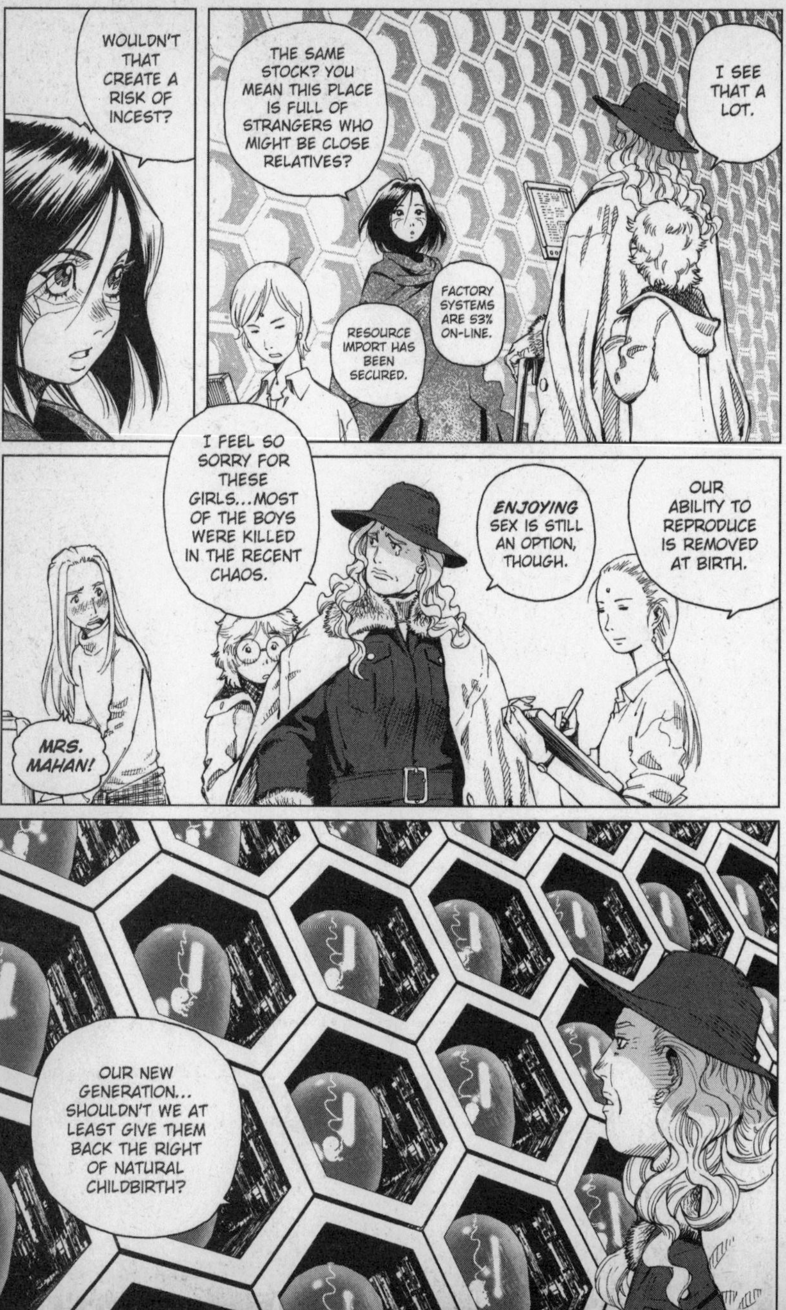
I SEE THAT A LOT.
THE SAME STOCK? YOU MEAN THIS PLACE IS FULL OF STRANGERS WHO MIGHT BE CLOSE RELATIVES?
FACTORY SYSTEMS ARE 53% ON-LINE.
RESOURCE IMPORT HAS BEEN SECURED.
WOULDN'T THAT CREATE A RISK OF INCEST?
OUR ABILITY TO REPRODUCE IS REMOVED AT BIRTH.
ENJOYING SEX IS STILL AN OPTION, THOUGH.
I FEEL SO SORRY FOR THESE GIRLS...MOST OF THE BOYS WERE KILLED IN THE RECENT CHAOS.
MRS. MAHAN!
OUR NEW GENERATION... SHOULDN'T WE AT LEAST GIVE THEM BACK THE RIGHT OF NATURAL CHILDBIRTH?

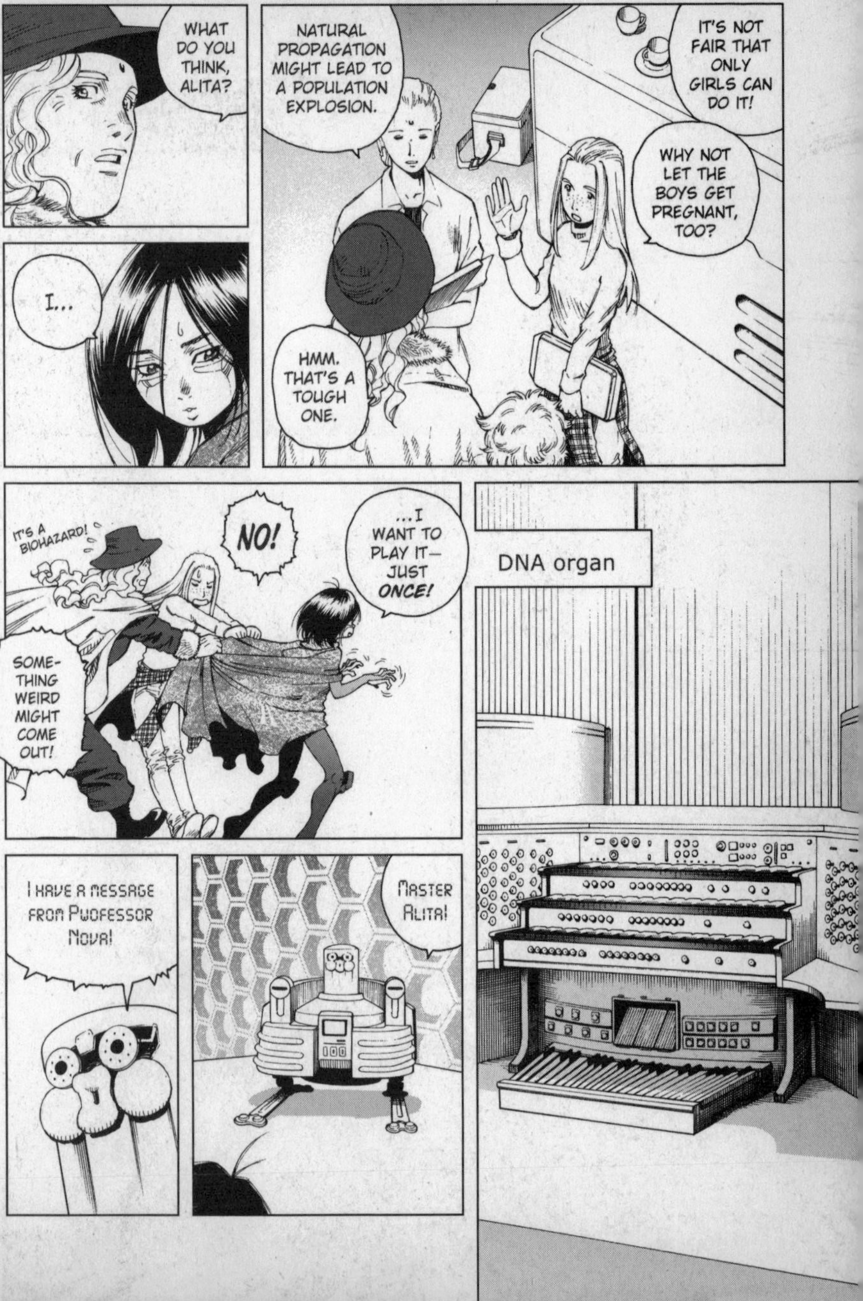
IT'S NOT FAIR THAT ONLY GIRLS CAN DO IT!
WHY NOT LET THE BOYS GET PREGNANT, TOO?
NATURAL PROPAGATION MIGHT LEAD TO A POPULATION EXPLOSION.
HMM. THAT'S A TOUGH ONE.
WHAT DO YOU THINK, ALITA?
I...
DNA organ
...I WANT TO PLAY IT—JUST ONCE!
NO!
IT'S A BIOHAZARD!
SOMETHING WEIRD MIGHT COME OUT!
MASTER ALITA!
I HAVE A MESSAGE FROM PWOFESSOR NOVA!

M.I.B. core, Disposal Division

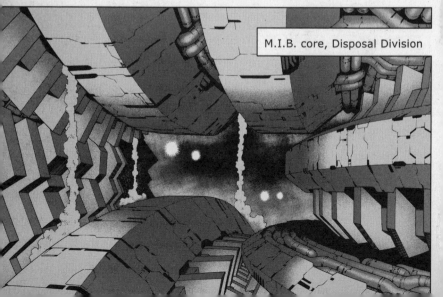

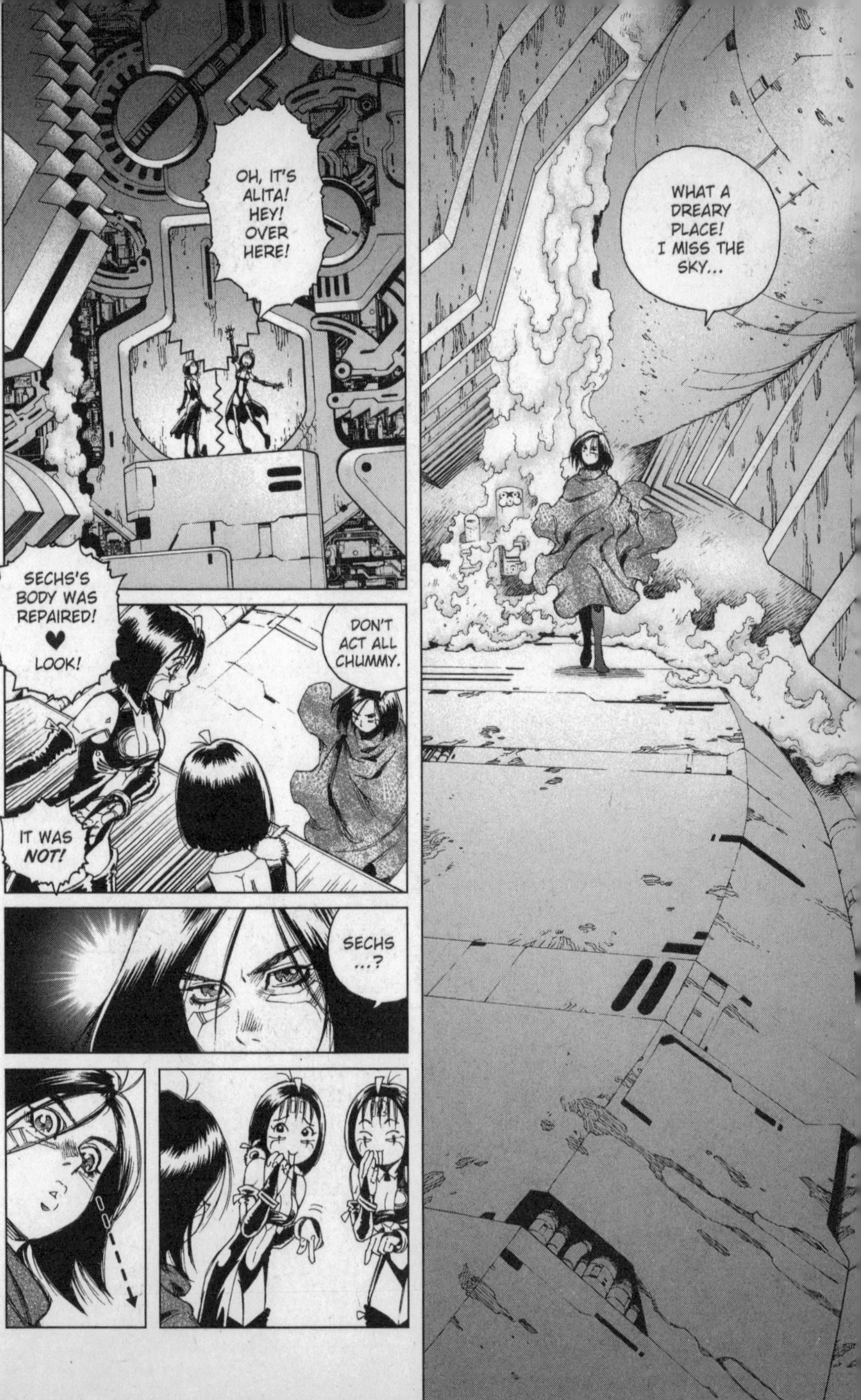
WHAT A DREARY PLACE! I MISS THE SKY...
OH, IT'S ALITA! HEY! OVER HERE!
SECHS'S BODY WAS REPAIRED! ♥ LOOK!
DON'T ACT ALL CHUMMY.
IT WAS *NOT!*
SECHS ...?

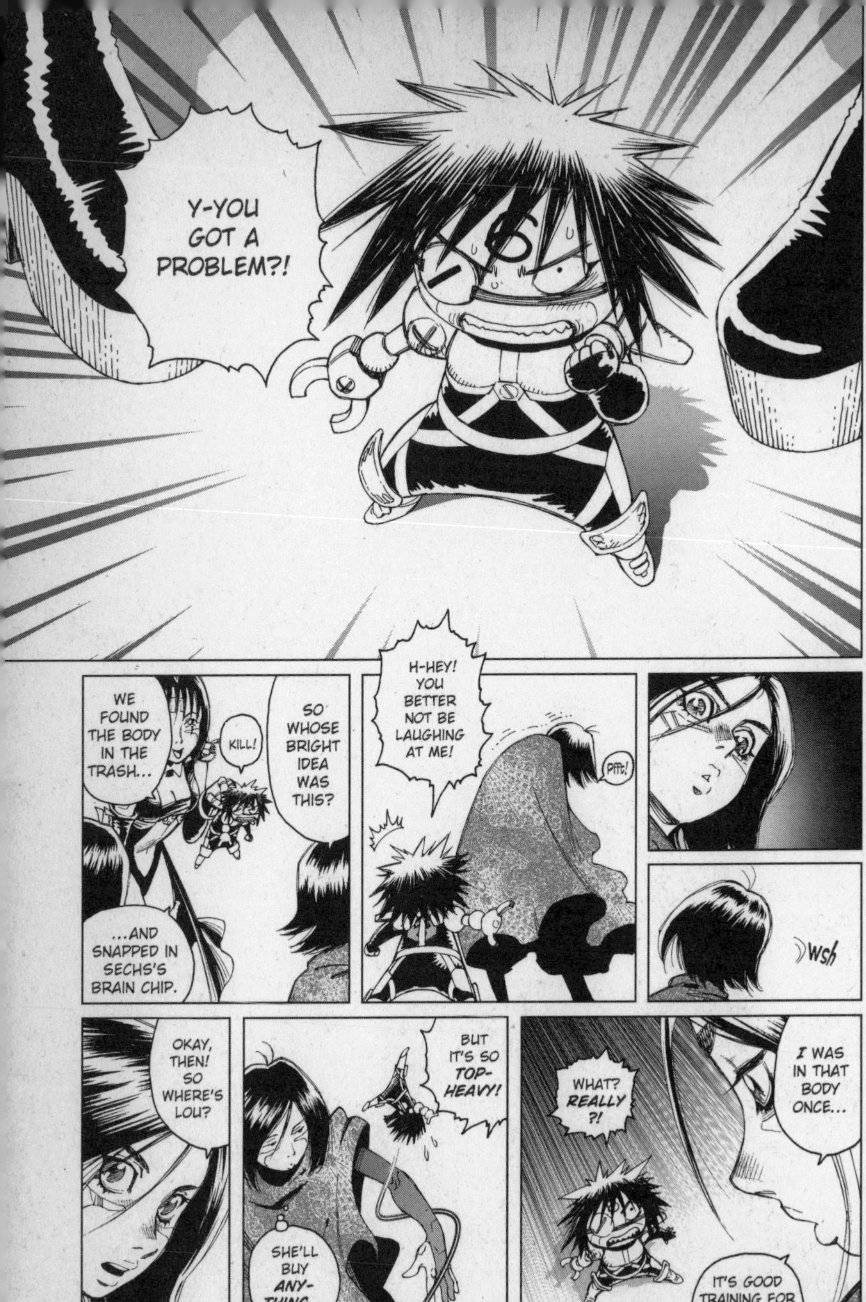
Y-YOU GOT A PROBLEM?!
SO WHOSE BRIGHT IDEA WAS THIS?
WE FOUND THE BODY IN THE TRASH...
KILL!
...AND SNAPPED IN SECHS'S BRAIN CHIP.
H-HEY! YOU BETTER NOT BE LAUGHING AT ME!
Pfft!
Wsh
OKAY, THEN! SO WHERE'S LOU?
BUT IT'S SO *TOP-HEAVY!*
SHE'LL BUY *ANYTHING...*
I WAS IN THAT BODY ONCE...
WHAT? *REALLY?!*
IT'S GOOD TRAINING FOR FIGHTING GIANTS LIKE DEN!

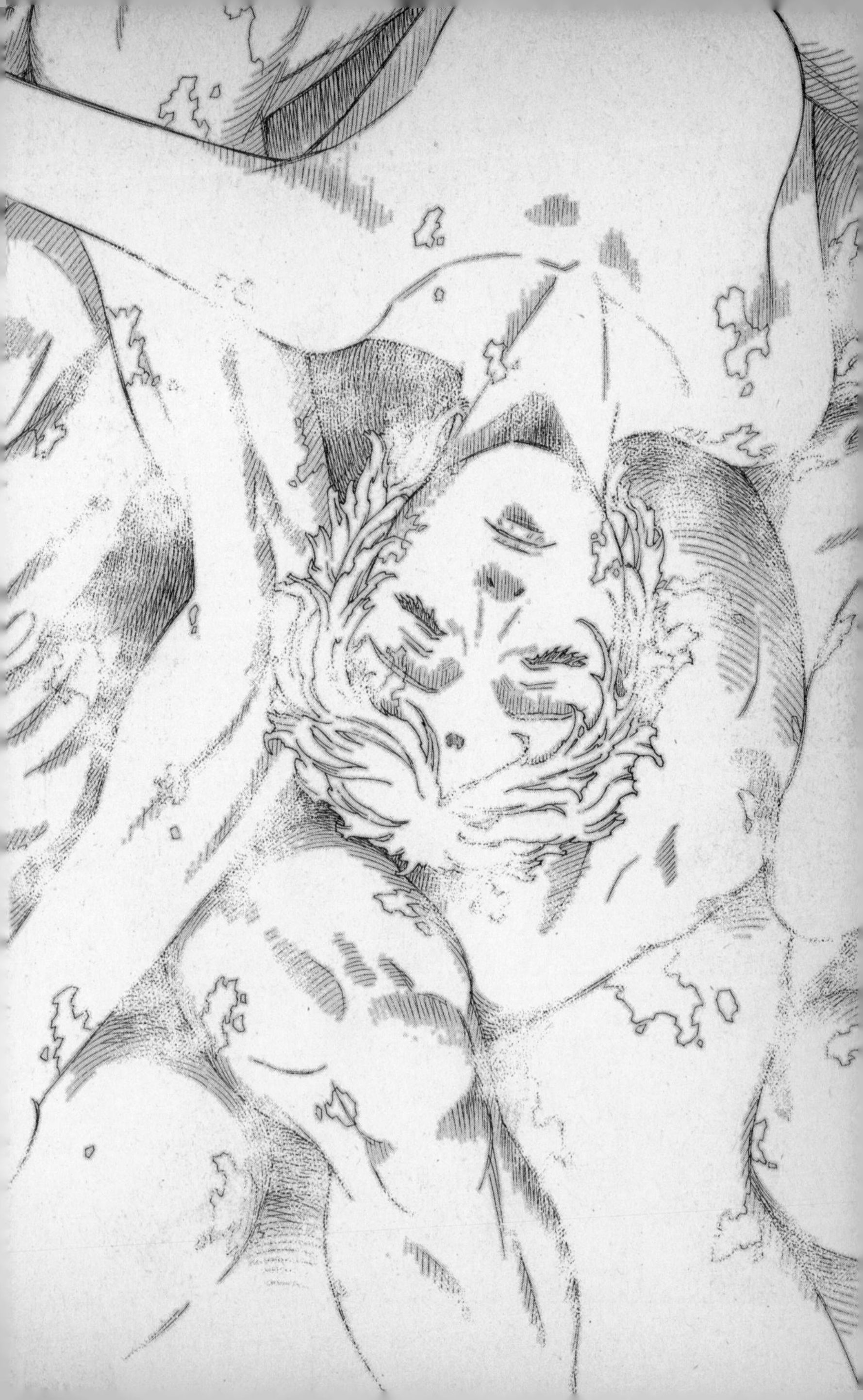

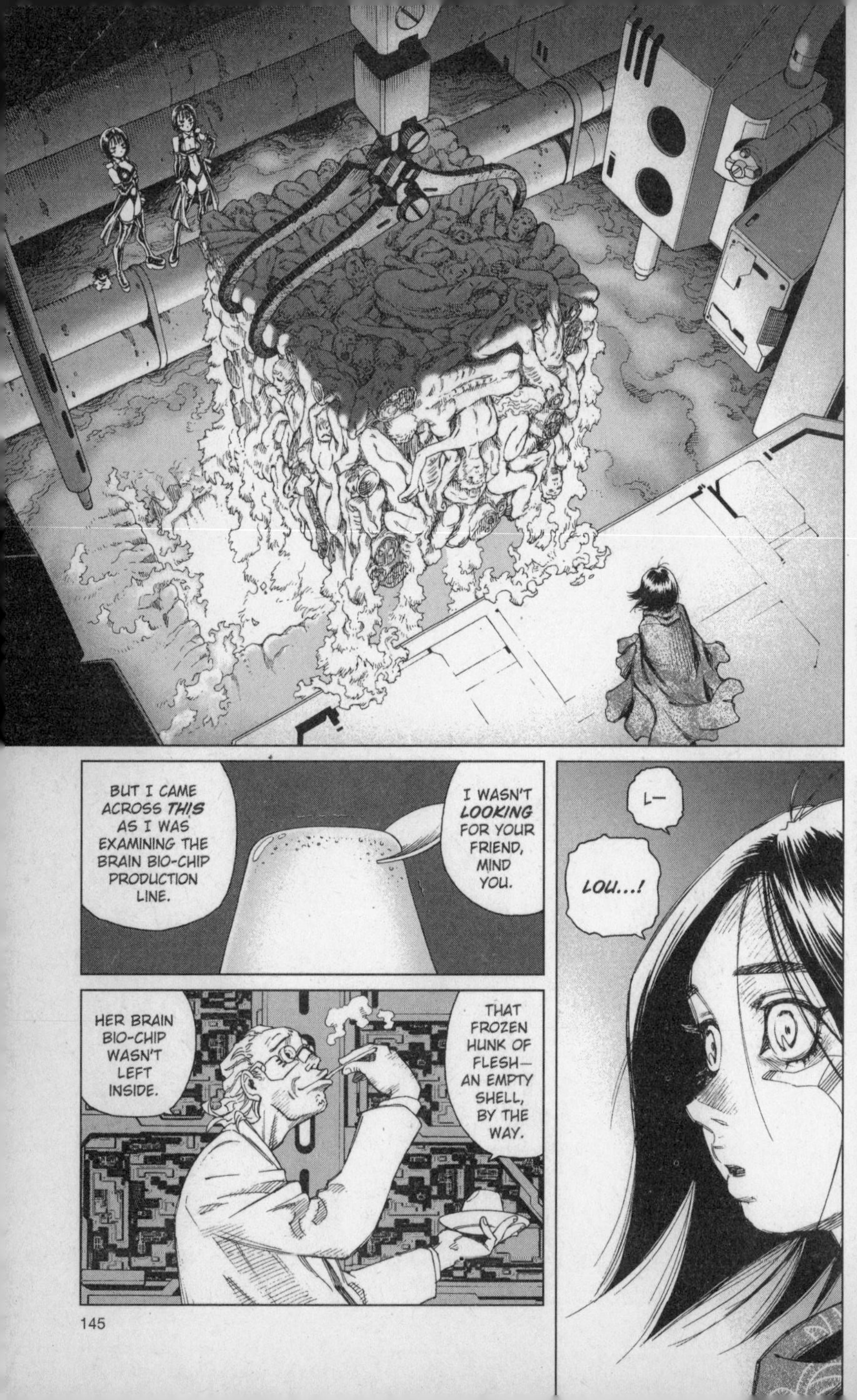
L—
LOU...!
I WASN'T LOOKING FOR YOUR FRIEND, MIND YOU.
BUT I CAME ACROSS THIS AS I WAS EXAMINING THE BRAIN BIO-CHIP PRODUCTION LINE.
THAT FROZEN HUNK OF FLESH— AN EMPTY SHELL, BY THE WAY.
HER BRAIN BIO-CHIP WASN'T LEFT INSIDE.

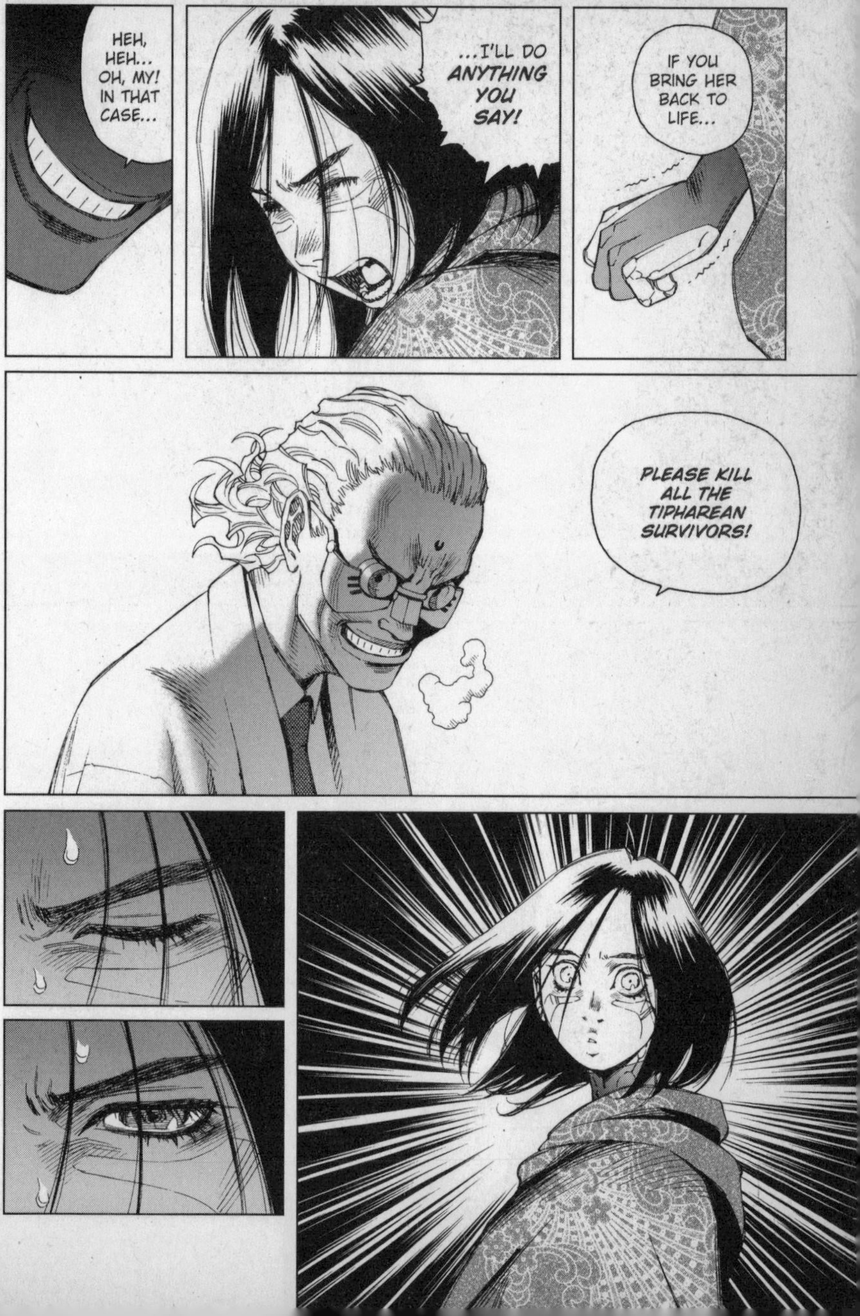
IF YOU BRING HER BACK TO LIFE...
...I'LL DO ANYTHING YOU SAY!
HEH, HEH... OH, MY! IN THAT CASE...
PLEASE KILL ALL THE TIPHAREAN SURVIVORS!

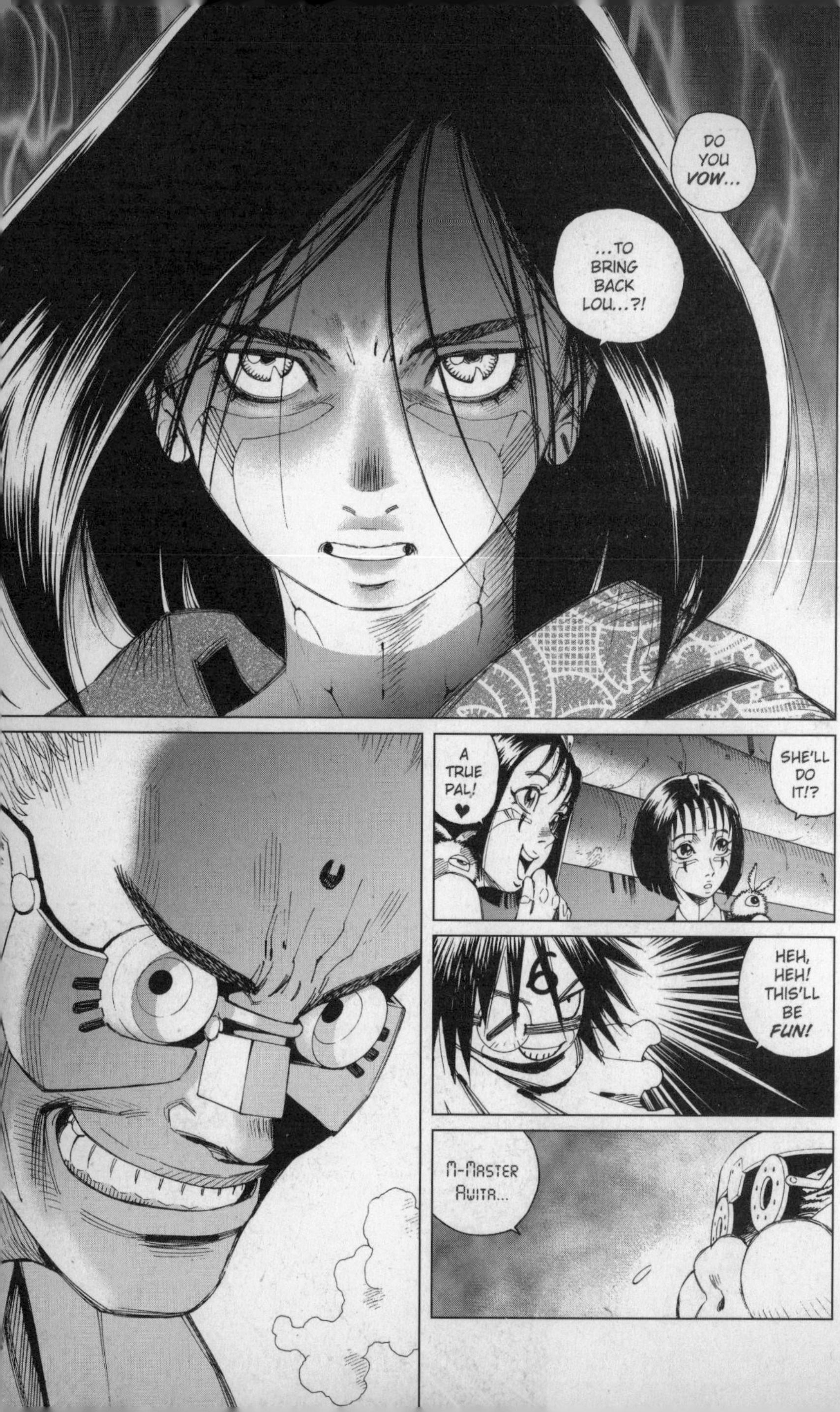
DO YOU VOW...
...TO BRING BACK LOU...?!
SHE'LL DO IT!?
A TRUE PAL! ♥
HEH, HEH! THIS'LL BE FUN!
M-MASTER ALITA...

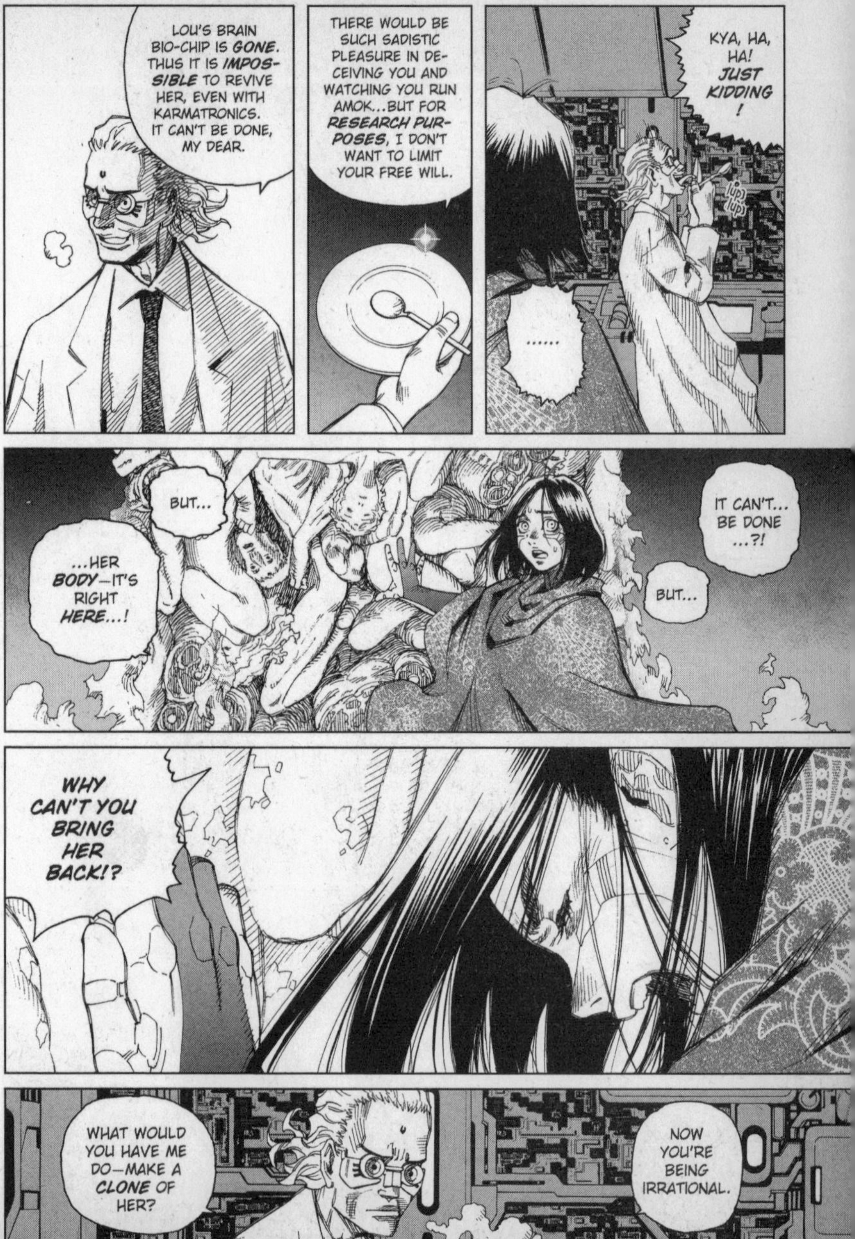
LOU'S BRAIN BIO-CHIP IS GONE. THUS IT IS IMPOSSIBLE TO REVIVE HER, EVEN WITH KARMATRONICS. IT CAN'T BE DONE, MY DEAR.
THERE WOULD BE SUCH SADISTIC PLEASURE IN DECEIVING YOU AND WATCHING YOU RUN AMOK...BUT FOR RESEARCH PURPOSES, I DON'T WANT TO LIMIT YOUR FREE WILL.
KYA, HA, HA! JUST KIDDING!
lup lup
......
IT CAN'T... BE DONE ...?!
BUT...
BUT...
...HER BODY—IT'S RIGHT HERE...!
WHY CAN'T YOU BRING HER BACK!?
WHAT WOULD YOU HAVE ME DO—MAKE A CLONE OF HER?
NOW YOU'RE BEING IRRATIONAL.

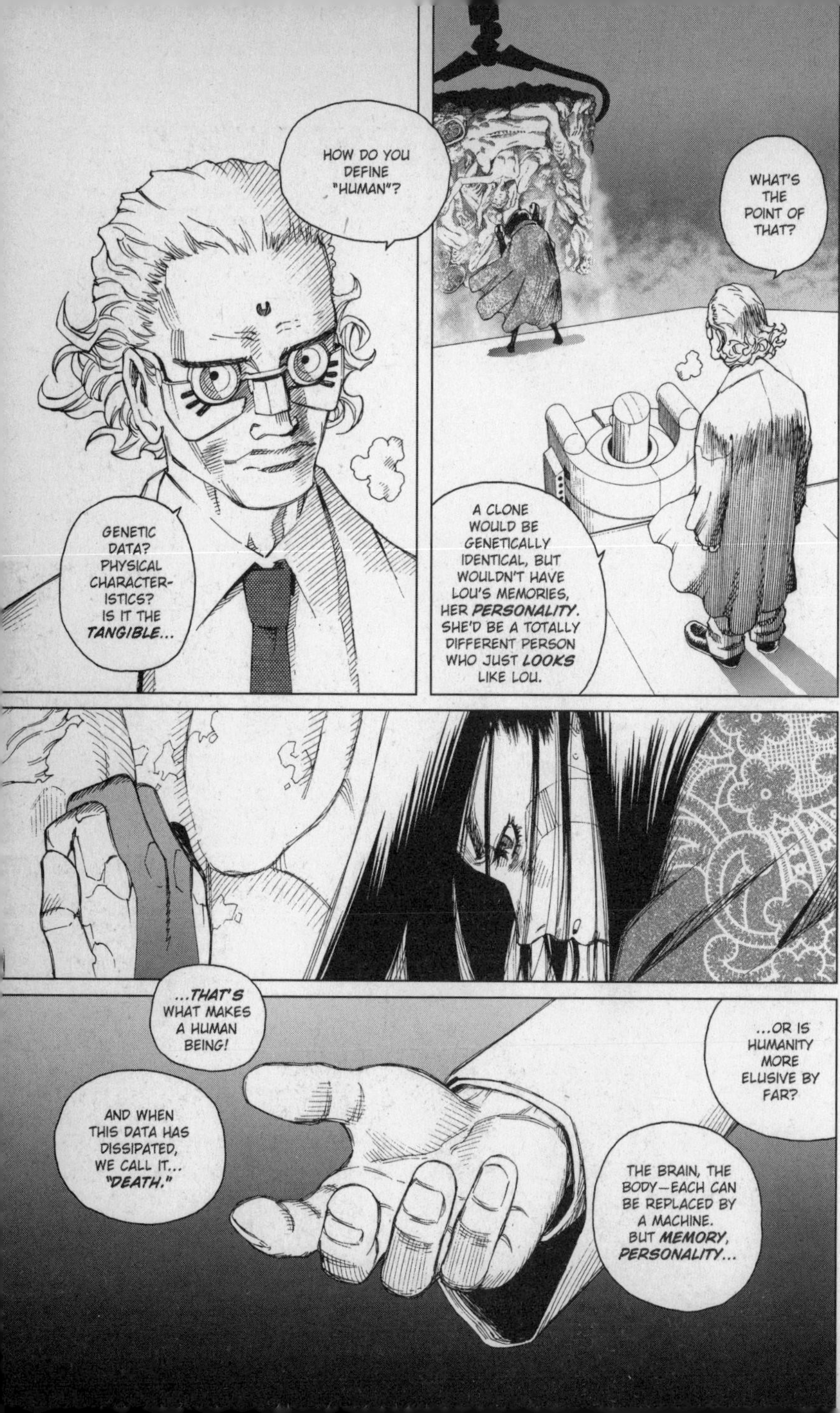
WHAT'S THE POINT OF THAT?
A CLONE WOULD BE GENETICALLY IDENTICAL, BUT WOULDN'T HAVE LOU'S MEMORIES, HER **PERSONALITY**. SHE'D BE A TOTALLY DIFFERENT PERSON WHO JUST **LOOKS** LIKE LOU.
HOW DO YOU DEFINE "HUMAN"?
GENETIC DATA? PHYSICAL CHARACTER-ISTICS? IS IT THE **TANGIBLE...**
...OR IS HUMANITY MORE ELUSIVE BY FAR?
THE BRAIN, THE BODY—EACH CAN BE REPLACED BY A MACHINE. BUT **MEMORY, PERSONALITY...**
...THAT'S WHAT MAKES A HUMAN BEING!
AND WHEN THIS DATA HAS DISSIPATED, WE CALL IT... **"DEATH."**

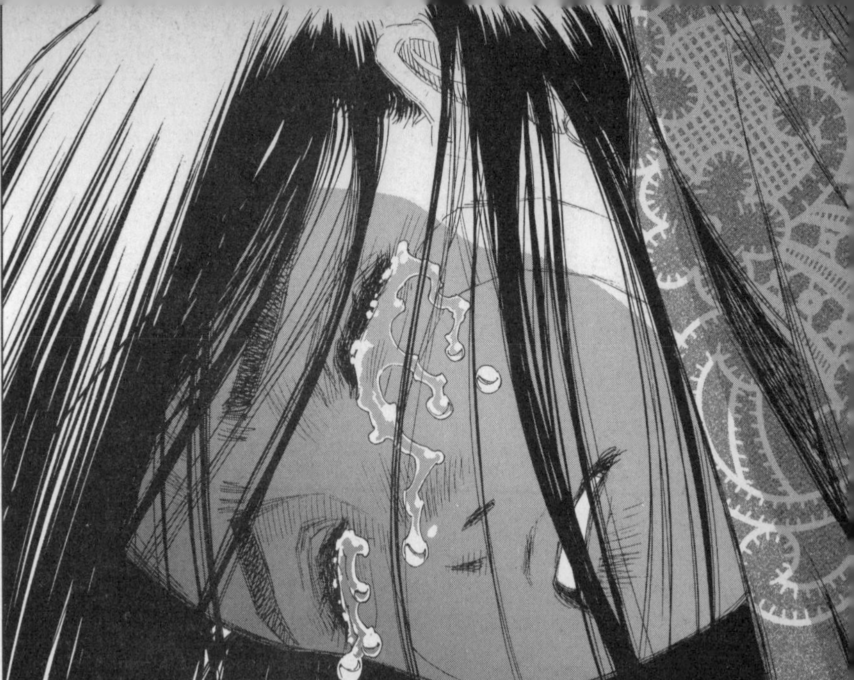

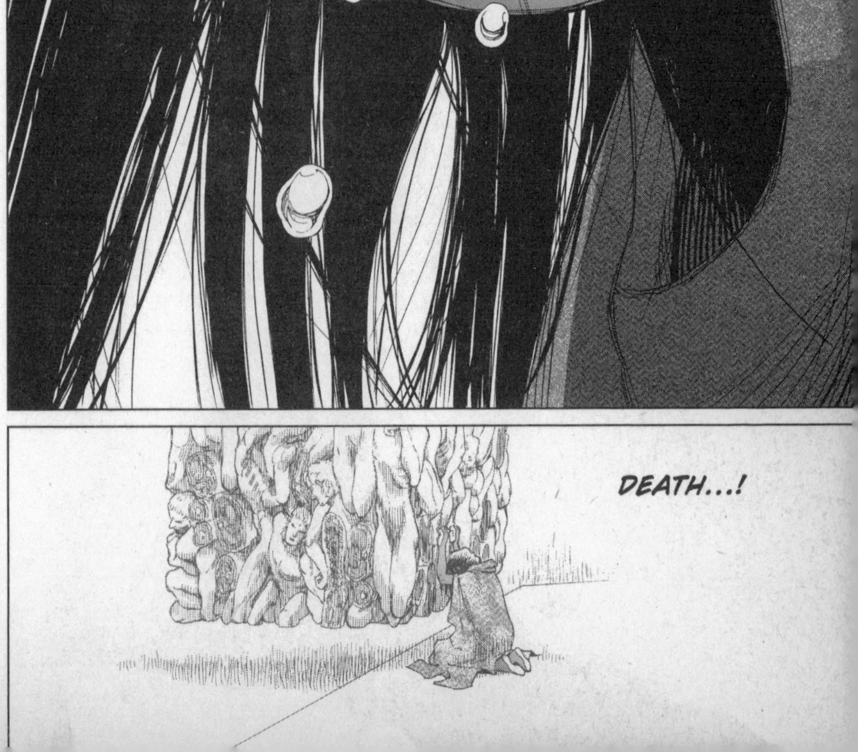
DEATH...!

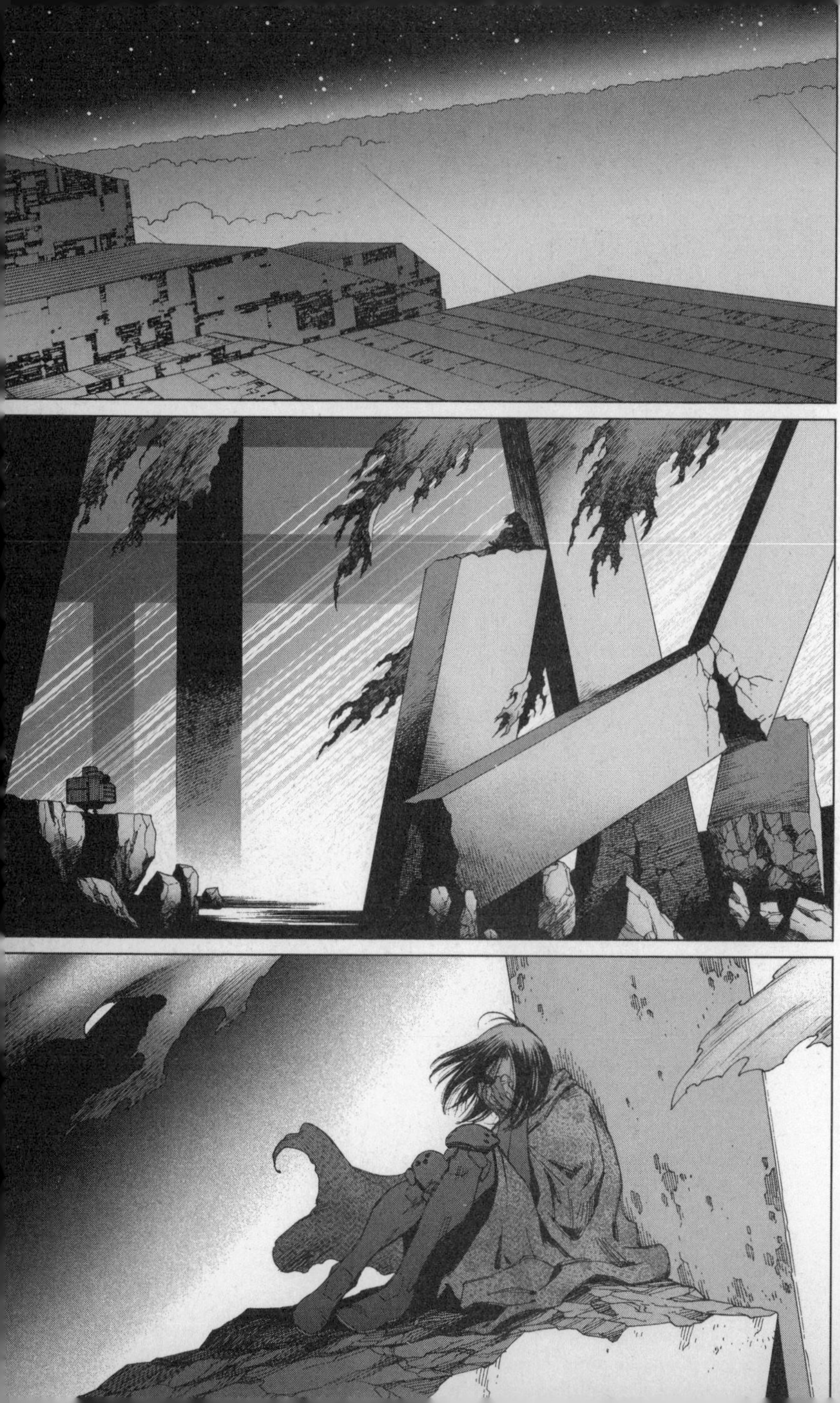

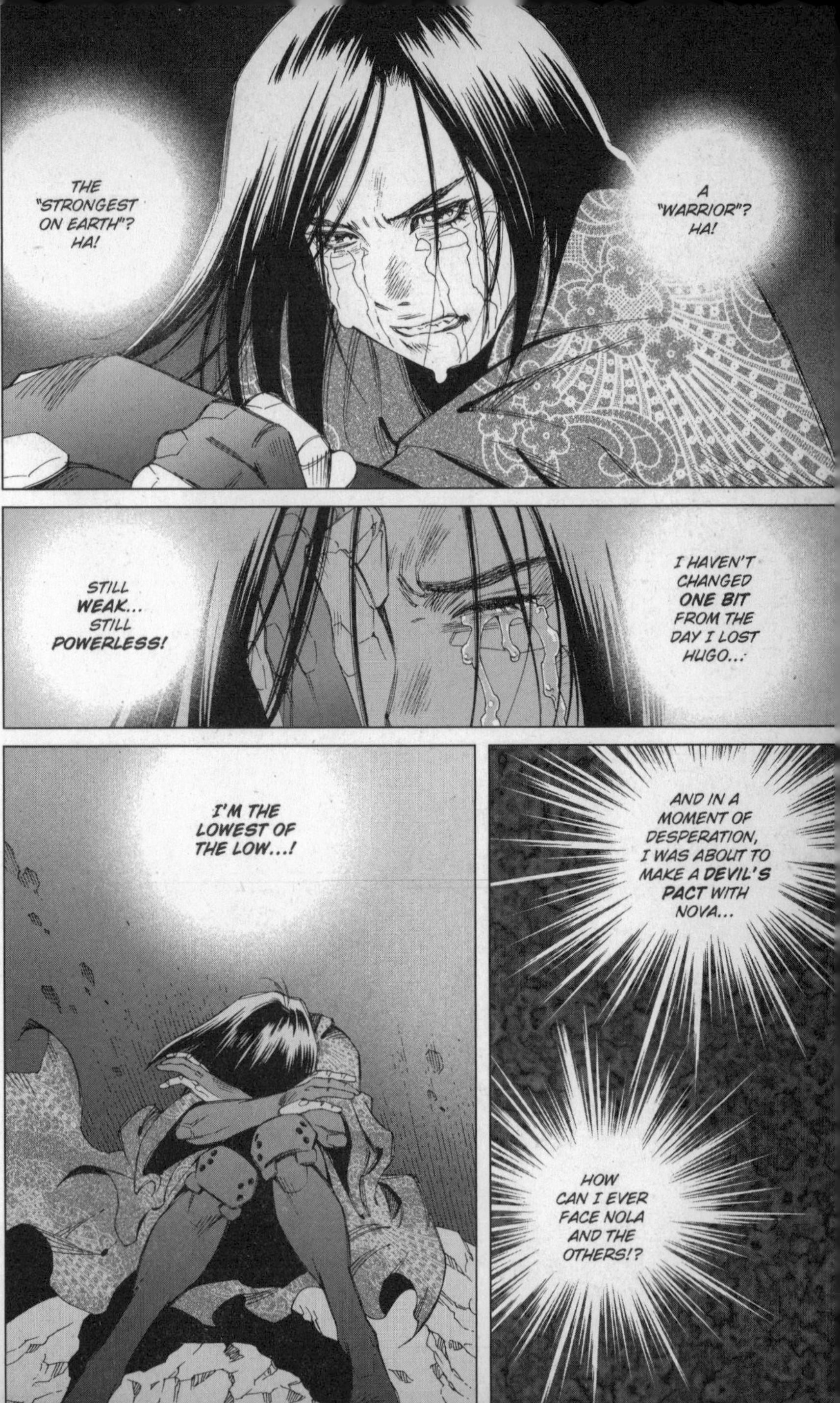
A "WARRIOR"? HA!
THE "STRONGEST ON EARTH"? HA!
I HAVEN'T CHANGED ONE BIT FROM THE DAY I LOST HUGO...
STILL WEAK... STILL POWERLESS!
AND IN A MOMENT OF DESPERATION, I WAS ABOUT TO MAKE A DEVIL'S PACT WITH NOVA...
HOW CAN I EVER FACE NOLA AND THE OTHERS!?
I'M THE LOWEST OF THE LOW...!

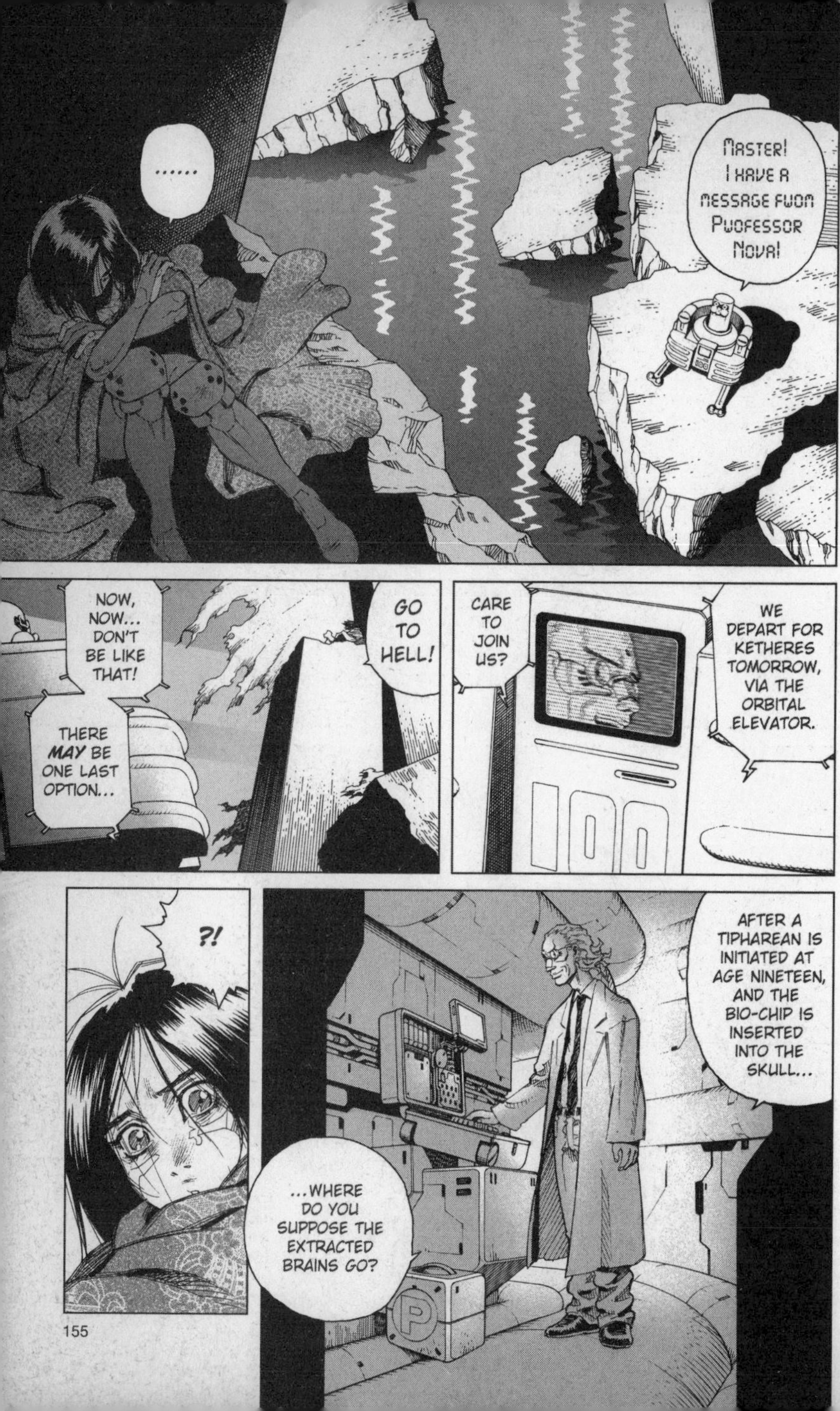
Master! I have a message fwom Pwofessor Nova!
......
WE DEPART FOR KETHERES TOMORROW, VIA THE ORBITAL ELEVATOR.
CARE TO JOIN US?
GO TO HELL!
NOW, NOW... DON'T BE LIKE THAT!
THERE *MAY* BE ONE LAST OPTION...
AFTER A TIPHAREAN IS INITIATED AT AGE NINETEEN, AND THE BIO-CHIP IS INSERTED INTO THE SKULL...
...WHERE DO YOU SUPPOSE THE EXTRACTED BRAINS GO?
?!

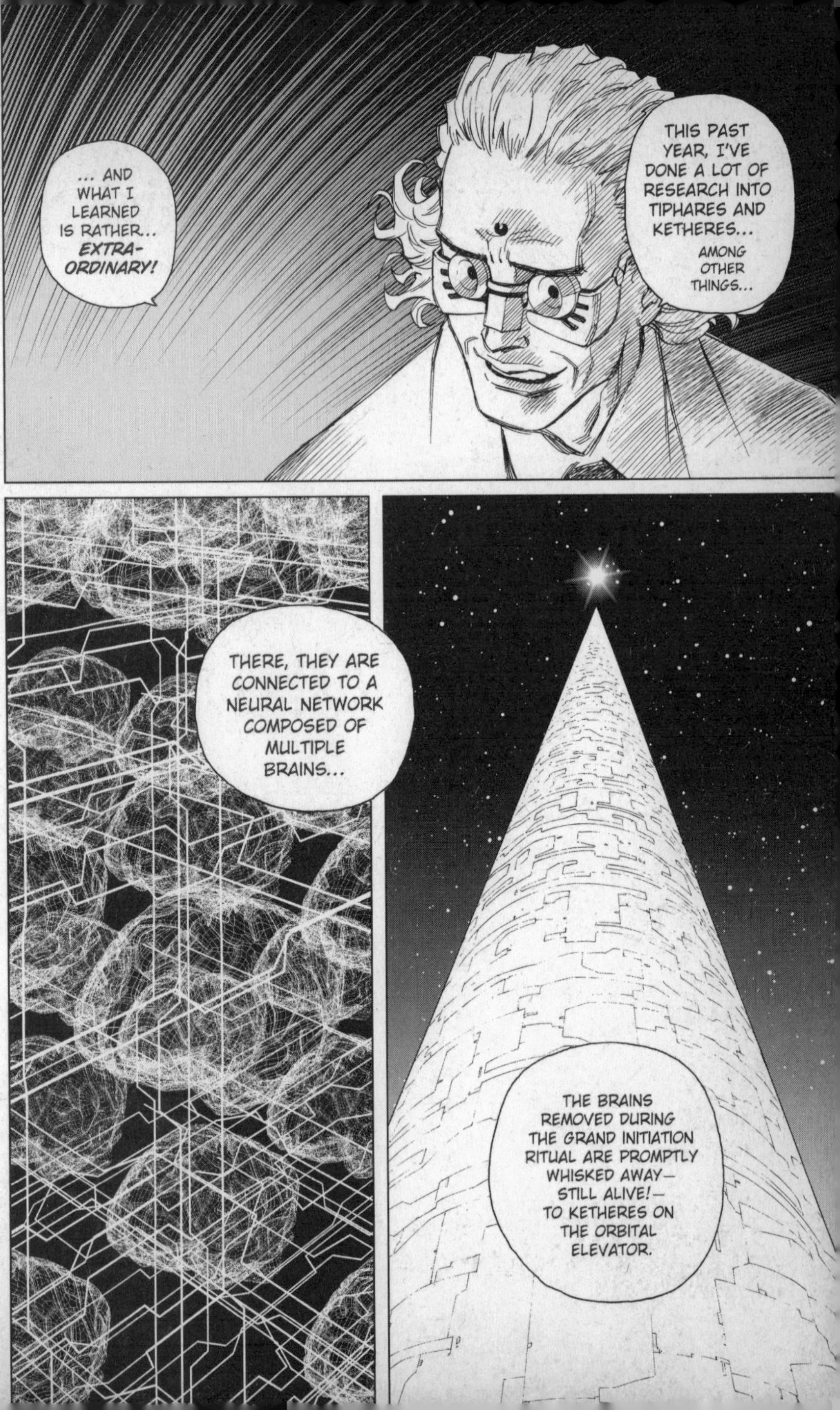
THIS PAST YEAR, I'VE DONE A LOT OF RESEARCH INTO TIPHARES AND KETHERES...
AMONG OTHER THINGS...
... AND WHAT I LEARNED IS RATHER... *EXTRA-ORDINARY!*
THE BRAINS REMOVED DURING THE GRAND INITIATION RITUAL ARE PROMPTLY WHISKED AWAY— STILL ALIVE!— TO KETHERES ON THE ORBITAL ELEVATOR.
THERE, THEY ARE CONNECTED TO A NEURAL NETWORK COMPOSED OF MULTIPLE BRAINS...

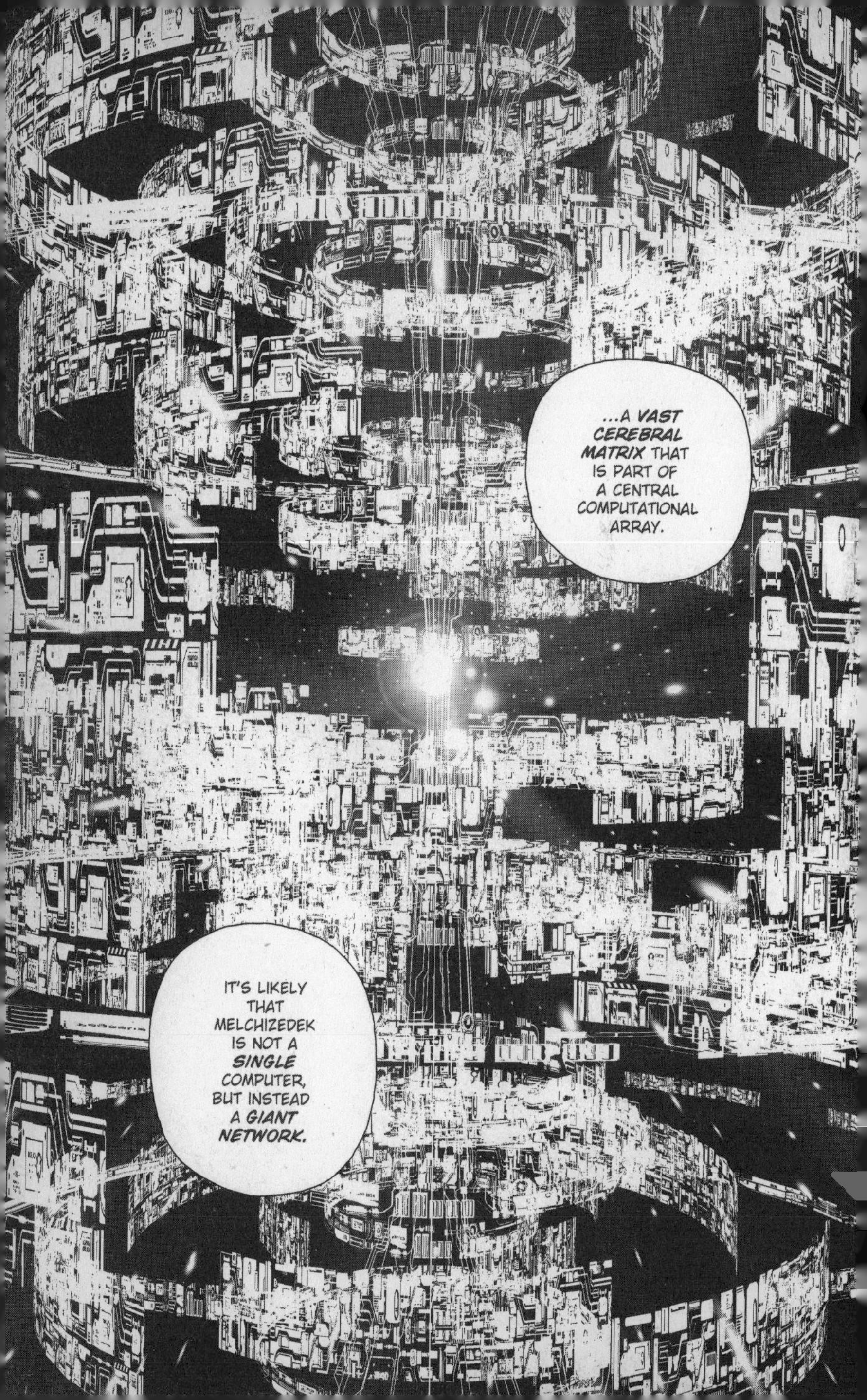
...A **VAST CEREBRAL MATRIX** THAT IS PART OF A CENTRAL COMPUTATIONAL ARRAY.
IT'S LIKELY THAT MELCHIZEDEK IS NOT A **SINGLE** COMPUTER, BUT INSTEAD A **GIANT NETWORK.**

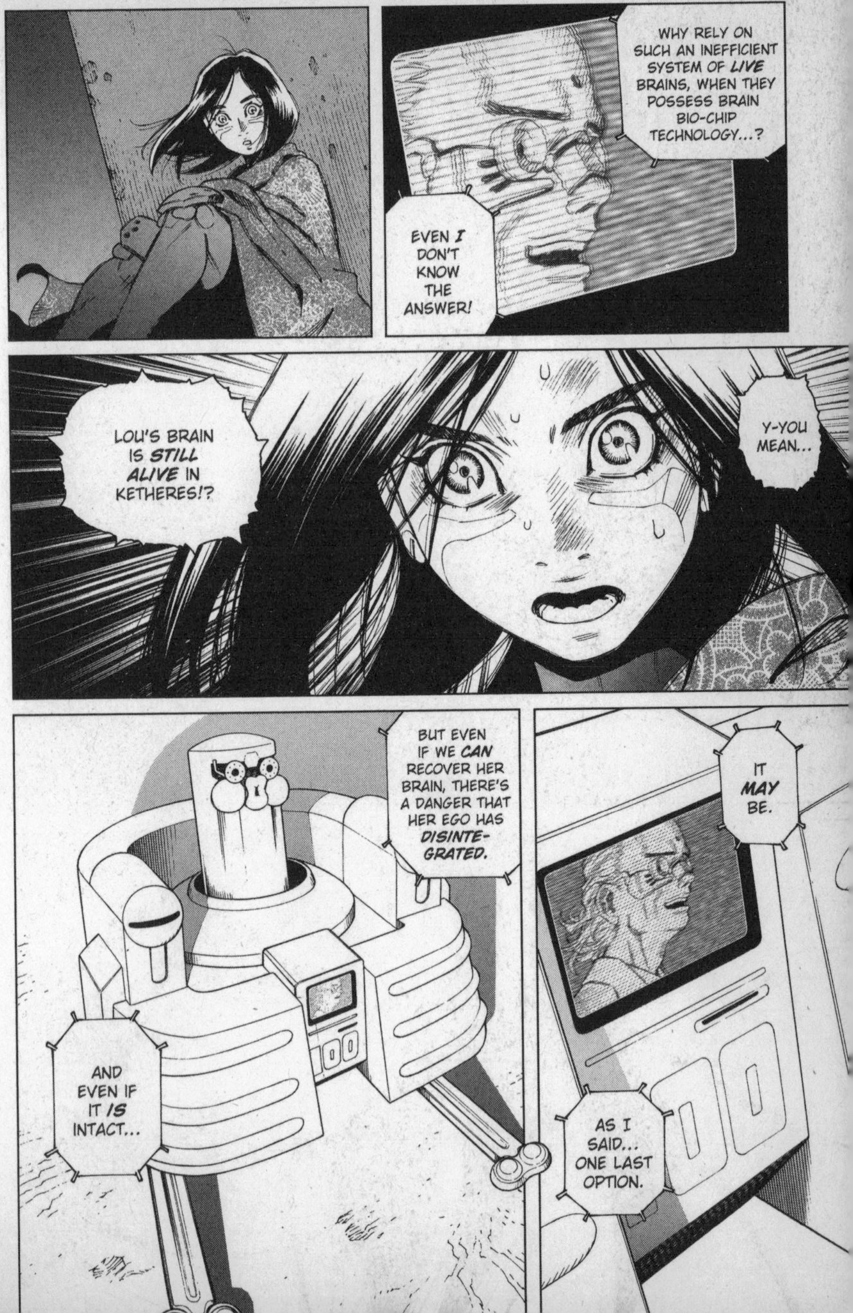
WHY RELY ON SUCH AN INEFFICIENT SYSTEM OF LIVE BRAINS, WHEN THEY POSSESS BRAIN BIO-CHIP TECHNOLOGY...?
EVEN I DON'T KNOW THE ANSWER!
Y-YOU MEAN...
LOU'S BRAIN IS STILL ALIVE IN KETHERES!?
IT MAY BE.
AS I SAID... ONE LAST OPTION.
BUT EVEN IF WE CAN RECOVER HER BRAIN, THERE'S A DANGER THAT HER EGO HAS DISINTEGRATED.
AND EVEN IF IT IS INTACT...

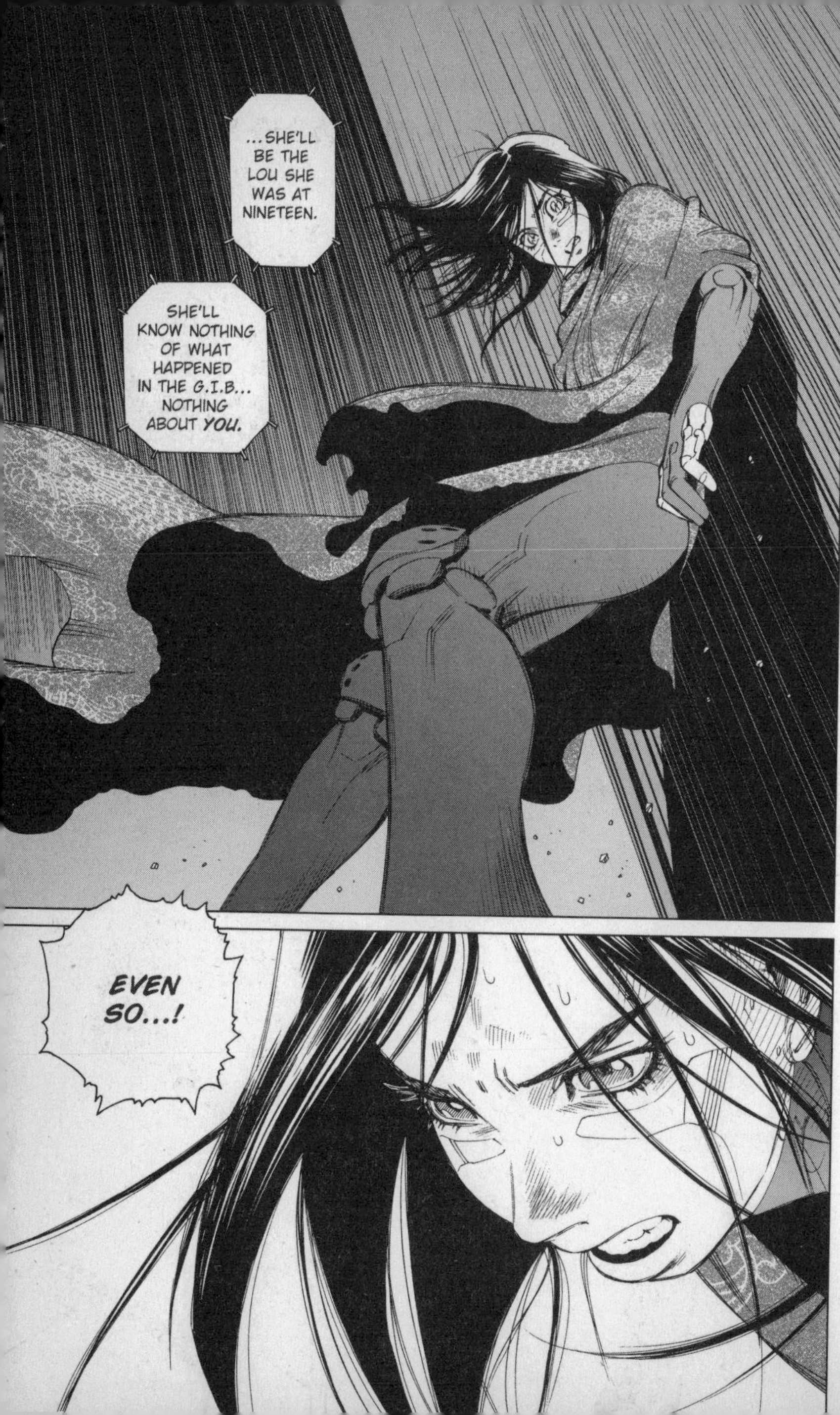
...SHE'LL BE THE LOU SHE WAS AT NINETEEN.
SHE'LL KNOW NOTHING OF WHAT HAPPENED IN THE G.I.B... NOTHING ABOUT *YOU.*
EVEN SO...!

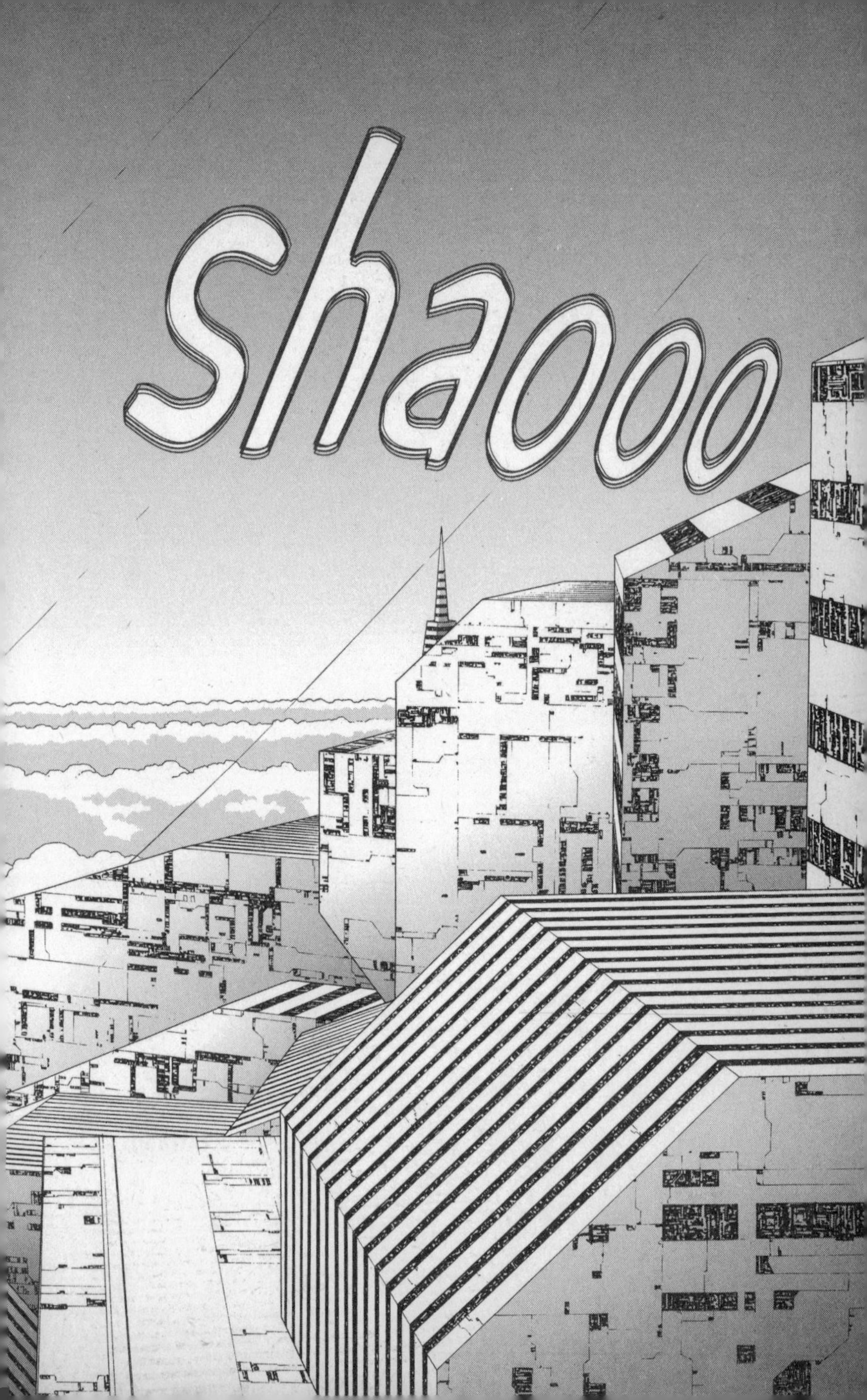
Shaooo

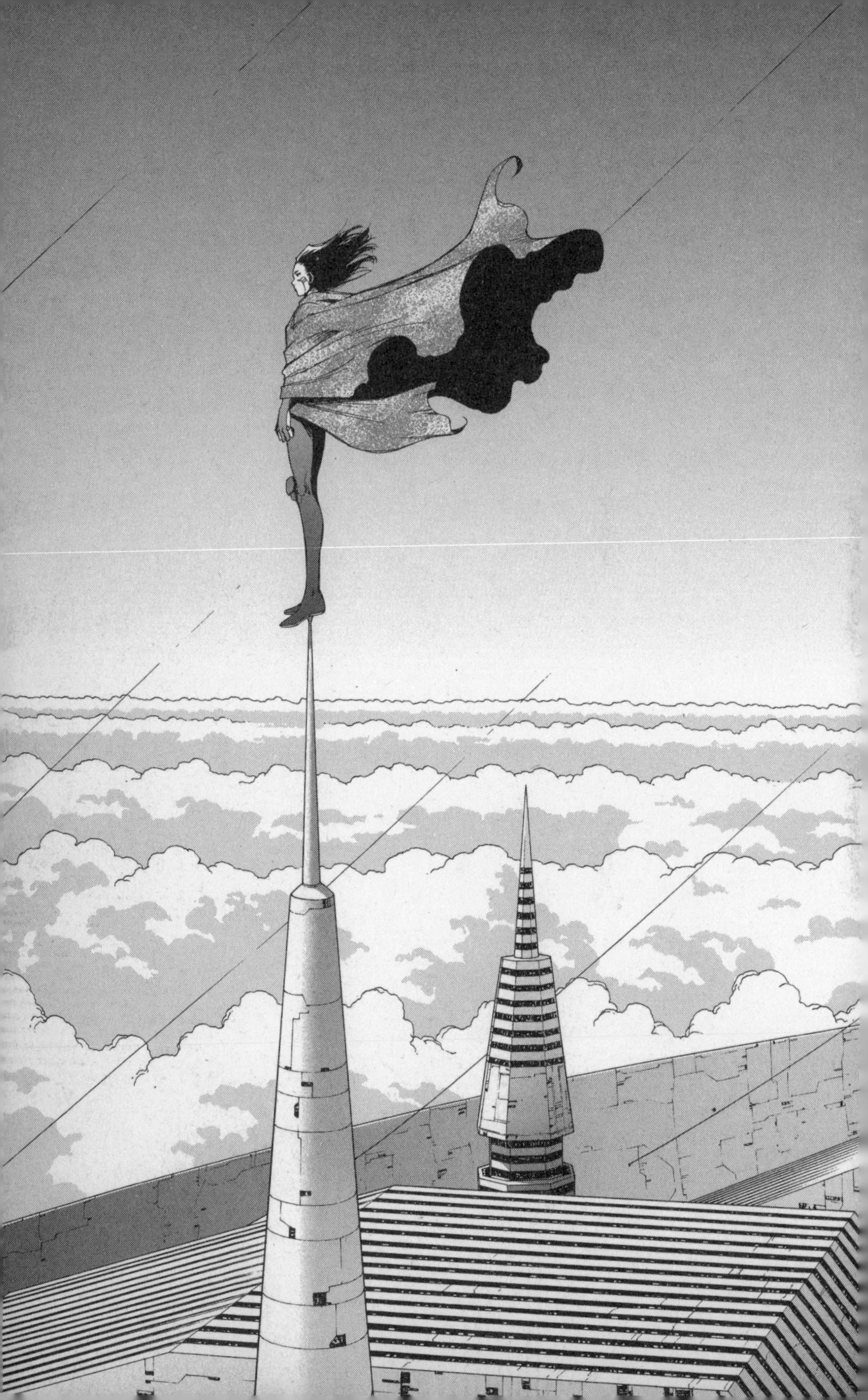

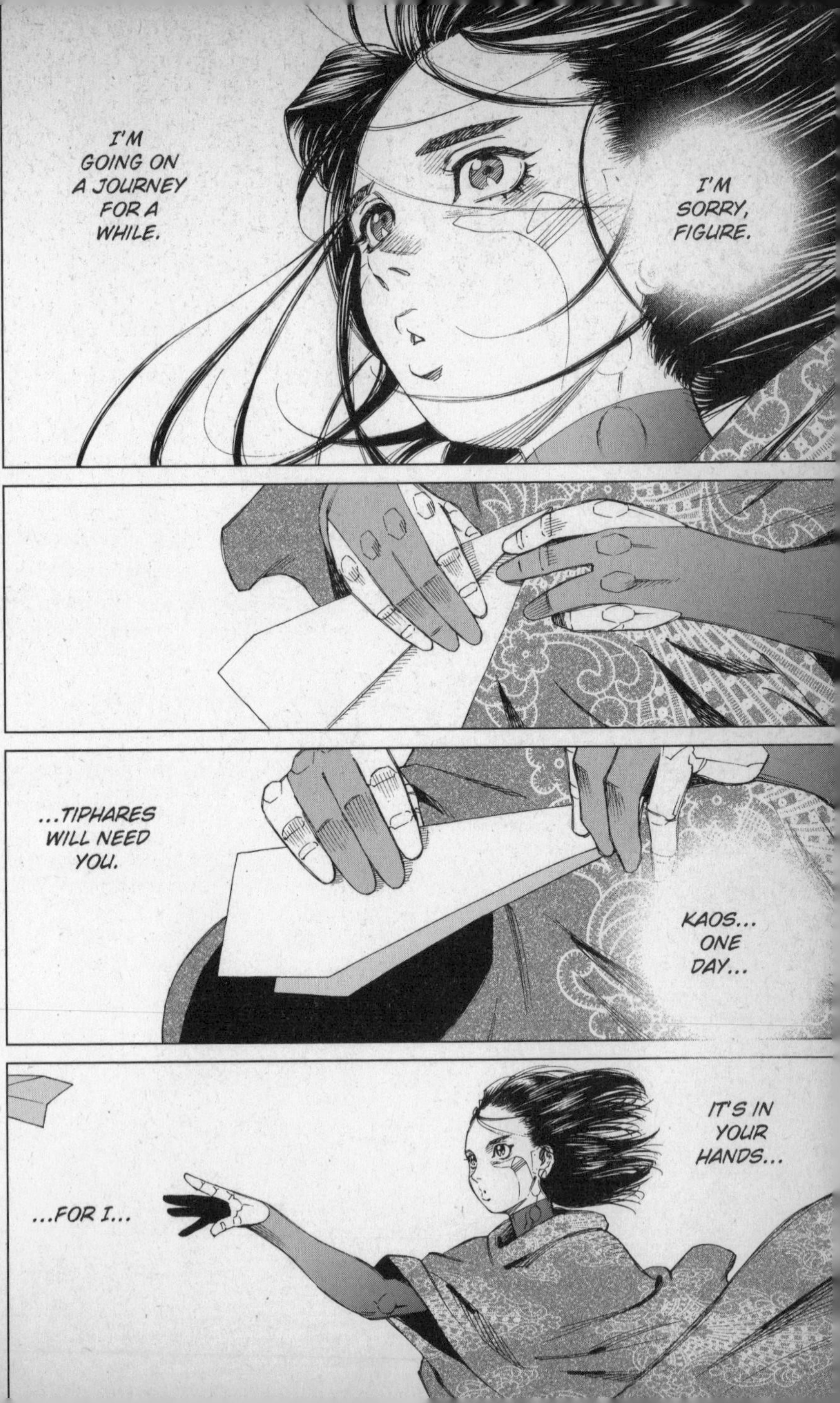
I'M SORRY, FIGURE.
I'M GOING ON A JOURNEY FOR A WHILE.
KAOS... ONE DAY...
...TIPHARES WILL NEED YOU.
IT'S IN YOUR HANDS...
...FOR I...

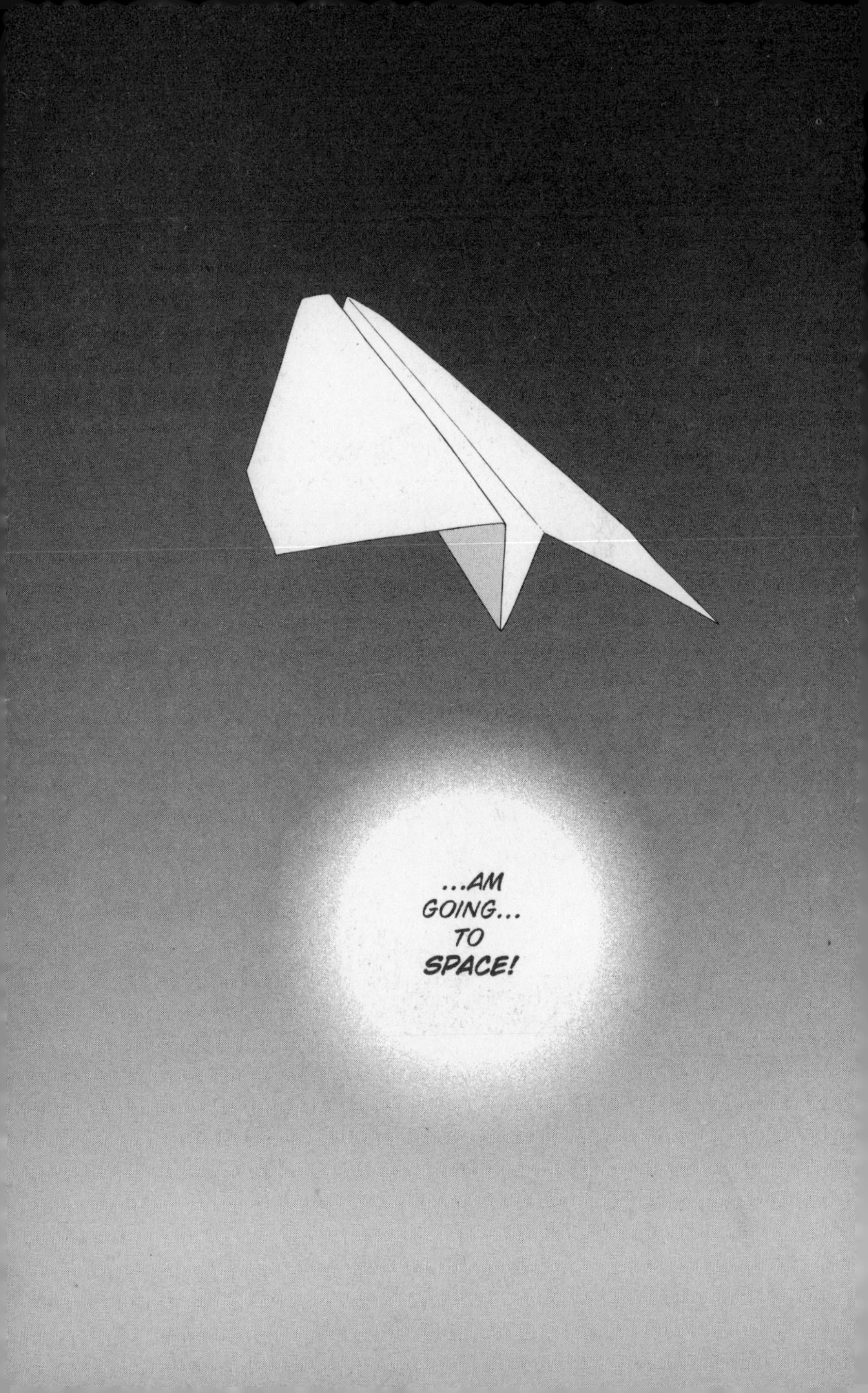
...AM GOING... TO SPACE!

PHASE 12

How Grave a Sin It Is to Dream

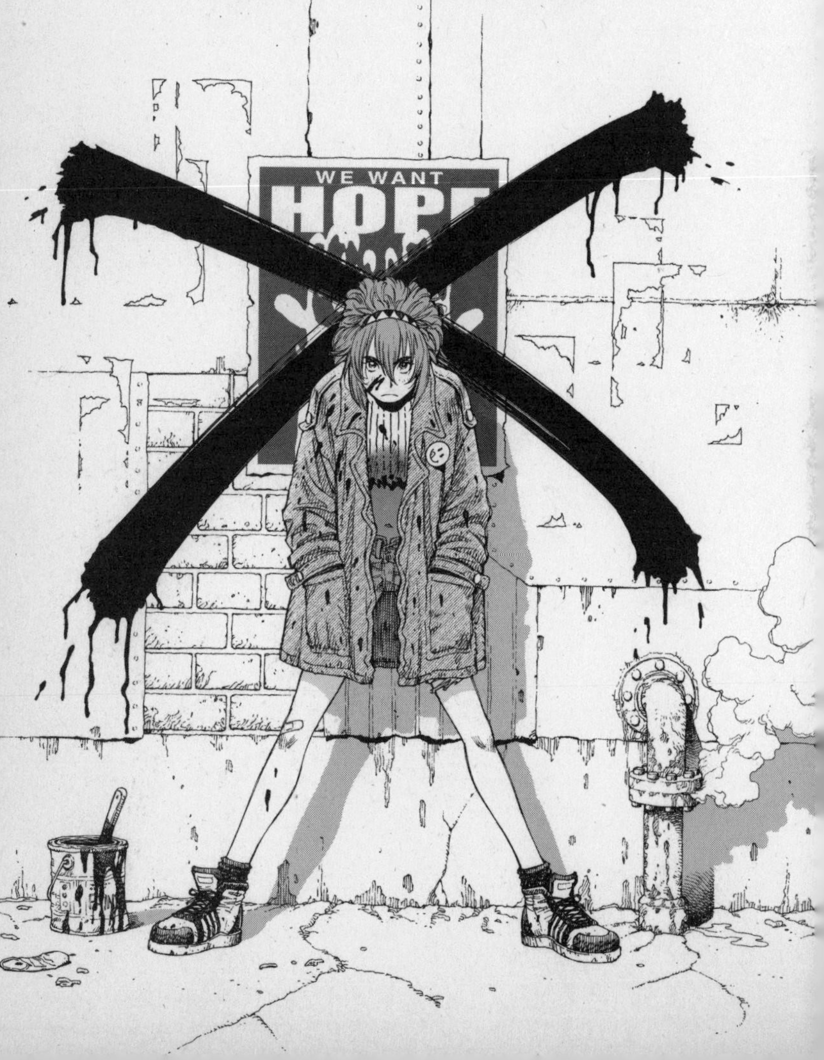
WE WANT
HOPE

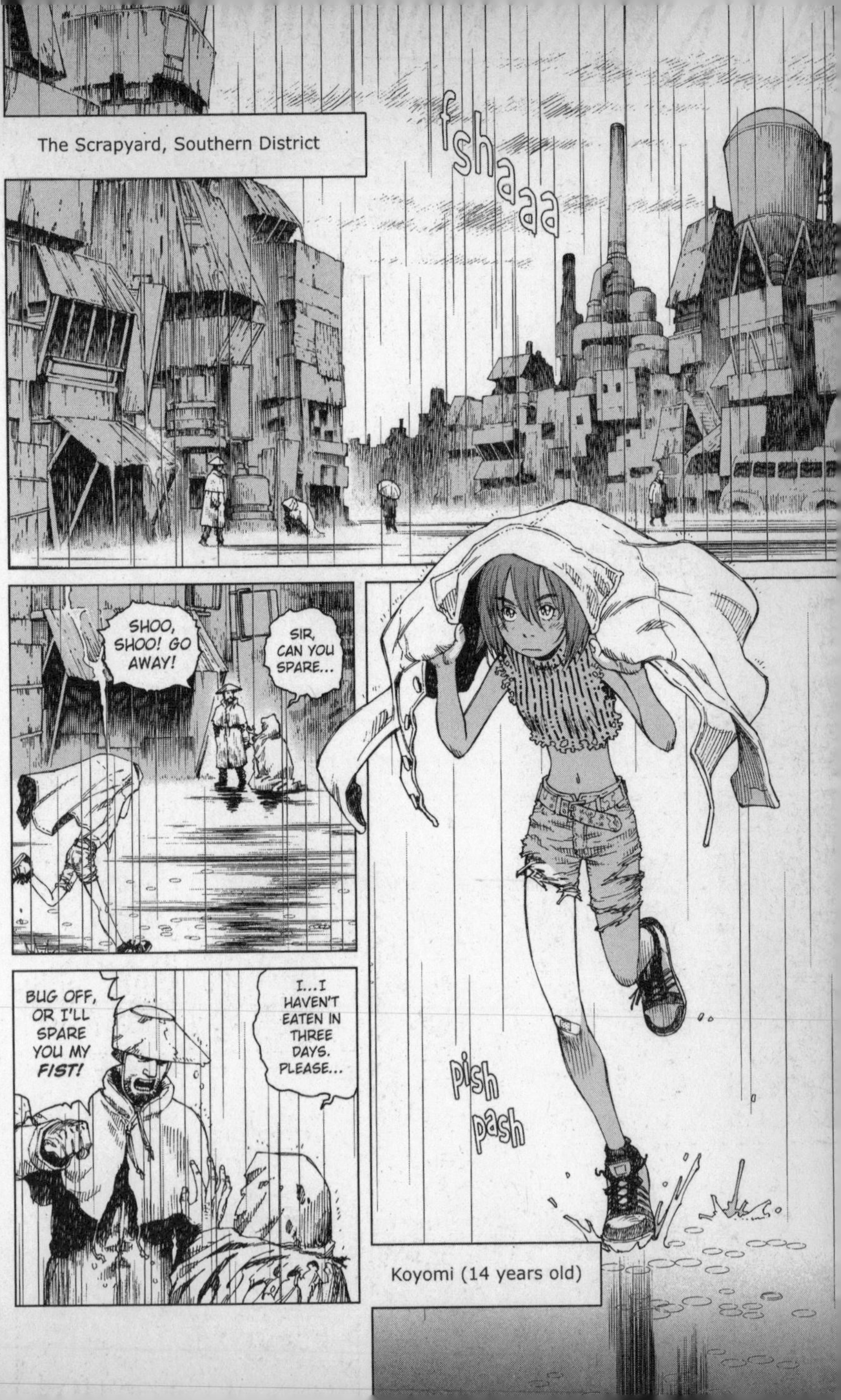
fshaaa
The Scrapyard, Southern District
pish pash
Koyomi (14 years old)
SIR, CAN YOU SPARE...
SHOO, SHOO! GO AWAY!
I...I HAVEN'T EATEN IN THREE DAYS. PLEASE...
BUG OFF, OR I'LL SPARE YOU MY *FIST!*

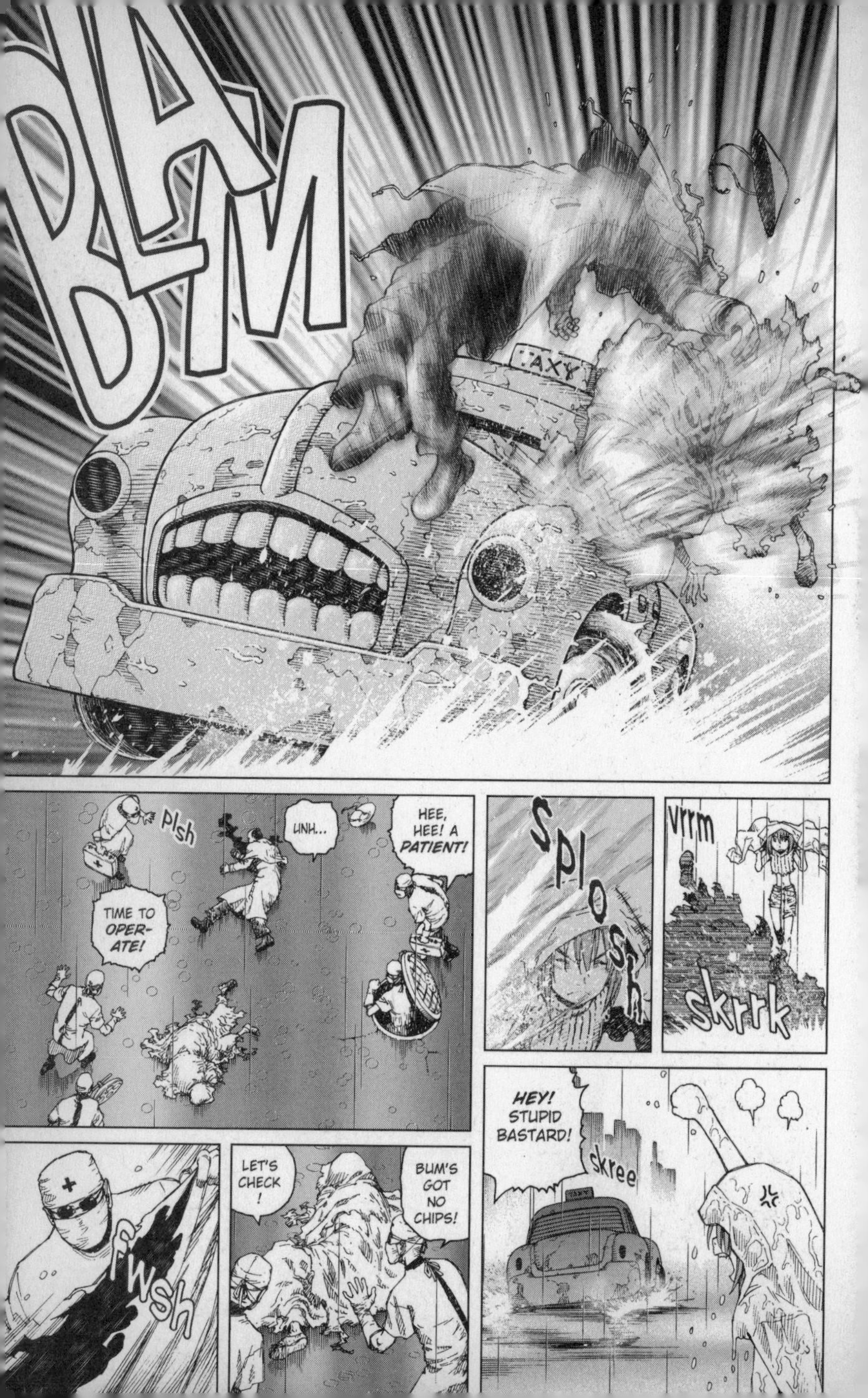
vrrm
skrrk
splosh
HEE, HEE! A PATIENT!
UNH...
plsh
TIME TO OPERATE!
HEY! STUPID BASTARD!
skree
BUM'S GOT NO CHIPS!
LET'S CHECK!
fwsh

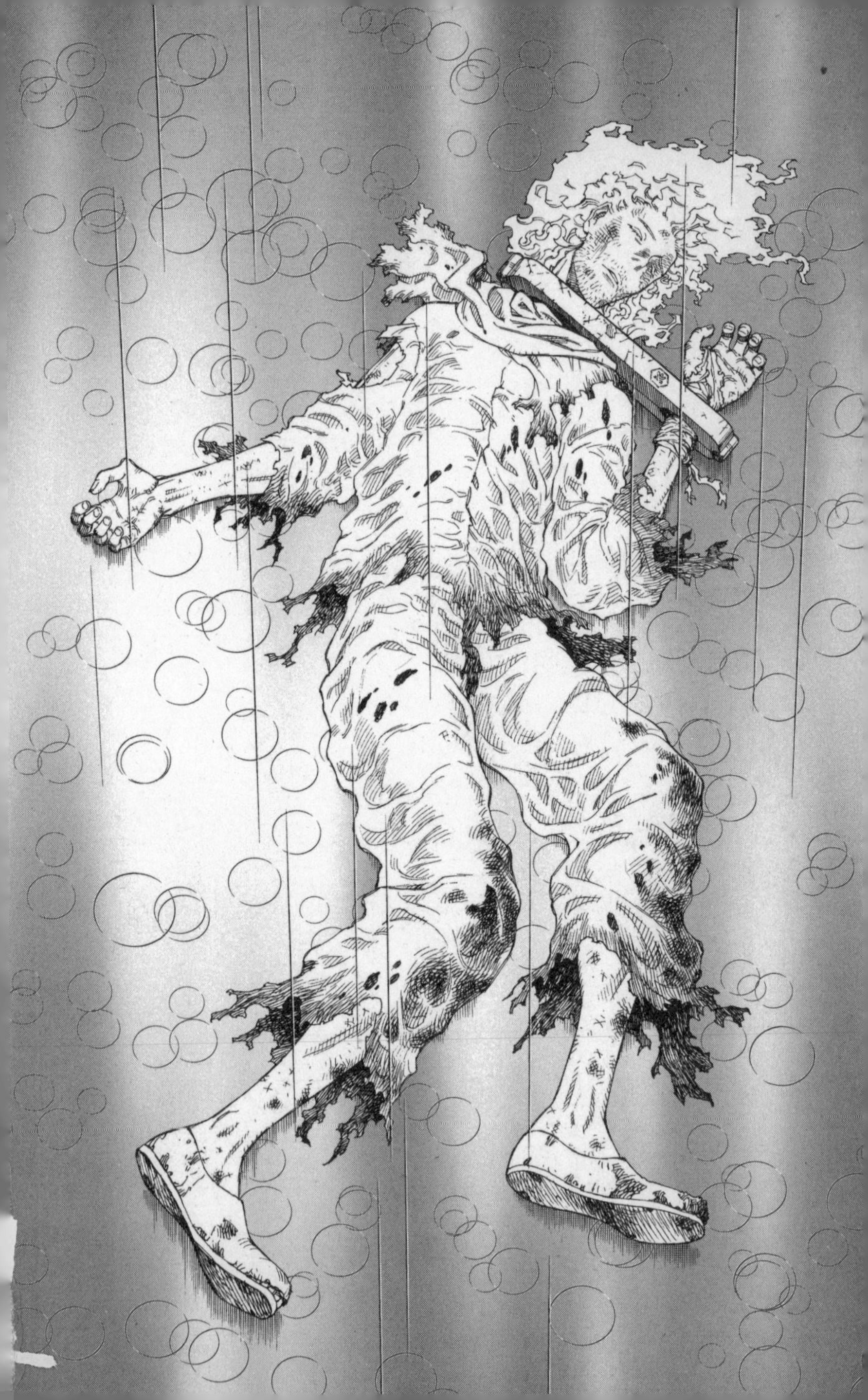

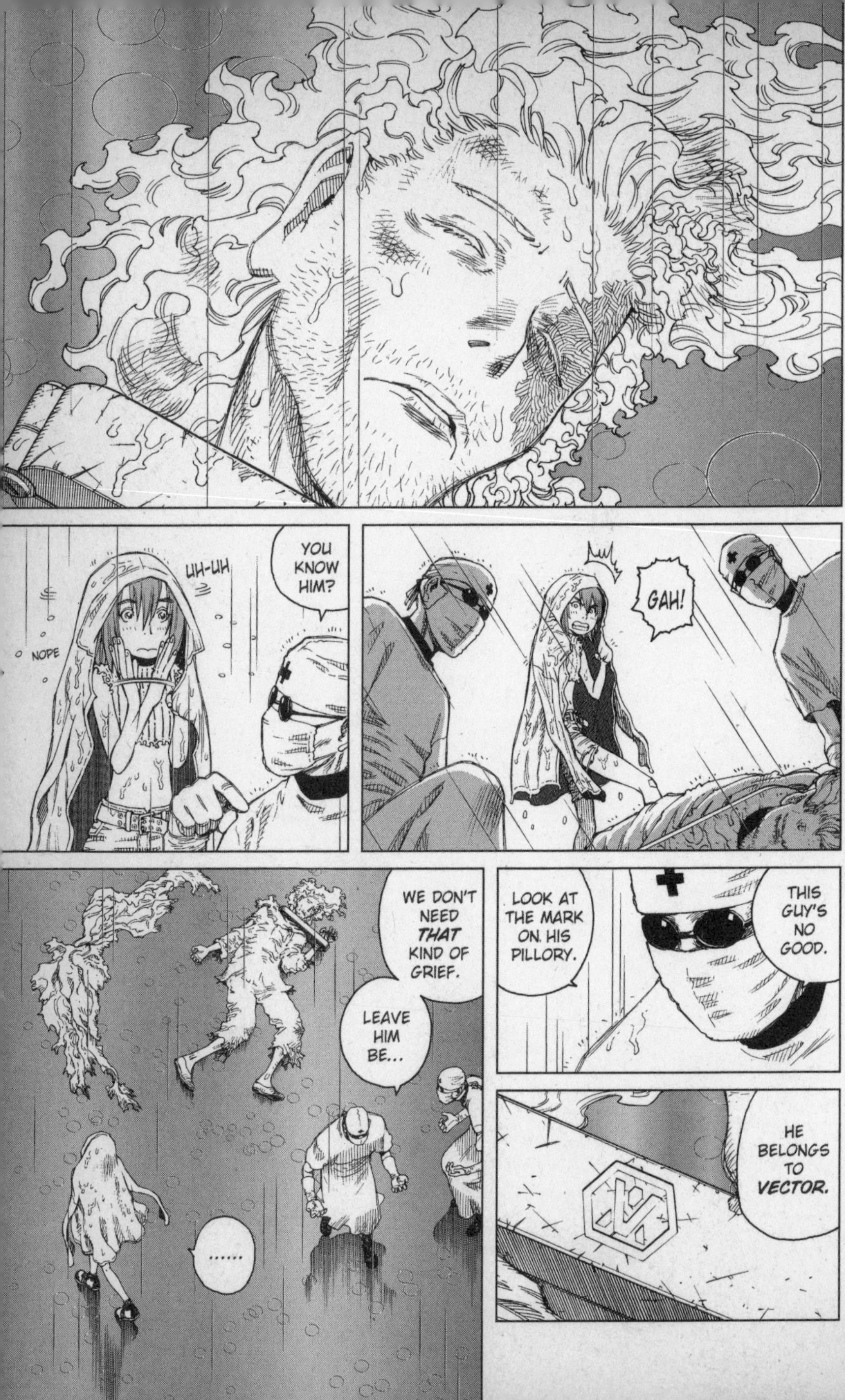
GAH!
YOU KNOW HIM?
UH-UH
NOPE
THIS GUY'S NO GOOD.
LOOK AT THE MARK ON. HIS PILLORY.
HE BELONGS TO VECTOR.
WE DON'T NEED THAT KIND OF GRIEF.
LEAVE HIM BE...
......

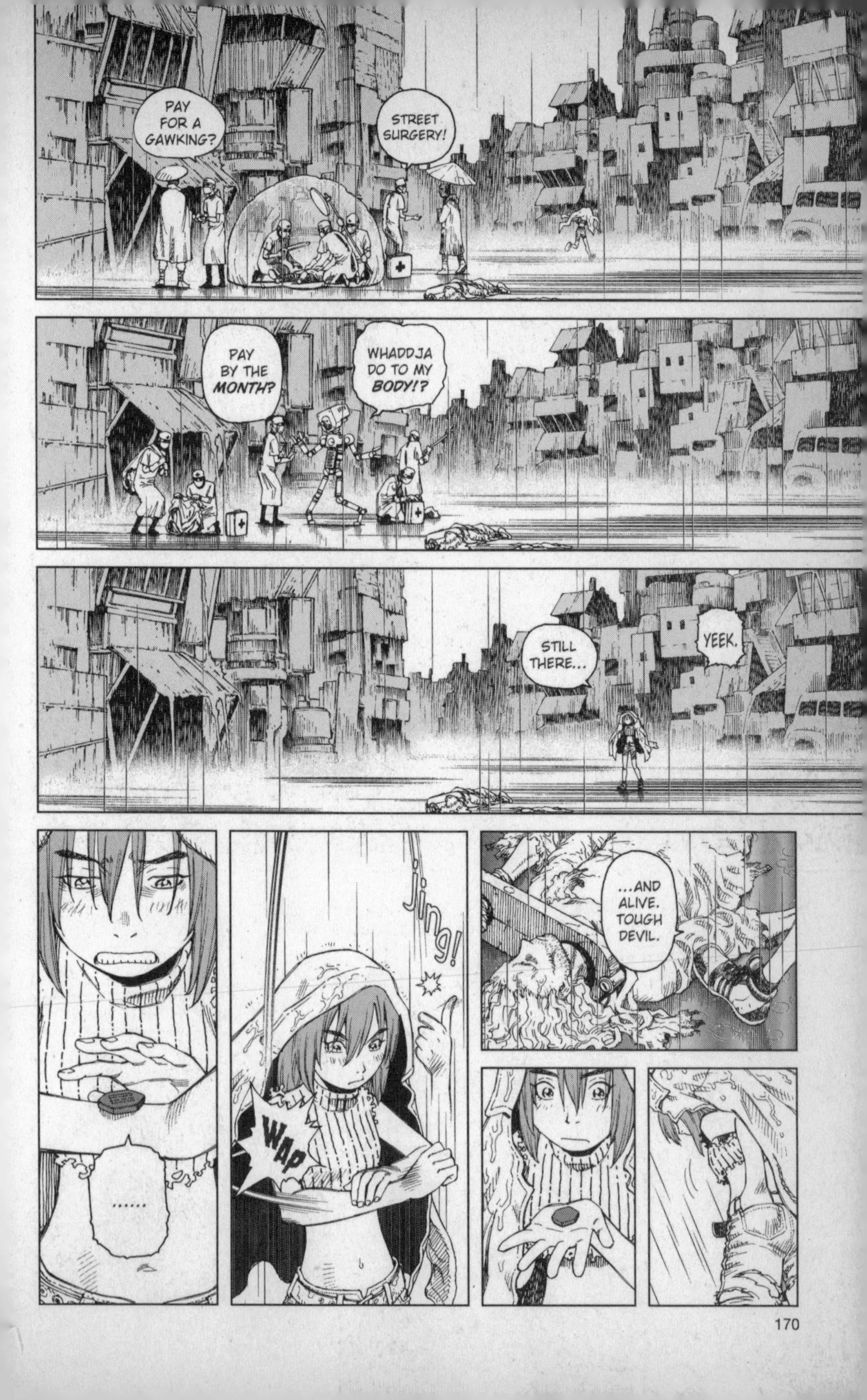
STREET SURGERY!
PAY FOR A GAWKING?
WHADDJA DO TO MY BODY!?
PAY BY THE MONTH?
YEEK.
STILL THERE...
...AND ALIVE. TOUGH DEVIL.
Jing!
WAP
......

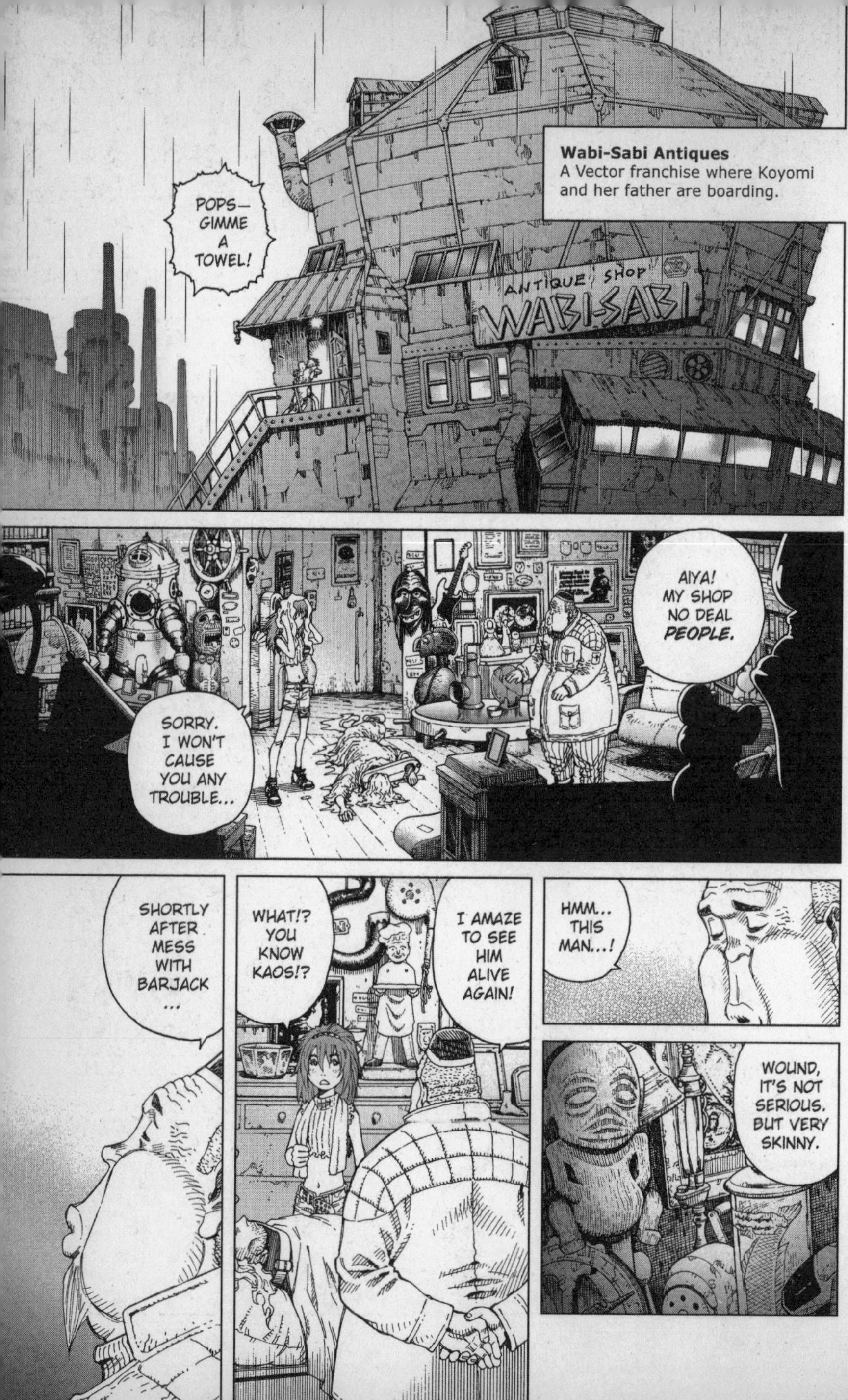
Wabi-Sabi Antiques
A Vector franchise where Koyomi and her father are boarding.
ANTIQUE SHOP WABI-SABI
POPS— GIMME A TOWEL!
AIYA! MY SHOP NO DEAL *PEOPLE.*
SORRY. I WON'T CAUSE YOU ANY TROUBLE...
HMM.. THIS MAN...!
WOUND, IT'S NOT SERIOUS. BUT VERY SKINNY.
I AMAZE TO SEE HIM ALIVE AGAIN!
WHAT!? YOU KNOW KAOS!?
SHORTLY AFTER MESS WITH BARJACK ...

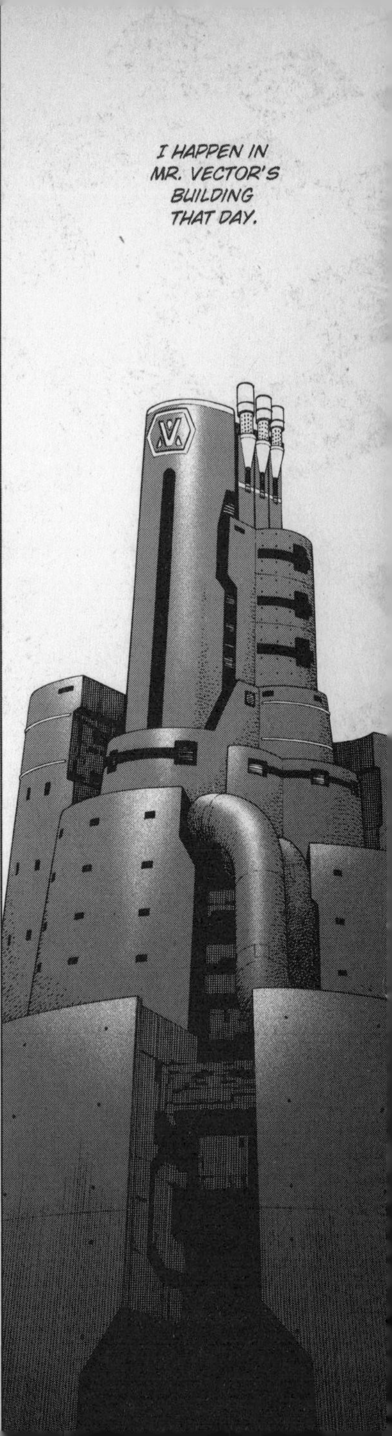
I HAPPEN IN MR. VECTOR'S BUILDING THAT DAY.

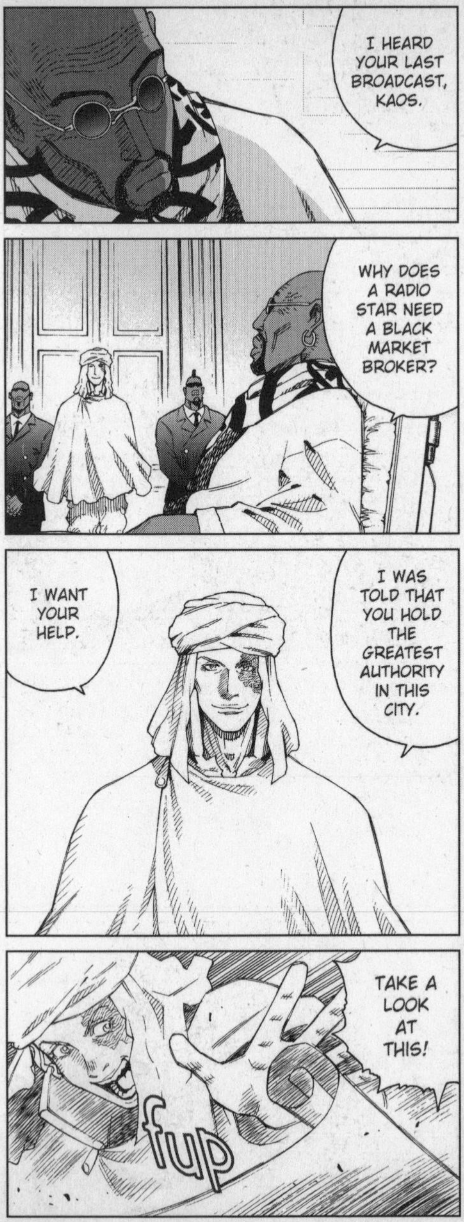
I HEARD YOUR LAST BROADCAST, KAOS.
WHY DOES A RADIO STAR NEED A BLACK MARKET BROKER?
I WAS TOLD THAT YOU HOLD THE GREATEST AUTHORITY IN THIS CITY.
I WANT YOUR HELP.
TAKE A LOOK AT THIS!
fup

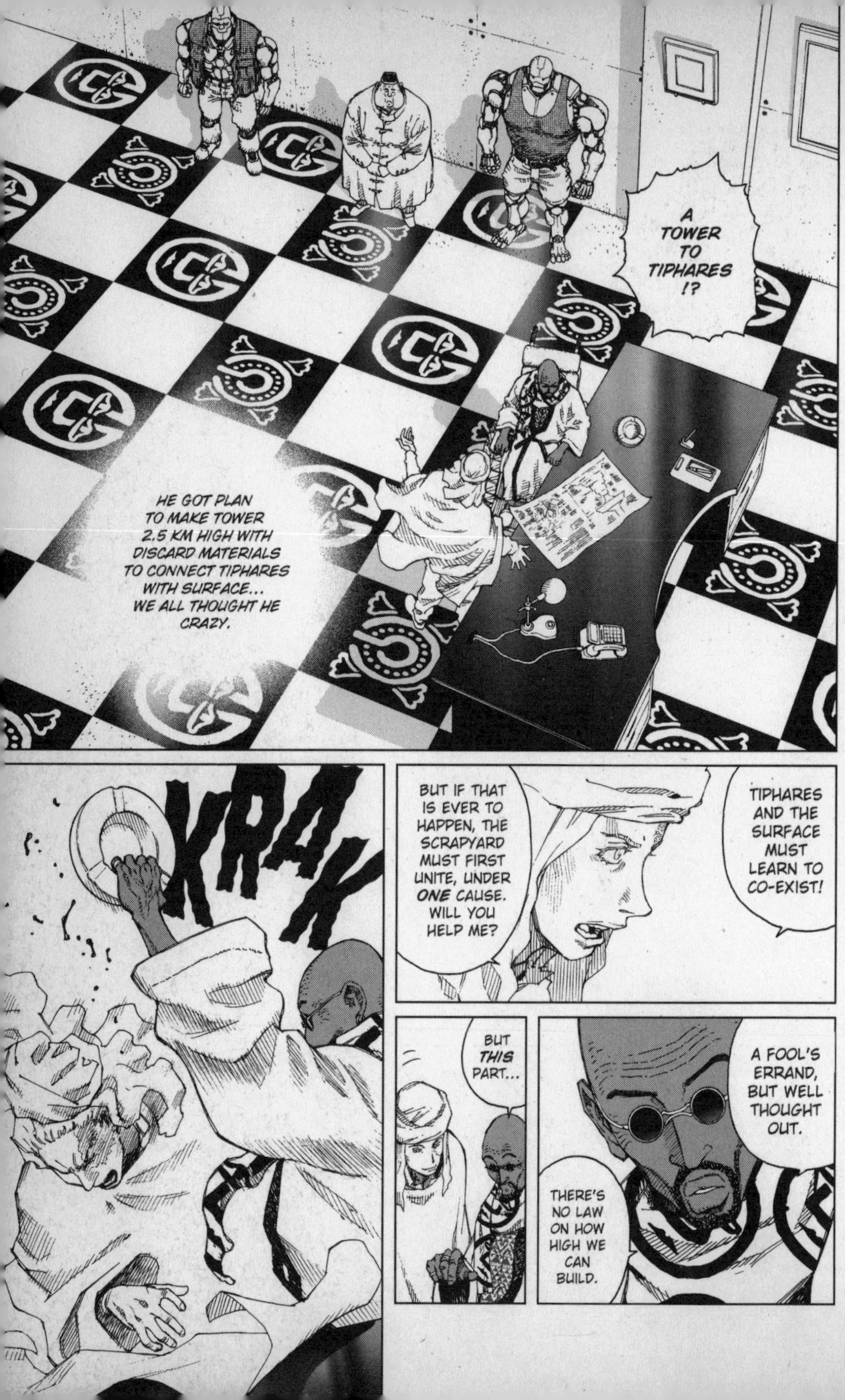
A TOWER TO TIPHARES !?
HE GOT PLAN TO MAKE TOWER 2.5 KM HIGH WITH DISCARD MATERIALS TO CONNECT TIPHARES WITH SURFACE... WE ALL THOUGHT HE CRAZY.
TIPHARES AND THE SURFACE MUST LEARN TO CO-EXIST!
BUT IF THAT IS EVER TO HAPPEN, THE SCRAPYARD MUST FIRST UNITE, UNDER ONE CAUSE. WILL YOU HELP ME?
A FOOL'S ERRAND, BUT WELL THOUGHT OUT.
THERE'S NO LAW ON HOW HIGH WE CAN BUILD.
BUT THIS PART...
KRAK

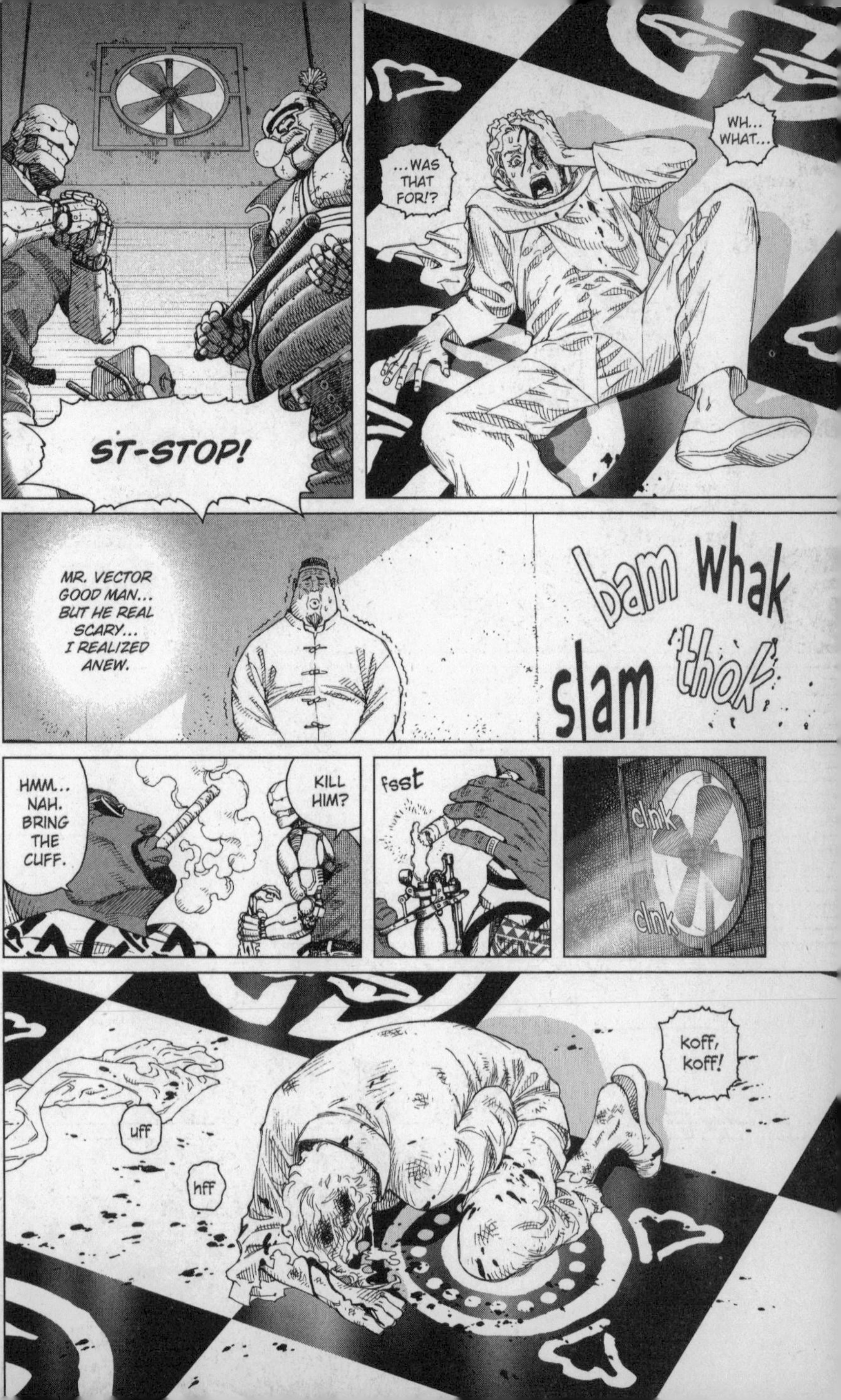
WH... WHAT...
...WAS THAT FOR!?
ST-STOP!
bam whak
slam thok
MR. VECTOR GOOD MAN... BUT HE REAL SCARY... I REALIZED ANEW.
clnk
clnk
fsst
KILL HIM?
HMM... NAH. BRING THE CUFF.
koff, koff!
uff
hff

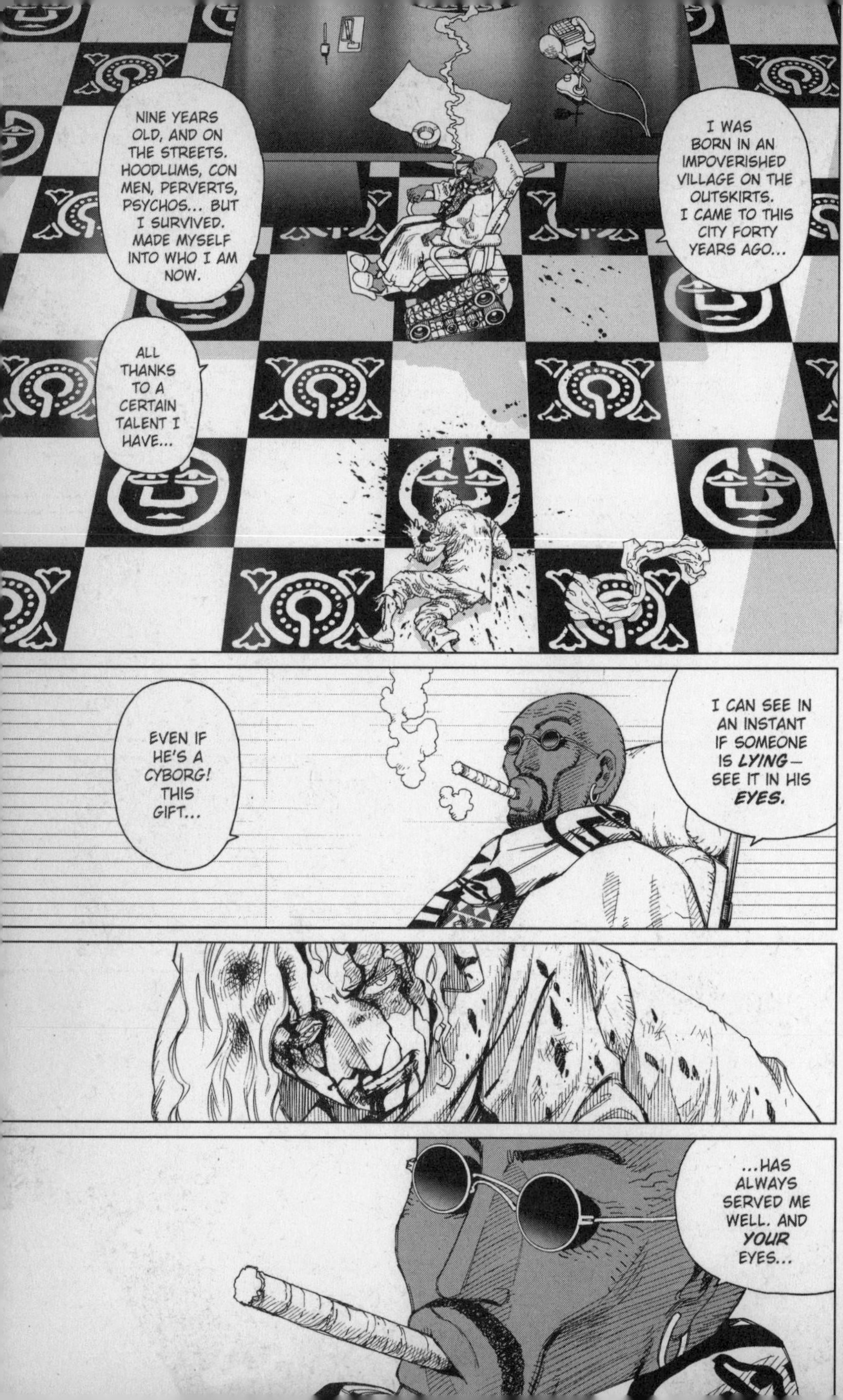
I WAS BORN IN AN IMPOVERISHED VILLAGE ON THE OUTSKIRTS. I CAME TO THIS CITY FORTY YEARS AGO...
NINE YEARS OLD, AND ON THE STREETS. HOODLUMS, CON MEN, PERVERTS, PSYCHOS... BUT I SURVIVED. MADE MYSELF INTO WHO I AM NOW.
ALL THANKS TO A CERTAIN TALENT I HAVE...
I CAN SEE IN AN INSTANT IF SOMEONE IS *LYING*—SEE IT IN HIS ***EYES.***
EVEN IF HE'S A CYBORG! THIS GIFT...
...HAS ALWAYS SERVED ME WELL. AND ***YOUR*** EYES...

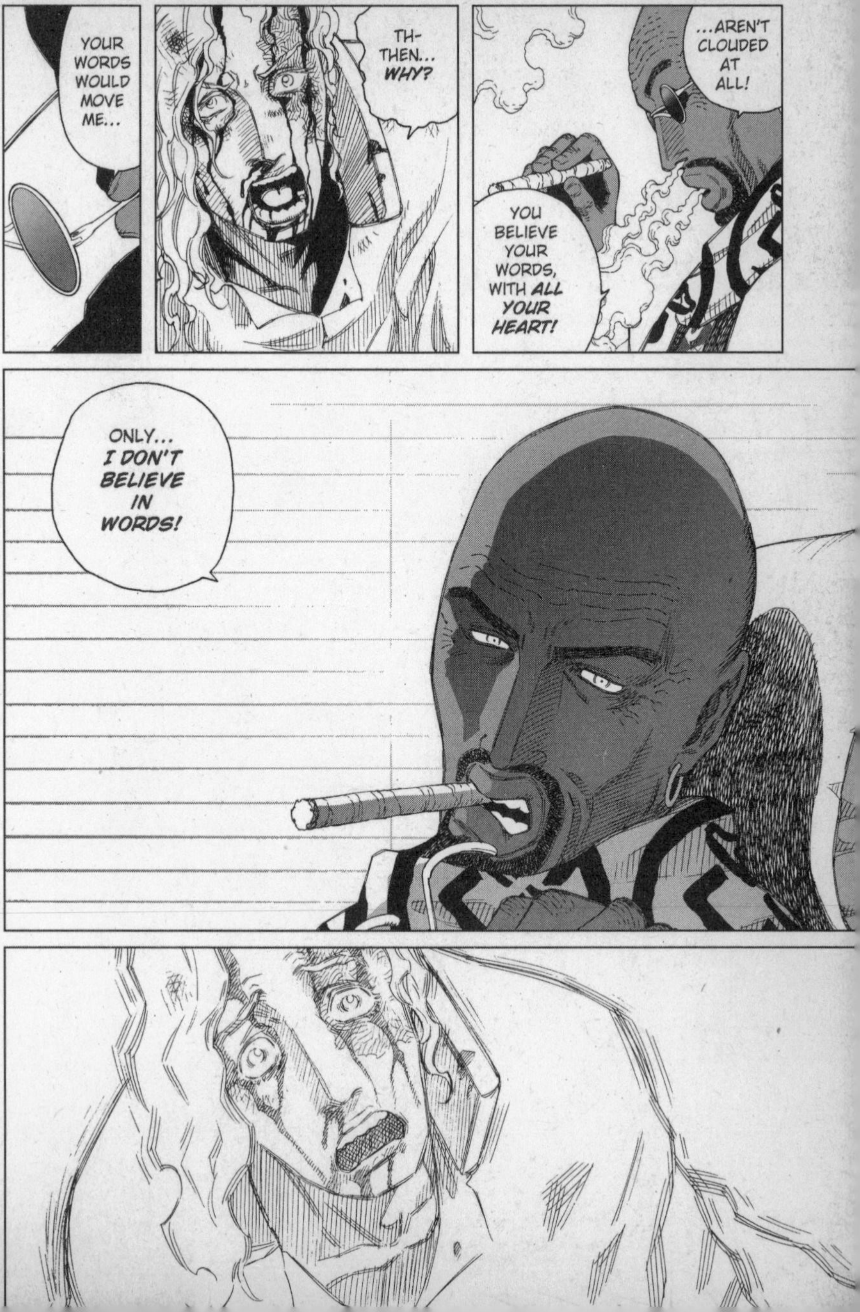
...AREN'T CLOUDED AT ALL!
YOU BELIEVE YOUR WORDS, WITH ALL YOUR HEART!
TH-THEN... WHY?
YOUR WORDS WOULD MOVE ME...
ONLY... I DON'T BELIEVE IN WORDS!

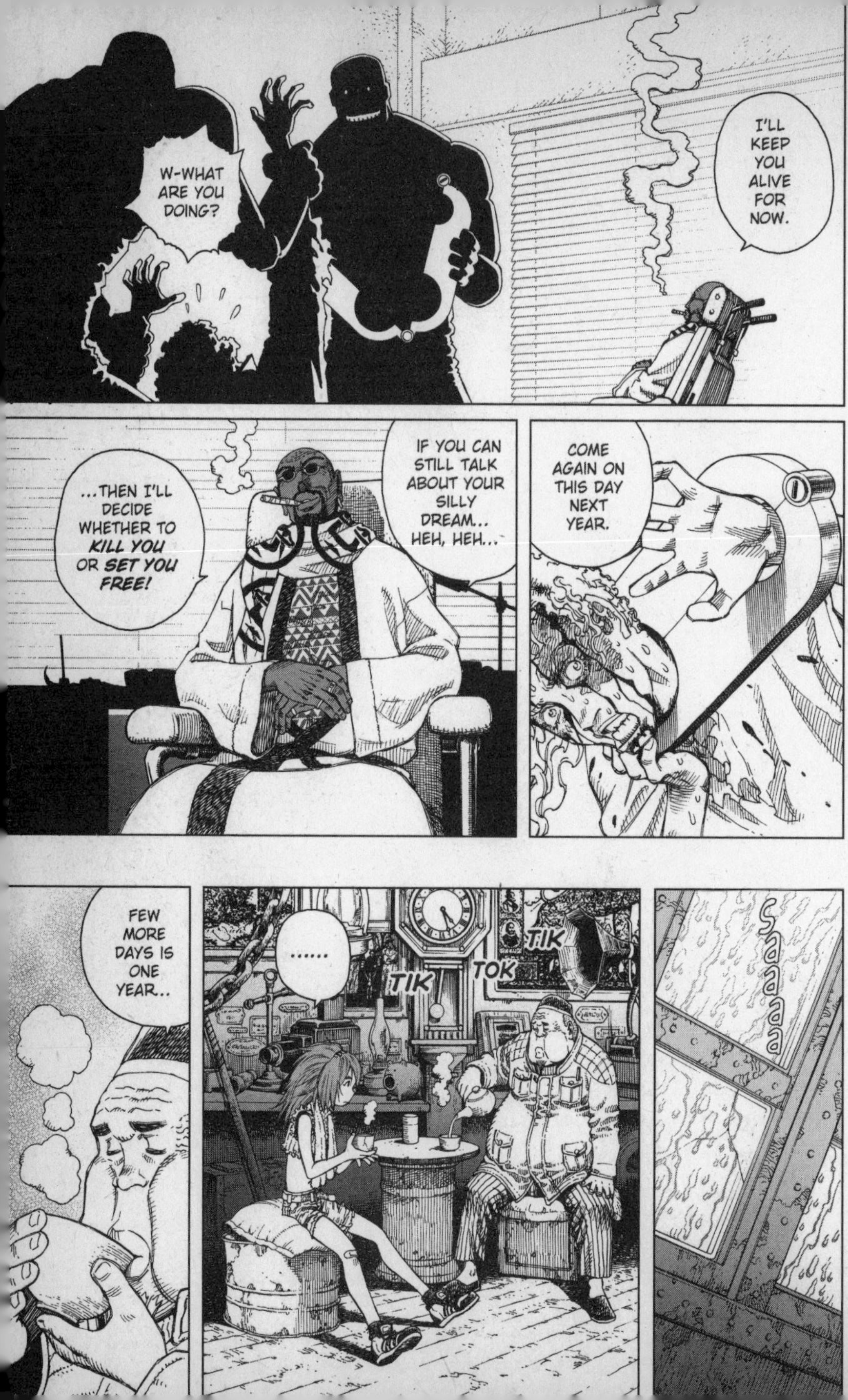
I'LL KEEP YOU ALIVE FOR NOW.
W-WHAT ARE YOU DOING?
COME AGAIN ON THIS DAY NEXT YEAR.
IF YOU CAN STILL TALK ABOUT YOUR SILLY DREAM... HEH, HEH...
...THEN I'LL DECIDE WHETHER TO KILL YOU OR SET YOU FREE!
Saaaa
TIK
TOK
......
TIK
FEW MORE DAYS IS ONE YEAR...

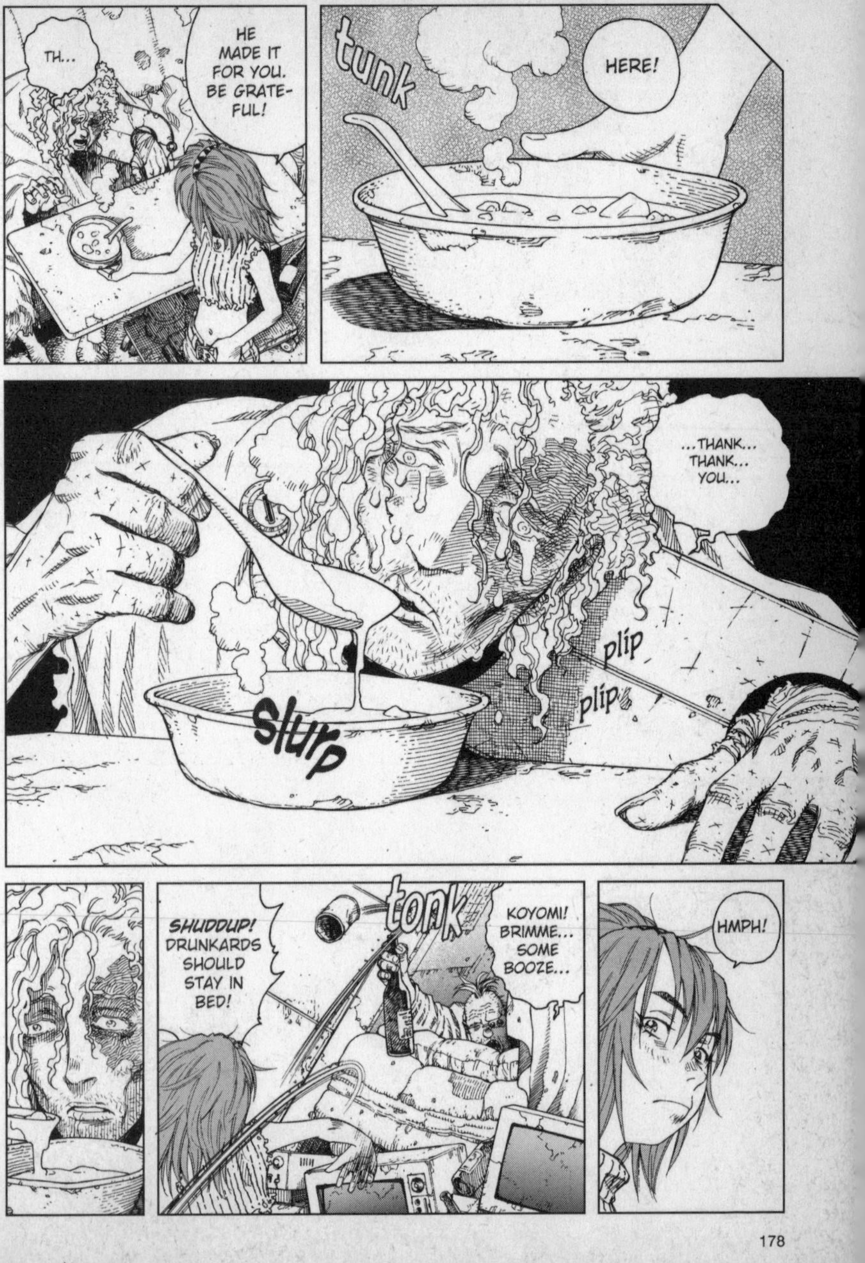

tunk
HERE!
HE MADE IT FOR YOU. BE GRATE-FUL!
TH...
...THANK... THANK... YOU...
plip
plip
slurp
HMPH!
KOYOMI! BRIMME... SOME BOOZE...
tonk
SHUDDUP! DRUNKARDS SHOULD STAY IN BED!

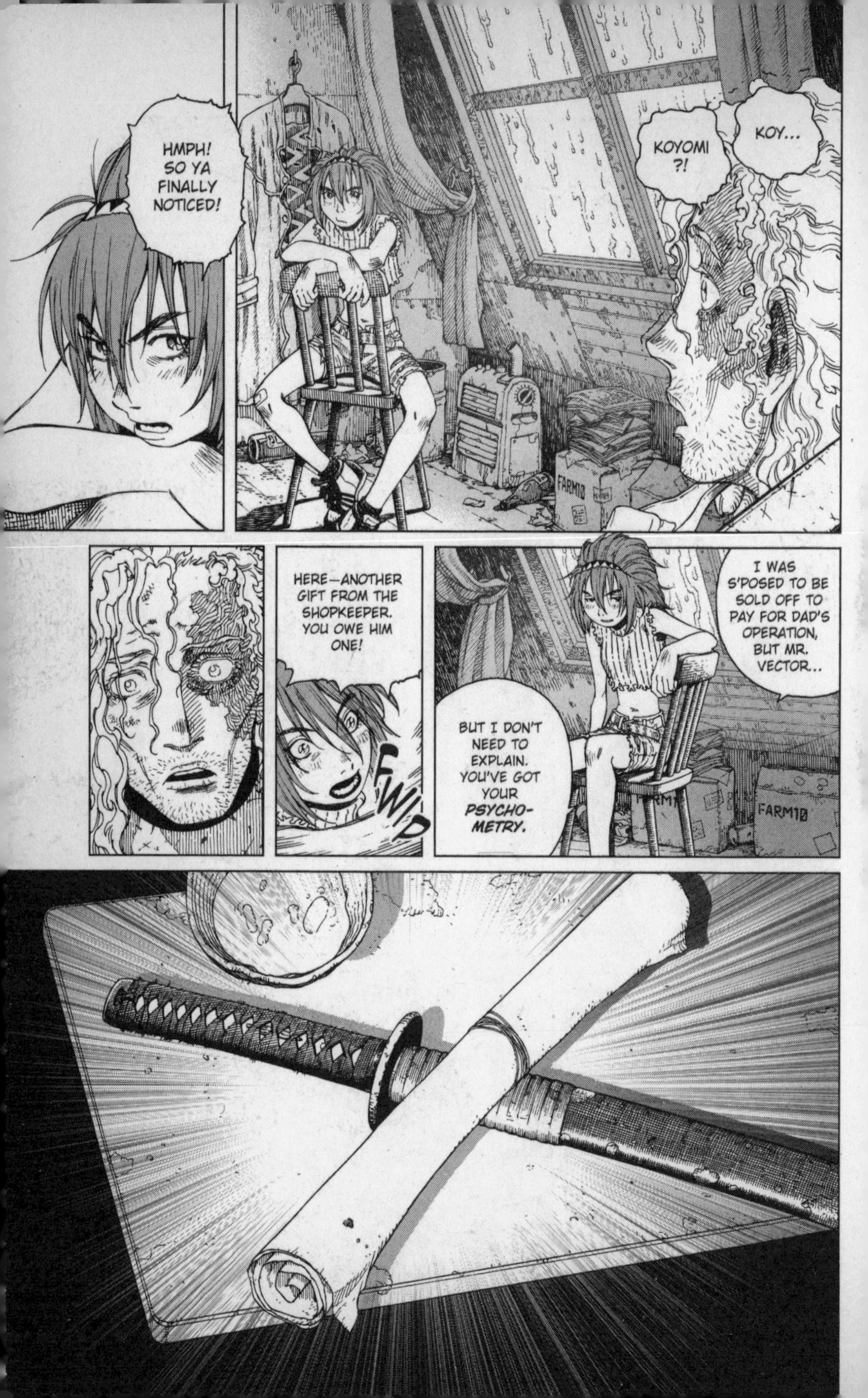
KOY...
KOYOMI ?!
HMPH! SO YA FINALLY NOTICED!
FARM10
I WAS S'POSED TO BE SOLD OFF TO PAY FOR DAD'S OPERATION, BUT MR. VECTOR...
BUT I DON'T NEED TO EXPLAIN. YOU'VE GOT YOUR *PSYCHOMETRY*.
FARM10
HERE—ANOTHER GIFT FROM THE SHOPKEEPER. YOU OWE HIM ONE!
FWIP

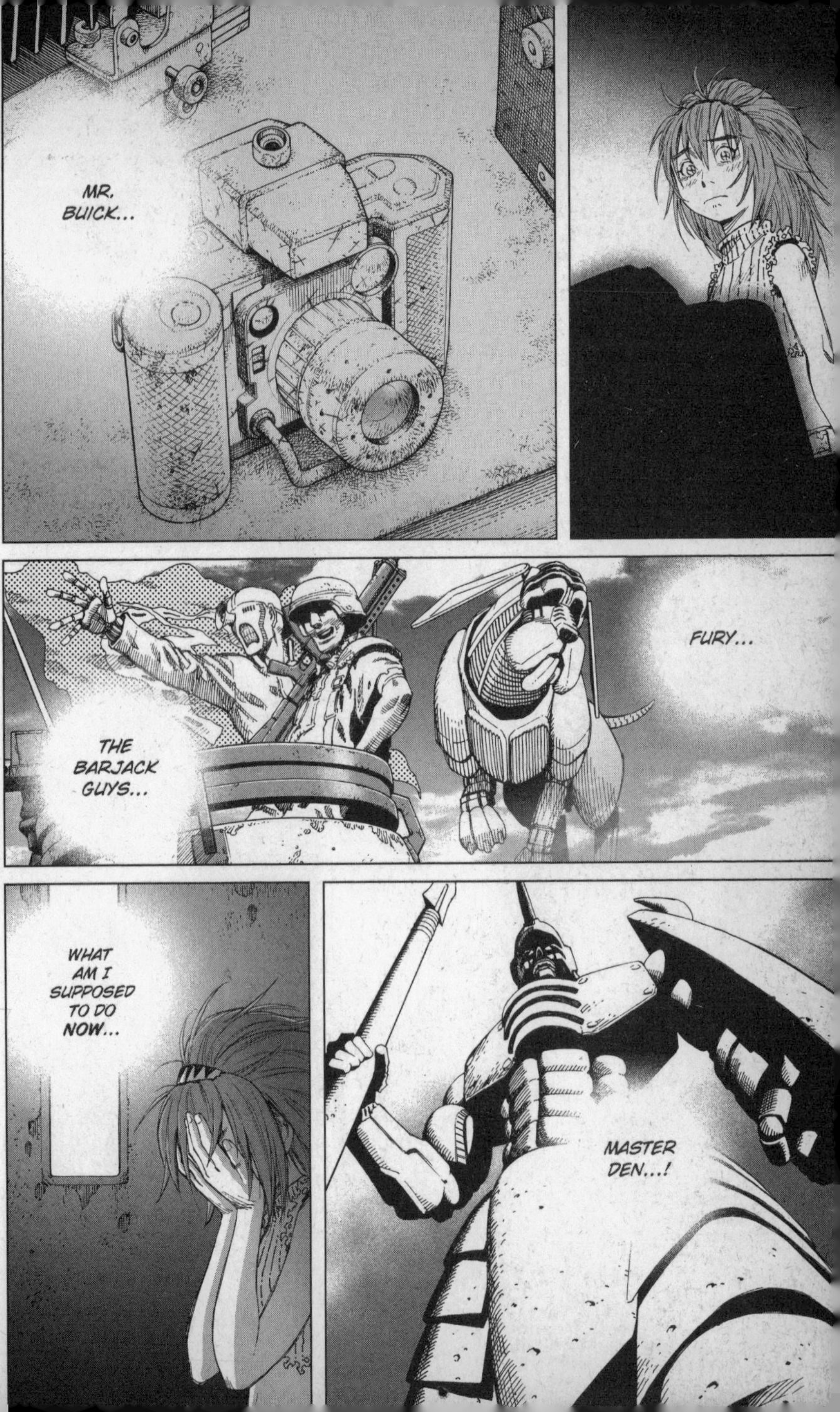
MR. BUICK...
FURY...
THE BARJACK GUYS...
MASTER DEN...!
WHAT AM I SUPPOSED TO DO NOW...

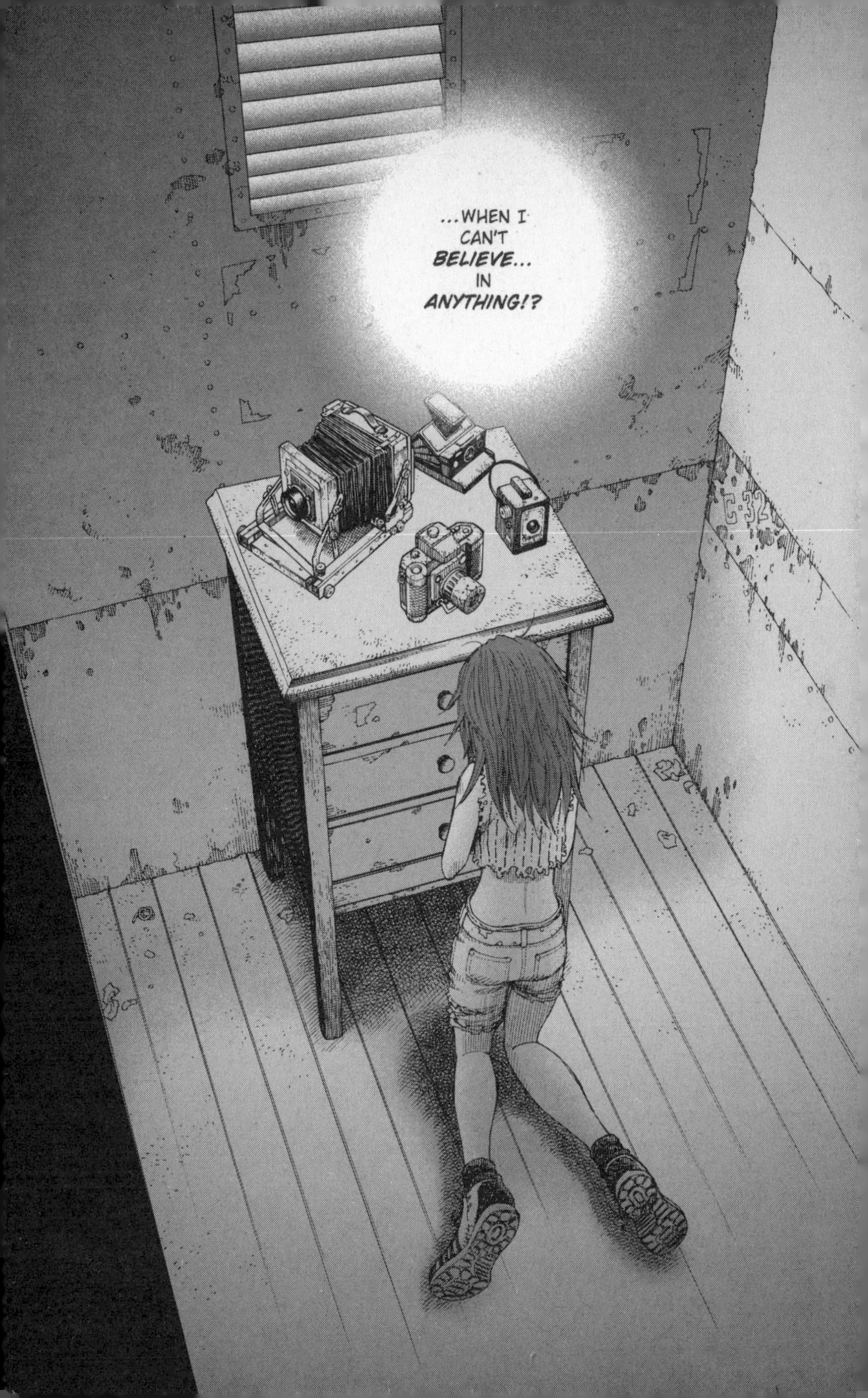
...WHEN I CAN'T BELIEVE... IN ANYTHING!?

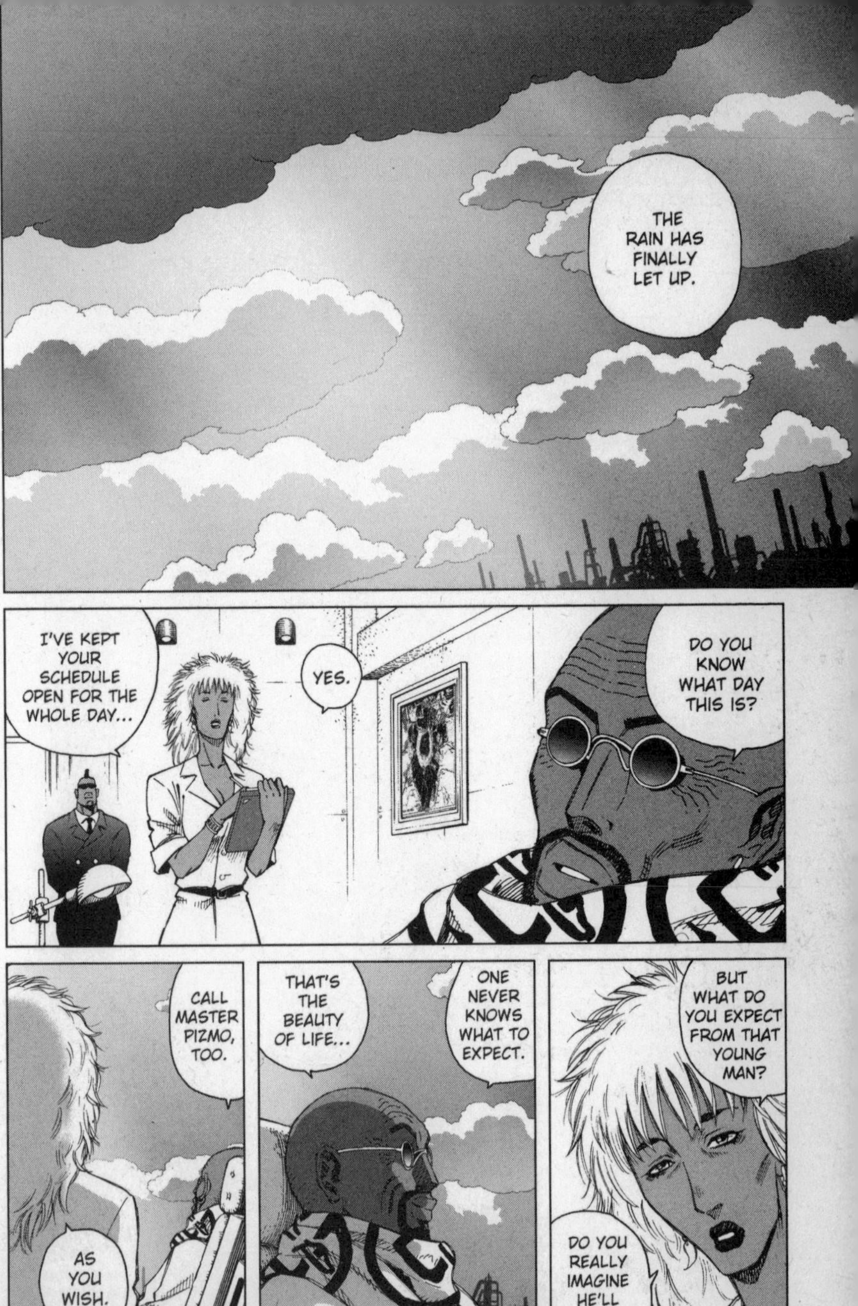
THE RAIN HAS FINALLY LET UP.
DO YOU KNOW WHAT DAY THIS IS?
YES.
I'VE KEPT YOUR SCHEDULE OPEN FOR THE WHOLE DAY...
BUT WHAT DO YOU EXPECT FROM THAT YOUNG MAN?
DO YOU REALLY IMAGINE HE'LL SHOW UP?
ONE NEVER KNOWS WHAT TO EXPECT.
THAT'S THE BEAUTY OF LIFE...
CALL MASTER PIZMO, TOO.
AS YOU WISH.

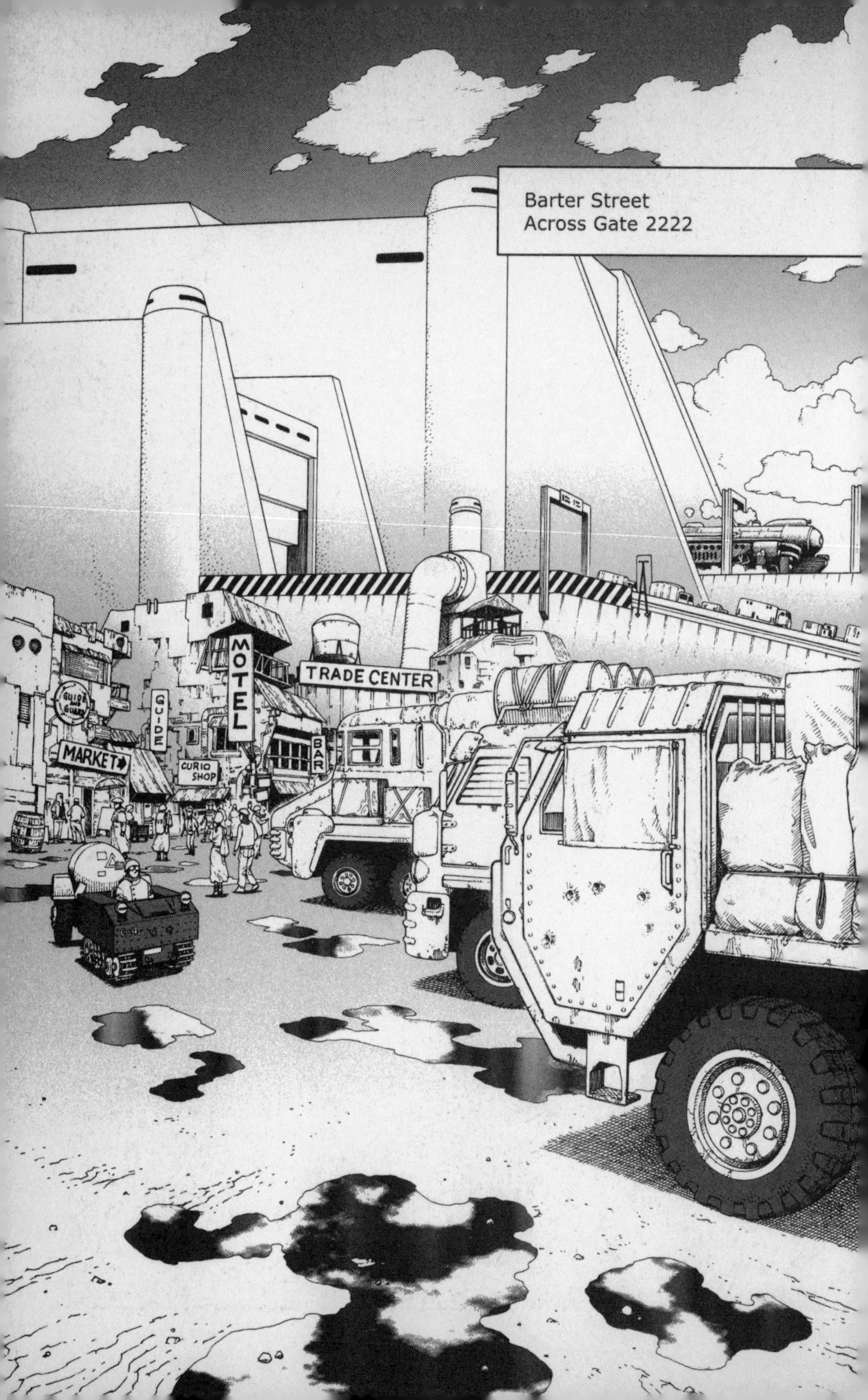
Barter Street
Across Gate 2222
MOTEL
TRADE CENTER
GUIDE
MARKET
CURIO SHOP
BAR

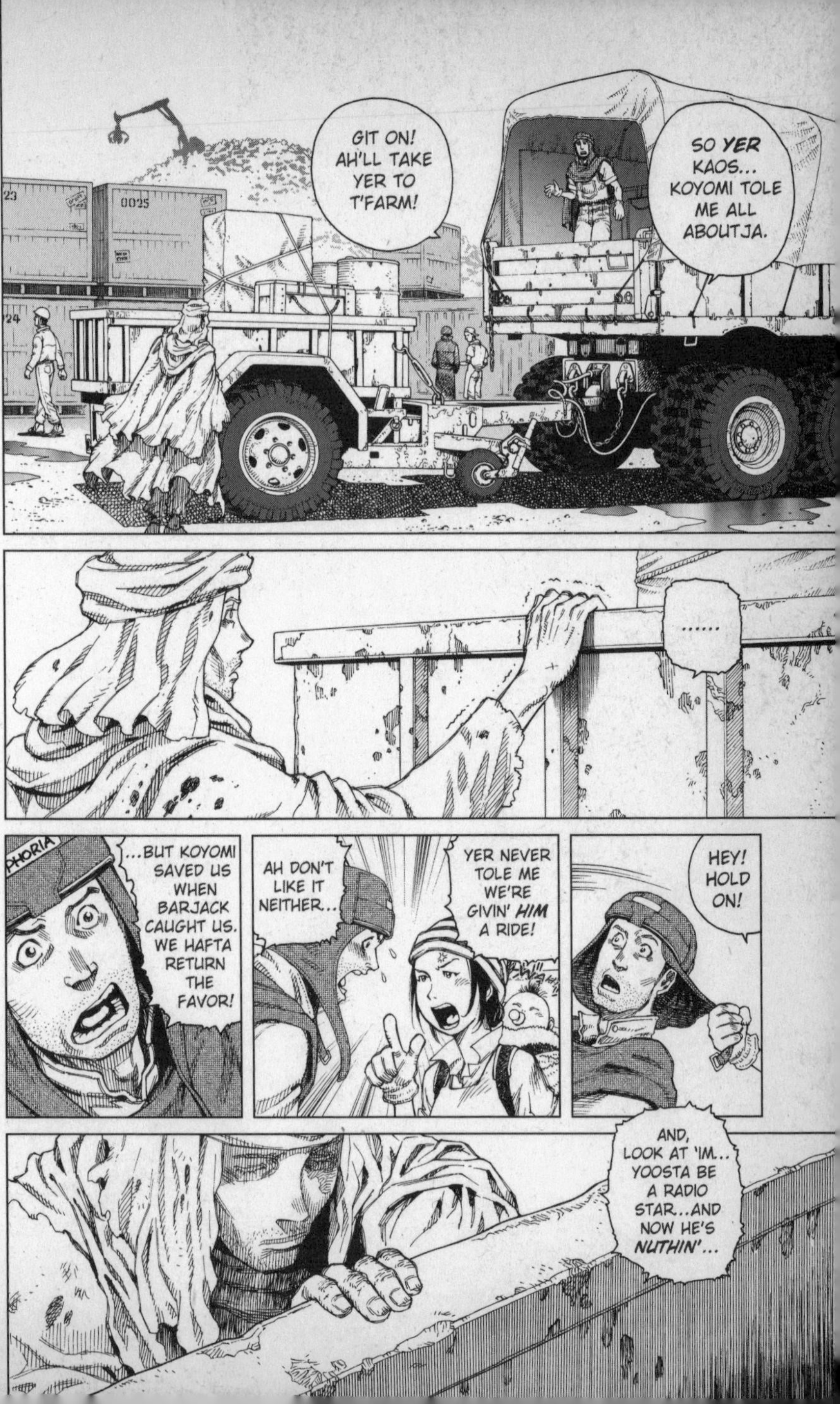
SO YER KAOS... KOYOMI TOLE ME ALL ABOUTJA.
GIT ON! AH'LL TAKE YER TO T'FARM!
......
HEY! HOLD ON!
YER NEVER TOLE ME WE'RE GIVIN' HIM A RIDE!
AH DON'T LIKE IT NEITHER...
...BUT KOYOMI SAVED US WHEN BARJACK CAUGHT US. WE HAFTA RETURN THE FAVOR!
AND, LOOK AT 'IM... YOOSTA BE A RADIO STAR...AND NOW HE'S NUTHIN'...

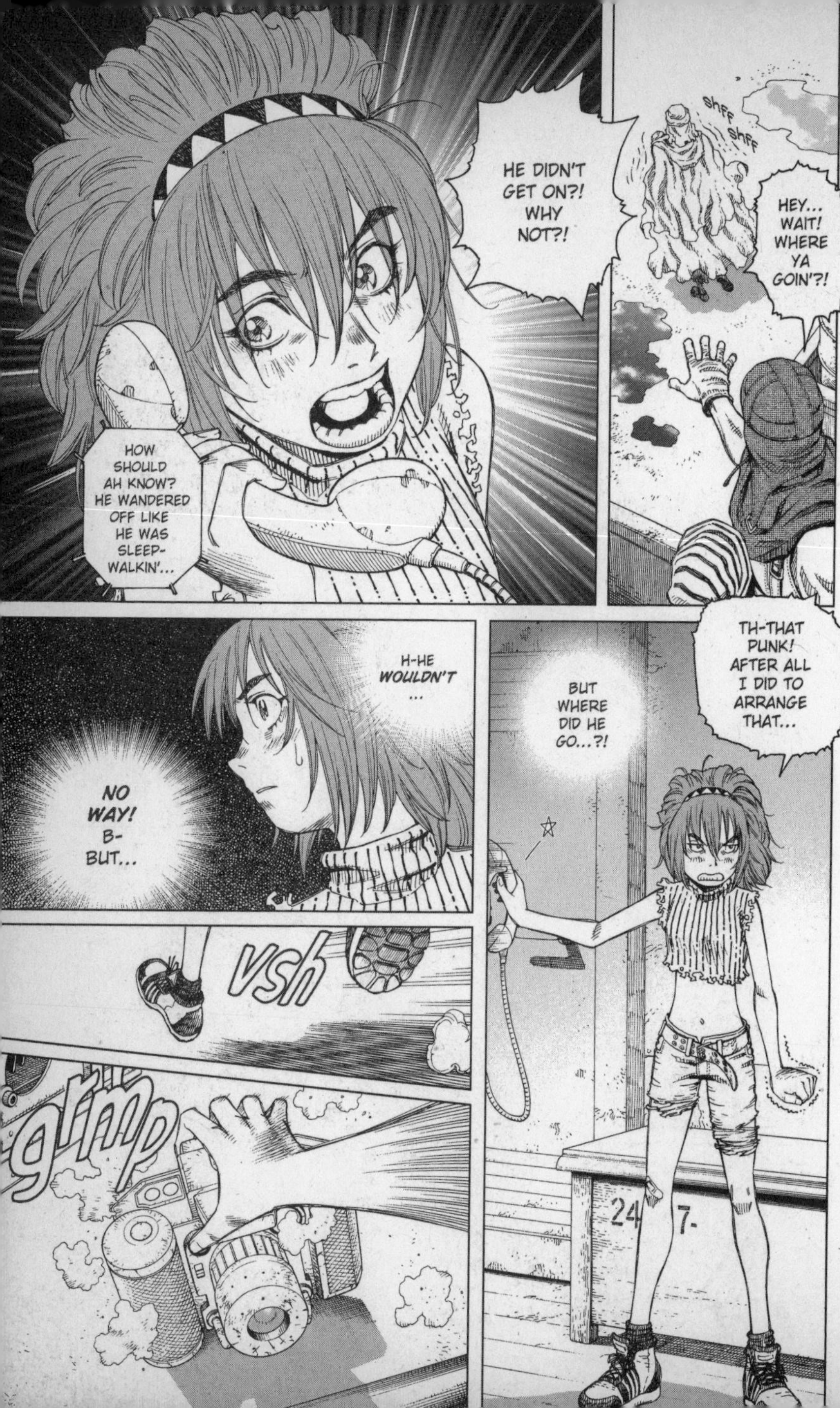
shff
shff
HEY... WAIT! WHERE YA GOIN'?!
HE DIDN'T GET ON?! WHY NOT?!
HOW SHOULD AH KNOW? HE WANDERED OFF LIKE HE WAS SLEEP-WALKIN'...
TH-THAT PUNK! AFTER ALL I DID TO ARRANGE THAT...
BUT WHERE DID HE GO...?!
24 7-
H-HE *WOULDN'T* ...
NO WAY! B-BUT...
vsh
glmp

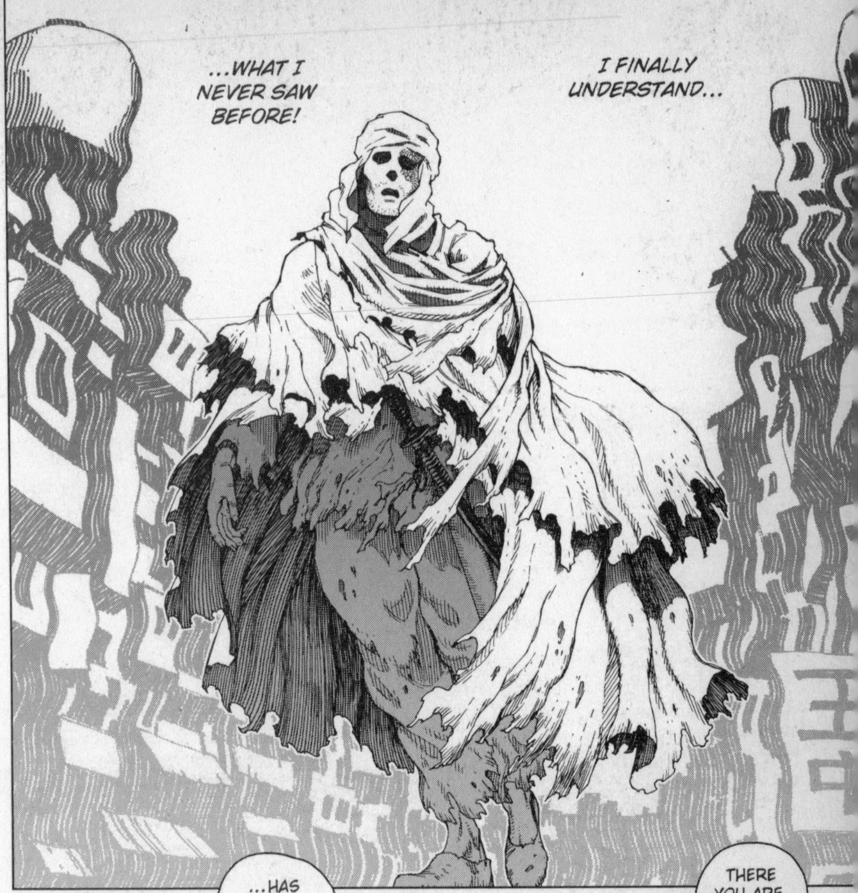
I FINALLY UNDERSTAND...
...WHAT I NEVER SAW BEFORE!
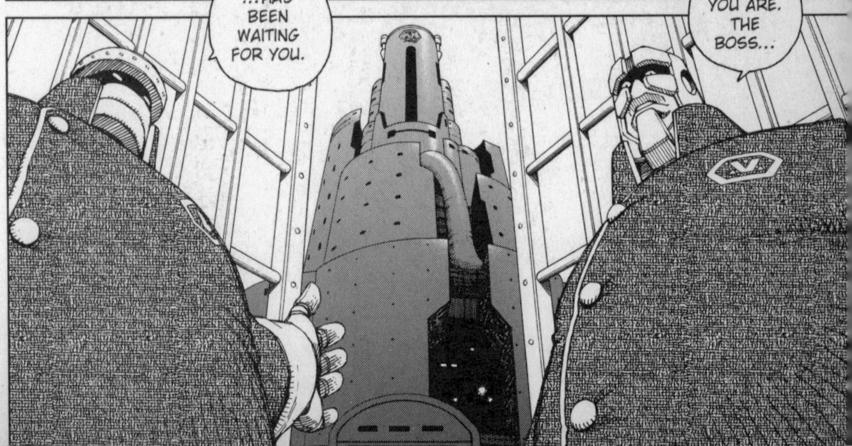
THERE YOU ARE. THE BOSS...
...HAS BEEN WAITING FOR YOU.

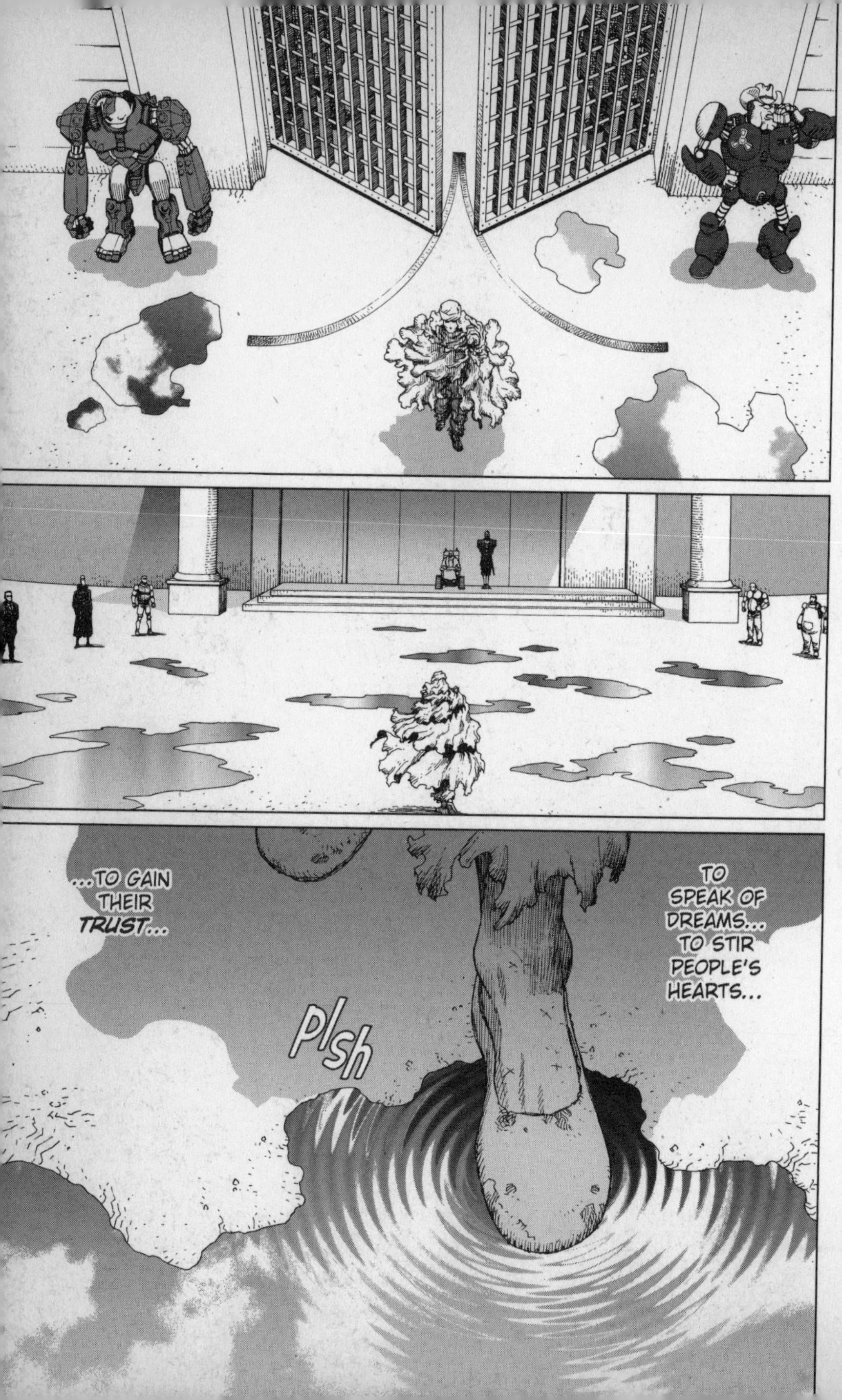
TO SPEAK OF DREAMS... TO STIR PEOPLE'S HEARTS...
...TO GAIN THEIR TRUST...
plsh

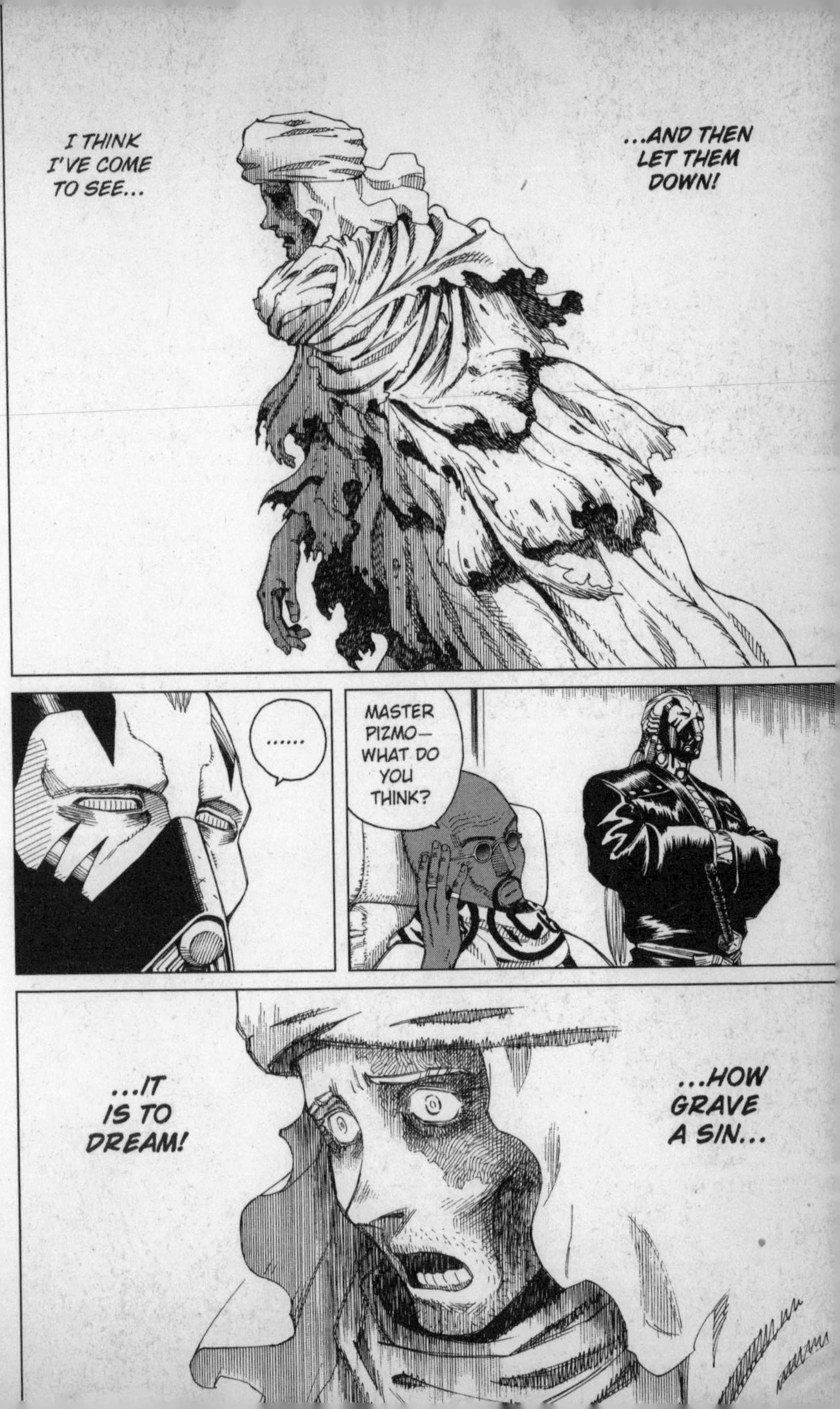
...AND THEN LET THEM DOWN!
I THINK I'VE COME TO SEE...
MASTER PIZMO— WHAT DO YOU THINK?
......
...HOW GRAVE A SIN...
...IT IS TO DREAM!

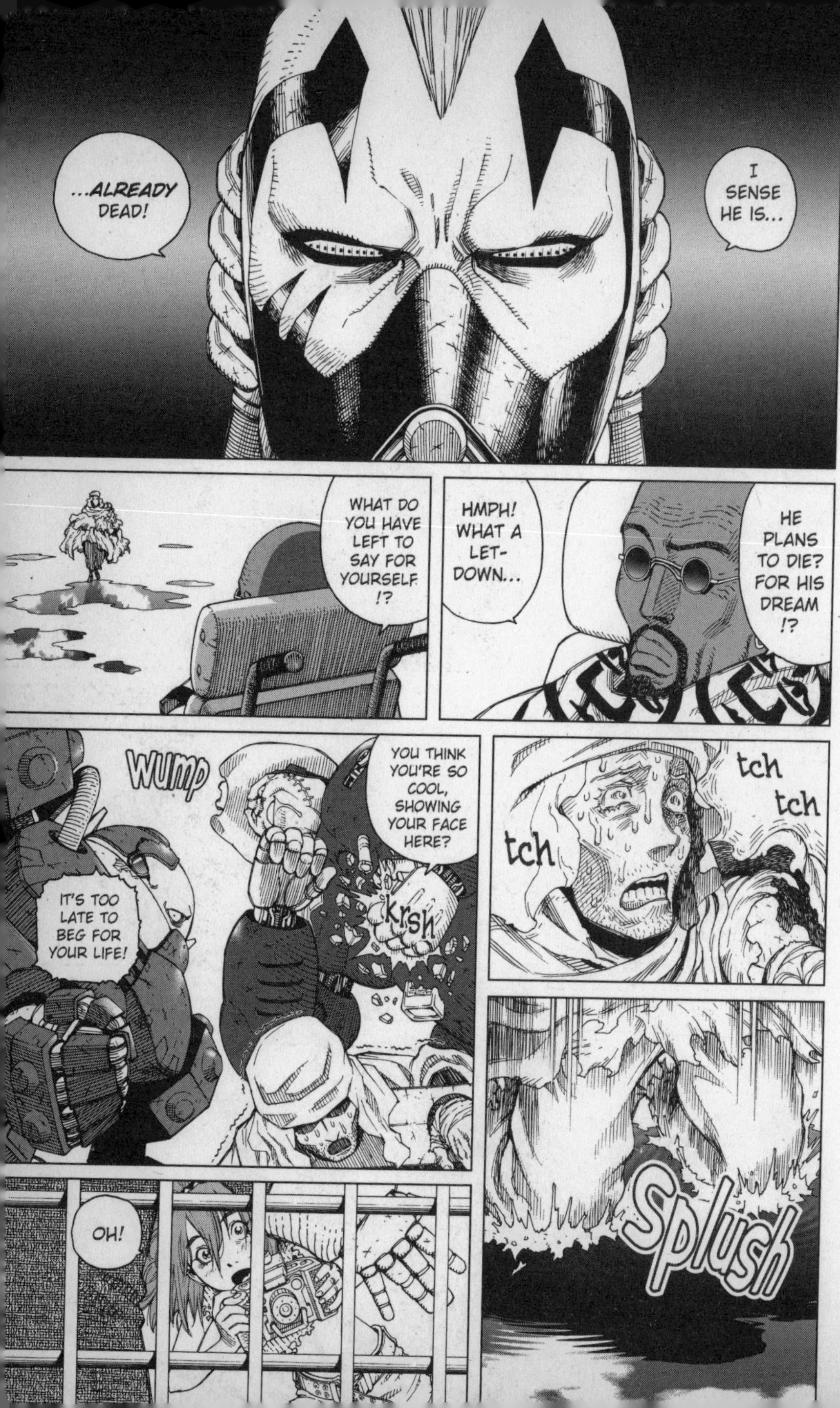
I SENSE HE IS...
...ALREADY DEAD!
HE PLANS TO DIE? FOR HIS DREAM !?
HMPH! WHAT A LET-DOWN...
WHAT DO YOU HAVE LEFT TO SAY FOR YOURSELF !?
tch
tch
tch
Splush
YOU THINK YOU'RE SO COOL, SHOWING YOUR FACE HERE?
wump
krsh
IT'S TOO LATE TO BEG FOR YOUR LIFE!
OH!

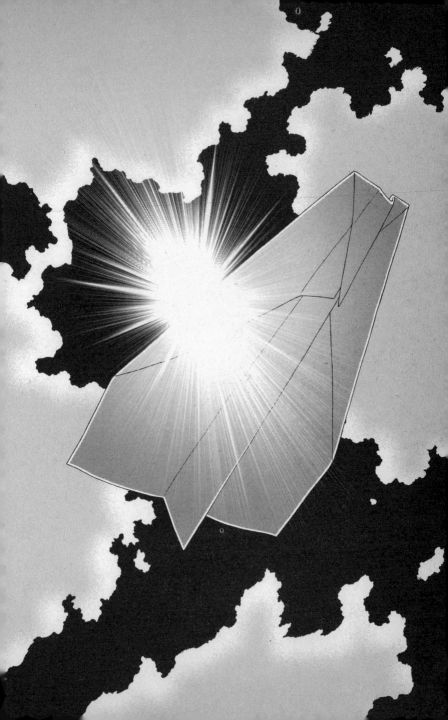

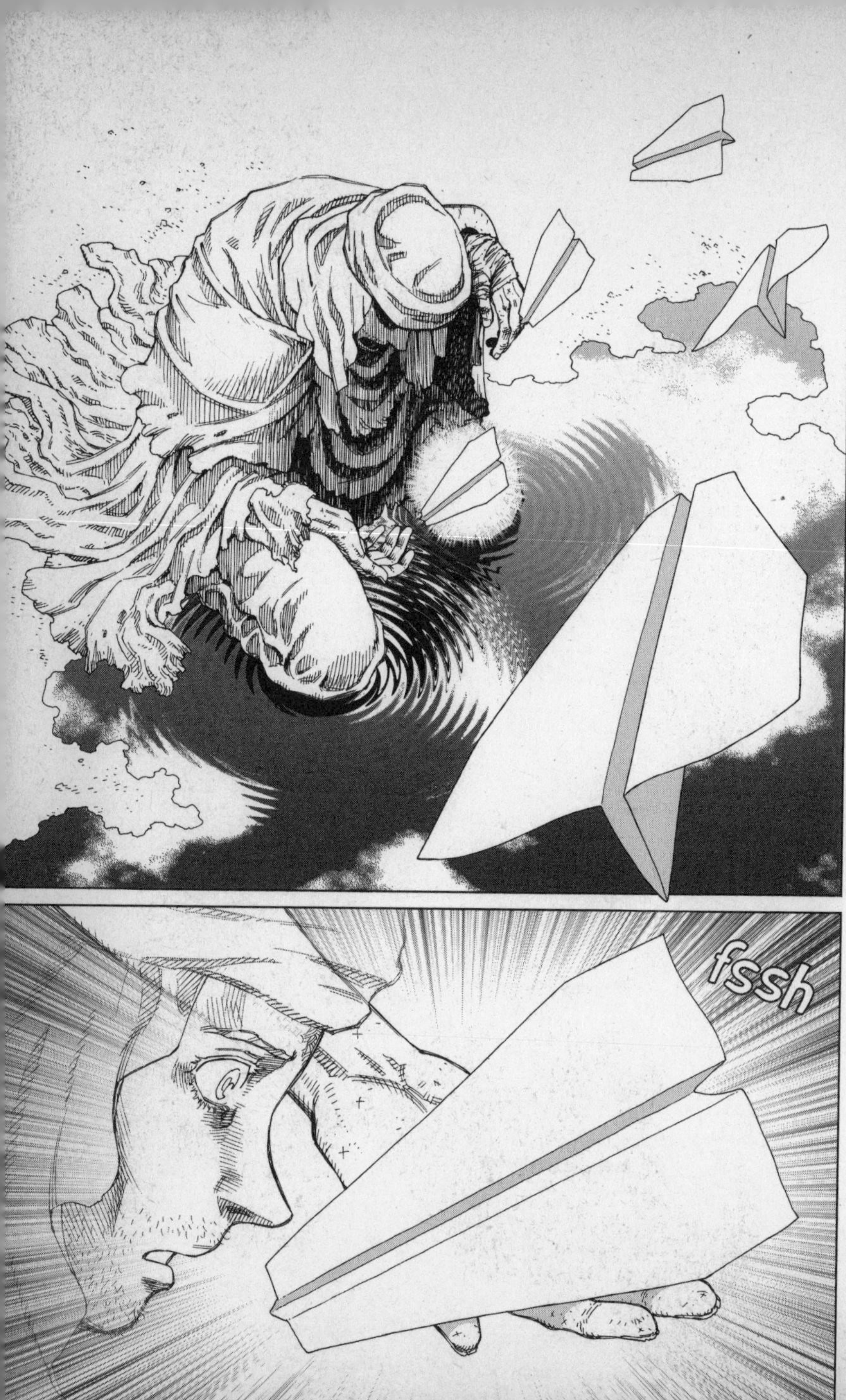
fssh

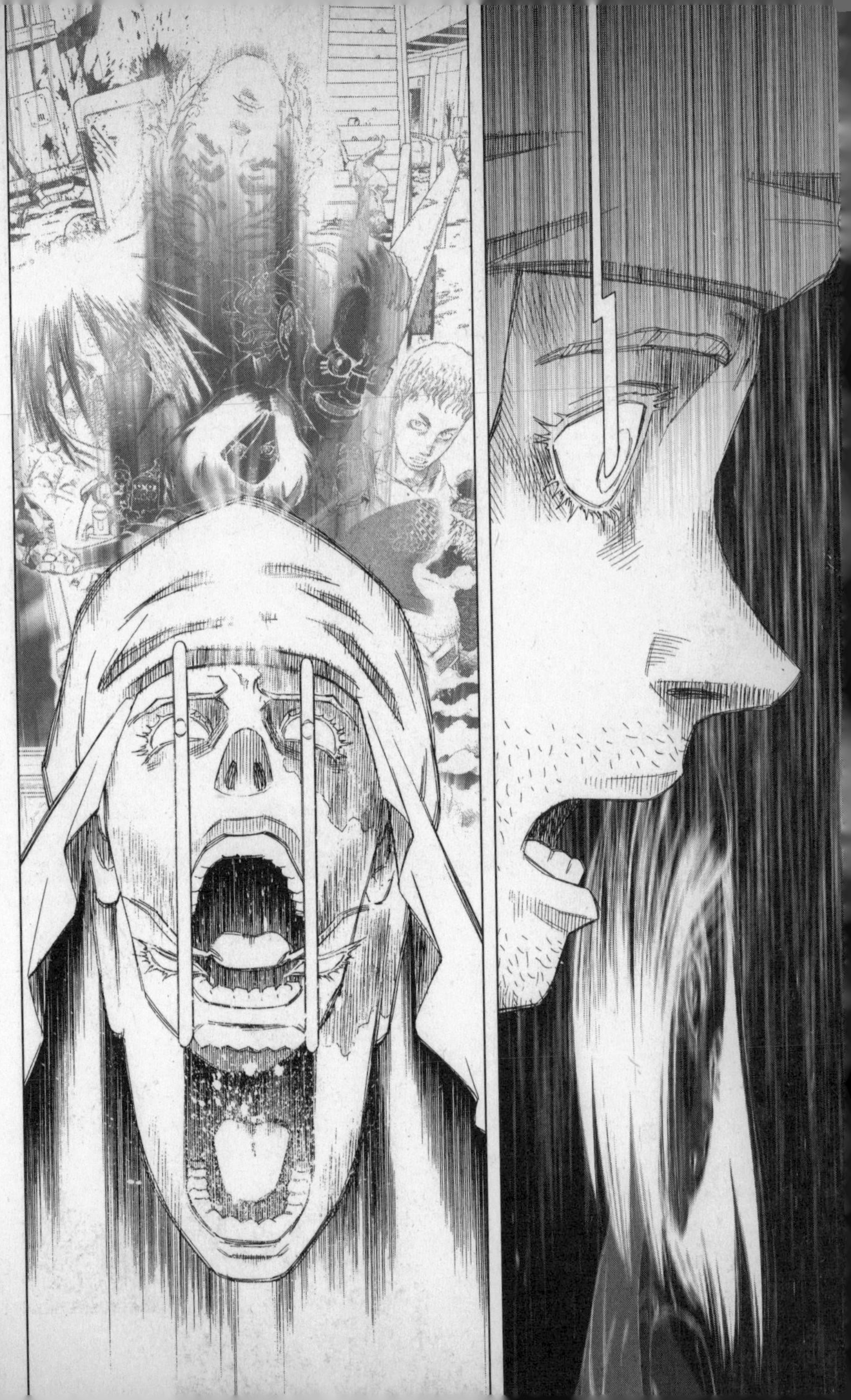

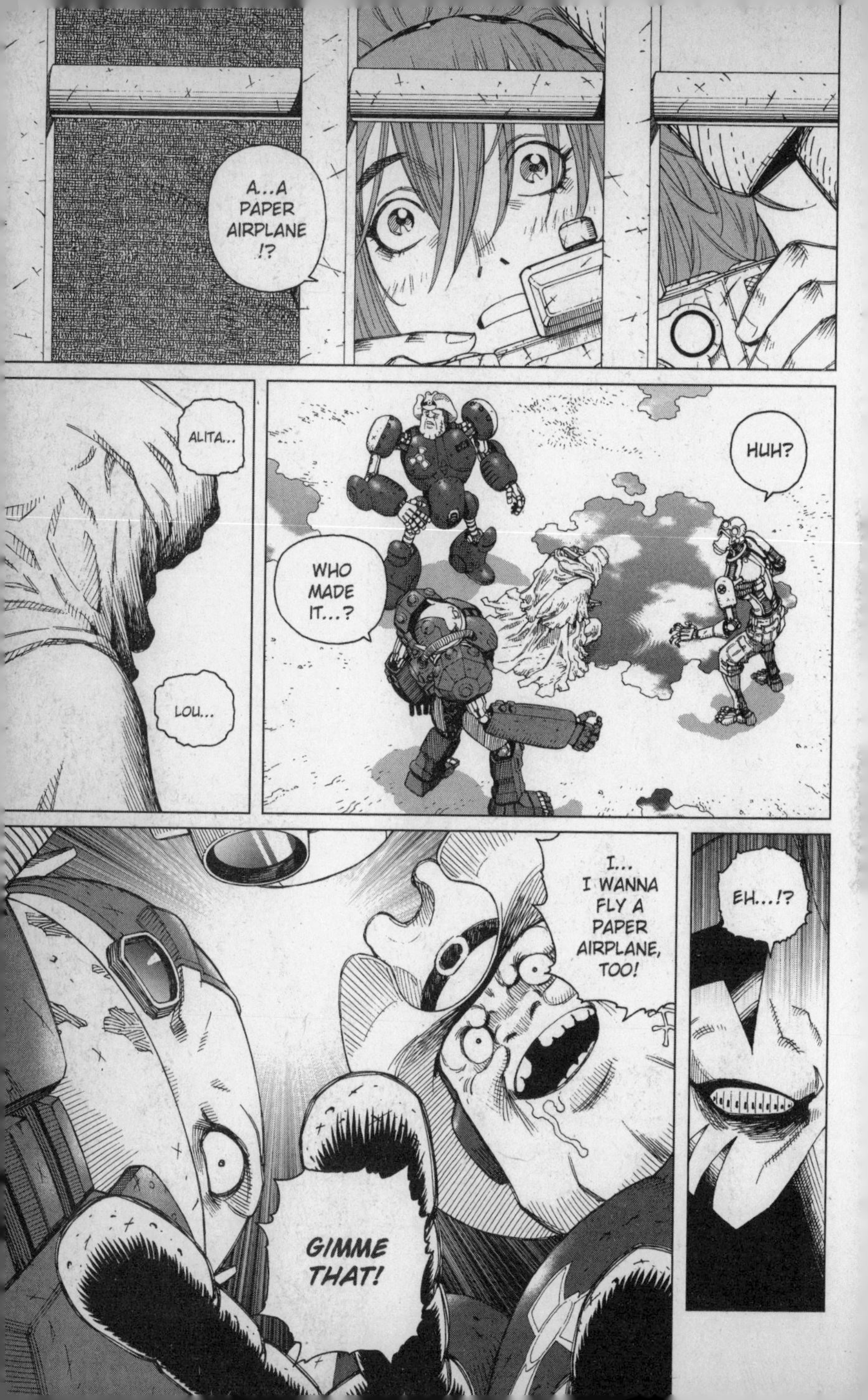
A...A PAPER AIRPLANE !?
HUH?
WHO MADE IT...?
ALITA...
LOU...
EH...!?
I... I WANNA FLY A PAPER AIRPLANE, TOO!
GIMME THAT!

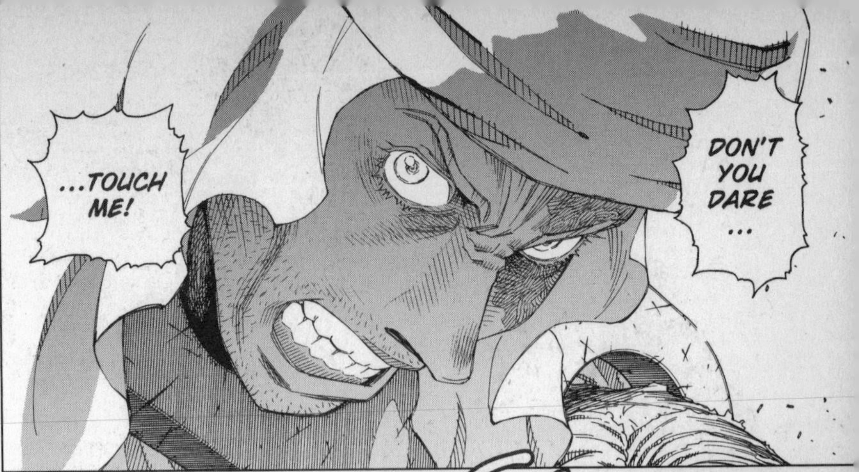
DON'T YOU DARE ...
...TOUCH ME!

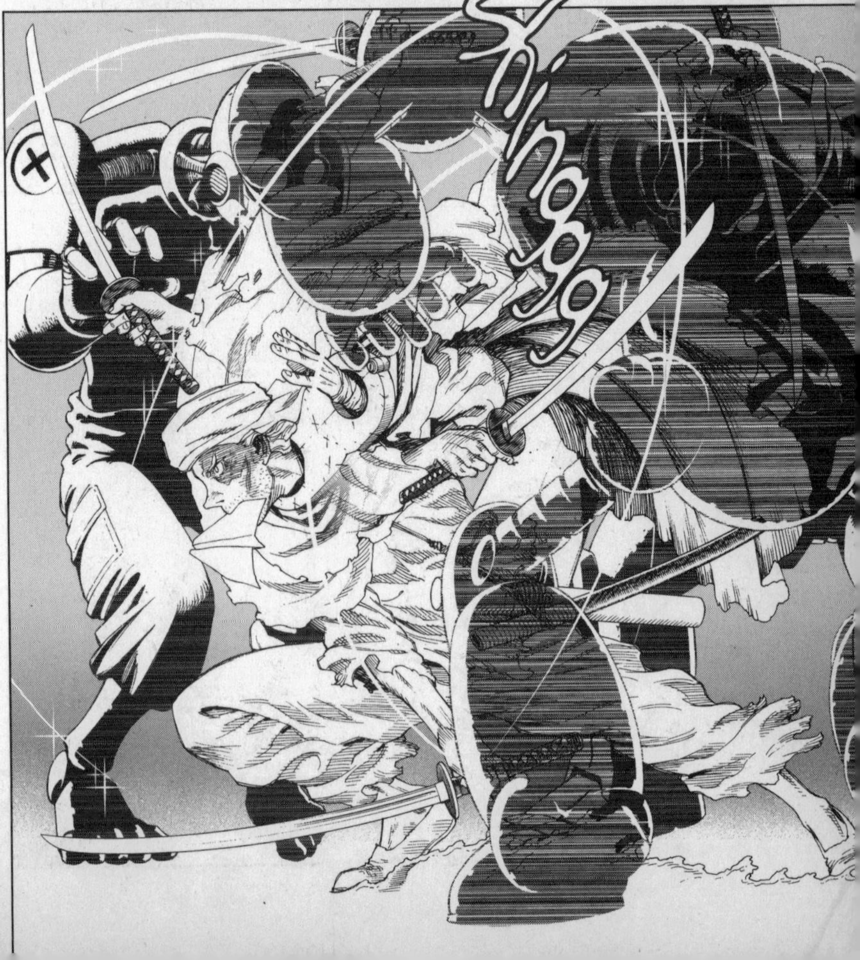
Shingg

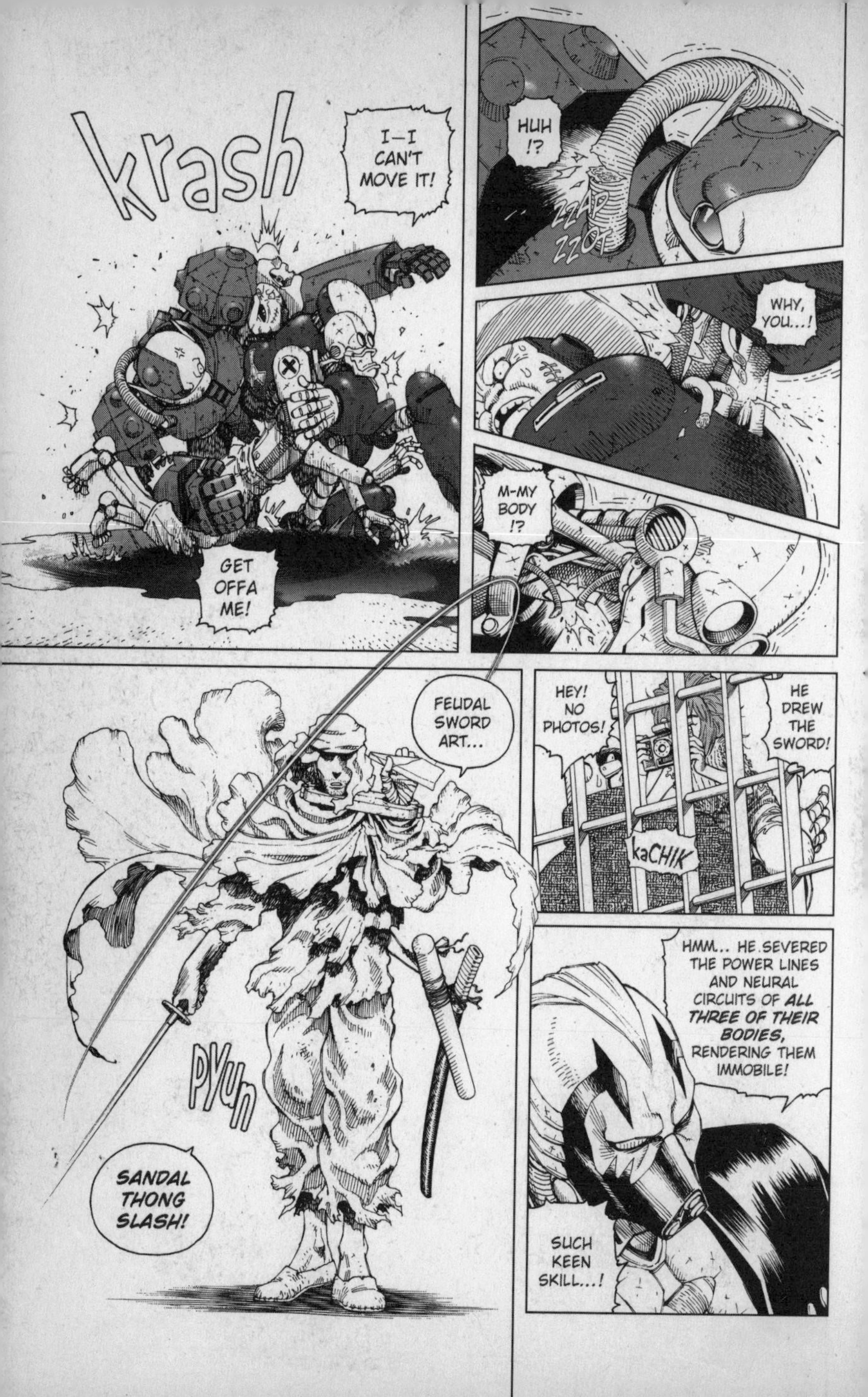
HUH !?
ZZAP
ZZOT
WHY, YOU...!
M-MY BODY !?
krash
I—I CAN'T MOVE IT!
GET OFFA ME!
HE DREW THE SWORD!
HEY! NO PHOTOS!
kaCHIK
HMM... HE SEVERED THE POWER LINES AND NEURAL CIRCUITS OF *ALL THREE OF THEIR BODIES,* RENDERING THEM IMMOBILE!
SUCH KEEN SKILL...!
FEUDAL SWORD ART...
PYUN
SANDAL THONG SLASH!

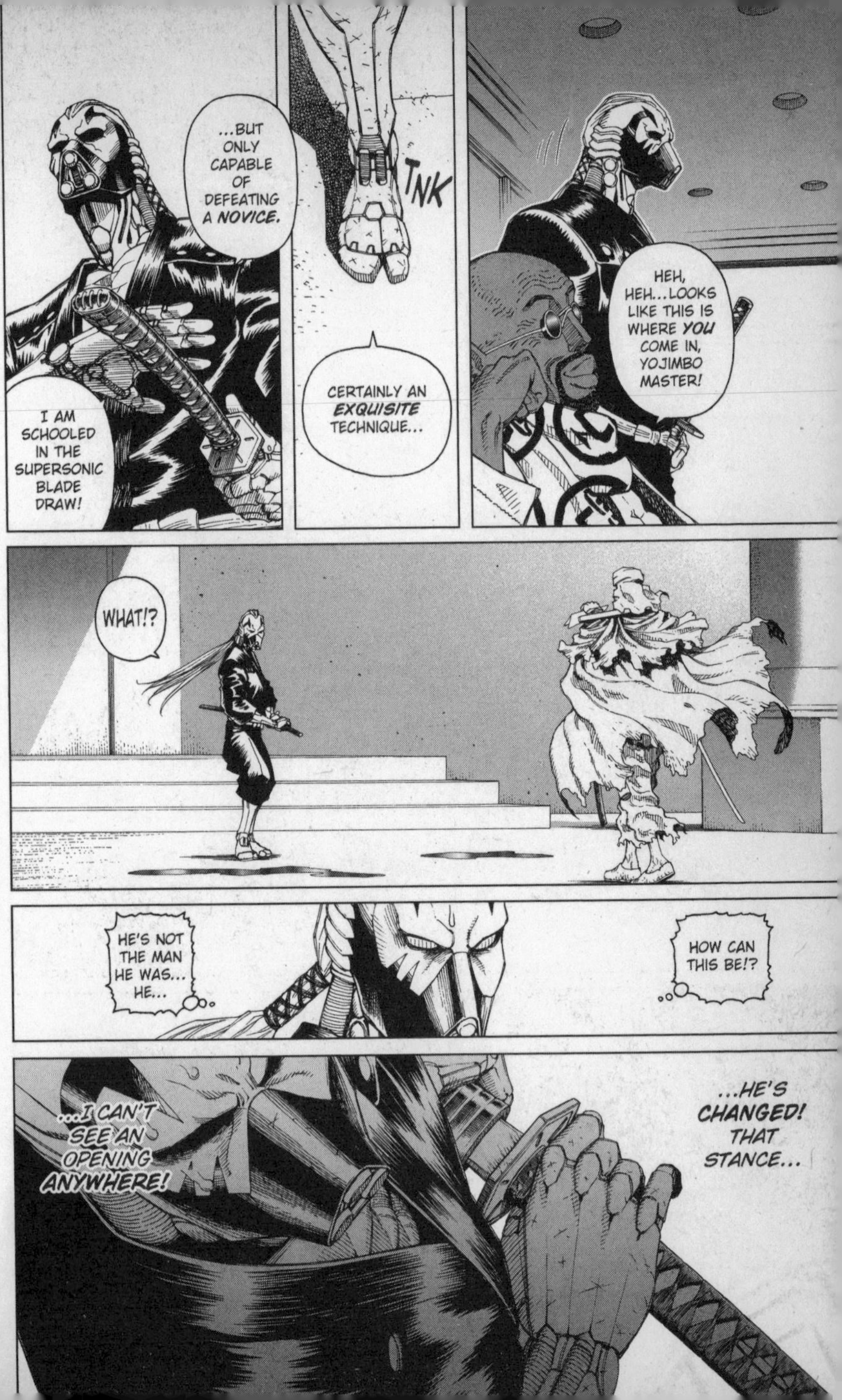
HEH, HEH...LOOKS LIKE THIS IS WHERE YOU COME IN, YOJIMBO MASTER!
TNK
CERTAINLY AN EXQUISITE TECHNIQUE...
...BUT ONLY CAPABLE OF DEFEATING A NOVICE.
I AM SCHOOLED IN THE SUPERSONIC BLADE DRAW!
WHAT!?
HOW CAN THIS BE!?
HE'S NOT THE MAN HE WAS... HE...
...HE'S CHANGED! THAT STANCE...
...I CAN'T SEE AN OPENING ANYWHERE!

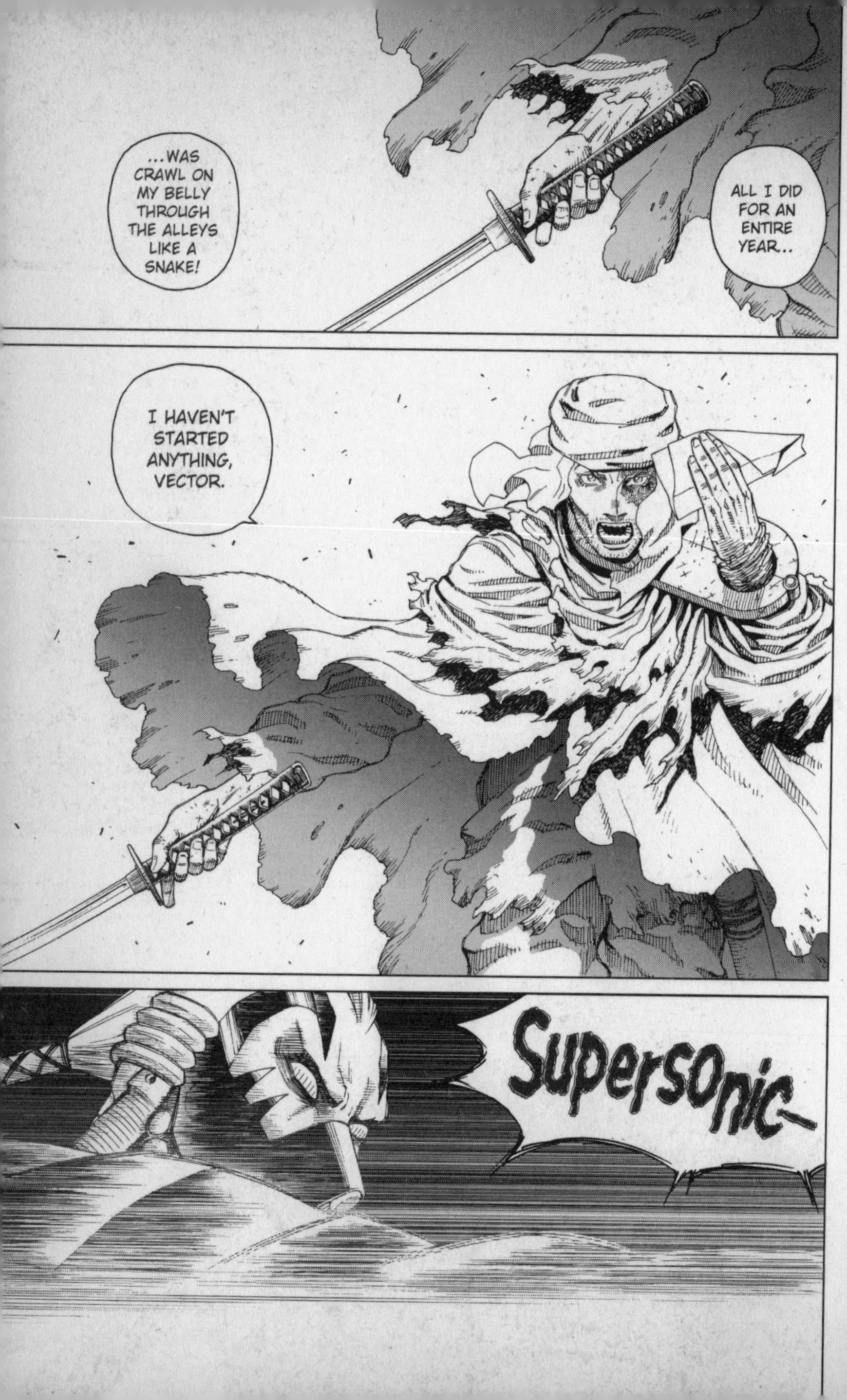
ALL I DID FOR AN ENTIRE YEAR...
...WAS CRAWL ON MY BELLY THROUGH THE ALLEYS LIKE A SNAKE!
I HAVEN'T STARTED ANYTHING, VECTOR.
Supersonic—

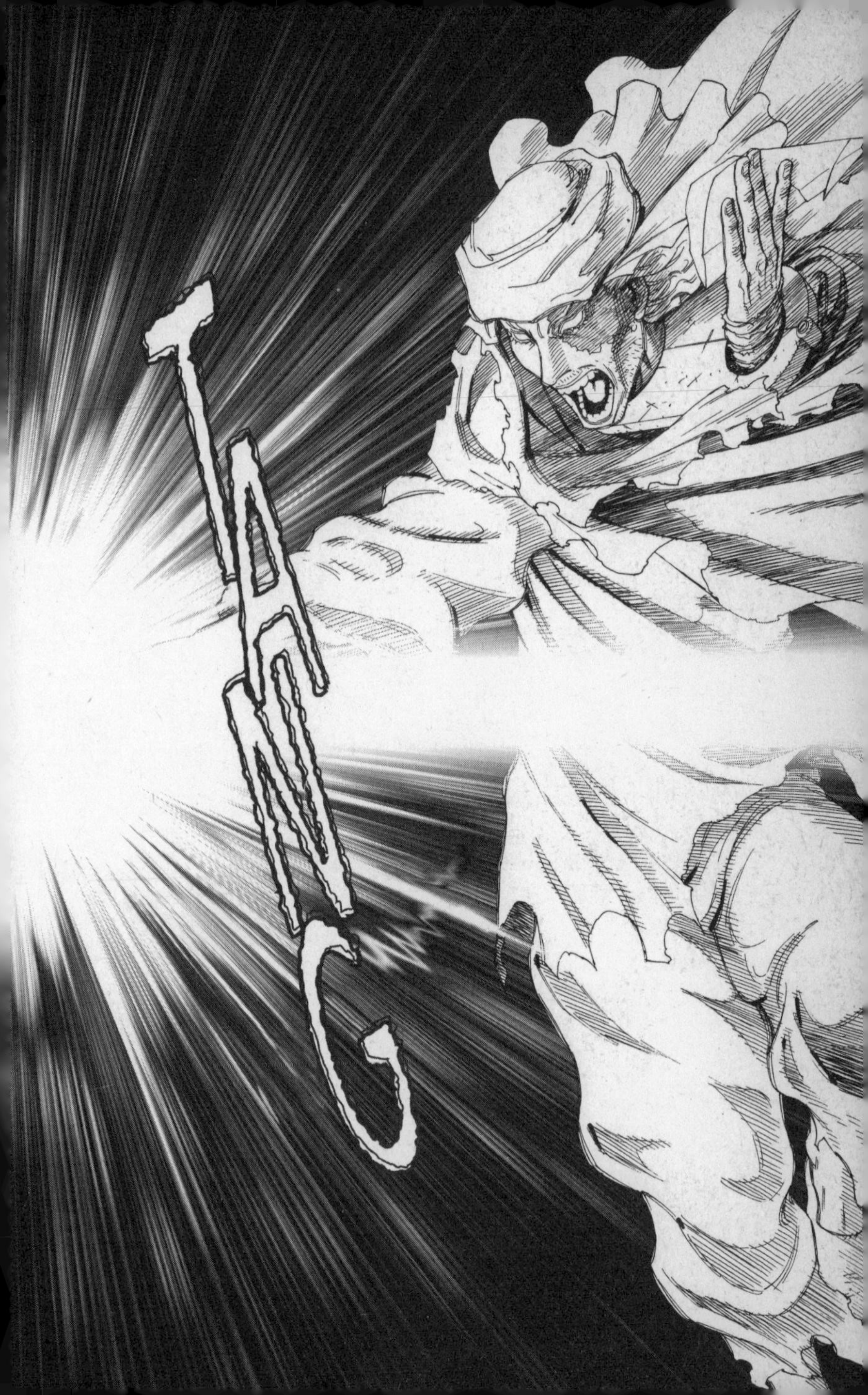

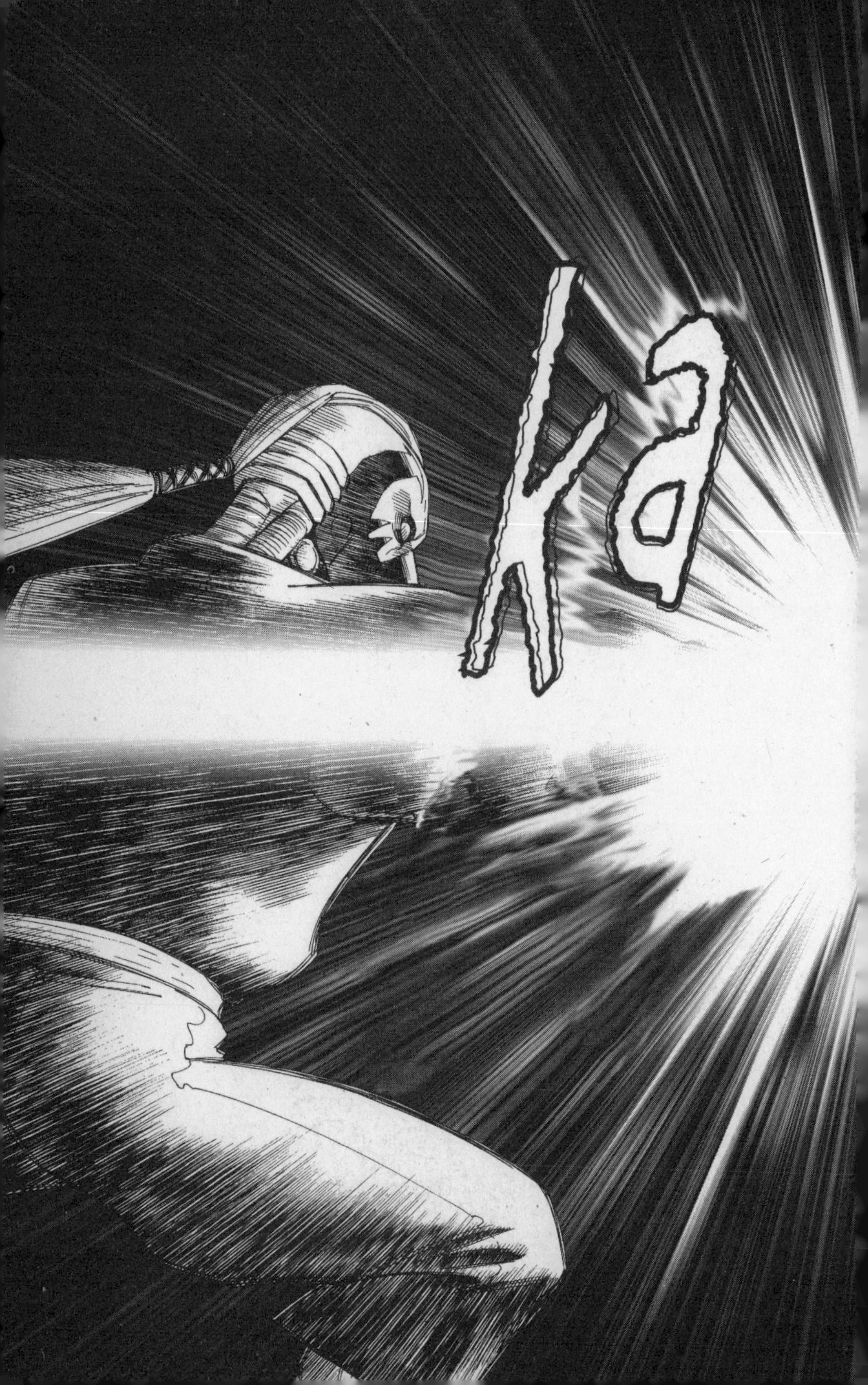
Ka

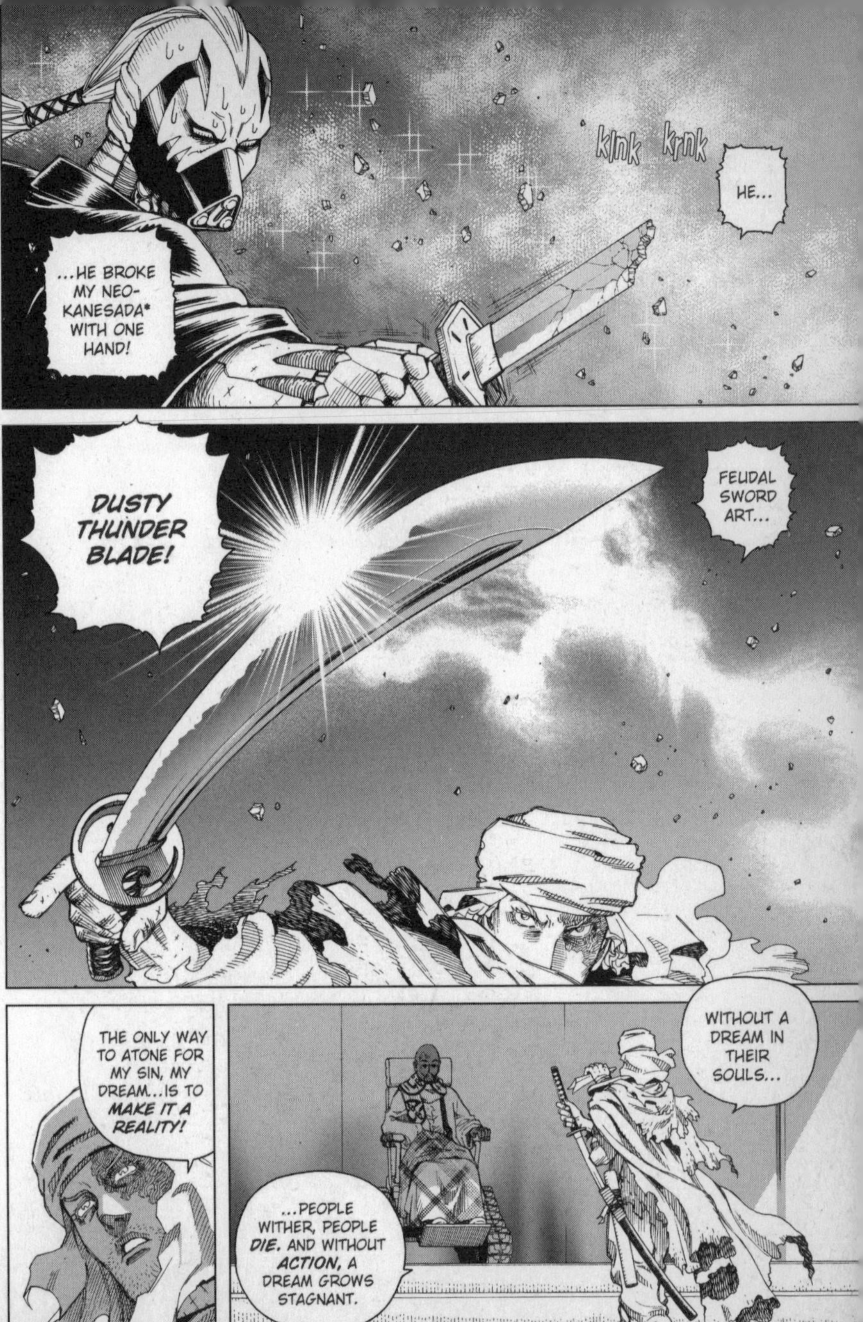
klnk krnk
HE...
...HE BROKE MY NEO-KANESADA* WITH ONE HAND!
FEUDAL SWORD ART...
DUSTY THUNDER BLADE!
WITHOUT A DREAM IN THEIR SOULS...
...PEOPLE WITHER, PEOPLE DIE. AND WITHOUT ACTION, A DREAM GROWS STAGNANT.
THE ONLY WAY TO ATONE FOR MY SIN, MY DREAM...IS TO MAKE IT A REALITY!

*Neo-Kanesada: Forged by the famed swordsmith Kanesada Izuminokami of Mino in the later years of the Muromachi era, and the favorite of Toshizo Hijikata, vice-captain of the Shinsengumi.

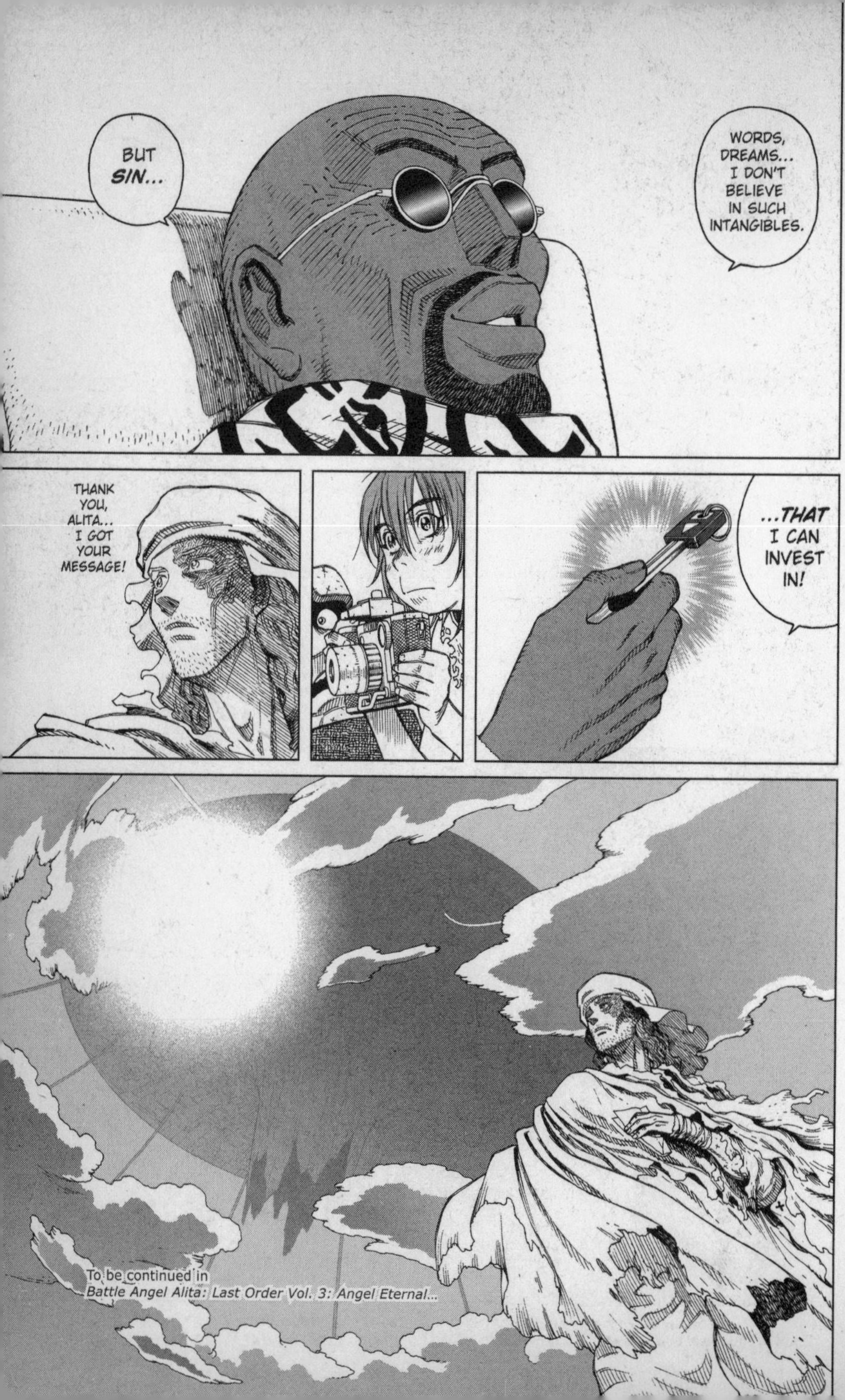
WORDS, DREAMS... I DON'T BELIEVE IN SUCH INTANGIBLES.
BUT *SIN*...
...*THAT* I CAN INVEST IN!
THANK YOU, ALITA... I GOT YOUR MESSAGE!
To be continued in
Battle Angel Alita: Last Order Vol. 3: Angel Eternal...

TIPHARES: ITS MORPHOLOGY

*Tiphares is shrouded in mystery.
Let's take a look back at what has been illuminated thus far
about the city in the sky.*

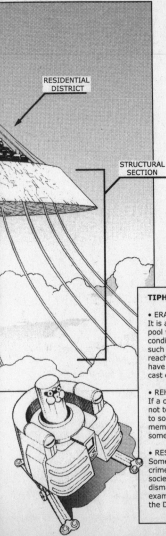

RESIDENTIAL
DISTRICT

STRUCTURAL
SECTION

Tiphares is roughly divided into three sections:

● RESIDENTIAL DISTRICT
All citizens live here. They are encouraged
to participate in sports, cultural events, and
academics—though scholarly pursuits are
restricted to abstract fields such as mathematics
and philosophy.

● STRUCTURAL SECTION
The physical support of Tiphares, this section
includes all equipment necessary for the upkeep of
a society, such as power supplies, food-processing
plants, and distribution networks.

● MEDICAL INSPECTION BUREAU CORE
Seen from above, the M.I.B. occupies the central
part of the concentric circles that shape Tiphares.
Citizens are normally not permitted access to this
fully automated zone, which houses the Initiation
Room, M.I.B. machines, an automated brain bio-
chip factory, the Mother Machine, the DNA organ,
Waste Management, and the orbital elevator port.

TIPHAREAN CLASSIFICATION OF CRIME AND PUNISHMENT

● ERADICATION OF GENETICALLY PREDISPOSED CRIME
It is accepted that there are genes even in the Tipharean gene
pool which predispose individuals to criminal behavior under certain
conditions. The actions and psychological profiles of citizens with
such genes are closely monitored. If their psychological status curve
reaches criminal threshold, they are taken into custody, even if they
have yet to commit an actual crime. Like Doc Ido, they are usually
cast out alive from the Dust Chamber beneath Tiphares.

● REHABILITATION OF BEHAVIORAL CRIME
If a crime is deemed both harmless to the functioning of society and
not to have arisen from criminal genes, the perpetrators are returned
to society after their brain bio-chips have been recalibrated. The
memory of the crime is erased, and their personality may change in
some cases.

● RESEARCH INTO IDEOLOGICAL CRIME
Some people, even without genetically predisposed tendencies to
crime, end up harboring ideologies that are thought to endanger
society. The brain bio-chips of such criminals are removed and
dismantled, and the thought processes that resulted in the crime are
examined. The body, considered genetically harmless, is returned to
the DNA bank of amino-acid soup.

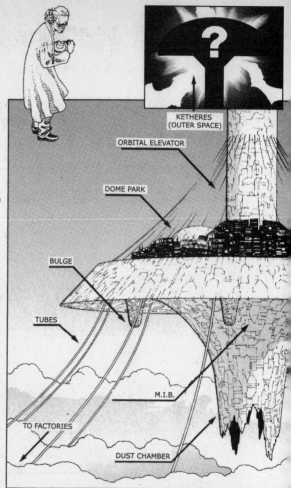

KETHERES
(OUTER SPACE)

ORBITAL ELEVATOR

DOME PARK

BULGE

TUBES

M.I.B.

TO FACTORIES

DUST CHAMBER

- **DOME PARK**
The largest park in Tiphares
houses Endjoy, the public
suicide booth Alita destroyed
in *Battle Angel Alita Vol. 9:
Angel's Ascension*. Jim
Roscoe used it as a base
camp for the children.

- **BULGE**
Three protrusions from the
lower part of Tiphares contain
giant Tesla coils, which use
electromagnetic waves to
control the weather
surrounding Tiphares.
These coils also create the
super-defensive weapon
Abaddon by manipulating
scalar waves to strike distant
targets with tremendous
(and unstoppable) energy.
(See *Battle Angel Alita Vol. 8
Fallen Angel*.) The G.I.B.
control room where Lou
worked was housed in one of
the bulges. Nova converted it
into his secret laboratory.

- **TUBES**
Transport tubes connect
the surface factories and
Tiphares. Eleven in all, the
twelfth was destroyed in an
accident over a century ago.

- **DUST CHAMBER**
Garbage generated in
Tiphares—including
inhabitants convicted of
genetically predisposed
crimes—is expelled here.
With strength, willpower, a
tenacious spirit, and a lot of
luck, such outcasts can
crash-land relatively intact in
the Scrapyard along with the
trash. Several, like Ido, have
survived their expulsion.

2001. 11. 21. Yukito.

- **THE ORBITAL ELEVATOR**
"Jacob's Ladder" extends beyond the atmosphere.
It supports Tiphares by perfectly balancing the gravitational
pull on the city with centrifugal force. Most of its mass is
composed of monomolecular wires made from carbon nano-
tubes. The temperature difference between outer space and
the atmosphere is also used to generate electricity—enough to
power both Tiphares and the Factories. The Orbital Elevator is
capable of shipping several hundred tons of cargo per day, but
now only transports Tiphorean brains harvested in the
Initiation Ceremony.

BLOOPERS

CATECHISM OF LIFE

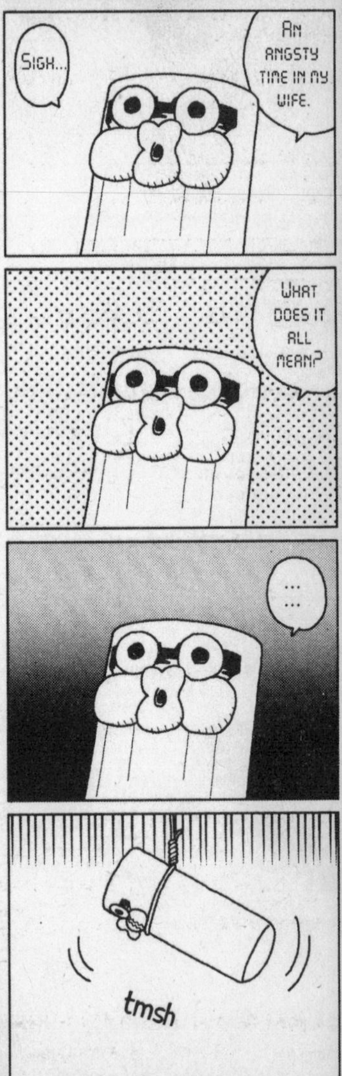
AN ANGSTY TIME IN MY WIFE.
SIGH...
WHAT DOES IT ALL MEAN?
... ...
tmsh

I saw those dolls that dance when you get mail...

I should've patented the idea!

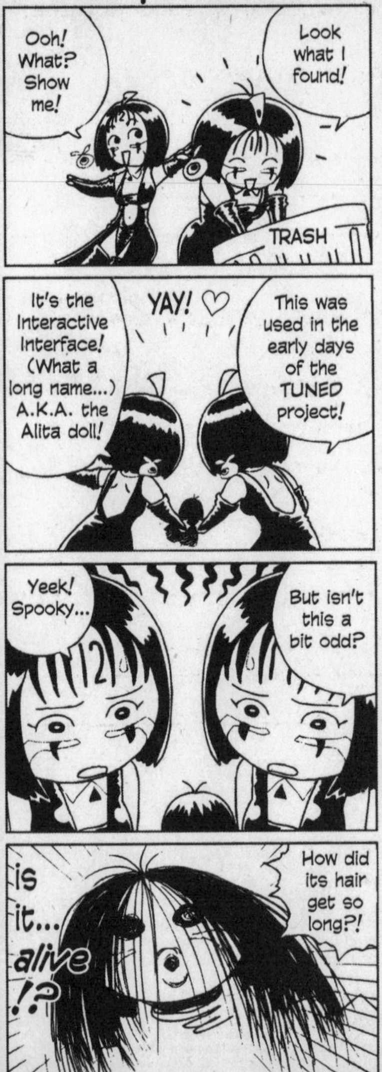
Look what I found!
Ooh! What? Show me!
TRASH
This was used in the early days of the TUNED project!
YAY! ♡
It's the Interactive Interface! (What a long name...) A.K.A. the Alita doll!
But isn't this a bit odd?
Yeek! Spooky...
How did its hair get so long?!
is it... alive !?